DISCIPLED

"GO THEREFORE AND MAKE DISCIPLES OF ALL THE NATIONS, BAPTIZING THEM IN THE NAME OF THE FATHER AND OF THE SON AND OF THE HOLY SPIRIT, TEACHING THEM TO OBSERVE ALL THINGS THAT I HAVE COMMANDED YOU; AND LO, I AM WITH YOU ALWAYS, EVEN TO THE END OF THE AGE. AMEN."

~ *MATTHEW 28:19-20*

DISCIPLED

JEREMY HORTON

HORTON PUBLISHING

Cover design by Hannah Linder Designs
Formatting template by Derek Murphy
Editing by Ashlyn McKayla Ohm

ISBN (paperback): 979-8-9868684-0-0
ISBN (ebook): 979-8-9868684-1-7
Library of Congress Control Number: 2023902726

First Edition: April 2023
City of Publication: Hot Springs, Arkansas

10 9 8 7 6 5 4 3 2 1

28 27 26 25 24 23

CONTENTS

DEDICATION

To my loving, supportive, selfless, Kingdom-minded wife, who continually stands with me for the furtherance of the gospel. I love you, Jillian.

INTRODUCTION

I cannot take it any longer. I must say those three words that start well, yet end tragically: saved, baptized, "pewscipled." Being saved by Jesus and baptized to follow Him is exciting, but reducing discipleship to only what you can glean by listening from a church pew is disheartening! Historically, you do not need another comparative church report that denotes how far Christianity has drifted from its solid roots. Statistically, it will do no good to sicken you once again with factual percentages that display the inconsistent lifestyle of a "professing" Christian as it derails from the standards of Jesus Christ our Lord. All the reports, statistics, and facts really speak volumes in a language that is more visible than vocal. That language is a Christian population today that has been predominantly discipled *without* the commands of Jesus Christ.

Bill Hull, my favorite voice on the subject of discipleship, offers a variety of comments that supplement my argument. In his book *The Disciple-Making Pastor*, Hull states:

> I have thrown down the gauntlet. I maintain that the evangelical church is weak, self-indulgent, and superficial, that it has been thoroughly discipled by its culture. As Jesus said, *"When a disciple is fully taught, he will be like his teacher"* (**Luke 6:40**). Furthermore, I believe the crisis of the church is one of product, the kind of people being produced. I propose the solution to be obedience to Christ's commission to "make disciples," to teach Christians to obey everything Christ commanded.[1]

Chris[2] fits this description perfectly. He came to me seeking answers to some Bible prophecy questions. Toward the end of our discussion, I asked him this question: "Have you been discipled?" I will never forget the look in Larry's eyes as he searched desperately to justify his church attendance, Bible knowledge, personality, and prayer life as an attempt to satisfy the demands of my question. When I realized that he was speechless, I proceeded with the scriptural source of my question, found in **Matthew 28:20**. Immediately, he broke down in tears. I was awed into silence at the penetrating power of Holy Scripture. In the wonder of that moment, I said to this Christian man, twice my age, "Larry, after you were born again and baptized, no one discipled you, did they?" He feverishly shook his head.

Sadly, the profile of Larry's Christian caliber is the norm for most believers today. They have not been discipled; the local church has failed them. That is precisely why churches are full of "Larrys" who are *pew*scipled—the essence of their walk with Christ is sermonized from a pulpit to a pew! Elaborating yet again on this subject, Bill Hull says:

> The test of a congregation, apart from personal holiness, is how effectively members penetrate the world. American churches are filled with pew-filling, sermon-tasting, spiritual schizophrenics, whose belief and behavior are not congruent...the truth we have sacrificed is the command for quality. The Great Commission has been worshiped, but not obeyed. The church has tried to get world evangelization without disciple making.[3]

Do you know what this means? We are reaping what we have been sowing. The result is a catastrophic, evangelistic disaster. The "reproduction" coming from the Body of Christ is as frightening and abnormal as a cow giving birth to a parakeet. However, Christianity did not start out this way. In fact, though neglected and dusty, the original plan that Jesus Christ Himself instituted is ready to be resurrected once again! What is that plan? What does it say?

Matthew 28:20 is THE plan. Jesus said it like this: *"teaching them to observe all things I have commanded you..."* Christ is telling His disciples to *reproduce* in others what He has *produced* in them. The way Christ expects this to happen is by teaching, observing, and commanding. Making disciples begins by teaching exactly what Christ has commanded, but not without observing His commands. This is critical in discipleship because *observe* (Greek *tereo*) means "to guard from loss; to keep your eye upon." The commands of Jesus must be received as something so valuable that they are guarded like treasure (Matthew 13:44), not as mere trivia to win a free T-shirt.

Adhering to the immediate principle taught in the Christian's **Matthew 28:20** mandate, Bill Hull beautifully expounds these rich truths:

> The imperative command of the text is *make disciples*. This is the formula for evangelizing the world and the methodology required to bring reproduction and multiplication to world mission. The Great Commission without multiplication is evangelism paralyzed from the neck down. By specifically commanding the making of disciples, Jesus specified the work product of the church. He did not say, "Make converts," or, "Make Christians." Being a convert or a Christian does not necessarily equal reproduction. Many Christians are spiritually sterile; many don't take the Gospel forward...Therefore, disciples solve the crisis at the heart of the church. Disciple making creates a quality product and an effective work force. This is God's plan for His church.[4]

So, in literal context, this means disciples are made, not born. Every Christian is expected to be experiencing an ongoing transformation *into* a disciple of Jesus Christ. And, again, this is correctly accomplished by disciples of Christ "instructing" *new* Christians to "guard and focus" that with which Christ has "enjoined or charged" them. Wow, what a catalyst for inborn change! Obviously, a new Christian has a regenerated heart, but not a renewed mind. This is why it is essential to be discipled, so that behavior is completely reprogrammed through submissive compliance with the commands of Jesus Christ.

This is Hull's excellent conception of what Jesus means by *making disciples*:

When Jesus said, "*Make disciples*," by necessity, the disciples understood it to mean much more than simply getting people to believe in Jesus. They had seen hundreds come and go; had witnessed the multitudes of the needy, the takers, and the superficial scramble after the spectacular; and knew that getting people to say, "Yes, I believe," was not enough. They had to interpret it to mean to make out of others what Jesus had made out of them...They needed to produce people committed to reaching the world, those through whom the Gospel could be multiplied...[Disciples] are born by the Spirit of God, with the right factory-installed equipment. Then they must be built, trained, taught, and led to commitment to Jesus Christ. Therefore, Jesus commanded more than evangelism; He commanded taking all Christians to His definition of a mature disciple...To the degree the church dedicates itself to disciple making it is obedient to Christ. Now the mission is in trouble because the church has stopped at the first step to disciple making. Too often the church wins and baptizes, but does not teach and train. The sad result is a lack of reproduction and multiplication. God desires that every Christian be His disciple. He wills that every Christian become spiritually reproductive.[5]

The summary of all I have shared with you is fascinating. Biblical, Christ-commanded discipleship will inevitably produce a light-bearing, salt-block Christian (**Matthew 5:13-16**) in society, not an immature, hypocritical, carnal, *pew*scipled believer. Jesus Christ our Lord does not deserve anything less. This entire book hinges upon one verse of Scripture—**Matthew 28:20**! There is nothing added. There is nothing taken away. There are neither manmade philosophies nor creative ideologies on discipleship. Rather, this book is merely the commands of Christ to His disciples. All that is needed now is the "raw cut" of what Jesus actually commanded.

So, if Jesus Christ gave the commands, and the disciples knew what the commands were, the obvious question to ask is: *what are those commands?* That is exactly what the following pages contain. In them you will find *every* implicit and direct command that Jesus gave *only* to His disciples, those "teachable moments" that were intended to be perpetuated. Think about that for a moment. These commands are the literal substance of your discipleship; you cannot be discipled without them. So, until you are discipled this way, Christ's intended way, you have not *truly* been discipled. Your life as a disciple depends on your willingness to discover these commands and then obey them.

Moreover, this book is broken down into a fifty-two-week (one-year) study guide for the purpose of continuing the *exact* discipleship model established in the church at Antioch (**Acts 11:26**), which will provide structure as you are discipled. Also, within each teaching, you will discover a recurring format that provides a structure for each command being studied:

The Command *Introduced*
The Command *Interpreted*
The Command *Illustrated*
The Command *Initiated*
The Command *Interrogated*
The Command *Indestructible*
The Command *Inquired*

Don't miss this: each of the above command categories is linked to a study question at the end of each teaching. For example, throughout the book, "The Command Introduced" always links to the following study question: "*In what passage(s) of Scripture do you find Christ's command on _____?*" Similarly, "The Command Interpreted" always links to this question: "*What is the accurate interpretation of _____ you have discovered?*" This linking continues in a consecutive descending order through each teaching.

Therefore, what you are about to read has the power to transform you into a fruit-bearing follower of Jesus, not a broad-minded, semi-committed professor of Christ. It is my prayer that you will take these commands from Jesus as a matter of life and death, endeavoring to reflect Christ's glory through your obedience to Him. Oh, may you truly be discipled the way Christ intended! Whatever you do, wherever you go, whomever you see, be *all* that Christ saved you to be! It is time for your transformation to begin (**Romans 12:2; Ephesians 4:23**).

SECTION A: CHRIST'S COMMANDS AS THEY RELATE TO THE DISCIPLE *PERSONALLY*

CHAPTER 1: THE *ATTITUDE* OF A DISCIPLE

"Let this mind be in you which was also in Christ Jesus, who, being in the form of God, did not consider it robbery to be equal with God, but made Himself of no reputation, taking the form of a bondservant, and coming in the likeness of men. And being found in appearance as a man, He humbled Himself and became obedient to the point of death, even the death of the cross" (**Philippians 2:5-8**). If you are going to emulate any characteristics of Jesus, you must begin with a transformation of your attitude. Do you realize what this means? You are being summoned to exchange your attitude for the mind (attitude) of Christ. To be blunt, you cannot keep your attitude; it must die today.

Why does it have to be this way? Simply because your entire way of thinking has been constructed for years in a spiritually lost condition. Everything you perceive about yourself, society, family, work, church, marriage, and pain is warped when compared to Jesus' perception of such topics. You see, when we were born again, you and I brought all of our preconceived "baggage" to Christ. It is through the process of being discipled that we willingly exchange that baggage for Christ's ways of handling things. In doing so, remember that Jesus does not call us to debate or question Him; He calls us to surrender and trust Him. This is how your attitude undergoes a complete renovation! The following chapter is devoted to displaying the commands that Jesus gave, in order to construct the necessary attitude needed for following Him. So, may the attitude develop in you which was also in Christ Jesus.

TEACHING # 1.1: BROKENNESS

Week 1

<u>This week's objective</u>: *To discover the beauty of brokenness, as well as learn how to live with such a broken attitude before the Lord Jesus Christ...daily.*

THE COMMAND INTRODUCED:

- **Matthew 5:4** "Blessed are those who mourn, for they shall be comforted."
- **Luke 6:21** "...Blessed are you who weep now, for you shall laugh."

THE COMMAND INTERPRETED:

This is an implicit command. When Jesus spoke these words, perhaps brokenness resounded in His voice. In the New Testament Greek language, the words "mourn" (*penthos*) and "weep" (*klaio*) mean "to grieve" and "to sob." Speaking to His disciples, Jesus had far more in mind than the crises of life, those which break and devastate you. Christ actually wants you to see the greater crisis at hand: your lost depravity without Him. He wants you to live life never forgetting that truth.

This is the essence of His command. He is commanding for you to grieve and sob over your separation from God because of sin's curse (**Romans 3:9-12**). When our depravity collides with His divinity, brokenness will ignite! Jesus is commanding you to abandon self-sufficiency, to admit you have no ability within, leaving you with no choice but to anchor yourself near the harbor of His grace. Jesus is commanding you to live daily with deep sensitivity to the reality of your lostness and hopelessness apart from His love. Consequently, His command for brokenness is not lacking in promises. Jesus assures you that He will comfort you (**John 14:18**) and flood you with laughter (**John 16:20**) in exchange for your brokenness. This kind of attitude toward Jesus keeps us far from prideful territory, sheltered safely in the arms of humility.

THE COMMAND ILLUSTRATED:

There are two examples in God's word that accurately exemplify brokenness: one a tax collector, the other a disciple. To start, read **Luke 18:9-14**. Do you see the brokenness in the tax collector? Scripture says that he "*stood afar off*" and did not "*raise his eyes to heaven*" and in a plea "*beat his chest.*" All of these are indications of a broken spirit, a degree of unworthiness erupting from his contrite heart.

Another example can be found with Jesus' disciple, Simon Peter. Turn to **Luke 5:1-11**. Have you ever had that kind of success from fishing? Peter interpreted the miraculous catch of fish as a reflection of the deity of Jesus Christ. In response, he fell down "*at Jesus' knees*" and cried, "*Depart from me, for I am a sinful man, O Lord!*" At that moment, Peter saw himself in the presence of Jesus as no more than a speck of dust or a fly on the wall near the throne of a King. More than simply feeling broken, he *knew* how undeserving he was to be in the same boat with Jesus.

THE COMMAND INITIATED:

As a disciple of Jesus, yearn for brokenness. Plead for it. A Christian life that functions in spiritual brokenness is one empowered by faith and not by flesh. This is the life that you are commanded to live. So, how do you "practice" brokenness? How is it jumpstarted in your life as a disciple?

In his book *The Blessings of Brokenness*, Dr. Charles Stanley gives an answer to these questions:

God's purpose is to break our will, not our spirit. His purpose is not to destroy us, but to bring us to a position of maximum wholeness, maturity, and usefulness in His kingdom. He wants us to yield control of our lives to Him. The last thing in the world that Peter wanted to give up was control. He wanted to dictate whether his feet would be washed, the terms by which he would prove Jesus was indeed walking on the water, the way Jesus was going to become the Messiah.

We are like Peter—each one of us has a very difficult time giving up control. We always want to have the final say. Brokenness is God's process of bringing us to the point where we not only don't have the final say, we have nothing to say, except to ask, 'Lord Jesus, what would you have me to do?'...Listen to what Peter eventually wrote: '*God opposes the proud but gives grace to the humble*' (**1 Peter 5:5**). He was quoting **Proverbs 3:34** in his letter. Peter *knew* the reality of that verse in his life...[1]

Oh, precious disciple, allow God to break you. Through circumstances or opportunities, bow at His feet and worship at His footstool. Don't protest the breaking process! Since you cannot create or "turn on" brokenness, discipline yourself to receive it without reservation but with anticipation that Christ loves broken people. Position yourself by releasing your fighting will, thus allowing Christ to break you, cleanse you, mold you, and use you (**2 Timothy 2:21**).

THE COMMAND INTERROGATED:

Since Satan is God's enemy, he is yours too. He has one objective for your life: destruction! As brokenness evidences itself in your heart, Satan will panic, because you are a great threat to him. Why? Simply because your heart is selfless, dependent, clinging to the command of Jesus to be broken. So, as you can guess, the devil will interrogate you in hopes that you will avoid a penitent heart before the Lord Jesus.

The primary approach Satan will take is self-sufficiency; this gives birth to pride. He will attack your mind, tempting you to think that you can reach a plateau with God, a point in your Christian journey at which you don't need His hand anymore to help you walk. Satan will try to make you believe in yourself, to glorify your fleshly abilities above your faith in God. He does not want you to have a broken spirit. Rather, he wants you to live as a "free bird," doing whatever you please, answering to nobody.

Independency debilitates a life-attitude of brokenness! As Satan attacks you, don't forget that God hates pride (**Psalm 119:21; Proverbs 6:17; 11:2; 13:10; 16:18; 21:4; Obadiah 1:3**). Learn from Uzziah, a man used of the LORD until his arrogance got the best of him (**2 Chronicles 26:16**). Learn from two kings, one named Nebucharnezzar and the other Herod, two men who pridefully exalted themselves so high until the LORD humbled them so low (**Daniel 4:30; Acts 12:23**). Dear disciple, listen and learn; follow Jesus.

THE COMMAND INDESTRUCTIBLE:

As your spiritual warfare is waged against Satan, God will both protect and equip you for the battle. Honestly, your only hope for defeating the devil in daily combat is by using God's Word (**Ephesians 6:17**). It is the only way the Lord Jesus fought against Satan (**Luke 4:1-13**). Just how powerful are the words of Jesus? *"Heaven and earth will pass away, but My words will by no means pass away"* (**Matthew 24:35**). They are indestructible! In fact, God's word is not only indestructible; it is also incorruptible (**1 Peter 1:22-25**).

Therefore, since Scripture is eternally invincible, you need a memory verse, a Scripture to use when (not if) Satan decides to launch attack on you. The goal here is to protect brokenness in your Christian life. That brings us to the perfect Scripture: **Psalm 51:17**. It says, *"The sacrifices of God are a broken spirit, a broken and a contrite heart—these, O God, You will not despise."* God longs for a heart permeated with brokenness. Stand on this Scripture if you ever sense your heart toward Christ becoming cold, distant, independent, or egotistical. Remember: it is never acceptable to *not* be broken—never. Seek the face of God with all your heart until He breaks you. There is no other standard. There is no other alternative. Brokenness must be the cry of your heart.

THE COMMAND INQUIRED:

What cannot be measured cannot be evaluated. Therefore, it is essential to measure your comprehension of Christ's command in this teaching, or else the devil will snatch away the "seeds" of

Scripture sown into your heart (**Matthew 13:19**). To keep this from occurring, write down your answers to the following questions as they correlate with the teaching this week:

In what passage(s) of Scripture do you find Christ's commandment on **brokenness**?

_____

_____

_____

What is the accurate interpretation of **brokenness** you have discovered?

_____

_____

_____

_____

_____

In your own words, what are some real-life examples in Scripture of **brokenness**?

_____

_____

_____

_____

_____

What steps of initiation did you learn to take in order for

brokenness to transform your life?

_____

_____

_____

_____

_____

_____

How will Satan attack you to hinder **brokenness** in your life?

_____

_____

_____

_____

_____

_____

What memory verse will you use to protect Christ's command of **brokenness** in your life? Write it out.

_____

_____

_____

_____

TEACHING # 1.2: HUMILITY

Week 2

<u>This week's objective</u>: *To grasp the true meaning of humility and to learn how to position your heart in order to walk humbly with the Lord God Almighty.*

THE COMMAND INTRODUCED:

- **Matthew 5:5** *"Blessed are the meek, for they shall inherit the earth."*
- **Matthew 18:1-4** *"At that time the disciples came to Jesus, saying, 'Who then is greatest in the kingdom of heaven?' Then Jesus called a little child to Him, set him in the midst of them, and said, 'Assuredly, I say to you, unless you are converted and become as little children, you will by no means enter the kingdom of heaven. Therefore, whoever humbles himself as this little child is the greatest in the kingdom of heaven.'"*
- **Luke 6:39-40** *"And He spoke a parable to them: 'Can the blind lead the blind? Will they not both fall into the ditch? A disciple is not above his teacher, but everyone who is perfectly trained will be like his teacher.'"*
- **Luke 10:17-20** *"Then the seventy returned with joy, saying, 'Lord, even the demons are subject to us in your name. And He said to them, 'I saw Satan fall like lightening from heaven. Behold, I give you authority to trample on serpents and scorpions, and over all the power of the enemy, and nothing shall by any means hurt you. Nevertheless do not rejoice in this, that the spirits are subject to you, but rather rejoice because your names are written in heaven.'"*

THE COMMAND INTERPRETED:

The first three commands from Jesus are implicit, while the

last command is direct. These commands leave no room for misinterpretation. Clearly, Jesus yearned for humility to be the nonnegotiable trait of His followers because He knew that without humility, the disciples could not properly follow Him. These commands provide you with a four-point panorama of what Jesus Christ wants to develop in a heart saturated with humility.

The first command (**Matthew 5:5**) teaches you that humility is *controlled.* Jesus used an original Greek word for "meek" (*praeis*) that has a meaning of being "gentle, mild, or humble." This means your entire Christian life operates under self-control, thus reflecting disciplined humility. Dr. Warren Wiersbe offers a great insight on this command:

> Meekness is not weakness, for both Moses and Jesus were meek men (**Numbers 12:3; Matthew 11:29**). This word translated "meek" was used by the Greeks to describe a horse that had been broken. It refers to power under control.[2]

What a great truth! Gentle humility does not define you as a weak coward or a pushover. Rather, it means you are blessed by God, choosing to restrain your emotions due to your reverential fear of God, out of desire to live like King Jesus. Humility is controlled.

The second command (**Matthew 18: 1-4**) teaches you that humility is *conditioned.* The disciples are concerned about rank; Jesus is not. The disciples want to know how to become the greatest; Jesus is looking for the least. Therefore, in a tone of slight correction, Christ compares humility to that of a little child. Why a child? Perhaps it is because a child conveys such simple, innocent faith. Also, a child is totally dependent on someone else for his survival. In addition, a child has nothing tangible to validate his worth. And lastly, a child has nothing with which to build his ego. With all this considered, the Greek word for "humble" that Jesus used (*tapeinoo*) means to "depress or humiliate." Walking with Christ calls for a lowering of yourself, a heart attitude bowed down in worship of Jesus. Truly, humility is conditioned; you must decrease as He increases (**John 3:30**).

The third command (**Luke 6:39-40**) teaches you that

humility is *comparative.* Jesus uses the example of *"the blind leading the blind."* The idea portrayed is that of a wake-up call: a destructive ditch (circumstance) awaits those who are influenced by the wrong leader. Christ is making an undisguised point—He wants you to see that He alone is your leader, and because He knows where He's going, He will lead you the right way. Follow Him—He will never stumble or fail.

Jesus continues this idea by using the Greek word "above" (*huper*), meaning to be "over, beyond." In context, Christ is teaching you that you are not and never will be over or beyond Him, independent of His leading or His shepherding. To settle for anything less is to be led by yourself, "blinded" by your own willful disguise. Therefore, true humility can only be compared to the Teacher, in that you can only be *"like the Teacher"* as much as you are willing to be led by the Teacher. Sit at His feet. Hear His Word. Obey His command. Humility is comparative.

The fourth command (**Luke 10:17-20**) teaches you that humility is *connected.* Can you imagine seventy gospel workers on one mission trip? It must have been exciting. They were laboring for Christ—building His Kingdom, spreading His love. However, there was a problem: success. Success? That's right. They had been so successful in what they had done *for* and *through* Christ that they experienced a devilish distraction *away from* Christ. The point is clear: be careful not to get so caught up in your "successes" for Christ that you neglect to honor the "success" that Christ made out of you. Do you know how Christ made you a success? He saved you from Hell; He loved your sin with His grace. That is why Christ immediately turns the attention of these seventy gospel workers to His statement: "*...rather rejoice because your names are written in heaven.*" Jesus is disconnecting false humility from focus on Kingdom successes and reconnecting true humility with blood-washed, soul-saving, roll-calling, salvation success (**Revelation 20:15; 21:27; Philippians 4:3; Hebrews 12:23**). Praise God! The first keeps our eyes on the works for Christ; the latter returns the focus to Christ. Therefore, true humility is connected.

THE COMMAND ILLUSTRATED:

There is a great example of humility involving a centurion in the Bible. Turn to **Matthew 8:1-13**. Clearly, the centurion was in an authoritative position professionally. And sometimes, such positions can be a tempting breeding ground for pride. But just the opposite was true with this man. Humility had invaded his heart because he recognized his power was useless to help his servant. Such is the key to humility. Immediately, he acted upon his humble attitude by begging Jesus to heal his servant. When Christ agreed to do so, the man hesitated with these words: *"Lord, I am not worthy that You should come under my roof. But only speak a word and my servant will be healed."*

That is how humility is supposed to look, talk, and act. It evidences itself in amazement that Christ would come near us and dwell among us (**John 1:14**). Humility finds total contentment in what Christ says; it needs no proof. The centurion's trust was in Christ's words rather than His miracles, for he knew that the miraculous would merely be a byproduct of the Word of God. Do you want Christ to brag on your humility before our Heavenly Father, to rejoice over the greatest faith He's ever seen displayed among mortals? If so, learn from the centurion. Learn to walk before Christ every day in amazement that He's willing to *"come under your roof."* Learn to follow Christ continuously, trusting for Him to just *"speak a word"* about your most impossible circumstance imaginable. Live before Christ in joyous wonder; trust Him with relentless faith; praise Him forevermore. Humble yourself (**James 4:10**).

THE COMMAND INITIATED:

The greatest men and women that have ever sought the Kingdom of God effectively have been those characterized by humility. They have been vessels of honor, fashioned perfectly for Christ's use and for His glory. Such a vessel was the humble servant of Christ Andrew Murray. Educated in Scotland and Holland, Murray spent the bulk of his life in South Africa as a pastor and missionary. Among the many books he authored, one stands out, particularly in regards to the current topic. Simply entitled *Humility*, this volume beautifully documents Murray's thoughts on the subject:

> It is only by the indwelling of Christ in His divine humility that we can become truly humble. We have our pride from Adam; we must have our humility from Christ. Pride rules in us with incredible power; it is ourselves, our very nature. Humility must become ours in the same way; it must be our true selves, our very nature. As natural and easy as it has been to be proud, it must become natural for us to become humble. The promise is "Where sin abounded, grace did abound more exceedingly." All Christ's teaching of His disciples, and all their vain efforts, were the needful preparation for His entering into them in divine power, to give and be in them what He had taught them to desire...May I urge the pressing need to seek a deeper conviction of the unique place that humility holds in the life of every believer. Let us consider how far the disciples were advanced while this grace was still lacking, and let us pray that other gifts may not so satisfy us that we never grasp the fact that that the absence of humility is no doubt the reason why the power of God cannot do its mighty work. It is only where we, like the Son, truly know and show that we can do nothing of ourselves that God will do everything. It is when the truth of the indwelling Christ takes the place it deserves in the experience of believers that the church will put on her beautiful garment and humility will be seen in her teachers and members as the beauty of holiness.[3]

Amen! Humility. Humility. Humility. Day after day, measure everything you do and say by the standards of the Lord Jesus. Think like Him; talk like Him. Every morning before you leave your home, bow before Christ and plead, "Humility today, Jesus. Nothing else. Make me like You." Act on the Scriptures that call for humility by your faith to practice them. As you are faithful to do so, Christ will honor your obedience and produce within you His divine humility...daily. What a bargain!

THE COMMAND INTERROGATED:

Beware. Satan is highly threatened by your humble attitude before the Lord our God. He's on the prowl and will do whatever is necessary to discreetly convince you to exchange your humility for pride. Pride is your obstacle, like a twisted vine rooted in your heart and sprouting from your speech. The greatest "target zone" for Satan's attacks is your mind (**2 Corinthians 10:4-5**) and heart (**Jeremiah 17:9**). This is your battleground, a fortress for either victory or defeat. Whatever you do, wherever you go, whomever you help, give God the glory, honor, and praise due unto His holy Name (**Psalm 115:1; 1 Corinthians 1:29**). Humbly, walk with the Lord. Boast only of Christ and Him crucified for your sins (**Galatians 6:14**). As you live your Christian life, remember that Christ-like humility is found in being a servant (**Philippians 2:5-8**) more than an applause-seeking people pleaser (**Galatians 1:10**). Again and again, cautious of your adversary the devil, remember: walk humbly with your God.

THE COMMAND INDESTRUCTIBLE:

Thank God that humility does not have to be squelched! To Christ's praise, there is a Scripture that you need as your memory verse to defeat Satan: **1 Peter 5:5**. It says, "*...be clothed with humility, for God resists the proud, but gives grace to the humble.*" Herein is contained your sword for battle, your ammunition for defense. God is commanding you to "dress up" every day in humility, to wear it as an example of your life with Christ. If you ever begin to sense a cocky attitude forming, repent and get dressed. If you know deep down that your heart is full of pride because of something great that you've done, admit that you've lied to yourself, repent, and get dressed. Humility is like wearing a mismatched sock: you may have it on, but don't let it show. Since you know God's will is for you to dress up in humility every day, then your freedom to obey is unlimited. God is for you (**Romans 8:31**) and one day, Satan will be under you (**Romans 16:20**). Until then, fight with the Word of our God.

THE COMMAND INQUIRED:

What cannot be measured cannot be evaluated. Therefore, it is essential to measure your comprehension of Christ's command in this teaching, or else the devil will snatch away the "seeds" of Scripture sown into your heart (**Matthew 13:19**). To keep this from occurring, write down your answers to the following questions as they correlate with the teaching this week:

In what passage(s) of Scripture do you find Christ's commandment on **humility**?

_____

_____

_____

What is the accurate interpretation of **humility** you have discovered?

_____

_____

_____

_____

_____

In your own words, what are some real-life examples in Scripture of **humility**?

_____

_____

_____

_____

_____

What steps of initiation did you learn to take in order for **humility** to transform your life?

_____

_____

_____

_____

_____

_____

How will Satan attack you to hinder **humility** in your life?

_____

_____

_____

_____

_____

_____

What memory verse will you use to protect Christ's command of **humility** in your life? Write it out.

_____

_____

_____

_____

TEACHING # 1.3: PASSION

Week 3

This week's objective: To both define and demonstrate the biblical passion that Christ ignites within the heart of a disciple who seeks Him intensely.

THE COMMAND INTRODUCED:

- **Matthew 5:6** *"Blessed are those who hunger and thirst for righteousness, for they shall be filled."*
- **Luke 6:21** *"Blessed are you who hunger now, for you shall be filled."*

THE COMMAND INTERPRETED:

These two commands are both implicit and identical, and, oh, are they full of meaning! Are you ready? All right, here's what you need to understand about these commands. There are four Greek words that demand your attention: *hunger, thirst, righteousness, and filled.*

The first Greek word "hunger" (*peinao*) is used metaphorically in the sense of "being famished, starving." The second Greek word "thirst" (*dipsao*) is used figuratively to dramatize the actual "act of being thirsty for something." The third Greek word "righteousness" (*dikaiosune*) stands for "justification." The fourth Greek word "filled" (*chortazo*) means "to gorge, to supply in abundance." In regard to passion, the first two words (hunger and thirst) call for its *practice*; the third word (righteousness) aims for its *prize*; and the fourth word (filled) results in its *promise*. So, what does all this mean? I am glad you asked.

The Lord Jesus Christ has defined how passion ignites in the hearts of His disciples. Do you see the picture He has painted for you? The object of this command is righteousness. Since its Greek meaning connects you to justification, this can be interpreted as a reflection of your relationship with Christ. How? You have been "justified" through the shed blood of Jesus Christ, standing in His righteousness alone (**Ephesians 2:13; Titus 3:5-7**). Why? All because you have no righteousness in and of yourself that is worthy of establishment (**Isaiah 64:6**).

So, to the degree that you rejoice in this reality, you burn deep inside to thrive in that "righteous," right-standing relationship with Christ. This is where passion is born. As you deny your flesh and pursue righteousness, you find yourself famished, starved, and thirsting for Christ (**Psalm 42:1-3**), longing to abide in a right relationship with Him. Then, the promise: "*You shall be filled!*" With what? His righteousness! In what manner? Abundantly drenched in a waterfall of His likeness, made to live in the floodplain of His glory (**John 10:10**). Amazing! That will make you want to shout! So, go ahead and give God the praise (**Psalm 47:1**).

THE COMMAND ILLUSTRATED:

One of the best Scriptures to correctly exemplify passion is found in **Matthew 15:21-28**. While the passage has as its focus a Phoenician woman's faith and miracle, pay close attention to the passion that propelled her toward it. According to the text, this lady had every obstacle against her to quench her passion. As a woman, she was considered less than men. As a Gentile, she held the status of an outcast. As if this weren't enough, she was ignored by the disciples, and her daughter was undergoing satanic attack!

Thank God her story demonstrates to you that in the midst of difficulty, passion does not abolish; it advances. This woman searched (**verses 21-22**), waited (**verses 23-24**), worshiped (**verses 25-26**), answered (**verse 27**), and received (**verse 28**), all by a faith flaming from coals of passion. She displays a beautiful picture of a passionate relationship with Christ, one that will gladly settle for "dog crumbs" just to be in His Presence and fall at His feet! Your passion for the Lord Jesus Christ must look no different. Like this woman, hunger and thirst for fellowship with Christ. Regardless of the obstacles that life and culture hurl at you, pursue passion. In spite of the people that talk about you, pursue passion. You want Christ; He wants you. Don't seek to generate an emotional surge in hopes of creating passion. Instead, in as undignified a manner as possible, hunger and thirst for Christ, His Word, His ways, His life. Then you won't find passion; it will find you.

THE COMMAND INITIATED:

The goal right now is for your passion in Christ to be something you live by more than something you dream about. It must come alive! But how? Christ. He's the solution. You see, it is your full surrender to Jesus that provides Him with the substance to accomplish His work in you (**Ephesians 2:10**). Your heart is like firewood, and Jesus has the match. It is through your willing availability that Christ ignites passion in proportion to your sacrifice (**Romans 12:1-2**).

In his book *The Courage to Be Christian*, Mike Nappa delivers excellent comments that show how this life of passion begins:

> If any cause is worth dying for, it is the cause of Christ. But even more, a relationship with God is worth *living* for! Still, a life lived in passionate devotion to Jesus is easier said than done. It costs more than we care to admit—everything we are and everything we have, minute after minute, hour after hour, day after day. Choosing that kind of life is difficult, and all the more so if you are blessed with an abundance of life's finer things. Don't believe me? Just ask the one we know as the rich young ruler. His story is told in **Mark 10:17-22**...Silence reigns in that moment. Jesus waits. The young man adds things up, but the tally finally gets too high. Sadly, he chooses the temporary instead of the eternal. He turns back on God and walks away—a rich man unwilling to part with his wealth, even for the prize of eternal life. Jesus presents that same demand to you and me today. He asks not only that we have the courage to die for Him; even more, He demands that we have the courage to *live* for Him. That means we give up all the right and title to anything we are and anything we own and place it in His hands. We courageously attempt to live out our daily experience in ways that are pleasing to Him, ways of integrity, honor, and truth. We freely walk away from sin and into His arms of

grace every moment, every hour, every day. We give up our dreams and ask God to give us His dreams instead. We pray daily for God's desire for our lives to become our own desire for our lives—whatever that means and whatever the cost. If only it were as easy to do these things as it is to talk about them! Fact is, we *can't* do them. We, in our own strength, face an impossible task if we want to pursue God with that kind of passion and abandonment. Only the strength of the Holy Spirit can empower us to live this kind of life for Christ, which means our primary responsibility is this: We must constantly plead for God's Holy Spirit to make this lifestyle possible—and then follow His leading when that power comes.[4]

Amen! That is how passion is uncovered and unleashed. It grows and grows as you devote yourself entirely to the cause of Christ. You embrace your identity in Christ and follow Him unashamedly...daily (**Luke 9:23**). You discard any habit, hobby, routine, or relationship that stands as a threat to your passion (**1 Corinthians 9:27**). Nothing is too great a cost when the passion begins moving in your heart like a runaway train! Oh, dear friend, just like the disciples, continue in your decision to forsake all and follow Jesus (**Luke 5:11**).

THE COMMAND INTERROGATED:

As always, Satan is on the prowl. He will do whatever is necessary to attack you in such a way as to hinder your passion for Christ altogether. Think about it: What could possibly be the primary obstacle to passion? What would keep its desire masked?

Complacency. That's it. Complacency is understood as sitting back, remaining overly contented with a lifestyle that evades passion for Christ. Complacency is choosing to exchange the narrow, difficult path that Jesus exemplified (**Matthew 7:13-14; 1 Peter 2:21**) for a life of disobedient ease (**Luke 12:13-21**). Satan is after your passion. Beware of the enticing distractions that he will set up to turn your focus away from the commands of Christ. That hellish rascal hates our Christ and all who follow Him. Watch out for his crafty assaults on your life that try to develop your passion more into fulfilling a hobby than into being a soulwinner! Satan's techniques are disguised and deadly, and he's bent on your absolute destruction. He's after your passion, so guard your heart (**Proverbs 4:23**) with your God-given shield of faith (**Ephesians 6:16**). Do not let your passion for Christ fall victim to the cunning trickery of your adversary, the devil.

THE COMMAND INDESTRUCTIBLE:

Hallelujah for the Word of God! There is a memory verse of Scripture that you must use to fight Satan: **Jeremiah 29:13**. The Lord says, *"And you will seek Me and find Me, when you search for Me with all your heart."* How much of your heart does He require? All of it. When will you find Him? Only when you are seeking Him.

You see, there will be days when Satan is attacking so strongly that you don't feel like seeking God or continuing your passion. You know those days—when everything is falling apart, when your job is not working out, when your health keeps fighting against you. Yes, there will be days along this journey with Christ that life gets tough. What do you do?

You stand your ground in spite of Satan's attack. You stand on the Rock of your salvation with your faith anchored steadfast to the Word of God—Jeremiah 29:13. In it is revealed the heart and will of God. He is calling out to you, inviting you to seek Him with all your heart, promising that you will find Him. God is asking you to enter the marathon of life and run toward Him, never losing sight of your passion and prize (**Philippians 3:7-14**). Cry out to the Lord, "O God, I choose to search for you!" The Lord knows the "want to" is a struggle when faced with Satan's attack. But He's there, waiting to rescue you and empower you to overcome and conquer (**Romans 8:37**), because God is for you (**Romans 8:31**) and is fighting your battle of complacency. God's Word will not fail! Memorize and quote the Scripture believingly in the face of any attack that targets your passion. You can do it, for it is Christ who strengthens you to do so (**Philippians 4:13**).

THE COMMAND INQUIRED:

What cannot be measured cannot be evaluated. Therefore, it is essential to measure your comprehension of Christ's command in this teaching, or else the devil will snatch away the "seeds" of Scripture sown into your heart (**Matthew 13:19**). To keep this from occurring, write down your answers to the following questions as they correlate with the teaching this week:

In what passage(s) of Scripture do you find Christ's commandment on **passion**?

_____

_____

_____

What is the accurate interpretation of **passion** you have discovered?

_____

_____

_____

_____

_____

In your own words, what are some real-life examples in Scripture of **passion**?

_____

_____

_____

_____

_____

What steps of initiation did you learn to take in order for **passion** to transform your life?

_____

_____

_____

_____

_____

_____

How will Satan attack you to hinder **passion** in your life?

_____

_____

_____

_____

_____

_____

What memory verse will you use to protect Christ's command of **passion** in your life? Write it out.

_____

_____

_____

_____

TEACHING # 1.4: SCRIPTURE

Week 4

<u>This week's objective</u>: *To assess the value of Holy Scripture and to learn how to apply its empowering truths in a daily walk with Christ.*

THE COMMAND INTRODUCED:

- **Matthew 5:17-19** *"Do not think that I came to destroy the Law or the Prophets. I did not come to destroy but to fulfill. For assuredly, I say to you, till heaven and earth pass away, one jot or one tittle will by no means pass from the law till all is fulfilled. Whoever therefore breaks one of the least of these commandments, and teaches men so, shall be called least in the kingdom of heaven; but whoever does and teaches them, he shall be called great in the kingdom of heaven."*

THE COMMAND INTERPRETED:

Jesus is giving a well-versed implicit command. Due to strong Jewish tradition, Christ briefed His disciples on the Law and the Prophets. He knew they had a connection to it, both through their forefathers and their culture. So, before they started accusing Him of heresy, Christ explained that He was not destroying the Old Testament Law of Moses, but *fulfilling* it. What does this mean? Christ is the fulfillment of the Law in all its aspects, for the Law pointed to the Messiah (Christ) to come for the nation of Israel. Yet, through His endorsement of the Law, Jesus was affirming the Old Testament as the inspired, inerrant, authoritative Word of God! Nothing will affect its validity until Christ says so. Jesus makes such an emphatic defense of the Scriptures because He has a greater plan in mind for His disciples.

That plan, in context, was to help the disciples rightly relate to the Word of God. Jesus strongly exhorted them to have a mighty foundation in the Holy Scriptures. To make this clear, Christ issued a paralleled contrast, with the Kingdom of Heaven as the backdrop: the *least* and the *greatest*. The former is seen as a failure; the latter is seen as faithful. Both have to do with the commandments of Scripture, so it is of paramount importance to understand what Jesus wants you to know about your relationship to Scripture.

There are two Greek words that govern correct interpretation of this command. The first word "breaks" (*luo*) means "to loosen or break up into." The second word "does" (*poieo*) means in a very wide sense "to make or do." Interestingly, in both classifications of being called least or greatest, the element of *teaching* is at the center. The people directly influenced through such teaching are either encouraged to break the commands or keep them. This can be both alarming and awesome, depending on the authenticity of the disciple.

Therefore, what Christ is saying to you as His disciple is that you analyze your relationship with Him by your relationship with Scripture. The two are synonymous! To break His commands is to loosen one's grip of obedience on His Word. Rather than causing someone to utterly depart from God all at once, this kind of disobedience leads people to break away in "little pieces" of rebellion, one at a time. Furthermore, the term "least" is better understood as an outcast, someone who has a form of godliness only (**2 Timothy 3:5**), who actually denies Christ by works that point to continual disobedience of Scripture (**Titus 1:16**). This means such a person is *not* a true disciple of Jesus; Christ warned us not to be surprised (**Matthew 7:21-23**).

On the other hand, when you position the Scriptures at the forefront of your life (**Deuteronomy 6:8**), you put into practice what they call for you to do. You begin living out your relationship with Christ as interpreted by His Word. This is a true disciple; this is you.

What are the characteristics of this obedience? First, a genuine disciple of Christ has crucified the flesh in order to follow Jesus (**Galatians 5:24**). Second, a genuine disciple of Christ has evidence that proves his or her new birth into God's Kingdom (**Matthew 7:15-20**). Last, a genuine disciple maintains a steadfast gaze upon doing the will of God (**1 John 2:15-17**). Amen! It is through your obedience to Scripture that the risen Christ lives His Word through you, thus growing you in grace, maturing you in love, and magnifying His Name.

THE COMMAND ILLUSTRATED:

Perhaps one of the greatest examples of being rightly related to the Scriptures is the Apostle Paul. After his conversion to Christ (**Acts 9:1-6**), Paul launched like a missile for the Kingdom of God (**Acts 9:20-22**). Throughout Christian history, there have been many believers who began just as strongly as Paul did but finished weak and defeated. However, this is not the case with Paul the Apostle. The best way to see his obedient relationship with Scripture is to look at the end of his time on earth.

Read **2 Timothy 4:6-9**. These words are believed by many to have been penned during the final days of the apostle. The language "*drink offering*" and "*departure*" indicates that Paul is nearing the end of his life. As you trace back through the Scriptures and take careful note of his life *after* coming to Christ, you will find that he was a true disciple. In fact, Paul was a model disciple for the entire Christian community of his day. Today, his exemplary lifestyle still serves as a standard for you and me. Paul lived the gospel and loved the Word of God! The apostle desired nothing more than Jesus' commands.

The greatest deathbed statement that any believer could make would be an echo of Paul: "*I have fought the good fight, I have finished the race, I have kept the faith.*" The Apostle Paul's mind was made up from the beginning. He did not treasure his life (**Philippians 1:19-21; Acts 20:24**), but willingly sacrificed his comfort, dignity and reputation for the sake of his love for Jesus Christ (**Philippians 3:7-14; 2 Corinthians 4:7-12, 16-18; 6:4-10; 11:22-29**). Why such a life? Because that is how much it costs to live by the gospel. Paul's life is a "price tag" of undignified, excuseless obedience. While it is easy to marvel at his devoted life, it is much easier to act in a cowardly manner and refuse any influence from it. Dear believer, as much as is in you, live by the gospel commands of our Lord Jesus Christ (**Romans 1:15**). Cling to the Word of God, and heed the Scriptures in your Christian life to the glory and praise of our Father.

THE COMMAND INITIATED:

There is no greater joy than faithfully practicing the teachings of Scripture and then experiencing its graceful, transforming power in your life. In order for you to gain a realistic perspective of God's Word and its place in your life, consider some insight from Dr. John MacArthur. In his book *Unleashing God's Word in Your Life*, he shares an intriguing thought:

> The Bible is an amazing book. It's amazing in that it stands up to many tests of authenticity. But beyond that, it's particularly amazing when looked at from a spiritual and moral perspective. The Bible claims to be alive and powerful. That's a tremendous statement. No other living book *exists*. There are some books that change your thinking, but this is the only book that can change your nature. This is the only book that can totally transform you from the inside out.
>
> There's a section in **Psalm 19:7-9** that is Scripture's own testimony to itself...**Psalm 19** says that the Scripture is "sure"—absolute, trustworthy, reliable—"making wise the simple." The Hebrew word translated "simple" comes from a root that speaks of an open door. Ancient Jewish people described a person with a simple mind as someone with a head like an open door: everything comes in; everything goes out...The Bible says it is able to make such a person wise. Wisdom to the Jew was the skill of daily living. To the Greek it was sheer sophistry—an abstraction. So when the Hebrew text says it can make a simple person wise, it means it can take the uninitiated, naive, uninstructed person who's undiscerning and unskilled and make him skilled in every aspect of daily living. What a fantastic promise![5]

The Word of our God is what you need; submit your entire mindset to Scripture. When Jesus came to John the Baptist to be baptized, John refused at first because it didn't make any sense (**Matthew 3:14**). Then, something happened. In response, Jesus rebuked him by saying *"permit it to be so now, for thus it is fitting for us to fulfill all righteousness"* (**verse 15**). The word "permit" in the Greek language means "to send away." Basically, Jesus was telling John to eliminate his preconceived ideas about what he thought was the "right" thing to do. Loosely translated, Jesus was saying, "John, throw away your opinion!" You know what? Some things never change. Christ also needs you to throw away your interpretation of how you think He wants you to serve Him. He doesn't need "our lip" (**Job 42:3**); He needs our surrender to the governing power of His Word. So, do just that. Freely and willingly allow obedience to Scripture to reprogram you into who you are saved to be in Christ.

THE COMMAND INTERROGATED:

Perhaps some Christians may think that Satan's primary method for hindering God's Word in believers' lives has to do with neglecting the reading of the Bible. Other Christians who do study their Bibles may feel Satan pounces on them the most as they attempt to memorize its verses. While these are ways Satan assaults believers, I assure you the lack of reading and difficulty of memorization are actually indications of defeat, not attack. Therefore, the greatest, most subtle way in which Satan attacks you regarding Scripture is assertively clear: *comprehension*.

Jesus said, "*When anyone hears the word of the Kingdom, and does not **understand it**, then the wicked one comes and snatches away what was sown in his heart. This is he who received seed by the wayside*" (**Matthew 13:19**). Do you see now how in vain it is to read and memorize Scripture if you do not "understand" it? Beware! Oh, precious disciple, Satan will do whatever is necessary to keep you from meditating on God's Word, because meditation produces comprehension.

Watch out for Satan's trickery as he labors deceitfully to provide you with opportunities that distract you from understanding Scripture. He will keep you too busy; put your foot down and make time. Don't try to appease your conscience by merely *reading* a Bible verse every day—comprehend it! Get up earlier. Go to bed later. Rearrange your lunch break at work. Do whatever is necessary to make sure God's Word is properly planted in the soil of your heart. If you don't, I assure you, Scripture "seeds" will fall by the wayside in your life; you will miss out on what God could have accomplished in you.

THE COMMAND INDESTRUCTIBLE:

I have some good news. Are you ready? Here it is: "But the anointing which you have received from Him abides in you, and you do not need that anyone teach you; but as the same anointing **teaches you**, concerning all things and is true, and is not a lie, and just as it has taught you, you will abide in Him" (**1 John 2:27**). Isn't that great? This is your memory verse. This is your weapon to defeat satanic forces of evil as they come against you when you are studying your Bible.

This "*anointing*" comes from the Holy One (**1 John 2:20**), Who is Jesus. And the actual anointing is the outpouring of the Holy Spirit in your life, to *teach* you the Scripture He wrote (**2 Peter 1:21**). Jesus said the Holy Spirit would lead you into all truth (**John 16:13**). No wonder John said it is "*true, and is not a lie.*" You have the Holy Spirit dwelling in you (**1 Corinthians 3:16**) for the purpose of teaching you the Scriptures, to provide you with the comprehension that Satan is bent on destroying. So, when you read a Scripture and don't "get it," quote **1 John 2:27** to the Lord in prayer. Jesus Christ will give you understanding in exchange for your confusion. Believe God for that to be your weapon to defeat Satan by God's invincible Word!

THE COMMAND INQUIRED:

What cannot be measured cannot be evaluated. Therefore, it is essential to measure your comprehension of Christ's command in this teaching, or else the devil will snatch away the "seeds" of Scripture sown into your heart (**Matthew 13:19**). To keep this from occurring, write down your answers to the following questions as they correlate with the teaching this week:

In what passage(s) of Scripture do you find Christ's commandment on **Scripture**?

_____

_____

What is the accurate interpretation of **Scripture** you have discovered?

_____

_____

_____

_____

_____

_____

In your own words, what are some real-life examples in the Bible of **Scripture**?

_____

_____

_____

_____

_____

_____

What steps of initiation did you learn to take in order for **Scripture** to transform your life?

_____

_____

_____

_____

_____

_____

How will Satan attack you to hinder **Scripture** in your life?

_____

_____

_____

_____

_____

What memory verse will you use to protect Christ's command of **Scripture** in your life? Write it out.

_____

_____

_____

_____

_____

_____

TEACHING # 1.5: PURITY

Week 5

This week's objective: To comprehend purity from God's perspective and to align your lifestyle in accordance with it.

THE COMMAND INTRODUCED:

- **Matthew 5:8** *"Blessed are the pure in heart, for they shall see God."*

THE COMMAND INTERPRETED:

This implicit command of Christ to His disciples evoked wonder and awe, for "seeing God" was both personally and culturally an intriguing thought. Such a comment by Jesus raised eyebrows and caused His listeners to seek understanding. Therefore, the focal points of this command lay in the phrases *"pure in heart"* and *"see God."*

To interpret this, we consider the prize before the pursuit. The prize, of course, is to see God. The Greek word Jesus used for "see" (*optanomai*) means "to gaze with wide open eyes at something remarkable." This Greek word is not like other words used in the New Testament, which usually refer merely to looking at something passively. Interestingly, this word Jesus used is better understood as experiencing God rather than actually "seeing" Him with the naked eye. But how?

Jesus provides the answer through the second focal phrase: *"pure in heart."* In "seeing" or experiencing God in all His glory, the heart is the springboard, while purity is the jump! You see, God commands us to love Him with all our heart (**Matthew 22:37**), but "purity" of heart is another subject. The Greek word Jesus spoke for "pure" (*katharos*) actually means "clean." A clean heart is a holy heart, which results in "seeing" the Lord (**Hebrews 12:14**). Therefore, as you "cleanse" your heart (**Psalm 119:9**) through Scripture, God

Himself dwells with you, abiding within you as you abide in Him. You know what this means, right? You experience God in the fullest sense of the word! Hallelujah!

THE COMMAND ILLUSTRATED:

There is a perfect example in Scripture for you to read. Turn to **John 1:43-51**. As Jesus was recruiting His disciples in the region of Galilee, He called Phillip, who in turn called a man by the name of Nathanael. Now, pay close attention to **verse 47**. Jesus, operating in His all-knowing ability, bragged on Nathanael by acknowledging him as having *"no deceit."* This means Nathanael was a man driven by love for God because he set his heart to seek the Lord (**Psalm 91:14-16**)!

Isn't it interesting that Christ knew Nathanael before he and Jesus ever met? This is a reminder that Jesus sees our hearts and examines our purity. You can't pretend to be something you're not, because Christ knows the real you. He longs to find your heart in similar shape to Nathaniel's—a heart governed by purity and not by deceit. It is this kind of heart that attracts Christ's Presence and receives the invitation to dwell with Him (**Psalm 24:3-4**).

THE COMMAND INITIATED:

In every command of Christ, action is always essential. Without question, as a disciple of Jesus, you desire to pursue purity in your life. There are no exceptions. For a roadmap of the direction to purity, consider Troy Cartmill. In his book *It's Time for Pure Hearts*, he comments with such simplicity on this necessary trait in the life of a disciple:

> After our spiritual birth we have a desperate need for our soul (mind, will, and emotions) to be refurbished. The stench of the world must be eliminated. Our *stinking thinking* must be replaced with the sweet aroma of God's word (**2 Corinthians 2:14**). The spiritual renovation begins by the renewing of our minds. The word *renew* means renovation; it comes from a root word indicating

repetition, intensity, and reversal...The power of repetition is a strength that separates the extraordinary from the ordinary. Athletes with God-given talents utilize the potency of repetition. Even though they have natural talents they must have a mindset of dieting, exercising, and training to the maximum to gain a competitive edge. They become intensely focused on reversing negative thinking, refusing to entertain a "born to lose" attitude. As Christians we should be like a boxer, buffeting and subduing our bodies. Our bodies (flesh) become submissive to God's word as our minds are renewed to the Word of God (**1 Corinthians 9:25-27**).[6]

So, after all has been said, it can be tied together with **Proverbs 23:7**: "*As a man thinks in his **heart**, so is he*." Clearly, the heart and the mind are greatly affected or infected by one another. Your heart is a sponge, soaking up that to which you expose it. On top of this, our natural depravity issues us an evil heart to begin with (**Jeremiah 17:9-10**), which is why we are exhorted to guard it (**Proverbs 4:23**). No wonder James is so passionate about the believer "cleaning up" in conjunction with approaching the Lord of glory (**James 4:8**). Indeed, your mind and your heart are eternally connected. Purify yourself daily from the filth of this world and society (**2 Corinthians 7:1**).

THE COMMAND INTERROGATED:

Satan is anything but pure; he is the epitome of evil, standing opposed to purity in all its forms. You have already learned that the heart and mind are synonymous in reference to the way they are used together in Scripture. So, since this is the case, how do you think Satan plots against you, to tempt you to fall from purity into a pit? Through attacks on your mind.

Satan's goal is to cleverly tempt you into a lifestyle of being carnally minded and not spiritually minded (**Romans 8:6**). The carnal mind is an idle mind, speaking idle words, living a defeated idle lifestyle. Since Satan attacks in seasons (**Luke 4:11**), it can happen faster than you realize, lulling a believer into a spiritually lazy sleep. Like Peter denying Jesus, so you as a disciple of Christ can find yourself living below your standards of integrity and yielding your fight for convictions. This is the way Satan works against you. Be on guard. Don't let him whisper lies into your mind that it is okay with God for you to compromise His Word for your fleshly appetites. Be careful not to let the devil persuade you to exchange your biblical worldview for a carnal, philosophical view of mankind. Satan is cunning; he is crafty. He will attack your mind— be on guard.

THE COMMAND INDESTRUCTIBLE:

How can you be on guard? How can you fight against Satan and actually experience victory? It's through the unchanging, all-powerful Word of God. Here's your memory verse to use in times during which purity is at stake in your heart: *"For the weapons of our warfare are not carnal but mighty in God for the pulling down of strongholds, casting down arguments and every high thing that exalts itself against the knowledge of God, bringing every thought into captivity to the obedience of Christ* (**2 Corinthians 10:4-5**).

You are encouraged to bring *every* thought into captivity and to measure it in obedience to Christ. Your mind is Satan's battleground and ultimately will defile your heart if you allow him to defeat you. But that's just it: you don't have to be defeated. Our Lord Jesus Christ has already won the battle for you (**1 John 3:8**). You are given both the right and the power to capture every thought that invades your mind and weigh it on the scales of obedience to Jesus. If it is a thought that Christ is not pleased with, confess it to Him out of obedience before it grows hellish roots down into your heart. Claim the Scripture over your attack. God's Word is your only hope in defeating the devil.

Whatever you do, stay focused on your heavenly course, meditating on things above (**Colossians 3:1-4**). Therein is the will of God for you, so claim it. If your eyes are fighting the evil lures of this world and society, then hold onto the Scripture in **Psalm 119:37**. In Christ, you are not a failure, you are a ransomed, blood-bought child of God! So live like it, talk like it, and think like it. Trust the Scriptures through every attack as you continue to press on toward the Kingdom of our God.

THE COMMAND INQUIRED:

What cannot be measured cannot be evaluated. Therefore, it is essential to measure your comprehension of Christ's command in this teaching, or else the devil will snatch away the "seeds" of Scripture sown into your heart (**Matthew 13:19**). To keep this from occurring, write down your answers to the following questions as they correlate with the teaching this week:

In what passage(s) of Scripture do you find Christ's commandment on **purity**?

_____

_____

_____

What is the accurate interpretation of **purity** you have discovered?

_____

_____

_____

_____

_____

_____

In your own words, what are some real-life examples in Scripture of **purity**?

_____

_____

_____

_____

_____

_____

What steps of initiation did you learn to take in order for **purity** to transform your life?

_____

_____

_____

_____

_____

How will Satan attack you to hinder **purity** in your life?

_____

_____

_____

_____

_____

What memory verse will you use to protect Christ's command of **purity** in your life? Write it out.

_____

_____

_____

_____

_____

_____

TEACHING # 1.6: PROVISION

Week 6

This week's objective: To discover the ways in which God provides for your needs and to learn how to reach out with your faith to receive His provisions.

THE COMMAND INTRODUCED:

- **Matthew 17:24-27** *"When they had come to Capernaum, those who received the temple tax came to Peter and said, 'Does your Teacher not pay the temple tax?' He said, 'Yes.' And when he had come into the house, Jesus anticipated him, saying, 'What do you think, Simon? From whom do the kings of the earth take customs or taxes, from their sons or from strangers?' Peter said to Him, 'From strangers.' Jesus said to him, 'Then the sons are free. Nevertheless, lest we offend them, go to the sea, cast in a hook, and take the fish that comes up first. And when you have opened its mouth, you will find a piece of money; take that and give it to them for Me and you.'"*

- **Luke 22:5-36** *"And He said to them, 'When I sent you without money bag, knapsack, and sandals, did you lack anything?' So they said, 'Nothing.' Then He said to them, 'But now, he who has a money bag, let him take it, and likewise a knapsack; and he who has no sword, let him sell his garment and buy one.'"*

THE COMMAND INTERPRETED:

One command is implicit, and the other is direct. First consider the implicit command found in the story of Jesus and Peter. In this context, Jesus is demonstrating to His disciple Peter that because He is the Messiah King, neither He nor His family (of which Peter is a member) owes taxes, for they are free from obligation to pay (who would dare ask the Creator to pay for something?). However, Jesus recognizes that His Kingship is not culturally appropriated. So, to keep from offending His onlookers, Jesus uses an awkward situation to teach a valuable lesson on provision. This lesson uncovers an amazing truth: although Jesus supplied the money, Peter had to actively retrieve the money. Just as Mary had to roll away the stone to experience God's miraculous resurrection of Lazarus (**John 11**), so Peter had to go fishing to receive God's unique provision for his need. Everything you have is dispensed from God's supply, but it is clear that Christ wants to involve you in the process of receiving your provision. A faith that believes is a faith that receives!

The second command is direct and unique. In its context, Jesus is nearing His Crucifixion. He commanded His disciples to prepare for this by taking their necessary supplies such as a moneybag, knapsack, sword, and sandals. Can you see why? It's because He will not be with them for a few days, at least not physically, to supply their needs. So, Jesus uses His soon-coming temporary absence from them to remind them of when they did not need such materials because He was with them, providing for them (**Luke 9:1-6; 10:1-24**). The key phrase in this direct command is that Jesus *"sent"* them with nothing, yet they lacked nothing. Jesus is teaching you as His disciple that when you're engaged in His Kingdom labor, you will lack nothing for your life journey. Supernaturally, God will provide your every need, every time, everywhere (**Matthew 6:33**)!

THE COMMAND ILLUSTRATED:

Perhaps one of the best-illustrated passages in the Bible on provisions is the story in **Acts 2:40-47; 4:32-35**. Soon after the coming of the Holy Spirit at Pentecost, the early church exploded in growth. And, of course, with the increase in people came an increase in the diversity of economic situations represented. While there are many examples of how the early Christians lived for Christ, one attribute shows clearly in this passage: they were selfless. You see, God often meets the needs of His people not only through a fish's mouth or a knapsack memory but also through His own followers. In this early church, people's possessions were of no value at all when compared to the neediness of a brother or sister in

Christ. People did not think selfishly; they truly loved their neighbor as themselves. And in today's modern church, that standard is not negotiable to change.

As profound as it sounds, the less you have, the more you can give (**Ecclesiastes 11:1**). In obedience to Christ's command, give, give, give. Distribute, within reason (not to the neglect of your family), your provisions to someone in need within your own congregation of the saints. Jesus has already said that He wants you to do that (**Acts 20:35**). Again, the key to learn here is that God provides through His own people, as well as through many other avenues, some supernatural. Praise be to our God of provision!

THE COMMAND INITIATED:

Frankly, you cannot truly appreciate the value of God's provision until you know what it's like in the valley of need. At this point, it would be good for you to read the Book of Ruth. That's right, the whole book...all four chapters. The faith Ruth put into action resulted in her provision. I like the way Janet Kobobel Grant puts it in her book *Trusting That God Will Provide*. Drawing from the Book of Ruth, Grant's comments supplement the understanding of provision:

> Ruth shows us how big her heart is when, at the beginning of the play, she travels away from all she knows. She leaves her country, her language, her friends and family, her customs, her gods, and the grave sites of her husband, brother-in-law, and father-in-law. Then she opens her heart to her mother-in-law, a new country, a new language, new customs, and a new God...As widows in the Hebrew culture, she and Naomi are in a precarious place—vulnerable, poor, and without a male relative's protection. So Ruth humbles her heart, bends her back, and develops calluses on her hands as she follows the barley harvesters, picking up what they have dropped...Ruth has discovered that, even in a new land, with no one to protect her and no resources to draw upon, God will provide...Through Ruth's story we learn that if the heart aches, God can satisfy its longing. If we have an empty

pantry, He can fill it. If we have bitter relatives, God can show Himself good even to them. If we feel vulnerable and unprotected, God will shelter us under His wings. If we have a sorrowful past, God can turn it into a joyful future. All this, if we will give Him our wholehearted devotion.[7]

Praise the holy Name of Jesus! God is your provider. He knows the needs you have before you even ask Him (**Matthew 6:8**). Hang on to your faith in Christ, the faith that moves mountains and conquers worry. As a child of God, put your faith in Christ into action, not to manipulate God's will but to maximize belief in His provision. This world has yet to see a child of the King not cared for by our Heavenly Father (**Psalm 37:25**). Stand on this truth as a disciple of Jesus.

THE COMMAND INTERROGATED:

While God is providing, Satan is plotting. Just think about it: when you are provided for, you are stable and satisfied. You are not tempted to worry about your sustenance, and you experience an overwhelming surge of contentment. All of these characteristics of a Christian who has been provided for by God are insulting to Satan. He cannot stand to see you prosper. He cannot stand to watch your Heavenly Father provide for your every need.

That brings us to a Scripture that insightfully summarizes Satan's agenda: **John 10:10**. "*The thief does not come except to steal, and to kill, and to destroy. I have come that they may have life, and that they may have it more abundantly.*" Jesus is elevating His role as the true Shepherd and contrasting it with a false shepherd, a wolf after the sheep...Satan, depicted as a thief with destruction on the mind. Please don't miss this: Satan is after you and would have no greater delight than to snatch your provision away from you, leaving you destitute and questioning your faith in Christ. Beware! This is how he operates, in hopes that you will blame God for what he himself actually did. Satan is a thief, a foe, a deceiver. He wants to sift you (**Luke 22:31-32**) and devour you (**1 Peter 5:8**). If he cannot get to your heart, he will try to get to your provision and strip you down (**Job 1**). These difficulties in life qualify as the tribulations Christ said we would endure (**John 16:33**), so hang on to your faith (**James 1:2-3**).

THE COMMAND INDESTRUCTIBLE:

The car breaks down. The dishwasher quits. The baby needs more medicine. There are more bills than there is money to pay them. What do you do? I assure you, worrying about these things will not change their realities. Since God knows all things, He knew you would have to endure such trials as these—provisions turned to problems. Therefore, in times of spiritual, material, or financial drought, claim the promise of your memory verse: *"And my God shall supply all your need according to His riches in glory by Christ Jesus"* (**Philippians 4:19**).

Amen! That verse will comfort your heart, strengthen your faith, and stimulate your voice to shout. As the Spirit of God was with Jesus in His wilderness (**Matthew 4:1**), so He is with you in every way the word can be defined (**Isaiah 43:2**). Do not ever think that Satan's attack catches God by surprise. The Lord knows the tests that Satan will take you through, and Christ will give you grace as you endure those tests and overcome (**1 John 5:4**). Don't entertain a fatalistic mindset, assuming that life just has to be the way it is for now. No, no, no!

You are a child of God, and your need is not met by your wishful thinking, but *"according to His riches in glory in Christ Jesus!"* The source from which God draws to meet your need is backed by all the royal riches of eternity. God dips into His heavenly supply to go out of His way to take care of you, His beloved child. So, stand firm on the Word of God, for it is your source of victory over Satan and all the demons of hell that come against you. Prevail, prevail, prevail!

THE COMMAND INQUIRED:

What cannot be measured cannot be evaluated. Therefore, it is essential to measure your comprehension of Christ's command in this teaching, or else the devil will snatch away the "seeds" of Scripture sown into your heart (**Matthew 13:19**). To keep this from occurring, write down your answers to the following questions as they correlate with the teaching this week:

In what passage(s) of Scripture do you find Christ's commandment on **provision**?

_____

_____

_____

What is the accurate interpretation of **provision** you have discovered?

_____

_____

_____

_____

_____

In your own words, what are some real-life examples in Scripture of **provision**?

_____

_____

_____

_____

_____

What steps of initiation did you learn to take in order for **provision** to transform your life?

_____

_____

_____

_____

_____

_____

How will Satan attack you to hinder **provision** in your life?

_____

_____

_____

_____

_____

_____

What memory verse will you use to protect Christ's command of **provision** in your life? Write it out.

_____

_____

_____

_____

_____

_____

TEACHING # 1.7: SWEARING

Week 7

This week's objective: To understand what it means to swear as well as to actively engage in a daily discipline to eradicate falsehood from your speech patterns.

THE COMMAND INTRODUCED:

- **Matthew 5:33-37** *"Again, you have heard that it was said to those of old, 'You shall not swear falsely, but shall perform your oaths to the Lord.' But I say to you, do not swear at all: neither by heaven, for it is God's throne; nor by the earth, for it is His footstool; nor by Jerusalem, for it is the city of the great King. Nor shall you swear by your head, because you cannot make one hair white or black. But let your 'Yes' be 'Yes,' and your 'No,' 'No.' For whatever is more than these is from the evil one."*

THE COMMAND INTERPRETED:

This is a direct command from our Lord Jesus Christ. To gain an accurate and concise interpretation of this command, you must respectively examine both the culture and the context.

First of all, Jesus began by using the Ten Commandments; the third commandment was His focal point (**Exodus 20:7**). The subject matter used here is swearing by or with God's Name. The Greek word "swear" (*omnuo*) means "to take or declare an oath." In other words, it carries with it the idea of something being either affirmed or denied by speaking an oath. The issue at hand was swearing falsely, which in turn was avoided only by performing all oaths to the Lord. The purpose behind this reverential commitment was the respect due to the Name of the LORD (Jehovah), the Name by which His children are called (**Jeremiah 15:16**). That's why the Old Testament made no apologies for any follower of the Lord who would not honor God's Name in his oaths (**Leviticus 19:12;**

Numbers 30:2; Deuteronomy 23: 21-23).

However, as interesting as it sounds, Jesus made a clear command in light of the Old Testament teaching: *do not swear at all.* So, rather than swearing under limited conditions, Jesus exhorted to do away with such speech entirely. Now, in context, understand that Jesus is not applying this to all types of oaths, such as those used in judicial and universal proceedings that do reverence the Name of God under oath (**Matthew 26:63-64**). Rather, the Lord Jesus emphatically commands His disciples to tell the truth in everything they do, to avoid a flippant attitude in their speech before Almighty God (**Ecclesiastes 5:1-7; Matthew 12:36-37**).

You see, in the culture of Jesus' day, His disciples were exposed to deceptive loopholes practiced by the Pharisees. In other words, since the Pharisees knew swearing by God's Name was binding, they would swear by anything other than God's Name (heaven, earth, Jerusalem, their heads). This means they would victimize people by convincing them of their camouflaged lies, while putting a "Band-Aid" on their guilty consciences for not telling the whole truth. This was a hellish crutch that hurt the Pharisees more than their hearers. But in reality, God's throne, footstool, city, and even human heads already represented Him as Creator, and therefore pulled Him into their deceptive sin and equated the use of His own Name anyway!

Therefore, do not swear at all. Jesus longs to have a disciple who will not swear deceitfully like a Pharisee (**Psalm 24:4b**). The entire content of your speech should be as pure and graceful as if you were under an oath anyway (**2 Corinthians 1:18-23**). Just tell the truth! And, as you are faithful to tell the truth, you will not feel the unnecessary pressure to back up your words with swearing. In our society, truthfulness is a delicacy. That's why you hear people making comments that swear over their mother's grave or promising to God they are telling the truth or calling God as their witness. This is wrong; this is sin. According to Jesus, it all stems from the evil one, Satan. Whatever you do as a disciple of Christ, get your speech under control (**Proverbs 10:19-20; Psalm 141:3**). Say yes. Say no. Speak the truth (**James 5:12**). That's all you need to say.

THE COMMAND ILLUSTRATED:

Perhaps there is no greater example in the New Testament of swearing than that of the Apostle Peter. Read **Matthew 26:69-75**. Peter serves as a prime example of what disobeying this command looks like. While the whole passage has incredible application, focus your attention particularly on **verses 72-74** for the sake of the teaching this week.

First of all, notice that Peter not only denies Jesus, but he does so with what? An oath. This means Peter used God's Name to cover up his allegiance because he was scared of being killed as a follower of Jesus (**Matthew 26:56**). People began to say that his speech betrayed him, meaning his language gave him away. Ironically, due to his unfortunate oath, his "*speech*" betrayed him in more ways than one. Finally, after Peter's shame reached its peak, he added *cursing* and *swearing* to his oath. While cursing is sinful and bad enough (**Romans 12:14; Colossians 3:8; Ephesians 4:29**), Peter topped it off by dragging God's Name through the filth of his oath and the scour of his swearing.

Remember, anytime, anywhere, to get your point across you never have to be so convincing as to use God's Name in vain. As a disciple, when you speak or use His Name, do so with reverence and worship. The Lord Jesus is worthy of your praise; keep it that way.

THE COMMAND INITIATED:

When you have both feet in your mouth, you don't have a leg to stand on. Oh, the discipline we lack when it comes to bridling our wagging tongues (**James 3:2-3**)! As a disciple, the greatest path to take in restraining your speech from swearing and vowing is to examine speech in and of itself. Words can be a horrendous dagger or a helping hand. Your speech is of primary importance to God. Every day, you must muzzle your mouth with the bridle of Scripture. You must speak what is edifying and encouraging to people whenever you have opportunity (**Colossians 4:6**) and whenever it's tough but necessary (**Proverbs 27:6**). From your devotion, your tongue is in motion. That is what Jesus desires.

However, this is not always the case, publicly or privately. A good voice on this subject is Max Lucado. In *The Inspirational Study*

Bible, he comments on this ancient subject of speech in a down-to-earth manner:

> Insensitivity makes a wound that heals slowly. If someone hurts your feelings intentionally, you know how to react. You know the source of the pain. But if someone accidentally bruises your soul, it's difficult to know how to respond.
>
> Someone at work criticizes the new boss, who also happens to be your dear friend. "Oh, I'm sorry—I forgot the two of you were so close." A joke is told at a party about overweight people. You're overweight. You hear the joke. You smile politely while your heart sinks...Someone chooses to wash your dirty laundry in public. "Sue, is it true that you and Jim are separated?" Insensitive comments. Thoughts that should've remained thoughts. Feelings which had no business being expressed. Opinions carelessly tossed like a grenade into a crowd...
>
> For when you start to think about insensitive slurs, you realize they come from an infamous family whose father has breeded generations of pain. His name? Egotism. His children? Three sisters: disregard, disrespect, and disappointment. These three witches have combined to poison countless relationships and break innumerable hearts. Listed among their weapons are Satan's cruelest artillery: gossip, accusations, resentment, impatience, and on and on...God's word has strong medicine for those who carelessly wag their tongues. The message is clear: He who dares to call himself God's ambassador is not afforded the luxury of idle words. Excuses such as "I didn't realize you were here" or "I didn't realize this was so touchy" are shallow when they come from those who claim to be followers and imitators of the Great Physician. We have an added responsibility to guard our tongues.[8]

THE COMMAND INTERROGATED:

There is no doubt whatsoever that Satan wins many battles within the parameters of speech among Christians. I heard it said many years ago in passing: "I am master of my unspoken words but slave to those which should have remained unsaid." How true this is; you cannot take back foul, intrusive words of regret. Satan is far too successful in this area of a Christian's speech. He has too many captives. Swearing by God's Name is an abomination to Christ; don't let Satan hold you in bondage. He doesn't know anything about truth, for he is by his own fallen nature a liar (**John 8:44**). But you, child of God, know the truth (**John 8:32**) and follow the Truth (**John 14:6**). So beware of Satan's envious attacks on your relationship with *truth*.

The best way to learn how to defeat your enemy is to study his methods of attack. By doing so, you prepare yourself for the battle. Imagine: if a criminal is hiding inside a building, and there seems to be no possible entrance to get to him, what should the police squad do? Well, we know it will do no good to spend their time shooting at a window or banging on a door or firing at a wall. The criminal is not in the window, at the door, or behind the wall— he's hiding farther in the building. Therefore, the police squad must go to where the criminal is, not fire haphazardly in directions where he is not. Likewise, in a spiritual sense, Satan will attack you in the same fashion. He will not attack your tongue to tempt you to speak perversely and insensitively, for like this example, that's not where he really is. Satan's going deeper; he's looking to attack the real you. So, rather than going for your tongue, he fires his hellish darts at your heart, to which your tongue is tied! Jesus explained this relationship between your heart and your speech (**Matthew 12:34**).

Dear disciple, be self-controlled and alert, for Satan will corrupt your heart (**Acts 5:3**) in order to corrupt your speech. He will tempt you to hold on to bitterness toward others instead of exchanging it for forgiveness. He will convince you through his lies to harbor feelings of anger and resentment inside your calloused heart instead of facing your offender the right way (**Matthew 18:15**). Guard your heart so that you can restrain your speech, or else you will eat its bitter fruit (**Proverbs 18:20-21**).

THE COMMAND INDESTRUCTIBLE:

Thank God, oh, thank God that He has given us His Word to defeat Satan and all the demons of Hell! We have His power to protect us and His victory to gain. Your memory verse to face Satan's attack is **Psalm 19:14**: *"Let the words of my mouth and the meditation of my heart be acceptable in Your sight, O Lord, my strength and my Redeemer."* Praise God; that says it all. Both your words and your heart come under review in this psalm. It is in these two aspects of your Christian life that you can gain God's favor and please Him. Herein is the capacity of faith (**Hebrews 11:6**).

As a child of God, stand firm in your proclamation of your memory verse. Satan must cower to the Word of the Lord. This is standard for the behavior of a disciple. This is how you follow in the footsteps of Christ (**1 Peter 2:21**), guarding your mouth from oaths, swearing, and all forms of perversity. As a disciple of Jesus, overcome (**1 John 5:4**).

In his book *God's Inspirational Promises*, Max Lucado simplifies this emulation of discipleship:

> Watch a small boy follow his dad through the snow. He stretches to step where his dad stepped. Not an easy task. His small legs extend as far as they can so his feet can fall in his father's prints. The father, seeing what the son is doing, smiles and begins taking shorter steps, so the son can follow. It's a picture of discipleship. In our faith we follow in someone's steps. A parent, a teacher, a hero—none of us are the first to walk the trail. All of us have someone to follow. In our faith we leave footprints to guide others. A child, a friend, a recent convert. None should be left to walk the trail alone. It's the principle of discipleship.[9]

To this you were called as a disciple of Jesus Christ (**John 8:31; 13:35; 15:8**). You can guard your heart and shut your mouth. You can both live and talk like Jesus. You can walk in His resurrection power. You can claim the promises of Scripture over your greatest temptations to lash back at oppressors. You can, you can, you can...through Christ (**Philippians 4:13**).

THE COMMAND INQUIRED:

What cannot be measured cannot be evaluated. Therefore, it is essential to measure your comprehension of Christ's command in this teaching, or else the devil will snatch away the "seeds" of Scripture sown into your heart (**Matthew 13:19**). To keep this from occurring, write down your answers to the following questions as they correlate with the teaching this week:

In what passage(s) of Scripture do you find Christ's commandment on **swearing**?

_____

_____

_____

What is the accurate interpretation of **swearing** you have discovered?

_____

_____

_____

_____

_____

In your own words, what are some real-life examples in Scripture of **swearing**?

_____

_____

_____

_____

_____

_____

What steps of initiation did you learn to take so that **swearing** will not destroy your speech?

_____

_____

_____

_____

_____

How will Satan attack you to instigate **swearing** in your speech?

_____

_____

_____

_____

_____

What memory verse will you use to protect Christ's command against **swearing** in your life? Write it out.

_____

_____

_____

_____

_____

_____

TEACHING # 1.8: PEACE

Week 8

This week's objective: *To discover what it really means to have peace with God and to learn how to live a life in which God's peace has you.*

THE COMMAND INTRODUCED:

- **John 16:33** *"These things I have spoken to you, that in Me you may have peace. In the world you will have tribulation; but be of good cheer, I have overcome the world."*
- **John 20:19, 21** *"Then, the same day at evening, being the first day of the week, when the doors were shut where the disciples assembled, for fear of the Jews, Jesus came and stood in the midst, and said to them, 'Peace be with you'...So Jesus said to them again, 'Peace to you! As the Father has sent Me, I also send you.'"*

THE COMMAND INTERPRETED:

Both commands are given in a direct tone from Jesus to His disciples. The key word Jesus uses with His disciples is the word *peace*. In both of these commands, the Greek word for "peace" (*eirene*) is a noun, and it means "quietness, rest." In fact, the root word for *eirene* is the word *eiro*, which means "to join, as to set at one again." Therefore, in literal translation, Jesus is calling for a retreat of the body, soul, and spirit (**1 Thessalonians 5:23**), one that "joins" the whole person of the disciple to the "quiet" solitude of "rest" (**Matthew 11:28-30**) found only in Himself.

Drawing from this clear interpretation, we can see that each command has its own application for the disciple. First of all, consider **John 16:33**. Remember, the disciples did not have to earn this peace because Jesus freely gave it to them (**John 14:27**). So, it is no surprise to hear Jesus reiterating that the disciples can access this peace, this rest, for He says it is found *"in Me."* Not *near* Jesus. Not *around* Jesus. Peace is *"in"* Jesus. That's exactly why the disciples had it so freely: because they were abiding *"in"* Christ (**John 15:4-5**).

Secondly, we see why Jesus encouraged His disciples with His peace, because of what followed in His statement—tribulation. He predicted they would abandon Him (**John 16:31-32**), and they did (**Matthew 26:56**). The only way the disciples could face their coming tribulations from the world was through the availability of this *"peace."* If Jesus overcame the world, then *joined in* His peace (*quietness, rest*), they could, too.

Last of all, consider the second command, **John 20:19, 21**. Resurrected and glorious, Christ made His first appearance to His disciples. It's interesting that the disciples heard about Jesus' Resurrection that day (**John 20:18**), but they didn't see Christ until that evening. Imagine, for those who believed, the anticipation in their hearts! Finally, Christ arrived and burst forth with, *"Peace be with you."* There was a specific purpose to His statement. He commanded peace because He noticed the atmosphere. It was one of fear—fear of the Jews. Such fear had driven the disciples into silent Christianity, isolated behind doors, disgruntled and discouraged until Christ the King appeared. From this, we learn that one of the intentions for Jesus ensuring peace with you as His disciple is to help you when your heart battles fear (**Psalm 27:1**).

Eventually, the disciples took heart. And then Christ said to their joyful spirits, *"Peace to you!"* Notice the exclamation mark, as compared to the period in verse **19**. Why is this? Simply because Christ is excited to connect His peace now from fear to commissioning: *"As the Father sent Me, I also send you."* Jesus was passing on the baton! You see, you need the peace of Christ with you as you fulfill your evangelistic mission as His disciple (**Matthew 28:18-20**), for the world will hate you and your testimony for Jesus (**John 15:18-19**). If persecution comes, don't give up, because Christ needs you in this world until He's done with you (**Matthew 5:14**). You are forever joined, made one, with His peace, no matter what situation you face for His glory (**1 Peter 4:12-14**).

THE COMMAND ILLUSTRATED:

While there are many passages concerning God's peace, there is one story that particularly stands out. Read **Mark 5:25-34**.

What did you notice about verse **34**? Peace. There it is again, and guess what? It's the same Greek word that Jesus used for His disciples in His commands. However, while He *gave* peace to His disciples, He *expected* peace from this woman. In other words, her miraculous healing from her twelve-year blood disorder was to be followed by a peace, a rest in Christ that would be equipped by Christ. Her peace was preceded by her faith! When Christ saw her faith, He endorsed it with His peace.

As you live your life committed to Jesus, you too must *"go"* in His peace. *Go* involves action. *Go* is fueled by motivation. If you are convinced that Christ's peace is in you and with you, then...go! No matter what you face as His disciple, Jesus' peace will not be exterminated. Christ will not change His mind and take it back. He knows you cannot face the tribulations of this world all by yourself. So He gives you His peace.

THE COMMAND INITIATED:

How exactly do you put the peace of God into action as a disciple? It's one thing to talk about it but quite another to practice it. When you believe that Christ's victory over your tribulations is sufficient, then you will see how His peace will silence your fears. One of the greatest voices on this subject is Dr. Billy Graham. In his book *Peace With God*, Graham offers comforting insight about peace for the earnest, receptive disciple:

> In summing up the superiority of the Christian life over all other ways of living we cannot overlook the advantage that the Christian will have for all eternity. Job said, *"If a man die, shall he live again?"* (14:14). He answered his own question when he said, *"For I know that my Redeemer liveth, and that He will stand at the latter day upon the earth"* (**Job 19:25**). What a prospect! What a future! What a hope! What a life! I would not change places with the wealthiest and most influential person in the world. I would rather be a child of the King, a joint-heir with Christ, a member of the Royal Family of heaven. I know where I've come from, I know why I'm here, I know where I'm going—and I have peace in my heart. His

peace floods my heart and overwhelms my soul! The storm was raging. The sea was beating against the rocks in huge, dashing waves. The lightening was flashing, the thunder was roaring, the wind was blowing, but the little bird was asleep in the crevice of the rock, its head serenely under its wing, sound asleep. That is peace: to be able to rest serenely in the storm! In Christ we are relaxed and at peace in the midst of the confusions, bewilderments, and perplexities of this life. The storm rages, but our hearts are at rest. We have found peace—at last![10]

Now that's plain English. Being a disciple of Jesus Christ is not an easy life, but it is rewarding. Can you see now why God's peace is a necessity? During the tribulations, valleys, and storms that Satan will launch at you, Christ is with you to calm and control those storms (**Mark 4:39**). Trust Him—He's with you to the very end.

THE COMMAND INTERROGATED:

By now, you have learned that Jesus literally wants to join you to a serene rest in Him, a quietness for your soul. This is true life in Christ, but never during this mortal life will it be without interruption. This is due to the attacks of our adversary, Satan.

If Christ gives you peace, what do you suppose Satan will do to disrupt it? I have one word for you: fear. When you are afraid, peace is the farthest thought from your mind. In the midst of fear, there exist panic, worry, and restlessness. In fact, when Satan attacks you with frightening circumstances, he hopes you will forsake Christ's peace and immerse yourself in fear. I assure you that a spirit of fear does not come from God (**2 Timothy 1:7**).

Never give into the lie that God is making you afraid, torturing you with a fear in order to teach you a lesson. Nonsense! If that were so, our loving heavenly Father would then be labeled abusive. Indeed, our Father has warned us that difficulty will come from following Christ (**Matthew 7:13-14**), but Satan is the one we must accuse as the source of our perilous attacks. Watch out, dear disciple. If you find yourself obsessed with fear from circumstances, the peace of God is deactivated within your heart, and faith is rendered powerless. It is while you are in this position that Satan can cleverly pin you down. Choose peace in spite of fears. Beware of this manner of Satan's attack.

THE COMMAND INDESTRUCTIBLE:

God's Word can be ignored, neglected, and even burned. But in an eternal sense, it will never be destroyed! God has the last word in all situations. So, it is with that privilege that you can once again trust in God's Word to provide you with artillery to crush Satan's assaults. Therefore, your memory verse for defending peace and defeating Satan is **Isaiah 26:3**: *"You will keep him in perfect peace, whose mind is stayed on you, because he trusts in You."*

That's the key! That's the treasure in the chest! As your mind is stayed or fixed on the Lord, God promises to keep you in perfect peace. It's not your abilities or your determination that God needs to "stay" on Him. He needs your mind to be *"stayed"* upon Him, which again is merely a reflection of your trust in Him. You see, as you trust in the Lord with all your heart (**Proverbs 3:5-6**), you are "pouring the concrete" for your mind. The mind is what Satan attacks heavily (**2 Corinthians 4:4**), but he cannot overcome it if, like concrete, it has been "set" on the Lord God Almighty. Furthermore, God not only gives you perfect peace, but He then promises to *"keep"* you in that peace. That will make you want to shout! The beauty of this is that God knows you cannot keep yourself in that peace; He is indeed your helper (**Psalm 121:1**).

Therefore, when the attacks of Satan begin to stack against you, do not fear. When you come home only to find that your house is in ashes, do not fear. When your boss tells you, "We're not going to need you any more after tomorrow," do not fear. When your spouse confronts you with divorce papers or your sixteen-year-old child is suddenly pregnant, do not fear. I assure you that Christ's peace is a "one-size-fits-all" kind of peace. You are not alone! Regardless of what you face, and however Satan hurls his hellish missiles at your mind and heart, keep your "mind stayed" on the Lord, trusting Him to work out the details. By the grace of God, you will overcome (**2 Corinthians 4:16-18**).

THE COMMAND INQUIRED:

What cannot be measured cannot be evaluated. Therefore, it is essential to measure your comprehension of Christ's command in this teaching, or else the devil will snatch away the "seeds" of Scripture sown into your heart (**Matthew 13:19**). To keep this from occurring, write down your answers to the following questions as they correlate with the teaching this week:

In what passage(s) of Scripture do you find Christ's commandment on **peace**?

_____

_____

_____

What is the accurate interpretation of **peace** you have discovered?

_____

_____

_____

_____

_____

In your own words, what are some real-life examples in Scripture of **peace**?

_____

_____

_____

_____

_____

_____

What steps of initiation did you learn to take in order for **peace** to transform your life?

_____

_____

_____

_____

_____

How will Satan attack you to hinder **peace** in your life?

_____

_____

_____

_____

_____

What memory verse will you use to protect Christ's command of **peace** in your life? Write it out.

_____

_____

_____

TEACHING # 1.9: LOVE

Week 9

<u>*This week's objective:*</u> *To assess the manner in which God has loved you, and with that assessment, to begin to practice the same manner of love toward people.*

THE COMMAND INTRODUCED:

- John 13:34-35 *"A new commandment I give to you, that you love one another: as I have loved you, that you also love one another. By this all will know that you are My disciples, if you have love for one another."*
- John 14:15 *"If you love Me, keep My commandments."*
- John 15:9-12, 17 *"As the Father loved Me, I also have loved you; abide in My love. If you keep My commandments, you will abide in My love, just as I have kept My Father's commandments and abide in His love. These things I have spoken to you, that My joy may remain in you, and that your joy may be full. This is My commandment, that you love one another as I have loved you...These things I command you, that you love one another."*

THE COMMAND INTERPRETED:

For the most part, these commands on *love* are direct; only one is by its nature implicit. In these commands, there are two Greek words that Jesus used for *"love."* The first word, *agape* (a noun), is best interpreted as the sacrificial love of God toward mankind. The second Greek word, *agapao* (a verb), describes the sacrificial love of a believer toward God and people. For a more exhaustive understanding, Dr. W. E. Vine provides a fascinating understanding of the theological significance of love:

Love can be known only from the actions it prompts. God's love is seen in the gift of His Son, 1 John 4:9-10. But obviously this is not the love of complacency, or affection, that is, it was not drawn out by an excellency in its objects, **Romans 5:8**. It was an exercise of the divine will in deliberate choice, made without assignable cause...Love has its perfect expression among men in the Lord Jesus Christ, **2 Corinthians 5:14; Ephesians 2:4; 3:19; 5:2**; Christian love is the fruit of His Spirit in the Christian, **Galatians 5:22**...Christian love, whether exercised toward the brethren, or toward men generally, is not an impulse from the feelings, it does not always run with the natural inclinations, nor does it spend itself only upon those for whom some affinity is discovered. Love seeks the welfare of all, **Romans 15:2**, and works no ill to any, **13:8-10**...it expresses the deep and constant "love" and interests of a perfect Being towards entirely unworthy objects, producing and fostering a reverential "love" in them towards the Giver, and a practical "love" towards those who are partakers of the same, and a desire to help others to seek the Giver.[11]

Isn't it amazing how much God loves you? Now, in your life as a disciple of Jesus, you are equipped by the Spirit of God to be an embodiment and dispenser of God's love. Moreover, this takes us back to the right foundation to build upon, which is the "*love*" called for by the two Greek words we began with. Since *agape* is a noun, it calls for a description. In contrast, since *agapao* is a verb, it calls for an action. Therefore, as a disciple of Jesus you need to know the context in which Christ expects for you to apply these commands.

Let's take the first command (**John 13:34-35**). Jesus gave a "new" commandment to His disciples; it was saturated in love. In fact, look at **verse 34** again. Every time Jesus mentioned the word *love*, He spoke of the active *agapao* love. Jesus was commanding His disciples to examine the "way" He loved them and in turn to actively communicate that exact type and pattern of love toward each other. That's it. Such unselfish simplicity serves as a protective shield from griping, arguing, judging, and complaining against one another. Dear disciple, to thwart the tendency of increasingly divided churches all over the world, obey this command...always. This is precisely why Jesus changed His word for "*love*" in **verse 35** to *agape*. The object here is "*all will know*." Christ wants every spectator with their cautious, curious eyes on Christianity to see love displayed by a true disciple. Therefore, your action of love (*agapao*) will translate into your description of love (*agape*). You can only produce what you practice.

The second command is both interesting and implicit (**John 14:15**). When Jesus said, "*If you love Me*," He was using the Greek word *agapao*. This marks a disciple who actively loves Jesus, not one who merely professes to do so. Do you remember this age-old question: what came first, the chicken or the egg? Well, here's another question for you: what comes first, love or keeping the commandments? The only way to correctly answer that question is to accurately examine this command. Notice what Jesus mentions first: love for Him. This means love actually precedes obedience to His commands, and therefore could not be a byproduct of "*keeping*" His commands. You see, if obeying Christ exceeds loving Christ, then that can lead to obligation without adoration. But, if your love for Jesus overrides your love for anything or anyone else, then "*keeping His commandments*" comes as easy as blinking your eyes! Therefore, love for Christ and obedience to Christ are distinguishable, yet inseparable.

Last of all, consider the third command (**John 15:9-12, 17**). The command that Jesus announces here is very direct: "*abide in My love*" (**verse 9b**). The type of love He is commanding us to abide in is an *agape* love, which is the Greek word expressing an unconditional, sacrificial love. Additionally, this Greek phrase is written in a tense that stresses a continual abiding, meaning it's a lifestyle, not an occasional effort. Jesus has already demonstrated to His disciples that such an ongoing, active love is possible—"*As the Father has loved Me, I also have loved you*" (**v. 9a**). Do you see the connection? Christ is commanding them to abide in His love *only* after acknowledging the way in which He has modeled *agape* love to them. This means Jesus only asks His disciples to do that which He has already done for them. Keeping His commands is the devoted, sacrificial *agape* love we express to Jesus as we abide in Him. Jesus promised His joy (**v. 11**) to fill our lives as we abide in Him and exhorted us to continue the practice of His *agape* love toward "one another" (**v. 12, 17**). As we abide, we love like Jesus.

THE COMMAND ILLUSTRATED:

A great example of this expression of love is found in Paul's third visit to the church of Corinth. Turn to **2 Corinthians 12:14-15**. The Apostle Paul was urgently pleading with the Corinthians. It is obvious that his previous visits were not too pleasant for him or the church, which explains why he brought one element back into focus before them: love. Paul says, "*...the more abundantly I loved you, the less I am loved*" (**verse 15**). Paul used the *agapao* form of love in his address to the Corinthians, as if he were trying to stir up the "*love*" he wrote to them about in his first letter (**1 Corinthians 13**).

Paul reinforces two reminders that you must not forget. The first is to love abundantly; the second is to love unconditionally. This is the call of a disciple of Jesus Christ! You love people abundantly, for that is how you are equipped by the Spirit of God (**Romans 5:5**). You love people unconditionally, for what reward do you have for only loving those who love you (**Matthew 5:46**)? In regards to *agapao* love, your entire life as a disciple needs to be poured out as an offering to people (**2 Timothy 4:6**). You are crucified to the world (**Galatians 6:14**), a servant to the selfish and the greedy. You are a distributor of God's love, in spite of how little you are loved back. Never forget this truth.

THE COMMAND INITIATED:

How important it is to imitate God by walking in His love every day (**Ephesians 5:1-2**)! The only way to truly initiate a lifestyle of God's kind of love is to make a choice to do so. Neither warm feelings nor strong willpower will help you here. Love, God's way, is a choice. You must decide. You must be willing to avoid measuring the success of your love by the people who pleasantly respond to it, for not all people will. Only you will give account to Christ for how well you loved others like He loved you.

In their book, *The Way of Agape*, Chuck and Nancy Missler hit the nail on the head within the contextual idea of God's love in the life of a disciple:

> God's love is the bond of completeness or wholeness. God's love through us is the finished product. **Colossians 3:14**

declares that *"above all these things we are to put on Agape, which is the bond of perfectness."* (Perfectness simply means completeness, or perfect union with Christ.) God's love is the completion, the perfection, and the finished product God longs for in each of us. If we obey Him, by loving Him first, His love will then be made complete and perfect in us. As God's love is allowed to grow in each of our lives, it will overshadow everything else. God's love is the mark of becoming a man and producing the finished product (**1 Corinthians 13:11**)...having God's love in our lives is the proof that we love Him. If we choose continually to lay down our wills and our lives to Jesus in order for Him to love others through us, that love is going to be the proof and the evidence that we do, indeed, love God. **John 14:21** asserts, *"He that hath My commandments, and keepeth them, he it is that loveth Me."*

God's love through us is the proof we have reached the goal of our instruction and the fulfillment of God's purpose in our lives. It is proof we have set aside, relinquished, and totally given ourselves over to Him in obedience. It's proof we are those open channels, carrying fruit from one place to another. Others are going to know that we belong to God just by hearing our words and seeing our actions. God's love filling our hearts and lives proves that we not only love God, but we have "passed out of death into life" (**1 John 3:10, 14**). God's love in our lives is to be preeminent, unsurpassed and superior to everything else in its importance to us. We must learn how to receive it, how to stay filled with it, and how to pass it on. Then and only then can we genuinely reflect God in all that we think, say, and do.[12]

You can fail. Your car can fail. Your heart can fail. But *love* will never, ever fail (**1 Corinthians 13:8**). There's nothing more secure, nothing more steadfast than the power of love. If something is that strong, it's worth building your life upon. Sometimes people will be mean, rude, and degrading towards you, in spite of the fact that you showered your love upon them. That doesn't mean love failed; it means it sacrificed! Keep loving people with the love of Christ, for such devotional love will move the heart of God.

THE COMMAND INTERROGATED:

There is one little yet spiritually atomic word that Satan loves to employ in the lives of Christians. That word is *bitterness.* Have you ever been bitter or vengeful towards someone who hurt you? In the midst of such bitter resentment aimed at another human being, it is impossible to love them with the love of Christ. That's exactly where Satan wants to do his damage in your life.

You see, you cannot love God and hate your brother (people). It's biblically impossible (**1 John 2:9-11; 3:14-15**). Satan will do whatever is necessary to bring division into your life, even in those relationships into which you thought it would never come (**Psalm 55:12-14**). Beware. When a potentially divisive issue arises between you and your "brother," go work it out immediately before Satan drives a wedge between you (**Matthew 18:15**). Do not let Satan win a battle that Christ has already won (**1 John 3:8**)! If the devil can provide a channel for bitter resentment to creep into your heart, he will. Resentment paralyzes love, and bitterness is the breeding ground for hatred, so you must be on guard. Do not forsake the love of Christ for any disguise of Satan. Remain steadfast (**Psalm 57:7**).

THE COMMAND INDESTRUCTIBLE:

Precious disciple, you are a child of God (**1 John 3:1**). Although Satan will interrogate the love of Christ in your heart, you don't have to give in to him. Destroy his hellish ways with the Word of our God. When facing times in your Christian life in which your love for Christ and others seems to be "cold" and distant (**Matthew 24:12**), you need a Scripture with which to fight.

While there are many Scriptures about *love*, there is one that you particularly need to use for your memory verse: **2 Corinthians 5:14-15**. That Scripture says, *"For the love of Christ compels us, because we judge thus: that if One died for all, then all died; and He died for all, that those who live should live no longer for themselves, but for Him who died for them and rose again."* Amen, praise God, hallelujah! The Greek word for "compels" (*sunecho*) means "to compress or keep in."

Therefore, the love of Christ literally should release itself in a pressurized explosion towards everyone, for *"He died for all."*

There is no prostitute, murderer, drunkard, adulterer, embezzler, or liar who does not deserve the same offer of the love of Christ that you have received. Every day of your life, keep the *"Christ died for all"* mentality close to your convictions. Dispense Christ's love with unending measures. Jesus died for you, rose again, saved you from your sins, and called you to Himself to be His disciple. What a privilege! What a Savior! May the love of Christ compel you...daily.

THE COMMAND INQUIRED:

What cannot be measured cannot be evaluated. Therefore, it is essential to measure your comprehension of Christ's command in this teaching, or else the devil will snatch away the "seeds" of Scripture sown into your heart (**Matthew 13:19**). To keep this from occurring, write down your answers to the following questions as they correlate with the teaching this week:

In what passage(s) of Scripture do you find Christ's commandment on **love**?

_____

_____

_____

What is the accurate interpretation of **love** you have discovered?

_____

_____

_____

_____

In your own words, what are some real-life examples in Scripture of **love**?

_____

_____

_____

_____

_____

_____

What steps of initiation did you learn to take in order for **love** to transform your life?

_____

_____

_____

_____

_____

How will Satan attack you to hinder **love** in your life?

_____

_____

_____

_____

_____

What memory verse will you use to protect Christ's command of **love** in your life? Write it out.

DISCIPLED

_____

_____

_____

_____

_____

_____

CHAPTER 2: THE *ALLEGIANCE* FROM A DISCIPLE

Indirectly, allegiance is a reflection of attitude. *"And whoever does not bear his cross and come after Me cannot be My disciple"* (**Luke 14:27**). The Lord Jesus Christ cannot be any clearer than He is here. Regarding discipleship, He does not stutter nor waver from truth. In fact, Christ leaves no room for misinterpretation by those who would view His statement as a suggestion or a possibility. It is so simple, yet absolute: some people *"cannot"* be His disciples. Why not? What's the problem? The problem for some "fake" believers is that they want the "blessings" of Jesus without the cost. They want a ticket to Heaven, but not a cross to carry. They want an easy life, not a narrow, difficult path (**Matthew 7:13-14**). For such people who have a contaminated view of Christianity, discipleship is not possible.

It's not that such people are not "good" enough. Jesus Christ simply has a standard, and it is not up for negotiation. He makes no exception for anyone. That is what this chapter is about. It focuses on the devotion of the disciple. It highlights the commands of Jesus to His followers that tested their allegiance to Him. Remember, multitudes followed Jesus, yet we see Him with only twelve disciples. Why? It is because people loved the spectacular, but when challenged with cross-carrying commitment to Christ, they scattered (**John 6:66**). Jesus Christ is not looking for pansies. He is not going to waste His time with the shallow-minded. Christ wants a "John the Baptist" heart that will decrease so that He can increase (**John 3:30**). Either you're in, or you're out (**Matthew 12:30**). Every fiber of your being is to be committed to Christ. This is what it means to be a disciple of Jesus. This is the selfless, Kingdom-minded vessel that is being transformed by His commands. This is who Christ is looking for. This is *you*.

TEACHING # 2.1: DEVOTION (PART 1)

Week 10

This week's objective: To define selfless, Kingdom-minded devotion through the vocabulary of Jesus Christ as well as personally surrender to such a lifestyle.

THE COMMAND INTRODUCED:

While there are multiple commands on devotion, there is a common theme connecting all of them: *following Jesus.* These commands are intertwined through all four Gospels but can be grouped together into commonalities that emulate what "following Jesus" means. Those categories are as follows:

1. <u>The poor in spirit</u>

- **Matthew 5:3; Luke 6:20** *"Blessed are the poor in spirit, for theirs is the kingdom of heaven."*

2. <u>The forsaking of family</u>

- **Matthew 8:21-22** *"Then another of His disciples said to Him, 'Lord, let me first go and bury my father.' But Jesus said to him, 'Follow Me, and let the dead bury their own dead.'"*
- **Matthew 10:34-37** *"Do not think that I came to bring peace on earth. I did not come to bring peace but a sword. For I have come to 'set a man against his father, a daughter against her mother, and a daughter-in-law against her mother-in-law;' and 'a man's enemies will be those of his own household.' He who loves father or mother more than Me is not worthy of Me. And he who loves son or daughter more than Me is not worthy of Me."*

3. <u>The cross to carry</u>

- **Matthew 10:38** *"And whoever does not take his cross and follow after Me is not worthy of Me."*
- **Luke 9:23; Matthew 16:24; Mark 8:34** *"Then Jesus said to His disciples, 'If anyone desires to come after Me, let him deny himself, take up his cross daily, and follow Me.'"*

4. <u>The light to shine</u>

- **Matthew 5:13-16** *"You are the salt of the earth; but if the salt loses its flavor, how shall it be seasoned? It is then good for nothing but to be thrown out and trampled underfoot by men. You are the light of the world. A city that is set on a hill cannot be hidden. Nor do they light a lamp and put it under a basket, but on a lamp stand, and it gives light to all who are in the house. Let your light so shine before men, that they may see your good works and glorify your Father in heaven."*

5. <u>The choice for life</u>

- **Mark 8:35-38; Luke 9:24-26; Matthew 10:39; 16:25-26** *"For whoever desires to save his life will lose it, but whoever loses his life for My sake and the gospel's will save it. For what will it profit a man if he gains the whole world, and loses his own soul? Or what will he give in exchange for his soul? For whoever is ashamed of Me and My words in this adulterous and sinful generation, of him the Son of Man will be ashamed when He comes in the glory of His Father with the holy angels."*
- **John 21:19** *"This [Jesus] spoke, signifying by what death [Peter] would glorify God. And when He had spoken this, He said to him, 'Follow Me.'"*

THE COMMAND INTERPRETED:

It is quite obvious that these commands of Jesus were given both directly and implicitly, depending on His purpose with His audience. In this teaching, the categories are listed in descending order to clearly present the process by which Christ actually calls and transforms His disciple. Such a process is Jesus' way to inform a

possible follower of the "fine print" at the bottom of His contract
(**Luke 14:28-33**). Christ wants people to count the cost! His pleading
call to those interested in being a disciple is actually a test of their
commitment. So, Jesus "tells all." His expectations are crisply stated
and not hidden.

First of all, He begins with the poor in spirit (**Matthew 5:3;
Luke 6:20**). It is worth noting that this was the first beatitude Jesus
proclaimed, as if to lay a foundation for the rest of His beatitudes.
This phrase "*poor in spirit*" has an interesting interpretation. The
Greek word for "poor" (*ptochos*) means "to crouch [like a beggar]."
The Greek word "spirit" (*pneuma*) means "breath," which in context
refers to the human spirit God "breathed" into man (**Genesis 2:7**).
Therefore, Jesus is teaching that the Kingdom of God belongs to
people who don't focus on building a kingdom of their own. It's for
those who purposely do not let their "*spirit*" get attached to the evil
of this world. That's why God gives grace to protect your spirit
(**Philemon 25**). By His grace, you keep yourself "*poor in spirit*,"
humbly crouching at His feet to worship instead of bowing to this
world's pride, ego, lust, power, and wealth. This is the beginning call
for those who are willing to forsake the "pleasures of this world" to
follow Jesus Christ (**Hebrews 11:24-26**).

Secondly, Jesus addressed the forsaking of family (**Matthew
8:21-22; 10:34-37**). As a disciple who is poor in spirit, you will learn
that not everyone will agree with your lifestyle change, especially
your family. Some of your greatest opposition to following Christ
may come from those you love the most. Do not be discouraged.
Christ Himself practiced this command before He gave it to His
disciples (**Matthew 12:46-50**). Remember, Jesus' purpose in
commanding this was not to utterly abandon or deny your family
members, for even Christ still acknowledged and cared for His own
mother at the cross (**John 19:27**). Rather, Jesus is commanding
loyalty! Christ is requiring that anyone wanting to be His disciple
must commit to loving Him more than they love any family
member. He is demanding your undivided attention, with no
distractions from lost or backslidden family members who try to
pull you down. This means refusing your family when their
requests would violate your relationship with Jesus. There can be no
compromise! Family can get in the way of serving God, or they can
serve alongside you. Either way, just choose Jesus.

Thirdly, Christ commands the cross to be carried (**Matthew 10:38; Luke 9:23; Matthew 16:24; Mark 8:34**). This command has as its objective goal *identification*. When you think of a cross, you naturally think of Jesus. In His day, when He commanded, *"Take up your cross,"* the disciples could only describe that command in one way: tough. In Roman law, people were often crucified on a cross, so the disciples knew to what Jesus was referring. They knew "carrying their crosses" was the only way to follow Him to His cross. Carrying their crosses was their way to unashamedly and courageously identify themselves with Jesus.

Today, as a disciple, you are commanded to carry your cross...daily. You are boldly called and commanded to identify yourself with Christ through your lifestyle. You do so by shouldering His life, His standards, His speech, His purity, His humility, and His commands upon your heart for all the world to see! To do so, you must deny yourself and dethrone your dignity, that you may embrace this cross devotedly. There is no other method. One Savior. One cross. One disciple—you.

Fourthly, Jesus commands your light to shine (**Matthew 5:13-16**). Not only are you to maintain your *"flavor"* in society, but you are to magnify the light of God in you (**2 Corinthians 4:6**) as well. Hypocrisy will fade your flavor (*influence*) and put out your "fiery" light of the Gospel (*witness*). Do not let this happen. You see, as a man can jump out of a plane because of the parachute on his back, so you can shine your light for Christ because of the cross on yours. Do you see the picture here? You do not shine your light for Christ so that you can carry your cross (identification); the process is actually reversed. You carry your cross, and by doing so, you are shining the light of Jesus. Everywhere you go, with everyone you meet, the light of His glorious Gospel radiates from your attitude, your smiles, your comments, your servanthood, and your compassion. A life shining with the light of Christ is that of a disciple whose reputation among men precedes him (**1 Thessalonians 1:8**). Others see the works that come as a result of your light, and they glorify God because of it. Oh, disciple, this is the joy that comes from such a lifestyle, and the joy of the Lord will strengthen you to continue shining (**Nehemiah 8:10; John 15:11**).

Lastly, the command is for you to realize devotion to Jesus is a choice for life (**Mark 8:35-38; Luke 9:24-26; Matthew 10:39;**

16:25-26; John 21:19). Following Christ is not something you "try out." Listen carefully: true, authentic salvation is not regretted (**2 Corinthians 7:10**), and in light of that salvation, the commands that follow are not a burden to the redeemed (**1 John 5:3**). Do not let anyone tell you anything different. Please understand that when you were saved by Christ, you did not "add" Jesus to your life and keep yours. You *"lost"* your life. You died to yourself so that you can live unto Christ (**Colossians 3:1-4; Romans 6:3-4**). Jesus and ALL that comes with Him became your life. You participated in a divine exchange—your life for Christ's life! There are no exceptions. You made a choice.

Those in the world today who cheapen this command are trying to *"save"* their lives as Jesus foretold. During His ministry, He addressed such people, identifying them as those who want to *"gain the world,"* yet lose their souls. These are the people who know the commands of Christ but are not willing to embrace them because they are *ashamed* of what those commands will chisel them into. On the Day of Christ's return, He will faithfully recompense His shame for these negligent, could-have-been disciples who were more attracted to the evil of this world than to the Christ who died for their sins.

Within this very hour, people have died only to wake up in the agonizing flames of Hell, the place for those who exchanged their souls for the world and not Jesus. What a tragedy! Discipleship is a choice, not an obligation. Like Peter, you "choose" to follow Jesus to the point of shame, ridicule, and even death (**John 21:19**). The invitation is to the poor in spirit, who will even forsake their love for family to give their loyal devotion to Jesus. The call is for those who will carry their crosses, so their light can shine into the lives of lost people all around (**2 Corinthians 4:3-4**). It is a choice for the rest of your life. Choose whom you will serve, whom you will follow (**Deuteronomy 30:19-20; Joshua 24:15**).

THE COMMAND ILLUSTRATED:

I hope that by now, you are convinced that the only way to truly follow Jesus is to devote your entire person to Him. By human nature, we like to see an example of what we are asked to do—the clothing of humility displayed on a mannequin before we try it on (**1 Peter 5:5**). To illustrate this devotion required by Jesus to follow Him, the Apostle Peter offers a great example. Read **Luke 5:1-11**.

Just like the other disciples, Peter was found and called. It is always clear that Jesus chooses us; we don't choose Him (**John 15:16**). This call for discipleship is actually a reflection of the sensitivity of our hearts before Christ. He's not searching for people to impress Him or advise Him, and He's not looking for the haughty or the snobby. Christ is looking for people in whom He can do a work, people who are not "too good" for His lifestyle. So Jesus found Peter.

Peter was involved in a non-spiritual task to teach him a spiritual lesson about Jesus. An unsuccessful day of fishing had a breaking point...the heart of Peter. When Jesus is in your boat, nothing is impossible (**Luke 1:37**)! Christ used this miraculous catch of fish (**verses 6-7**) to snatch Peter's attention. In response, this man emptied himself of his own opinions and submitted to Christ's word (**verse 5**). When he saw the nets breaking and the boats sinking, Peter broke, too: *"Depart from me, for I am a sinful man, O Lord!"*

Jesus had found someone who was "poor in spirit," someone who had nothing to offer Jesus but his own sins. Perfect! That's what Christ was looking for, a man like Peter who would not flaunt his flesh in the Presence of the Savior (**1 Corinthians 1:31**). So Jesus told him not to fear, but to focus on his new mission for fishing (**verse 10**), one in which Jesus, not Peter, would clean these "fish." So, along with his broken spirit, Peter forsook all (family, agendas, abilities, ego) to follow Christ (**verse 11**). *All* means *all*. As you read through the Gospels, you notice that the Apostle Peter was inconsistent in carrying his cross and shining his light. It wasn't until after Christ's Ascension that Peter began to faithfully carry his cross and shine his light at Pentecost (**Acts 2-4**). However, in spite of Peter's back-and-forth attitude, he was solid on one point: choosing Christ for life (**John 6:66-69**). And through the disciple's times of struggle, Christ knew that one day Peter would be faithful (**Matthew 16:18**).

As a disciple of Christ, emulate Peter's example. Like Peter, you will be faced with times of testing, times that your faith will be strengthened. However, like that of all humans, Peter's example is marred. He wavered all throughout Christ's ministry, hot one day and cold the next. He often spoke before he listened to Jesus. Instead of emulating Peter's less desirable qualities, pay attention to his faithfulness. You must imitate God (**Ephesians 5:1**) and the godly leaders He puts in your life that imitate Jesus Christ (**1 Corinthians 11:1**). It's the Lord Jesus that you want to be like (**Colossians 2:6; 1 John 2:6**) and think like (**Philippians 2:5**). Build your entire character around Him.

TEACHING # 2.2: DEVOTION (PART 2)

Week 11

This week's objective: To define selfless, Kingdom-minded devotion through the vocabulary of Jesus Christ as well as personally surrender to such a lifestyle.

THE COMMAND INITIATED:

The only way to put this command of Christ into motion personally is to examine your lifestyle now. As a new believer, you probably have already been "cleaning temple" in your speech, habits, and friendships (**2 Corinthians 7:1**) in order to embrace the life of a disciple. Such baggage weighs us down (**Hebrews 12:1-2**) so that we cannot carry our cross. By now, I pray that Christ has already been transforming you more and more by His Word. Scripture is the sculpting tool and the cleansing water of a disciple (**Psalm 119:9**). Christ is calling you to take what you know about the demands for a disciple and put it into practice. Follow faithfully.

J. Oswald Chambers knew very much about a disciple's faithful pursuit of Jesus. In his book *The Joy of Following Jesus*, Chambers details a befitting description packed with the evidence of true discipleship:

> When we respond to Christ's call to discipleship, we enter His school and place ourselves under His instruction. Originally "Christian" and "disciple" were interchangeable terms, but they cannot be so used today. Many who would wish to be classed as Christians are unwilling to comply with Christ's stringent conditions of discipleship. Jesus never led His disciples to believe that the path of discipleship would be prime rose-strewn. He coveted men and women who would follow Him through thick and thin. He was aiming more for quality than for quantity, so He did not tone down His requirements in order to gain more recruits...Jesus said

to the Jews who had believed in Him, *"If you continue in My word you are truly My disciples..."* (**John 8:31**). This gives us the inward view of discipleship, permanent continuance in the words of the Master, the attitude of scholar and teacher. Where that is absent, discipleship is nominal and lacks reality. What is the significance of "My word" in the passage? In a sense it is distinguishable from Himself, for He is the living Word. The sense here, however, is that of the whole tenor and substance of His teaching. It stands for His message as a whole, not favorite passages or pet doctrines but the whole range of His teaching...To continue in His Word (or "to hold to His teaching,"...) was to make it their rule of life in daily practice. Our discipleship begins with the reception of the Word. Continuance in the Word is the evidence of reality.[1]

Again, as you can tell from Chamber's comments, it is the living, vital, refreshing Word of God that you need as Christ's disciple. The purpose in your needing Scripture is for growth (**1 Peter 2:2**) and sanctification (**John 17:17**). You can never be the disciple Christ is looking for apart from His commands. Precious disciple of Jesus, continue in His Word, never looking back (**Luke 9:62**). It will be worth it all (**Hebrews 11:24-26**).

THE COMMAND INTERROGATED:

What do you think Satan's weapon of attack is to derail your devotion to Christ? Do you think it is money? Lust? Envy? While there are many ploys he can wedge between you and your devotion to Jesus, there is one that stands above all the rest: *time.*

You see, this beautiful gift is by far the most valuable commodity that God gives you (**Ecclesiastes 3:1, 11**). You can waste time, or you can use time. Now that you gave your life to Jesus Christ, your time is His time. You're on His watch. That's what surrender does for a disciple. No matter where you go, what you do, or who you converse with, your aim is to use God's time wisely to promote Christ's gospel in everything.

This is where Satan comes in. He will do whatever is

necessary to sway you into using your time for anything other than Kingdom labor for the Master. He will disguise it with excess in hobbies and relationships or mask it with over-commitment in sports and recreation. Do you see the problem that develops? Your time for Christ becomes minimized due to your investment in too many other priorities. It takes time to study, learn, and practice the words of Christ. This is our command (**Colossians 3:16**), not our option! How can we continue in the words of Christ if we are so diverted by an excess in worldly distractions? These enjoyments are not wrong or sinful in themselves, but they can become so if our time tips ninety percent in their direction and ten percent toward discipleship with Christ. Beware of these crafty, deceptive ways of the devil to pollute your time with more earthly pursuits than Kingdom goals (**Matthew 6:33**). Again I say it: beware.

THE COMMAND INDESTRUCTIBLE:

Oh, thank God for the power-punch of His holy Word. There will be times during your Christian walk with Jesus when you find your devotion under Satan's pressurized heat. There will be days that taking up your cross devotedly is harder to do than ever before. Why? It is because of the intensity of Satan's attack, as his demonic spirits oppress you in hopes of turning your devotion into distraction. You need a verse of Scripture to combat Satan and encourage yourself in the Lord. Here's one for you: **2 Corinthians 5:9**. It says, *"Therefore we make it our aim, whether present or absent, to be well pleasing to Him."* This is your invincible memory verse to live by and fight with.

You're not going down in the "hall of faithlessness" for wasting your time on things in this life that did nothing for building up the Kingdom of God. Your memory verse serves to protect you from such a regretful life. You see, devotion to Christ has an enduring yet rewarding element to it. It means, "Don't give up, because the best is yet to come." That should be the "carrot" dangling before your eyes of faith as you devotedly plow the souls of men in this life, only to reap a harvest in the next (**Hebrews 11:27**). Stay focused on devotion. You continually catch your second wind as you look unto Jesus, because He's already run this race, plowed this field, and lived this life. He's the model! Like Paul, with Heaven in your scope, you make it your aim to stay devoted to Jesus. Present or absent from this life, it doesn't matter; your aim is to please Him because He is your Lord and your Master. In this way, your love for Christ becomes evident (**1 Corinthians 8:3**). Your devotion is not up for compromise; continually abide in His Word (**1 John 2:3-5**).

THE COMMAND INQUIRED:

What cannot be measured cannot be evaluated. Therefore, it is essential to measure your comprehension of Christ's command in this teaching, or else the devil will snatch away the "seeds" of Scripture sown into your heart (**Matthew 13:19**). To keep this from occurring, write down your answers to the following questions as they correlate with the teaching this week:

In what passage(s) of Scripture do you find Christ's commandment on **devotion**?

_____

_____

_____

What is the accurate interpretation of **devotion** you have discovered?

_____

_____

_____

_____

In your own words, what are some real-life examples in Scripture of **devotion**?

_____

_____

_____

_____

_____

_____

What steps of initiation did you learn to take in order for **devotion** to transform your life?

_____

_____

_____

_____

_____

_____

How will Satan attack you to hinder **devotion** in your life?

_____

_____

_____

_____

_____

_____

What memory verse will you use to protect Christ's command of **devotion** in your life? Write it out.

TEACHING # 2.3: PERSECUTION

Week 12

This week's objective: To define what Kingdom assault is and to learn how Christ commands you to react when you are faced with it as a believer.

THE COMMAND INTRODUCED:

- **Matthew 5:10-12; Luke 6:22-23** *"Blessed are those who are persecuted for righteousness' sake, for theirs is the kingdom of heaven. Blessed are you when they revile and persecute you, and say all kinds of evil against you falsely for My sake. Rejoice and be exceedingly glad, for great is your reward in heaven, for so they persecuted the prophets who were before you."*
- **Matthew 10:16-20; Luke 12:8-12** *"Behold, I send you out as sheep in the midst of wolves. Therefore be wise as serpents and harmless as doves. But beware of men, for they will deliver you up to councils and scourge you in their synagogues. You will be brought before governors and kings for My name's sake, as a testimony to them and to the Gentiles. But when they deliver you up, do not worry about how or what you should speak. For it will be given to you in that hour what you should speak; for it is not you who speak, but the Spirit of your Father who speaks in you."*

THE COMMAND INTERPRETED:

These commands from our Lord Jesus have both an implicit and direct tone to them. In the area of persecution, Jesus wanted His disciples to know what He expected from them in response to attacks from unbelievers.

The first command (**Matthew 5:10-12; Luke 6:22-23**) begins implicitly and finishes directly. Following Christ means embracing His lifestyle. Such a way of life is offensive to unbelievers because your shining light exposes their darkness (**John 3:19-20**). The inevitable result is persecution against those who exhibit Christ's "*righteousness*" in their conduct. Jesus is implying that the Kingdom of Heaven belongs to people like this, who have no kingdom of their own in this world. They have truly forsaken all to follow Christ. This persecution is properly identified with reviling. The Greek "revile" (*oneidizo*) means "to defame; taunt." Such reviling was explained when Jesus said people would "*say all kinds of evil against you falsely.*" Therefore, Jesus does not want His disciples to be caught off guard; expect this kind of verbal persecution.

Such insight bridges the command at hand: "*Rejoice and be exceedingly glad.*" This is how you are to react when someone persecutes you for your faith in Jesus Christ. You are to be excited (**Acts 5:40-42**)! Why? Simply because you have a reward for enduring the persecution. Did you hear that? Christ actually wants to reward you (**Hebrews 11:6, 24-26**). By way of encouragement, Jesus says that the prophets have experienced the same persecution for righteousness' sake. This means there is a cloud of witnesses (**Hebrews 12:1**) that have already been subjected to the same defaming treatment you are. Therefore, Jesus' command is to rejoice in the face of persecution, not retaliate against it.

The second command (**Matthew 10:16-20; Luke 12:8-12**) is direct and to the point. Christ wanted His disciples to know that they were on a mission, one that was paved with difficulty (**Matthew 7:14**). As a disciple, you fit the profile. You, like the twelve disciples, are sent out as sheep in the midst of tenacious wolves. What a gruesome, frightening picture that triggers in your mind! However, it is necessary, for light (sheep) must penetrate darkness (wolves) in spite of hardship, just as Jesus did among dark-hearted fishermen in Capernaum (**Matthew 4:15-17**).

Obedience to go forth is not without admonition for you, the disciple: "*Be wise as serpents and harmless as doves.*" What did Jesus mean by that? The Greek "wise" (*phronimos*) means "thoughtful, discreet, cautious," and the Greek "harmless" (*akeraios*) translates as "unmixed, innocent." The command here for you, the disciple, is to live your Christian life in a state of both wise cautiousness (**Ephesians 5:15**) and innocent, pure blamelessness as you keep yourself "unmixed" or unspotted from the world (**James 1:27**). The purpose for this command is revealed by what Jesus says in **verses 17-18**. This defines the tribulation in the world (**John 16:33**) that is promised, coming from authorities or dignitaries or your next-door neighbor. Satan works through the sons of disobedience (unbelievers) to harm you.

Jesus knows us so well! He knows that passion for Him does not eradicate the human tendency to gravitate toward fear, which is not from God (**2 Timothy 1:7**). Therefore, He commands you to not panic when faced with these trials and persecutions, especially when you are called upon to speak and stand up for Christ. Do you see why? It is because Christ promises that the Holy Spirit will speak for you. Therefore, the command to you as Christ's disciple is to be bold in your faith, combining wisdom with fearlessness. In the face of persecution, we are not to back down in fear but to stand in faith by the power of the Holy Spirit, Who will speak through you.

THE COMMAND ILLUSTRATED:

The Apostle Peter knew this to be true. Turn to **Acts 4:1-22**. This is a fabulous example of what Jesus is commanding you to do when faced with persecution. Peter and John were both arrested for their involvement in the lame man's healing at the gate of the Temple (detailed in **chapter 3**). As Jesus said, His disciples would stand before councils and rulers to be persecuted. But do you also remember how Christ said the Holy Spirit would give them the words to say? Who is filling Peter in **verse 8**? Exactly!

Peter is your example. He, a vessel like you, provides you with confidence in the Holy Spirit to help you in your time of persecution. I have been persecuted many times for sharing the Gospel of Jesus with people. I have been run out of stores, scolded by people to whom I was witnessing, and nearly arrested one time in a hospital parking lot. I tell you the truth, dear disciple: *never* did I lack the words to say. It is true: the Holy Spirit of God gives you the words in such a critical moment of standing for Christ! As you obey the command, you will find yourself rejoicing and telling others (**Acts 4:23**) about what happened to you; it encourages you to witness for Christ even more. Just always remember that the persecution is not against you personally; rather, it is against the Christ who lives within you (**Galatians 2:20**). So don't become discouraged, but be encouraged that you are counted worthy (**Philippians 1:27**) to suffer for His Name.

THE COMMAND INITIATED:

Most of the persecution that takes place among Christians is predominantly verbal. However, a lot of verbal persecution results in physical persecution. Naturally, this brings into question the unknown extent of such persecution. No matter what form persecution takes, it results in some form of fracture brought into our lives as we follow Jesus. So, as we follow Christ, it means that we are willing to be uncomfortable, to shed your dignity, to speak when intimidated. This is the cost of being a disciple (**Matthew 16:25**). Your life is no longer your own; you gave it to Jesus Christ (**Colossians 3:4**)!

John Foxe offers a compelling old English account of martyr Hugh Latimer in his book *Foxe's Book of Martyrs*. Speaking of Latimer, Foxe states:

> Beginning afresh to set forth his plough he labored in the Lord's harvest most fruitfully, discharging his talent as well in divers places of this realm, as before the King at the court. In the same place of the inward garden, which was before applied to lascivious and courtly pastimes, there he dispensed the fruitful Word of the glorious Gospel of Jesus Christ, preaching there before the King and his whole court, to the edification of many. In this his painful travail he occupied himself all King Edward's days, preaching for the most part every Sunday twice. Though a sore bruised man by the fall of a tree, and above sixty-seven years of age, he took little ease and care of sparing himself. Every morning, winter and summer, about two of the clock, he was at his book most diligently. Master Latimer ever affirmed that the preaching of the Gospel would cost him his life, to the which he cheerfully prepared himself.[2]

What a disciple of Jesus Christ! Refusing to renounce his faith in Christ, Latimer was eventually burned at the stake. Persecution is normal for a devoted, Christ-exalting Christian life (**2 Timothy 3:12**). It comes with the package; it's part of the lifestyle. As a disciple of Jesus, don't bow down to the fear of man. Stand for Christ, no matter what the cost; for to live is Christ, and to die is gain (**Philippians 1:21**). It's the gain of Christ that far surpasses losses we may experience while following Him. The gospel has a way of scattering all who do not want to follow your Jesus with you. So be it. Persecution now, glory on its way. It shall be worth it all (**2 Corinthians 4:17**)!

THE COMMAND INTERROGATED:

Persecution is Satan's way of dealing with your godliness. Anything you do or say for Jesus Christ insults him. Your faith is a threatening fragrance in the demonic atmosphere of spiritual warfare. Perhaps the greatest toll Satan will take on you through persecution is discouragement. He will try to beat you down—spiritually, physically, emotionally, and psychologically. The devil wants to keep you lukewarm, straddling the fence of your convictions and Christ's commands.

Be very, very careful not to become discouraged if you are persecuted for righteousness' sake. When you share the gospel with someone and they spit in your face, cursing you, don't become upset and retaliate. When you stand up for Christ in a conversation and someone scornfully mocks you, don't become saddened and depressed. When you passionately share Christ with a friend, who in turn curses you or pushes you, don't be discouraged and give place to the devil's lie of "failure." You haven't failed. Instead, you've been faithful.

You see, Satan wants you to believe that rejection is an indication of failure. He will constantly bombard your mind with depressing incidents and seemingly discouraging conversations. Don't let him do that! Remember: in God's eyes, you are called and commissioned to be faithful, not successful according to our culture's definition. Leave the results up to the Lord God. Your success is found in planting God's Word in someone's life, not in reaping immediately. Jesus just wants disciples to labor in the harvest (**Matthew 9:37**).

Whenever you suffer for Christ, Satan will pounce on the opportunity to discourage you. You don't have to give in (**Psalm 42:11**). Never, ever take persecution personally. It's always an assault against our Christ. Satan has been on the loose since the beginning in the Garden of Eden with relentless attacks against God and His people. Stand up for Christ, but be very alert for Satan's vicious plots against you.

THE COMMAND INDESTRUCTIBLE:

If you live by the gospel, you will be persecuted. Persecution is common for you as a disciple. There's no way around it. Since Satan will be lurking daily to discourage you, a memory verse from God's Word is essential to combat him and drive him away. That verse of Scripture is **1 Peter 4:14**. It says, *"If you are reproached for the name of Christ, blessed are you, for the Spirit of glory and of God rests upon you. On their part He is blasphemed, but on your part He is glorified."* Praise the Lamb of God! Isn't that wonderful news? Why are you *"blessed"* for suffering for Christ? It is because the Holy Spirit of God rests upon you during those times. People's attack against you is actually a blasphemous attack against Jesus. Their blaspheming results in your glorification of Christ. What a deal!

When (not if) you face persecution, stand on **1 Peter 4:14**. Quote it. Shout it. Sing it. To your accusers and attackers, it will seem that you have lost your mind. Oh, but you know you haven't. You use God's indestructible Word to fight against persecution. Fight against discouragement with an encouraging reminder that you have a divine "support group" suffering with you (**1 Peter 5:9**). As believers, we're in this together! All that Christ asks of you as His disciple is to be faithful throughout your persecutions (**Revelation 2:10**). Casual Christianity is not invited to such a lifestyle. A disciple makes up his mind to suffer for Christ because he views his sufferings as nothing worthy to be compared to what Jesus suffered for him. A disciple has no agenda, no reservations. He's all for Christ, regardless of the cost. His life is not his own. Jesus owns him (**Romans 6:18**), and he joyfully and willfully endures persecution for the glory of God (**James 1:2-3**). This is your call, your profile, as a disciple.

THE COMMAND INQUIRED:

What cannot be measured cannot be evaluated. Therefore, it

is essential to measure your comprehension of Christ's command in this teaching, or else the devil will snatch away the "seeds" of Scripture sown into your heart (**Matthew 13:19**). To keep this from occurring, write down your answers to the following questions as they correlate with the teaching this week:

In what passage(s) of Scripture do you find Christ's commandment on **persecution**?

_____

_____

_____

What is the accurate interpretation of **persecution** you have discovered?

_____

_____

_____

_____

_____

In your own words, what are some real-life examples in Scripture of **persecution**?

_____

_____

_____

_____

_____

What steps of initiation did you learn to take in order for **persecution** to transform your life?

_____

_____

_____

_____

_____

How will Satan attack you to hinder **persecution** in your life?

_____

_____

_____

_____

_____

What memory verse will you use to protect Christ's command of **persecution** in your life? Write it out.

_____

_____

_____

_____

TEACHING #2.4: PRAYER (PART 1)

Week 13

<u>*This week's objective:*</u> *To value the privilege of access to converse with the Father, as well as to learn the purposes behind Jesus' command to pray.*

THE COMMAND INTRODUCED:

- **Matthew 6:5-13; Luke 11:1-8** *"And when you pray, you shall not be like the hypocrites. For they love to pray standing in the synagogues and on the corners of the streets, that they may be seen by men. Assuredly, I say to you, they have their reward. But you, when you pray, go into your room, and when you have shut your door, pray to your Father who is in the secret place; and your Father who sees in secret will reward you openly. And when you pray, do not use vain repetitions as the heathen do. For they think that they will be heard for their many words. Therefore do not be like them. For your Father knows the things you have need of before you ask Him. In this manner, therefore, pray: Our Father in heaven, hallowed be Your name. Your kingdom come. Your will be done on earth as it is in heaven. Give us this day our daily bread. And forgive our debts, as we forgive our debtors. And do not lead us into temptation, but deliver us from the evil one. For Yours is the kingdom and the power and the glory forever. Amen."*
- **Matthew 7:7-11; Luke 11:9-13** *"Ask, and it will be given to you; seek, and you will find; knock, and it will be opened to you. For everyone who asks receives, and he who seeks finds, and to him who knocks it will be opened. Or what man is there among you who, if his son asks for bread, will give him a stone? Or if he asks for a fish, will he give him a serpent? If you, then, being evil, know how to give good gifts to your children, how much more will your Father who is in heaven give good things to those who ask Him!"*

- **Matthew 26:41; Mark 14:38; Luke 22:40** *"Watch and pray, lest you enter into temptation. The spirit indeed is willing, but the flesh is weak."*
- **Mark 11:25-26; Matthew 6:14-15** *"And whenever you stand praying, if you have anything against anyone, forgive him, that your Father in heaven may also forgive you your trespasses. But if you do not forgive, neither will your Father in heaven forgive your trespasses."*
- **John 14:13-14; 16:24** *"And whatever you ask in My name, that I will do, that the Father may be glorified in the Son. If you ask anything in My name, I will do it...Until now you have asked nothing in My name. Ask, and you will receive, that your joy may be full."*

THE COMMAND INTERPRETED:

For you as a disciple of Christ, prayer is to your Christian life what gasoline is to a car. Therefore, it should be no surprise that Jesus gives several commands on the subject, most of which are direct but some of which are implicit. The interpretation of these commands is vital in order to form a proper relationship to the principles of prayer. Oh, disciple, you cannot afford to settle for a mediocre prayer life. Pay close attention to what Jesus is teaching and commanding you as His disciple regarding prayer.

The first command (**Matthew 6:5-13; Luke 11:1-8**) has a familiar tone to it—namely, the Lord's Prayer. You have probably heard this prayer repeated among small groups of believers or even in the locker room before a football game. Unfortunately, many people have "prayed" the prayer without appreciating its underlying meaning. As a disciple, you need to know what Christ was teaching here and how you are to apply that teaching.

Jesus was teaching you two things: the *wrong* way to pray and the *right* way to pray. Wrong praying is synonymous with hypocrisy. Christ taught that people who love to be "seen and heard" praying are hypocrites, obviously because they have no real desire to talk with the Father. Likewise, Jesus added that these same people (hypocrites) pray using vain repetitions; that is, their words are empty and have no sincere, heartfelt meaning to them. They pollute prayer into a "show-and-tell" performance, seeking to impress men with their fancy words and legalistic recitations that never reach the throne of God. Jesus' command (**Matthew 6:8**) is direct to you as a disciple. Do not play the hypocrite in prayer.

The right way to pray was explained by Christ through both model and manner. The model Jesus instructs you to emulate in "right" praying, in contrast to wrong praying, is to go into your room and shut the door when you pray (**Matthew 6:6**). This is an invitation to private prayer between you and the Lord, the kind that Christ has a way of "*rewarding*" openly because it was done in secret.

In addition to this, Jesus told His disciples, "*In this manner, therefore, pray...*" So, we see that Christ moved His disciples from the model to the manner of prayer. The manner of prayer is really a reference to the content of your praying. Jesus is giving you some "substance" to be used when praying to the Father. As the command goes in **Matthew 6**, prayer is to "*our Father in Heaven*," and His Name is to be "*hallowed*" or revered as holy (**verse 9**). You are to pray in agreement with His Kingdom and His will in mind, for both Heaven and Earth (**verse 10**). You are also to believe God for His financial and material supply of your "*daily bread*" (**verse 11**). Another characteristic of your praying is that it is to be inclusive of forgiveness, both for yourself and for those who have mistreated you (**verse 12**). In addition, you are to pray in sensitivity to the reality that "*temptation*" and the "*evil one*" are lurking, by faith believing God's protection to "*lead you not*" into those hellish snares the devil has for you (**verse 13a**). Finally, you are to pray with an acknowledgment that the Father is credited with "*the kingdom, the power, and the glory forever*" (**verse 13b**), reminding yourself that it is truly an honor to be on the Lord's side in this evil world (**Romans 8:31**). This is the manner in which a disciple should pray.

The second command (**Matthew 7:7-11; Luke 11:9-13**) is quite direct, but not without permission. Jesus is commanding, yet permitting, you to ask, seek, and knock. Each command is completed by a promise. When you "*ask*," the Lord gives to you what you have been asking for. When you "*seek*," you find what you have been seeking. When you "*knock*," your request is entirely opened for you to receive. Now, of course, this kind of praying is not done to manipulate God's will or to get your way selfishly with a prayer, but to position God's will appropriately (**1 John 5:14-15**). As you do, Christ is inviting you to enter the full permission you have to pray like this and to reap whatever it is He wills for you.

How can this be? If this is true, then a disciple can conclude that prayer is not meant to be mysterious; Christ actually wants to bless you and answer your prayers! Amen (**Psalm 103:2**)! You see, that is why Jesus shifted an illustration of real life into your path. He implied that it would be unthinkable for a man to give his child a rock if he asked for a piece of bread, or a serpent if he asked for a fish. Jesus used this example to validate the reality that a parent wants to give his child the best gift he can. Likewise, Jesus commands us to persistently ask (*not beg*) because our Father, too, wants *"to give good things"* to His children who ask Him! This does not mean you get what you want but rather that you receive what the Father wants you to have. Be careful not to prostitute this command with unhindered, fleshly gratification by focusing your prayers more on the "blessing" than the "Blesser." Do more bowing than you do begging. Focus more on praying simply to pray than praying just to prosper. Furthermore, God's people often do not receive God's blessing because of their doubt (**James 1:7-8**) and their selfishness (**James 4:3**). Oh, disciple, yes, the Father wants to give to you and bless you as His child, but remember to obsess yourself more with Him as your Father than with His blessing.

The third command (**Matthew 26:41; Mark 14:38; Luke 22:40**) is direct and to the point. Jesus does not merely command you to pray, but to *"watch"* and pray. Why? Because temptation is a trap baited with Satan's hellish deceit, by which the enemy waits for you to be ensnared. Interestingly, the Greek word "watch" (*greggoreuo*) means "to keep awake." Sounds like spiritual coffee to me! Christ is adding this component to your prayer life for a reason. He is saying to you as His disciple to stay alert, because your flesh is weak prey for temptation to sink its teeth into. Do you see the literal idea presented? Jesus is not saying to look out for temptation while you are praying as much as He's saying your praying should include a "cry for help" to be alert, awakened to the temptations around you.

The fourth command (**Mark 11:25-26; Matthew 6:14-15**) is about as blunt of a statement as you will hear from the Lord Jesus. While prayers that confess sin are forgiven (**1 John 1:9**), those offered while the supplicant harbors sin are unanswered (**Psalm**

66:18). In this case, prayer is brought into direct connection with relationships with others. The issue at hand is not if people don't like you but if you *"have anything against anyone."* Without stuttering, Jesus commanded that if you pray to the Father with a grudge against another person, you are exhorted to forgive that person so that God can forgive you. If you remain bitter and angry at the person you choose not to forgive, then God does not forgive your sins either. Why? Simply because we are expected to forgive and show the same mercy Christ Jesus has shown to us (**Colossians 3:13**). There are no exceptions; this is the allegiance expected from a disciple. The Lord Jesus has ordained this method for you to stay in right relationship with people in general (**Matthew 18:15-17**). As a disciple, you are not permitted to hold anything against anyone because God did not hold your sins against you. Since the depth of His love will forever transcend and exceed your love, you are forever held to His standard of mercy and forgiveness. The extent of love is a true indicator of the converted, born-again disciple with the attitude and allegiance of Jesus Christ (**1 John 3:14**).

The fifth command (**John 14:13-14; 16:24**) mimics the second command in that Christ instructs us to *ask*. The difference in this command compared to the second command is actually twofold. First of all, you as the disciple are told to *"ask"* the Father in Jesus' Name so that *"the Father may be glorified in the Son."* So the One to Whom we pray is the Father, but if we ask Him for anything, we ask in the name of His Son, Jesus. That makes you wonder how many prayers you hear closing with the words "In Jesus' Name I pray..." that haven't actually asked the Father for anything. Remember, you're dealing with the Name of Jesus Christ, a holy Name, an awesome Name, a glorious Name. Moreover, the purpose of asking anything in Jesus' Name is to glorify the Father, and this is accompanied by the promise that Christ will *"do"* whatever you have asked.

Second, your *"asking"* the Father is not complete without your *"joy being full."* Amazing! Do you see a picture here? This fifth command is about asking, similar to yet differing from the second command. The climactic image Christ is portraying for you the disciple is that asking in His Name glorifies the Father, assures you of your request, and rightfully contributes to an abundant joy that is full and abounding! Who would have thought "asking" could be so rewarding? This command from Christ is not up for debate but available for the disciple who will take Him at His word. Obey and receive; you have been given permission.

THE COMMAND ILLUSTRATED:

There is an excellent example in Scripture that captures the truths presented in these five commands of Jesus about prayer. The passage is found in **Acts 7:54-60**. The disciple of Jesus is Stephen, the martyr. Stephen was accused of blasphemy and arrested in **Acts 6**. Like Peter, he went on trial and stood boldly before the council for his faith in Jesus Christ. However, he was stoned to death. What parallels these commands with this passage is Stephen's prayer in **verses 59-60**.

All five of Jesus' commands on prayer reflect different principles, but among those commands is a connection with Stephen's prayer: forgiveness of those who trespass against us (**Luke 11:4**). This was exactly the attitude of Stephen as he was being stoned to death: *"Lord, do not charge them with this sin."* Rather than boasting God's grace in their faces and lashing back at his attackers, Stephen humbly and mercifully viewed the sin of the people as a sin against Christ alone. Dear disciple, when you pray, do you have a clear conscience, one that does not condemn you because of known sin? Can you really pray out of a clean heart before God because you know that you have nothing against anyone? If so, praise the Lord God Almighty. If not, like Stephen, do not hold people's wrongdoings against them. Learn from this example. You can pray all day long with the right model and manner, in the right way, asking, seeking, and knocking, watching as you pray, and even praying in Jesus' Name, but if you have bitter, unforgiving resentment against someone else, all praying is in vain! As a disciple of Jesus Christ, this is a part of your lifestyle. You cannot carry your cross if you're going to carry this burden. Release it to the Lord (**1 Peter 5:6-7**) and forgive the person who wronged you. Don't sacrifice your prayer life for stubbornness or excuses. You can do this, for Christ Himself strengthens you so that you can. Trust Him.

TEACHING # 2.5: PRAYER (PART 2)

Week 14

<u>*This week's objective*</u>: *To value the privilege of access to converse with the Father, as well as to learn the purposes behind Jesus' command to pray.*

THE COMMAND INITIATED:

Prayer is truly a privilege. As a disciple of Jesus, you need to know how to pray. As you journey through this Christian life, you will find yourself in some situations that will cause you to praise God in prayer and some that will compel you to cry out to God in prayer. Life as a Christian is like this continuously. Therefore, it is very important for you as a disciple to know how to appreciate the real motive behind your praying. Dr. Ken Hemphill offers you an intriguing insight about your prayer life. In his book *The Prayer of Jesus*, Hemphill dissects prayer into what it is and what it is not:

> God does answer prayer. I know it from experience. Besides that, the Scripture is full of instances where God's people prayed and He responded exactly as they had asked. *However, having our requests granted is not the primary goal of prayer.* Prayer is not simply the process of giving God our wish list. Many times we ask for things that seem to be what we need, but we later recognize that—had we gotten them—they would have been far from our best interests. God does not exist merely to give us what we want. *Neither is prayer a way to alert God to our needs.* As we'll see later in this Bible passage, God knows our needs even better than we do, and He needs no formal reminders about where we are and what we're up against. Prayer is in no way a squeaky wheel designed to manipulate God into remembering us. *One of the most primary purposes of prayer is to spend time in conversation*

with our Father. And when this is our goal, we can pray at all times guaranteed that it will be rewarded. Will it be answered the way we want it to? Maybe. But will it be rewarded by bringing us into the Father's presence? Absolutely. *You see, prayer is not about answers. Prayer is about reward.* I'm telling you, this understanding of the purpose of prayer will begin to revolutionize the way you approach God. It will cause you to marvel at the miraculous privilege of being able to engage in intimate conversation with the Creator of the universe. By His own grace and design, He has chosen to become our Father. He has opened the windows of heaven and allowed us to spend hours at a time in His awesome presence...this fellowship is hardly limited to what we usually consider our "prayer time" but is truly a constant, continuous, moment-by-moment relationship with God.[3]

You are created to glorify your Creator (**Romans 1:20, 25**). You see, when Jesus Christ died and His blood flowed from His body, the Temple veil split in half (**Matthew 27:51**) because His sacrifice as the Lamb of God was sufficient, inaugurating Him as our Great High Priest (**Hebrews 4:14-15; 9:11-15**). Praise God! By the blood of Jesus, we draw near (**Ephesians 2:13**) and enter into the holiest place of all, the Presence of God (**Hebrews 10:19-20**). Oh, with the precious blood of Jesus, the Body of Christ (church) has been purchased (**Acts 20:28**), redeemed (**Ephesians 1:7**), and justified (**Romans 5:9**). You and I no longer stand condemned in our sins, but now by the justifying power of Christ's blood, we are finally at peace with God (**Colossians 1:20; Romans 5:1**). The "war" in our souls, the enmity against God, is over (**James 4:4**)! With this kind of understanding and appreciation, you cannot allow prayer to become a duty, burden, or obligation. Every time you pray, remember what it cost Jesus for you to enjoy such status.

THE COMMAND INTERROGATED:

Now that you see as a disciple how important prayer is in

your relationship to Christ, you can also see how much Satan would love to sever your divine line of communication. Well, the good news is that the devil will never be able to do that, for he is a defeated foe in light of the cross of our Christ. However, in this mortal life, he will, like a rat in the attic, do whatever is necessary to nibble at the line of communication between you and the Father.

Hebrews 4:16 is a commonly quoted verse of Scripture that explains the permission Christians have in prayer. It says, *"Let us therefore come boldly to the throne of grace, that we may obtain mercy and find grace to help in time of need."* While some might think a lack of time is Satan's primary corruption to disengage a disciple's prayer life, this verse illuminates an assault that far exceeds even a shortage of time to pray. Think about it: the topic of this verse is *"time of need."* The promise for this is twofold: that you will *"obtain mercy"* and that you will *"find grace to help."* Now, remember, all of this is in the context of prayer. Can you see how Satan would be more attracted to this area of a disciple's life than merely by corrupting his time to pray?

Listen very carefully. Throughout your Christian life, you will continually find yourself in a time of need. Yes, your heavenly Father knows your needs (**Matthew 6:8**) and will meet your needs (**Philippians 4:19**), but that doesn't mean Satan will not try to deceptively do it for you. Be very, very cautious. While you are obtaining the LORD's mercy for your need, Satan wars against your heart and mind, exerting himself to either hinder such help from coming to you or to distract your mind and tempt you to seek help from someone or something else that is not of the LORD. *"Be sober, be vigilant: because your adversary the devil walks about like a roaring lion, seeking whom he may devour"* (**1 Peter 5:8**).

THE COMMAND INDESTRUCTIBLE:

It is obviously impossible for you to have a vibrant relationship with Christ without also enjoying a passionate prayer life. Both living for the Father and having dialogue with Him go synonymously hand in hand. Since Satan will never stop attacking you in the area of prayer, you must be on guard with God's Word to encourage you and help you fight through his attacks. A wonderful memory verse for you to tuck into your heart (**Psalm 119:11**) is **Luke 18:1**. As Luke was writing his Gospel account, you can hear the assertiveness in his voice as he recalled what Jesus was doing in regards to prayer: "*Then He spoke a parable to them, that men always ought to pray and not lose heart.*"

There's a verse of Scripture in the Bible that commands Christians to "pray without ceasing" (**1 Thessalonians 5:17**). This memory verse validates what Jesus is requesting. You are to always be in a state of prayer; that is, you should be constantly conversing with God throughout each day. Yes, your praying begins in your room with the door shut, but it continues all day long as you spend time with the Father. Can you see the picture of dependability stroked on the canvas of your heart? Repeatedly talking with God breeds a childlike trust in God. That's what the Father wants from you as His disciple. You are to always be praying—at your desk, in the store as you shop, in the car while you drive (eyes open, please!), and in the waiting room while you, well, wait! This is what allegiance is all about as a disciple. Being rightly related to the Word of God and to prayer is essential for a disciple. If you find yourself "losing heart" to pray, bow down wherever you are and pray! Pour out your heart. With all reverence and fear of God, tell the Father exactly what's on your heart so that He can relieve the burden and you can pray freely. Claim **Luke 18:1** as your memory verse, reminding yourself of what Jesus, your Lord and Master, expects of you as His disciple. Pray. Pray. Pray.

THE COMMAND INQUIRED:

What cannot be measured cannot be evaluated. Therefore, it is essential to measure your comprehension of Christ's command in this teaching, or else the devil will snatch away the "seeds" of Scripture sown into your heart (**Matthew 13:19**). To keep this from occurring, write down your answers to the following questions as they correlate with the teaching this week:

In what passage(s) of Scripture do you find Christ's commandment on **prayer**?

_____

_____

What is the accurate interpretation of **prayer** you have discovered?

_____

_____

_____

_____

_____

_____

In your own words, what are some real-life examples in Scripture of **prayer**?

_____

_____

_____

_____

_____

What steps of initiation did you learn to take in order for **prayer** to transform your life?

_____

_____

_____

_____

_____

_____

How will Satan attack you to hinder **prayer** in your life?

_____

_____

_____

_____

_____

What memory verse will you use to protect Christ's command of **prayer** in your life? Write it out.

_____

_____

_____

_____

_____

TEACHING # 2.6: FASTING

Week 15

This week's objective: To explain the discipline of fasting as well as the purpose behind it as it is practiced in the Christian life.

THE COMMAND INTRODUCED:

- **Matthew 6:16-18** *"Moreover, when you fast, do not be like the hypocrites, with a sad countenance. For they disfigure their faces that they may appear to men to be fasting. Assuredly, I say to you, they have their reward. But you, when you fast, anoint your head and wash your face, so that you do not appear to men to be fasting, but to your Father who is in the secret place; and your Father who sees in secret will reward you openly."*

THE COMMAND INTERPRETED:

This is definitely a direct command from Jesus. When Jesus issued this decree of fasting to His disciples, they were already very familiar with its well-known practice. They had learned by way of the Mosaic Law that fasting was standard for the priests and the Pharisees. However, Jesus went beyond the externals of the practice to emphasize the motive behind our fasting.

Perhaps you're asking yourself, "What exactly is fasting?" The Greek word Jesus used for "fast" (*nesteuo*) literally means "not eating; to abstain from food." Basically, fasting is disciplining yourself to do without something (food) for the sole purpose of seeking the Lord God Almighty (**Psalm 27:8**). Like an unhappy employee, you go on "strike" against the gratifying indulgences of your flesh (hunger) in pursuit of a deeper, closer relationship with the Lord God (**Isaiah 55:6**). Therefore, fasting is supplemented with prayer and meditation upon God's Word. You fast as often as you choose to; there are no legalistic guidelines. Again, the motive behind your fasting is the primary factor that will determine how seriously God will view your fasting.

The motive behind any action is always worthy of evaluation. The Lord Jesus interprets this command for us by identifying the hindrance to it: *hypocrisy*. Clearly, Christ commands for you not to imitate the *"hypocrites."* The Greek word Jesus used for hypocrites (*hupokrites*) means "an actor under an assumed character; pretender." It carries the literal meaning of wearing a mask such as people don for a costume party. A hypocrite is someone who is fake or superficial. The real, genuine part of them is in disguise, but Christ sees right through them. The Lord Jesus identifies what is portrayed by a hypocrite's mask, such as a sad countenance intentionally disfigured to draw attention to himself. The reward of such people is the sympathy and applause of men, leaving no reward from God. Do not be like these pretenders!

Rather, the Lord Jesus specifically spelled out His clear command for you as His disciple when you fast. Did you notice that Jesus used *"when"* you fast, not *"if?"* Fasting is supposed to be a normal part of your Christian life; start practicing. In order to be genuine disciples and not hypocrites, Jesus' disciples were commanded to anoint their heads and wash their faces. Why? *"So that you do not appear to men to be fasting."*

It's the same principle as when you wake up each morning and take a shower. The water from your shower wakes you up. Afterwards, you do not appear to be asleep anymore, nor do you look as if you just awoke. Jesus is being very sensitive to the reality of physiological changes in the human body as a result of ignoring hunger pains. When you are hungry, there is either a growl coming from your belly or your face. Oh, disciple, hear the Lord Jesus. Splash some water on your face, wet your head, and do whatever is necessary to keep people from knowing that you are fasting before the Lord your God. Encouragingly, Jesus says that if you keep this your and His little secret, He will reward you. Now that's divine bribery! The reward is not cookies and milk or a New York steak. The reward is Christ. If this discipline has not already ignited a spiritual fire in your life as a disciple, may it be so from this day forward.

THE COMMAND ILLUSTRATED:

The Bible is full of incredible examples of fasting, in both the Old and New Testaments. In the context of Jesus and His disciples, one of these proves to be the most beneficial for this teaching. It is found in **Matthew 9:14-17**. Do you remember John the Baptist, the forerunner of Jesus? He was responsible to launch Jesus' ministry, to prepare the people for the appearance of Christ (**Matthew 3**). Well, John the Baptist had many "disciples" (followers) who believed his message of repentance in preparation for the soon coming of the Messiah (Jesus). Ignorantly, the men in **Matthew 9** were oblivious to the fact that they were looking and talking with the Messiah John proclaimed! Rather than addressing their ignorance, Jesus answered their question, for it was more important at the moment it launched.

Jesus gave the analogy of a wedding party. In regards to the bride and groom, the reception following the wedding is inevitable. There is so much joy and celebration because of the wedding, all of which is accompanied by "*eating*" and "*drinking*" together to commemorate the happiness of the wedding guests. Do you see Jesus' point? Likewise, as long as He, the Bridegroom, was with His disciples (bride), there was no need to fast because of the joy and celebration of unity with the Presence of Christ.

Furthermore, using an old patch and old wineskins in comparison to new ones, Jesus illustrated that you cannot "patch" the *old* Mosaic Law of fasting onto the *new* Covenant truth of fasting. Now that Christ the Bridegroom has been taken away (**Acts 1:9-11**), you are to be fasting during this earthly life, seeking the Lord and enduring patiently the trials and persecutions of your life as a disciple. Oh, but one day, we shall resume a "fast-free" relationship with Christ (**Matthew 26:29; Revelation 19:6-9**). Praise the Lord our God!

THE COMMAND INITIATED:

How tragic it would be for you as a disciple to know that Christ your Lord expects for you to fast, and then to not put it into practice! It is really simple: exchange days or hours without food for prayer and seeking the Lord through His Word. Now, of course, there's nothing simple about fighting your flesh to endure, but the decision itself could not be easier. Like the Nike™ slogans you have probably seen in stores and on television, just do it! As Christ's disciple, you will find that the reward of fasting will outweigh the rigorous hunger pangs that accompany it.

Donald Whitney has an impressive grasp on the subject of fasting. In his book *Spiritual Disciplines for the Christian Life*, Whitney assertively explains what fasting really is. He quotes Cornelius Plantiga, Jr., and follows with personal insight:

> Self-indulgence is the enemy of gratitude, and self-discipline usually its friend and generator. That is why gluttony is a deadly sin. The early desert fathers believed that a person's appetites are linked: full stomachs and jaded palates take the edge from our hunger and thirst for righteousness. They spoil the appetite for God...Christians in a gluttonous, denial-less, self-indulgent society may struggle to accept and to begin the practice of fasting. Few disciplines go so radically against the flesh and mainstream of culture as this one...A biblical definition of fasting is a Christian's voluntary abstinence from food for spiritual purposes. It is *Christian*, for fasting by a non-Christian obtains no eternal value because the discipline's motives and purposes are to be God-centered. It is *voluntary* in that fasting is not to be coerced. Fasting is more than just the ultimate crash diet for the body; it is abstinence from food for *spiritual* purposes...There's more to a biblical fast than abstaining from food. Without a spiritual purpose for your fast it's just a weight-loss fast...And without a purpose, fasting can be a miserable, self-centered experience...There's something about fasting that sharpens the edge of our intercessions and gives passion to our supplications. ...The Bible does not teach that fasting is a kind of spiritual hunger strike that compels God to do our bidding. If we ask for something outside of God's will, fasting does not cause Him to reconsider. Fasting does not change God's hearing so much as it changes our praying.[4]

Whitney put it so well! You see, when you fast as a disciple, remember that it begins with a voluntary discipline but continues with spiritual purpose. Fasting without purpose will cause you to act merely to fulfill an obligation or to appease your conscience. God's commands should never burden you (**1 John 5:3**). As a part of your allegiance to Christ, count it a pure joy to fast before Him, the King of Kings! Also, remember that your fasting is not done to impress God or gain His favor and blessings. As you initiate true, biblical fasting into your life as a disciple, never forget that it is more a privilege than it is a hardship. Seeking Jesus Christ and finding Him will always be an honor.

THE COMMAND INTERROGATED:

Go ahead—take a wild guess. What do you think Satan would love to do to sway you from fasting? Believe it or not, it's not putting food in front of you, for food is to be received with thanksgiving from God (**1 Timothy 4:4-5**). Cleverly, the devil attacks the greater root of the source. You see, he knows that fasting is more about the absence of self than it is about the absence of food. It's not the food you deny; instead, you deny *yourself* (your flesh) to abstain from the food. Why? To pursue the Lord Jesus without wavering distractions.

It is not Satan's goal to load you with food every day in hopes of distracting you. He's more cunning than that. Rather, he wants to keep you satisfied with a lukewarm lifestyle, one that is full of "self" and that is wrapped up in the satiety of spiritual stagnation. This is the attack of Satan against a disciple. If you allow yourself to be controlled by the amenities of life to the point that fasting becomes viewed as frightening and burdensome, he's got you pinned down! He has your fleshly appetites just where he wants them. Choose **Luke 9:23**. The devil will do whatever is necessary to convince your mind to depend on yourself and delay in prayer. Fasting to you would then become something "other Christians" engage in. Beware. Do not allow that hellish spirit to fire up the selfishness inside your sinful, mortal flesh. By the grace of God, rule over your flesh (**Romans 6:14**), deny yourself, and fast.

THE COMMAND INDESTRUCTIBLE:

As a disciple of Jesus Christ, you need a memory verse of Scripture that will serve as divine artillery against Satan. Such an invincible weapon is found in **Ezra 8:23**: *"So we fasted and entreated our God for this, and He answered our prayer."* Ezra and the children of Israel were about to embark on a long, dangerous journey. They needed protection against the enemies that would come against them. So what did they do? Fast. Guess what? The Lord honored their fast and granted them the protection they needed.

Fasting is to prayer what oxygen is to lungs: they cannot be separated. Scripturally, fasting was always accompanied by prayer. God hears you when you pray. Oh, child of God, hear and believe the Word of the Lord. During your long Christian pilgrimage, you will encounter Satan and his attacks often. He'll go away for seasons (**Luke 4:11**), but he always comes back again (**James 4:7**). Jesus wants His command to take root as a discipline in your life as His disciple. Claim the memory verse. Hide it in your heart and allow it to be the adhesive to your walk with Christ. Always, especially in times of attack, be found by the Lord quoting and believing by faith His indestructible Word!

The promise is to you what it was to Ezra: God answers prayer. Fast and pray—your prayer will be answered. You don't know when or how. But you do know God will not ignore a disciple in fasting and prayer before Him. Fast according to the Word. Fast with the Word. Fast.

THE COMMAND INQUIRED:

What cannot be measured cannot be evaluated. Therefore, it is essential to measure your comprehension of Christ's command in this teaching, or else the devil will snatch away the "seeds" of Scripture sown into your heart (**Matthew 13:19**). To keep this from occurring, write down your answers to the following questions as they correlate with the teaching this week:

In what passage(s) of Scripture do you find Christ's commandment on **fasting**?

_____

_____

What is the accurate interpretation of **fasting** you have discovered?

_____

_____

_____

_____

_____

In your own words, what are some real-life examples in Scripture of **fasting**?

_____

_____

_____

_____

_____

What steps of initiation did you learn to take in order for **fasting** to transform your life?

_____

_____

_____

_____

_____

_____

How will Satan attack you to hinder **fasting** in your life?

_____

_____

_____

_____

_____

What memory verse will you use to protect Christ's command of **fasting** in your life? Write it out.

_____

_____

_____

_____

_____

_____

TEACHING # 2.7: FAITH (PART 1)

Week 16

<u>*This week's objective:*</u> *To explore the meaning of faith, assess its current value in life, and begin to develop a lifestyle that reflects it.*

THE COMMAND INTRODUCED:

- **Matthew 17:16-20** "'*So I brought him to Your disciples, but they could not cure him.' Then Jesus answered and said, 'O faithless and perverse generation, how long shall I be with you? How long shall I bear with you? Bring him here to Me.' And Jesus rebuked the demon, and it came out of him; and the child was cured from that very hour. Then the disciples came to Jesus privately and said, 'Why could we not cast it out?' So Jesus said to them, 'Because of your unbelief; for assuredly, I say to you, if you have faith as a mustard seed, you will say to this mountain, 'Move from here to there,' and it will move; and nothing will be impossible for you.*'"
- **Mark 11:20-24; Matthew 21:18-21** "*Now in the morning, as they passed by, they saw the fig tree dried up from the roots. And Peter, remembering, said to Him, 'Rabbi, look! The fig tree which You cursed has withered away.' So Jesus answered and said to them, 'Have faith in God. For assuredly, I say to you, whoever says to this mountain, 'Be removed and cast into the sea,' and does not doubt in his heart, but believes that those things he says will be done, he will have whatever he says. Therefore I say to you, whatever things you ask when you pray, believe that you receive them, and you will have them.*"
- **John 20:27b** "*Then he said to Thomas, 'Reach your finger here, and look at My hands; and reach your hand here, and put it into My side. Do not be unbelieving, but believing.*"

THE COMMAND INTERPRETED:

These commands are, for the most part, direct. The subject of *faith* is by far the most essential element that Jesus Christ imparted to His disciples. Faith is what connects all the commands of Jesus. If all the commands of Christ were books, *faith* would be the ink. If all the commands were smoke, *faith* would be the fire. One is a result of the other. Therefore, as you can tell, *faith* is the necessity for the practice of all Christ's commands; yet at the same time, it is itself a command. Never forget this: your *faith*fulness to obey Christ's commands will always be linked to the quality of your *faith* in the Christ of the commands.

The first command (**Matthew 17:16-20**) positions its use in a disciple's relationship to **people**. Earlier in this Scripture passage, Jesus was transfigured in His glory on a mountain in front of Peter, James, and John. After this "mountaintop" revival, Christ descended into the valley of need. A man from a multitude came running to Jesus, pleading with Him to heal his demon-possessed son. Interestingly, this man also informed Jesus that he had already brought his son to the remaining nine disciples who stayed behind while Peter, James, and John were gone with Jesus. The devastating news he gave Jesus was that the other nine "*could not cure him.*" This very incident is precisely why the command here relates to people.

Where was the disciples' faith? Why could they not cure the demon-possessed young man? Was there a glitch in their faith? The response of Jesus is paramount. Christ was very upset and frustrated, and of course He had every right to be. Do you know why? Because of **Matthew 10**. Just seven chapters earlier Christ gave them power to do for others what they did not do that day for the young man. There was a breakdown somewhere, and Christ hit the nail on the head: "*O faithless and perverse generation...*" His reaction targeted the real source, their faith. The Greek word for "faithless" (*apistos*) means "untrustworthy; without faith." The Greeks were notorious for referencing such a word to describe a heathen. At the same time, the Greek word for "perverse" (*diastrepho*) means "to distort; corrupt; turn away." Can you see why this was a rebuke that put these disciples in their place? Literally, Jesus was calling these nine disciples untrustworthy, corrupt heathens! Such comments coming from Christ reveal His righteous indignation against doubt and unbelief.

In addition to Jesus' righteous anger towards His disciples,

He followed His bold statement with a question: *"How long?"* This was not an address to the multitudes nor to the pleading father. This was a question for His disciples. A lack of faith had reached a boiling point with Christ. At that moment, it was as if Jesus were saying, "How much longer do I have to endure this? You people just don't get it. You're getting on my nerves." It is like being around an annoying person, or even worse, a foul odor. Have you ever had to change a baby's diaper? Have you ever smelled rotten food by accident? Have you ever passed through a town with a paper mill? You see, the point is that Christians are called to be the aroma of Christ (**2 Corinthians 2:14-16**). In a spiritual sense, disciples are to "smell good" wherever they go. But these nine disciples who lacked faith reeked! Therefore, Christ's nauseated remarks serve as a reminder that a disciple's lack of faith doesn't hurt him as badly as it hurts others; the demon-possessed boy suffered the consequences for the disciple's faithless attitude. As a disciple, exercise your faith for the glory of Christ.

Did you notice what happened next? Jesus took charge, demonstrated faith in the Father, and healed the boy. Out of sheer embarrassment, the nine disciples came to Jesus secretly, sincerely asking why they failed. Jesus' reply was so simple, yet so blunt: *"Because of your unbelief."* What do you suppose their belief was in? It was in themselves. They had healed and played the exorcist so many times that they became dependent on themselves and their natural abilities. Learn a valuable lesson here: never become so accustomed to "serving Jesus" that you try to do so without Him. Your effectiveness to build the Kingdom and help people will only be as good as your faith. Jesus' use of a mustard seed reminds you that He's not impressed with how *much* faith you say you have. Instead, He's only interested in the *quality*. Christ is looking for undaunted, pure faith—the kind that is mountain-moving, the kind that laughs confidently in the face of impossible odds. Disciple, how is your *faith*?

The second command (**Mark 11:20-24; Matthew 21:18-21**) positions its use in a disciple's relationship to *prayer.* Jesus used a fig tree to get His point across about the lesson of faith. With His disciples watching, one day Jesus saw a fig tree that had leaves on it but no fruit. This is to say that it exhibited a form of life (leaves) but did not do what it was created to do (bear fruit). Such is the case even today with deceptive people who have a form of godliness (leaves) but lack what counts (salvation)—2 Timothy 3:5; Titus 1:16. Jesus cursed the unfruitful fig tree just as He will curse phony Christians at the Judgment (**Matthew 7:21-23**).

Now, believe it or not, although fruitfulness is included in this command, it is not the heart. The main point Jesus is making to you is what He stated to an inquisitive, stupefied Peter: "*Have faith in God.*" Perhaps Peter would have loved to listen intently to the details of the agricultural phenomenon, but Jesus did not explain to Peter how or why He cursed the fig tree. He did not detail the science behind it. Rather, Christ merely used the awe and wonder of the decayed fig tree as a bridge to teach His disciples about faith. Just as it seemed impossible and unbelievable for that to happen, so Christ wanted His disciples to know the beauty of "believing" the impossible into reality.

As a disciple, you cannot overlook the aspect of prayer among these impossibilities. We're talking about faith as interpreted by speaking. Speaking? That's right. Notice how Jesus referred to "whoever *says*" and "those things he *says*" and "whatever he *says*." One verse—three references to the phrase *says*. If that doesn't convince you, just read the next verse (**Mark 11:24**). It is clear: doubt leads to drought. Doubt in the heart will result in a drought of answered prayer. What confidence this gives you as Christ's disciple to pray His Word and believe Him for the results! The key is believing and receiving. Granted, this is not intended to be a manipulative tool for self-gratification; that is, this is not a tactic to get what you want. Instead, it is a discipline to pray in faith, believing in what you do not see as if you see it already, as Abraham did (**Romans 4:13-22**). Avoid doubt. Embrace faith. Live in victory (**1 John 5:4**).

Lastly, the third command (**John 20:27b**) positions its use in a disciple's relationship to **persistence**. Can you imagine what it must have been like to be Thomas, gazing not only into the eyes of the resurrected Christ but also at His wounds? Breathtaking! Captivating! Rather than clinging to the risen Jesus, His disciples doubted Him, especially Thomas. While the others eventually believed, Thomas was the hard-headed one, bent on not believing until he could "*see*" for himself that Jesus was alive. Even though Christ was by no means required to "prove" Himself to Thomas, He did, meeting Thomas at his own point of weakness. That weakness was his faith.

Can you see why Thomas's faith was so weak? Imagine being one of the twelve disciples: for the past three years, you have left all, including family, careers, and friends, to follow this Man. Suddenly, He's crucified, and that's it. Now, what do you do? How do you pick back up with your life before you met Him? That's exactly how Thomas must have felt. The disciples gave up everything and everyone to follow Christ, and now He was gone? Though it is no excuse for weak faith, you can understand their despair. This is why the Resurrection of Jesus Christ changed everything! Now, the disciples had hope. He really was the Messiah. Sins really were forgiven. Eternal life really would take place. It was time to go tell the world! Such a reaction is more than fitting for a believer in light of Christ's Resurrection. However, that is where we find Thomas wavering.

As he addressed Thomas's faith, Jesus commanded, *"Do not be unbelieving, but believing."* Thomas's reply (**John 20:28**) indicates that he never took Jesus up on His offer to touch His wounds. He merely said, *"My Lord and my God!"* At that moment, Thomas's faith was revived. That is why this command is all about persistence. If the disciples had faith before Christ died, then how did they not have it after He died? Simply because they did not remain persistent in exercising it. Dear disciple, listen carefully: use your faith, or it will stagnate. Faith that does not persist in believing and fulfilling the commands of Jesus will find itself turning to the traditions of men for help. It will result in glorification of fleshly wisdom above heavenly wisdom (**James 3:13-17**). As a disciple of Christ, discipline yourself to live by faith, not by sight (**2 Corinthians 5:7**). By doing so, you protect yourself from being controlled by your visible surroundings while you follow by faith your invisible God (**Hebrews 11:27**). There is no real joy in Christ and His commands until you persistently live in faith...daily.

THE COMMAND ILLUSTRATED:

The Bible records hundreds and hundreds of examples of faith. While it is difficult to choose one to address, there is one that stands out as a foundational understanding more than an experiential connection. The passage is found in the "faith" chapter of the Bible, **Hebrews 11:1-3**.

Here you find the literal, biblical definition of *faith*. How can you contain a substance if you are still hoping for it? How can you see evidence of something you do not yet behold? That is faith. That should be your life. This is exactly how the elders (people of God) lived their lives before you. They are the members of the great cloud of witnesses that begins the next chapter (**Hebrews 12:1**). It is by this same faith that Christianity embraces the belief, by faith, of how the universe was created. Faith says that everything you see with your eyes was made by and with that which you cannot see. Amazing! This mentality of faith describes perfectly how you are to live as a disciple of Christ. Using God's Word, you are to speak and believe Christ's plan, will, and direction for everything you do, everywhere you go, and everyone you meet. It is the only way a disciple can please his Master, Jesus (**Hebrews 11:6**). Strive for a lifestyle of relentless, mountain-moving faith.

TEACHING # 2.8: FAITH (PART 2)

Week 17

This week's objective: To explore the meaning of faith, assess its current value in life, and begin to develop a lifestyle that reflects it.

THE COMMAND INITIATED:

Putting your faith into action is the best way to grow in Christ, which is done in relation to His Word (**1 Peter 2:2**). Remember, faith is just as necessary to live for Christ as a chain is necessary to pedal a bicycle. There is nothing like living by faith! Whatever God's word says about marriage, family, finances, careers, forgiveness, anger, sexuality, and even government, your surrender to the Word of God in these areas testifies your faith through them. Such authentic faith is like the igniting of a fire, allowing the lives of those around you to be warmed from the touch of God's Presence through you.

In his book *Faith to Live By*, Derek Prince offers a clear and explosive point of view in the arena of faith:

> Faith lifts us above the realm of our own abilities and makes God's possibilities available to us. Faith connects us to two unseen realities: God and His word. As we maintain a relationship with God through faith, we are enabled to endure and to overcome the tests and the hardships that confront us in our daily lives. These, in turn, become opportunities for God to reveal His goodness and His glory. There is an ongoing tension between faith and sight. Our old nature is at home in the world of the senses, and it demands to see. As Christians, we need to cultivate the new nature, which is able to trust God and His word without demanding other evidence.[5]

Can it be any clearer than that? Faith is not demanding for God to give you what you want because you say you believe in Him.

Instead, faith is your childlike trust in your heavenly Father who promises to give you, His child, what He knows you need (**Matthew 6:8; 7:11**). Christ does not operate on need alone; He reacts to faith. Release yours to the glory of God.

THE COMMAND INTERROGATED:

Satan loves to destroy faith. In fact, it is undoubtedly his primary objective, for if he successfully deactivates an active faith, you will be spiritually paralyzed and rendered immobile for Christ's Kingdom. It is clear that Satan is after your faith more than anything else based on the account of Jesus and Peter in **Luke 22:31-32**. Did you read it? Pay close attention to the word *sift*. The Greek meaning (*siniazo*) translates "to take through a sieve; riddle." Basically, Satan wants to mulch you, to grind you on a chopping block! Excuse such a graphic picture, but that is a grammatical fact of this passage. Notice that Jesus' concern for Peter was not necessarily his sifting but his shifting. Christ was more concerned that Peter's faith would fail as a result of his sifting. Jesus didn't want Peter to shift in his faith away from Him, for it would only hurt the brethren that looked to Peter for leadership. Beware of Satan's attack against your faith. Do not put your faith in what you see, for if you do, your faith will be anchored insecurely and can be destroyed by Satan. Therefore, keep your faith only in Christ and His Word, aimed toward His Kingdom (**2 Corinthians 5:10**). Do not let Satan block your aim. Stay faithful, and allow your faith to move him out of your way.

THE COMMAND INDESTRUCTIBLE:

The Word of God is your sure foundation, your hope for defeating Satan every time. Stand strong in your belief that God is for you (**Romans 8:31**) and that you are more than a conqueror in Christ (**Romans 8:37**). Day after day, as you fight against the ways of Satan, you will need a memory verse that will bring to your attention the commands of Christ on the subject of *faith*. While there are many, perhaps the most meaningful Scripture for you to memorize in order to fasten Christ's commands on faith is 1

Corinthians 2:5. It boldly proclaims, *"That your faith should not be in the wisdom of men but in the power of God."*

If that doesn't make you want to shout, nothing will! Every day of your mortal life, may you breathe this verse of Scripture. All throughout your life, men and women alike will give you seemingly "wise" advice about your decisions. If that advice has no Scriptural basis to it, do not trust in the *"wisdom of men."* It is a detour, a callous to your faith. As a disciple of Jesus, anchor your faith in the power of God only. Do not merely know what the Scriptures say; live what they say. Then the power of God is released from Heaven on behalf of your faith, and it is God's power that will make the difference in everything you do and say.

This is the fitting lifestyle of those justified by faith (**Habakkuk 2:4**). By this faith, you have access to the grace of God (**Romans 5:2**), where you will find the peace of God (**Philippians 4:6-7**). By this faith, you do not waver back and forth, because you believe in the powerful promises of God to see you through (**Hebrews 10:23, 38**). By this faith, the fiery trials you endure throughout life actually purify your faith and "shine it up" as a dazzling light for all to see (**1 Peter 1:7**). And, one day, the hustle and bustle will be done. The heartaches and disappointments will be terminated. The attacks of Satan and the people he uses will cease. Yes, there will be a day that this faith by which you live will be rendered unnecessary and come to an end: when you reach your heavenly finish line (**1 Peter 1:9**). As long as there is breath in your body, fight this good fight of *faith* until the day you die (**2 Timothy 4:7**).

THE COMMAND INQUIRED:

What cannot be measured cannot be evaluated. Therefore, it is essential to measure your comprehension of Christ's command in this teaching, or else the devil will snatch away the "seeds" of Scripture sown into your heart (**Matthew 13:19**). To keep this from occurring, write down your answers to the following questions as they correlate with the teaching this week:

In what passage(s) of Scripture do you find Christ's

commandment on **faith**?

_____

_____

_____

What is the accurate interpretation of **faith** you have discovered?

_____

_____

_____

_____

_____

In your own words, what are some real-life examples in Scripture of **faith**?

_____

_____

_____

_____

_____

_____

What steps of initiation did you learn to take in order for **faith** to transform your life?

_____

_____

_____

_____

_____

How will Satan attack you to hinder **faith** in your life?

_____

_____

_____

_____

_____

What memory verse will you use to protect Christ's command of **faith** in your life? Write it out.

_____

_____

_____

_____

_____

_____

TEACHING # 2.9: GIVING

Week 18

This week's objective: To discover the act of worship that comes from releasing God's blessing to others, and to appreciate the purpose underlying such devotion.

THE COMMAND INTRODUCED:

- **Luke 6:38** *"Give, and it will be given to you: good measure, pressed down, shaken together, and running over will be put into your bosom. For with the same measure that you use, it will be measured back to you."*

THE COMMAND INTERPRETED:

This is nothing short of a direct command from the Lord Jesus. In the context of the passage, Christ had previously paralleled judging, condemning, and forgiving. Using these three topics as a bridge, He moved right into the aspect of giving. The only difference is that Jesus explained to His disciples not only the command to be a giver but also the blessing that comes from giving.

The only way to gain a comprehensive, accurate interpretation of Jesus' command on giving is to look at the background. From a cultural standpoint, the command to *give* was inevitably connected to the marketplace of Jewish culture. In the way that we go to the store to buy groceries, Jews went to the marketplace to purchase grain. The actual grain, as Jesus illustrates, was dealt in a substantial measure, pressed down, shaken up, and then abundantly poured into the lap (bosom) of the customer. In fact, the Jews intentionally wore long robes in preparation for their trip to the marketplace. These robes served to carry the overflow of the grain they purchased.

Do you see the interesting connection of *giving* to grain? The Greek word for *"give"* is properly translated in its broadest sense, needing no further clarification. Moreover, it is highly important to notice that Jesus spent the greatest amount of this command focusing on the result of obeying the command and not on the command itself. Notice that Jesus' actual command here is to give, not receive. Giving is the duty. Receiving is the blessing. The motive of giving is to obey the command of Christ, not to be blessed. However, the benefit of giving is that Christ will bless you since you have blessed Him and others through your generous giving.

Isn't that interesting? As a disciple, this has incredible meaning for you. Jesus wants you to know that as long as you give, He will give to you. Your supply will never lack (**Philippians 4:19**)! Again, remember, you give out of your obedient love for Jesus, and He blesses you out of recognition of your obedience and His love for you (**Matthew 7:11**). Intriguingly, the *less* you have, the *more* you give. In other words, the less you keep for yourself because of your generosity to others, the more you are blessed from the generosity of your Father. The cycle of giving becomes a perpetual chain of supply and demand from the heart of God. Please remember, as long as you are caught giving (not hoarding), *"it will be given to you."* That's a promise from the Lord Jesus, not a possibility! The *"measure"* (amount) of your giving is also promised to be *"measured"* back to you. If you give a little, you reap a little. If you give a lot, you reap a lot. Therefore, based on the principle of the *"measure,"* you reap what you sow (**2 Corinthians 9:6-15**).

THE COMMAND ILLUSTRATED:

One of the best examples in the entire Bible on giving is actually found in the Old Testament. Turn to **Exodus 36:1-7**. Under the leadership of Moses, the time had come to build the sanctuary of the Tabernacle for the children of Israel to worship Jehovah God. However, there was a condition to its being built. That condition is found in **35:29**. A freewill offering was an act of giving characterized by people's *"willingness of heart."* That means their heart attitude to give was right and not corrupted by obligation or necessity. Simply put, the children of Israel gave because they wanted to give. As a result, they gave so much (financially and materially) that Moses had to actually instruct the people to stop giving! Amen. This story provides you as a disciple with what Christ is looking for in your giving to Him. Such an attitude is validated as "cheerful giving" in **2 Corinthians 9:7-8**. In light of this mindset, you can see a twofold understanding behind your giving to God.

First of all, *giving is accomplished by consequences*. In other words, there are unpleasant ramifications for those who hoard their blessings. This understanding is what propels people to obedience. The reason for this is simple: everything you have has been given to you from your heavenly Father. Everything (**James 1:17**)! Since you did nothing to earn God's blessing, you are not entitled to withhold God's blessing. However, in spite of this reality, people often do harbor their resources out of greed. As a disciple, do not ignore the fact that you are still susceptible to a greedy heart (**Proverbs 15:27; 1 Timothy 6:10; Proverbs 3:28**). Furthermore, if at any time you attempt to resort to selfishness and stinginess in regards to God's blessings, you will be awakened by unpleasant but necessary chastisement from the Lord (**Proverbs 11:24b; Proverbs 28:27; Ecclesiastes 5:13; James 5:3**). Such chastening is certainly not intended to hurt you but to serve as a tool to correct your heart into a position to give again (**Hebrews 12:5-11; Revelation 3:19**). However, as long as you remain in a continuous state of generous giving, you will never have to deal with such chastening. The act of giving itself immobilizes greed entirely.

Secondly, *giving is awarded by faith*. This constitutes and supplements the entire command of Christ in **Luke 6:38**. Faith is what pleases the Father (**Hebrews 11:6**). He acts upon faith more so than upon need alone. And, of course, there is a starting point at which you begin to operate in faith as you give. Such a beginning is found by pure obedience alone. Your obedience is preceded by your faith, yet not separate from it at all. This means your faith in Christ's command to *"give"* translates into your obedience to this command.

This obedience to give has two primary targets: your finances and your local church. In dealing with money alone, I have heard it said by J. Oswald Sanders, "The basic question is not how much of our money we should give to God, but how much of God's money we should keep for ourselves." You see, the attitude you have with your money will determine your attitude toward the giving of your money. The way God expects you to give your money back to Him is by recognizing that you are commanded to (**Proverbs 3:9**) and by believing that it is His method for funding the resources behind local church ministry (**Malachi 3:8-10; 1 Corinthians 16:2**).

As you begin to financially give out of faith and obedience, your release leads to your replenishment. You see, as Christ already said, when you give, "*it will be given to you.*" Your giving is accompanied by God's promises to "replenish" you so that you can enjoy His blessing and then give more and more out of your blessing (**Ecclesiastes 11:1; Proverbs 11:24a, 25**). Ultimately, such Kingdom giving is welcomed by Kingdom reward (**Luke 18:22; Matt. 6:19-21**). Reward? That's right. Jesus Christ will reward you with the treasures you build up in Heaven through a refusal to greedily set your heart and mind on the treasures of this world (**Colossians 3:1-4**). Remember, you cannot take anything from this world with you to Heaven, so why not give it all away throughout your life (**1 Timothy 6:6-7**)? Therefore, beginning with your finances, give. Continuing to your material resources, give. Extending even to your time, give. Money, food, clothing, time—it all belongs to God, and as a steward of such blessings, be faithful (**1 Corinthians 4:2**) to give as Christ has given to you.

THE COMMAND INITIATED:

Giving calls for practice. Oftentimes you see people who cling to their money so tightly that it would take an act of Congress for them to share it with anyone. I heard a story years ago about a little girl whose father gave her two dollars. He then told her the condition that she had to obey for receiving the money: "One dollar is for you to buy anything you want, and the other dollar is to give to the Lord on Sunday." She agreed to the conditions. Soon after this, all she could think about was candy, so she went down the street to a store. As she was joyfully skipping along, she tripped and fell down, causing one of her dollars to be caught in the wind and blown into a storm drain by a curb. After she dusted herself off, she began to look at her remaining dollar bill and the storm drain, thinking about what her daddy had said. Finally, she looked up to the sky and said, "Lord, I'm sorry I just lost your dollar."

Although this is a humorous story, it is regretfully true. Giving is so often perceived as a burden, as losing something. When there is no joy to give, there will only be sorrow and grief. As Christ's disciple, do not mimic this attitude in your giving.

You have learned thus far the motive and the meaning behind giving; now it's time to see it in action. Stephen F. Olford wrote a book called *The Grace of Giving*. In his book, Olford expounds on the churches in Macedonia in **2 Corinthians 8:1-9**. He unveils a beautiful picture of the Macedonians' giving and articulately applies this to disciples today:

> Paul's conception of giving is a lofty one. To him giving is a grace, a ministry of the Holy Spirit that is wrought in personal experience and worked out in practical expression. Wherever he planted churches the apostle made it his business to instruct the people of God in the doctrine of Christian giving...Dr. J. H. Jowett has said, "Ministry that costs nothing accomplishes nothing." Paul takes care to show that it was not in circumstances of prosperity that the saints in Macedonia gave their liberal offering. Some severe tests of affliction had come on these local churches (**Acts 16:20; 17: 5,13; Philippians 1:28; 1 Thessalonians 1:6; 2:14; 3: 3-9**) and they had been reduced to what is described as "deep poverty" or, more literally, "down-to-the-bottom poverty." But in all their affliction and poverty there was joy and liberality. This is true sacrifice, and they had learned it from their matchless Savior, "who for the joy that was set before Him endured the cross, despising the shame" (**Hebrews 12:2**). Dr. Roy L. Laurin tells of a Christian businessman who was traveling in Korea. In a field by the side of the road was a young man pulling a rude plow while an old man held the handles. The businessman was amused and took a snapshot of the scene. "That is curious! I suppose

these people are very poor," he said to the missionary who was interpreter and guide to the party. "Yes," was the quiet reply, "those two men happen to be Christians. When their church was being built, they were eager to give something toward it; but they had no money. So, they decided to sell their one and only ox and give the proceeds to the church. This spring they are pulling the plow themselves." The businessman was silent for some moments. Then he said, "That must have been a real sacrifice." "They did not call it that," said the missionary, "they thought themselves fortunate that they had an ox to sell!" When the businessman reached home, he took the picture to his pastor and told him all about it. Then he added, "I want to double my giving to the church and do some *plow* work. Up until now I have never given God anything that involved real sacrifice." The Macedonians gave with joy and liberality. Theirs was sacrificial giving.[6]

Amazing and humbling. That is a real-life illustration of what your giving should look like as a disciple. It should be sacrificial (**2 Samuel 24:24-25**). It should be joyful. It should be a privilege! Always have your attitude in check when you are in a position to give. You know enough now about what giving is and how you can give. Now, put your giving heart into practice. It is time for your lifestyle to reflect your understanding of biblical, sacrificial giving.

THE COMMAND INTERROGATED:

Satan loves to corrupt the minds of godly givers and turn them into staunch hoarders. There are many stereotypes that may be coming to your mind about the way that Satan affects Christians' giving. Perhaps you are thinking it deals with being greedy and thus not giving at all. Also, you may be thinking that it involves Christians who do give but do so for the wrong reason, such as to receive praise and attention. While these examples are indeed ways that Satan attacks the integrity of your giving, they are not his primary tools at all.

The greatest way that Satan interrogates your giving has to do with your heart, not your amount. He wants to tempt you to become dishonest with your giving. He wants you to hold back more than Christ would have you keep. This is giving to the Lord out of a dishonest heart (**Leviticus 19:36; Proverbs 16:11; 20:10, 23; Micah 6:11**). Satan loves to persuade your mind to give just enough to the Lord to appease your conscience and keep the rest to spend on yourself and your pleasures (**James 4:3; 5:1-5**). Beware of the devil's plots and traps! A beginning point for your financial giving is ten percent of your income, but it is by no means limited to that. A baseline for your material giving is according to the need of your neighbor in proportion to your ability to meet it. No matter what, Satan will try to contaminate your giving in these areas, tempting you to hold back more than what is right, both financially and materially. Such rebellion cost Ananias and his wife Sapphira their lives for lying to the Holy Spirit (**Acts 5:1-11**). Oh, disciple, watch out for the evil snares of Satan as he comes against the truthfulness of your heart in giving. Be very careful.

THE COMMAND INDESTRUCTIBLE:

Since Satan has no intention of leaving you alone, you need a verse of Scripture to wage war against him in conquering power. Your memory verse to protect your heart and maintain a giving attitude is **Acts 20:35**. It says, "*...And remember the words of the Lord Jesus, that He said, 'It is more blessed to give than to receive.'*" Can you see the irony in that word from Jesus? While it is easy to think of the blessing as only contingent upon receiving, it is mind-boggling to consider being "*blessed*" only if you give your blessings away. What is so wonderful about this Scripture for you to memorize is that it demands attention to the type of "blessedness" Jesus is referring to. The Greek term "blessed" (*makarios*) is the same word Jesus used in the Beatitudes (**Matthew 5:1-12**). It is a reference to the greatest happiness that a mortal man can attain. It is a blessedness that is not consumed with finances or materialism but is instead linked only to the giving away of such resources. Christ declares that this blessed state of your life is only possible to experience if you are willing to give.

Even in the natural world, haven't you ever felt good inside when you gave a child some of your leftover candy, or perhaps blessed a stranger with an extra ticket you had to a game? If that delights your heart in the natural, imagine the supernatural realm of giving—that is, when you give out of devotional obedience to Christ and not merely out of moral good. There is a blessedness that is promised to you when you give this way. The only way to guard your heart from becoming too materialistic is to give. There are necessities in life that you need, and then there are amenities in life that you don't need. As a disciple, find your balance between the two. Do not be overindulgent; give yourself away with the love of Christ compelling you! Quote **Acts 20:35** in confidence when you can be a blessing to someone. Practice giving out of your poverty, not just in times of your prosperity. You will be blessed by the Father in ways you cannot repay. Cheerfully, sacrificially, joyfully...give.

THE COMMAND INQUIRED:

What cannot be measured cannot be evaluated. Therefore, it is essential to measure your comprehension of Christ's command in this teaching, or else the devil will snatch away the "seeds" of Scripture sown into your heart (**Matthew 13:19**). To keep this from occurring, write down your answers to the following questions as they correlate with the teaching this week:

In what passage(s) of Scripture do you find Christ's commandment on **giving**?

_____

_____

_____

What is the accurate interpretation of **giving** you have discovered?

_____

_____

_____

_____

_____

_____

In your own words, what are some real-life examples in Scripture of **giving**?

_____

_____

_____

_____

_____

What steps of initiation did you learn to take in order for **giving** to transform your life?

_____

_____

_____

_____

_____

How will Satan attack you to hinder **giving** in your life?

_____

_____

_____

_____

_____

What memory verse will you use to protect Christ's command of **giving** in your life? Write it out.

_____

_____

_____

_____

_____

_____

TEACHING # 2.10: MARRIAGE

Week 19

<u>This week's objective</u>: *To evaluate the teaching of marriage as it relates to a disciple.*

THE COMMAND INTRODUCED:

- **Matthew 5:31-32** *"Furthermore it has been said, 'Whoever divorces his wife, let him give her a certificate of divorce.' But I say to you what whoever divorces his wife for any reason except sexual immorality causes her to commit adultery; and whoever marries her who is divorced commits adultery."*
- **Matthew 19:10-12** *"His disciples said to Him, 'If such is the case of the man with his wife, it is better not to marry.' But He said to them, 'All cannot accept this saying, but only those to whom it has been given: For there are eunuchs who were born thus from their mother's womb, and there are eunuchs who were made eunuchs by men, and there are eunuchs who have made themselves eunuchs for the kingdom of heaven's sake. He who is able to accept it, let him accept it.'"*

THE COMMAND INTERPRETED:

Both commands from Jesus are implicit yet distinct. Jesus is not commanding a disciple to marry; you can be a disciple of Christ whether you are married or not. The idea that Christ is presenting to His disciples involves both those who are married and those who are not yet married.

First of all, for those who are married, Jesus addressed the context of divorce. In the Old Testament, divorce was issued in the form of a certificate (**Deuteronomy 24:1-4**) only in certain cases as it appeared necessary. In the New Testament, Jesus shed light on one obvious fact: people who divorce more than likely will remarry. Therefore, under the new covenant, Jesus said divorce can only be acceptable if there were grounds for sexual immorality. The Greek phrase "sexual immorality" (*porneia*) refers to "adultery; harlotry." It is being sexually involved with someone other than your spouse. Moreover, if a man divorces his wife for any reason other than sexual immorality, Jesus said that he would be the cause for her to remarry and thus commit adultery in doing so. To make matters worse, Jesus also said that the man who marries the woman who is unnecessarily "divorced" also commits adultery because she should not be divorced to begin with. So, in sum, Jesus established a very high standard of marriage, one that could incur grounds for remarriage only in the most extreme of circumstances.

Secondly, for those who are not yet married, Jesus taught the right perspective. After the disciples heard Jesus "lay down the rules" for marriage and divorce, they did not think anybody should get married since they could not easily divorce. That's when Jesus introduced the principle of *celibacy*, which is to lead an intentional, single life that is governed by the choice to remain unmarried. The key word in this implicit command is *eunuch*. In Bible times, a eunuch was a castrated male, meaning someone who eradicated their sexual identity to allow full lifetime concentration to their calling and position.

According to Jesus, there are three types of eunuchs: those born that way (called or gifted—1 **Corinthians 7:7**); those who made themselves (self-inflicted) eunuchs for men (to serve in a palace of authority); and those who made themselves (self-denial) eunuchs for Christ (to serve the Lord with undivided attention). Again, this is truly a calling or a gifting to only the people whom the Lord strengthens for it to be. It is definitely not for everyone (**1 Corinthians 7:1-2**).

As a disciple, if you are not married but are not able to remain unmarried because of your physical desire for sexual intimacy, it is better for you to marry one day (**1 Corinthians 7:8-9**). However, as the Apostle Paul states over and over, getting married means you will not be able to serve Christ as you could if you remained unmarried (**1 Corinthians 7:33-34; Luke 14:20**), unless a spouse commits to Christ with you.

Likewise, those who are unmarried serve the Lord in more freedom than those who are (**1 Corinthians 7:32, 35**). Therefore, the point Jesus is commanding is for you not to divorce if you are married (**1 Corinthians 7:10-16, 27**) with the exception of sexual immorality. Again, Christ is inviting you to be His disciple regardless but not without facing and accepting these commands as a part of the package deal.

THE COMMAND ILLUSTRATED:

A great example in the Bible of the ideal husband-wife relationship between disciples is that of Aquila and Priscilla (**Acts 18:2, 18, 26; Romans 16:3; 1 Corinthians 16:19**). Aquila and his wife Priscilla were both tentmakers with the Apostle Paul, and based on these Scriptures, they were not "dead weight" to Paul during his missionary journeys. Actually, they helped him and encouraged him along the way. This dynamic duo even used their own home to host worship services with other Christians. Here you see the beauty of being equally yoked together in Christ (**2 Corinthians 6:14**).

As a disciple of Jesus, it is of utmost importance that, if you intend to marry, you pray that the Lord will send you a spouse that is spiritually compatible with your passion and convictions concerning Christ. Do not settle for less! If you are already married, build your relationship upon Jesus daily. If this is not an option due to a rebellious, careless, unbelieving spouse, surrender yourself to God's Word whether you are the wife (**1 Peter 3:1-6**) or the husband (**1 Peter 3:7**). Allow Christ, through your submission to Him as your Lord, to work in the heart of your spouse in ways you cannot. No matter what, strive to have a relationship similar to that of Aquila and Priscilla. And remember, it is not their marriage relationship that you try to emulate, but rather Christ Himself that makes a marriage glow.

THE COMMAND INITIATED:

The ideal Christian marriage is always pursued by any Christian couple. As a disciple of Jesus, you have to learn to balance your devotion to Him and your devotion to your spouse. It is a tough job! Of course, by way of choice, God is first always (**Matthew 6:33; 22:37**). There are to be no exceptions. Your loyalty to your spouse and family should always come in second place. Why? This is because you cannot have a healthy relationship with your spouse if you do not have one with the foundation of the marriage, Jesus Christ (**Psalm 127:1; Matthew 7:24-27**). For those disciples today that are not married yet, this seems so intimidating because of the apparent strain it will place on one's relationship with Jesus. If this describes your feelings or those of some other disciple you know, do not despair! Jesus Christ our Lord chose His disciple, Peter, to build His church upon (**Matthew 16:18**), yet Peter was a married man (**Mark 1:30**). You see, you can be married and still serve Jesus. Your relationship with Christ and your spouse can equally soar!

The goal is to have a marriage with your spouse without sacrificing devotion to your Lord Jesus. Can such a marriage actually exist? In her book *Marriage Without Regrets*, Kay Arthur extracts the biblical understanding and appreciation of the way a marriage should be handled:

> After God created Eve, He presented her to Adam. Now, how do you suppose Adam might have responded? We might guess he would say something like, "Wow!" Or maybe, "Where have you been all my life?" Actually, we don't have to guess. Scripture gives us his precise words: "This is now bone of my bones, and flesh of my flesh; she shall be called Woman, because she was taken out of man" (**Genesis 2:23**)...What is the significance of Adam's words? It seems obvious, doesn't it. When God presents Eve to Adam, that very act makes it an issue of stewardship for Adam. After all, the woman was created by God for man and presented to him. Surely such a gift from God brings with it some serious accountability...Once God presents Eve to Adam, the first thing you hear from Adam's lips is the unshakable recognition that Eve is part of him—not just an appendage tacked on, extraneous baggage, but a deep and profound sense of identification. How important this is to marriage—identifying with one another, owning one another, treasuring one another...In marriage as God

intended it to be, the man and woman become an expression of the other, even as between the heavenly Father and His Son. Jesus was the glory of the Father. He told Philip, "He who has seen Me has seen the Father." Not only did God establish the marriage relationship with the principles of stewardship and identification built in, He also made it clear that this was a relationship that would have priority over all other relationships...Marriage supersedes the relationship of a child to his parent, especially a son to his mother and father, because in marriage husband and wife are joined. With these words, Scripture acknowledges for all time the priority of the husband-wife relationship. The man is to leave his father and mother and cleave (like glue!) to his wife.[7]

There is nothing that will transcend the marriage relationship any better than a close, God-fearing adherence to the Scriptures that designed marriage. As a disciple of Christ, if you are unmarried, you have total freedom to serve Christ without any potential hindrance from a spouse. If you are married, be careful not to view marriage pessimistically. Rather, view it with the perspective that, since there are two of you, you can get twice as much accomplished now that you are "one flesh" serving Christ. Amen!

THE COMMAND INTERROGATED:

It is no secret that Satan loves to destroy marriages. The divorce toll is rising, not declining. How does he do it? What avenue does the devil take to bring a marriage down? While Scripture says very little about the process of Satan's attack on a marriage, it does say something about the lack of self-control in marriage (**1 Corinthians 7:5**). One of the mandates in marriage is that sexual fulfillment between the man and woman is a desire surrendered to one another (**1 Corinthians 7:2, 4**). If there should be a period of abstinence between the husband and wife, it is to be joined by fasting and prayer until the couple comes back together. During this span of time, Satan intensifies his attack! Perhaps a man and wife have an argument before going to work. Satan will cunningly maneuver a fuming wife toward a kind, gentle-talking, good-looking man by the coffee pot. He knows how to entice you and viciously play on your emotions. Beware of his subtle attacks. If you are married, fighting and arguing will damage your sexual union with your spouse. With those desires surfacing after long spans of abstinence, Satan will tempt your vulnerability to the point of having an affair. Never, ever, convince yourself that you are the exception to the rule. Again, if you are married, keep your marriage bed undefiled (**Hebrews 13:4**) and your relationship sizzling!

THE COMMAND INDESTRUCTIBLE:

For the disciple who is married, your relationship with your spouse is worth protecting. Since Satan is on the prowl to destroy you and your marriage, you are left with no choice but to use a Scripture to defeat him vigorously. The memory verse for all male disciples is **Ephesians 5:25**, which says, "*Husbands, love your wives, just as Christ loved the church and gave Himself for her.*" The memory verse for all female disciples is **Ephesians 5:22**, which says, "*Wives, submit to your own husbands, as to the Lord.*"

These two Scriptures sum up a biblical marriage relationship. If you are a husband, this is your blueprint for your relationship to your wife. There are no other guidelines. There is no other standard. As I have heard it said before, "If you want to be king of your castle, your wife must be the queen of your heart." The standard of love you are to display is "*as Christ loved the church.*" That's sacrificial, not selfish. You are her servant, not her daddy! Likewise, if you are a wife, you are to voluntarily submit yourself to your husband's leadership in your life. Your submission allows him to freely exercise his Christ-appointed position as a spiritual leader in the home. Don't nag or hinder him. In this way, both the husband and wife show loving, caring affection toward each other (**1 Corinthians 7:3**). As a disciple of Jesus, if you are married, this is your model. In like manner, this is the exact way that Christ treats you. Since Christ is so closely connected to the marriage relationship, how you love your spouse is really an indicator of how you love Jesus. The two are inseparable.

THE COMMAND INQUIRED:

What cannot be measured cannot be evaluated. Therefore, it is essential to measure your comprehension of Christ's command in this teaching, or else the devil will snatch away the "seeds" of Scripture sown into your heart (**Matthew 13:19**). To keep this from occurring, write down your answers to the following questions as they correlate with the teaching this week:

In what passage(s) of Scripture do you find Christ's commandment on **marriage**?

_____

_____

_____

What is the accurate interpretation of **marriage** you have discovered?

_____

_____

_____

_____

_____

In your own words, what are some real-life examples in Scripture of **marriage**?

_____

_____

_____

_____

_____

_____

What steps of initiation did you learn to take in order for a godly **marriage** to transform your life?

_____

_____

_____

_____

_____

How will Satan attack you to hinder your **marriage**?

_____

_____

_____

_____

_____

What memory verse will you use to protect Christ's command of **marriage** in your life? Write it out.

_____

_____

_____

_____

_____

_____

TEACHING # 2.11: REST

Week 20

This week's objective: To value the meaning behind God's protective rest for His children as well as to learn to position ourselves in the path of His rest.

THE COMMAND INTRODUCED:

- **Mark 6:31-32** *"And He said to them, 'Come aside by yourselves to a deserted place and rest a while.' For there were many coming and going, and they did not even have time to eat. So they departed to a deserted place in the boat by themselves."*

THE COMMAND INTERPRETED:

This is a direct command from the Lord Jesus to His disciples. To put it plainly, they were traumatized throughout the course of the day because their beloved brother, John the Baptist, had recently been beheaded (**verses 24-29**). After the funeral, the disciples came to Jesus, wearied emotionally and physically from the multitudes of people and the expedition tour of laboring for Christ (**verses 7-9, 12-13, 30**). Recognizing their physical and spiritual fatigue, Christ countered with the command to *"rest."*

By way of practical interpretation, this scene of Jesus and His disciples resembles a retreat, not a vacation. What's the difference? Well, a *vacation* is taken to empty yourself (vacate) of stress and tension buildup; a *retreat* is pursued to fill yourself up because you are already emptied out and tired. It is the act or process of withdrawing to a place of peace, privacy, and security, while caressed by solitude. You see, Kingdom labor invokes God's favor. A retreat is God's idea, His protective rest to help you avoid spiritual defeat in your life as a disciple. Praise God, this command is a concession of renewal for you! As you faithfully labor for Jesus, you will grow weary and tired. Ministering to people in Christ's power is an honor, but it has a way of draining you physically

(**Mark 5:30**). It is the will of Jesus to grant you stellar refreshment so that you can continue in your labor for Him. Based on this command, there is an undeniable, comprehensible pattern that you are commanded to follow to embrace His rest.

First of all, it begins with an *invitation*. Jesus said, "*Come aside...*" The Greek "come" (*deute*) means "to go; respond in presence to a summon." The Greek "aside" (*idios*) translates "according to one's own; privacy." Jesus wants His disciples to abandon their weary load. His invitation is a personal appeal indicative of His care for you. Christ loves you and understands the toll Kingdom labor takes on you. So He summons you to a private retreat; He calls for you (**Matthew 11:28; Isaiah 55:3; Psalm 55:22**).

Secondly, the command introduces the idea of *isolation*. Jesus specified, "*...by yourselves.*" Do you see the permission granted in this verse? Christ is giving the "green light" to break from the multitudes. This is not to be seen as a retirement from living for Christ but rather as a recharge to be strengthened by Christ. The Lord Jesus wants you to isolate yourself with Him. He doesn't want you to bring the multitudes with you. The bottom line is that Jesus is trying to eliminate all possible distractions and interruptions from your mind and heart (**Psalm 19:14; 119:15**). Like a husband that does not "bring work home" with him, a disciple is commanded to leave the bumps and bruises of ministering to people with the multitudes while "resting" in Christ's presence.

Thirdly, the command calls for a *location*. Jesus directed His disciples to "*a deserted place...*" It is interesting to note that the Greek word for "desert" (*eremos*) literally refers to a "wilderness; wasteland or uninhabited expanse." Jesus knew that His disciples had to have an actual place to take a break from ministering. He understood that although people had the best intentions in coming to them, the demand would make solitude impossible. Therefore, a location was imperative to Jesus. As His disciple, you need a "*desert*" place to spend time with Jesus. You need a hideout, a private place where you and the Lord commune together (**Psalm 91:1; 63:1-3; 84: 1-2**). Jesus demonstrated this to us with His Father. In the Gospels, we see Him frequently retreating to a quiet place to abide with God the Father. So, where is your "*desert*" place? If you haven't obeyed this command yet, choose a location today. Some options might include inside a room or a closet in your house, under a tree in your yard, or at a nearby park. The point is that you find a location that is like a wasteland: uninhabited by people so there can be no interruptions.

Lastly, the command results in *restoration*. Jesus identified the purpose of the command by ordering His disciples to "...*rest a while*." It makes a lot of sense now, doesn't it? Jesus gave the *invitation*, conditioned by *isolation*, in vain without a *location*, with the goal of your *restoration*. What a thoughtful Savior! The Greek word Jesus used for "rest" (*anapauo*) means "to repose by exemption; refresh through ease." Christ is wanting you to take a break sometimes. He knows you love Him, but He also knows you are not called to be a superman or superwoman. Your physical strength has limitations, and by admitting this you are not being a spiritual weakling. It is biblically okay to stop for a breather in your work for Christ. In fact, based on Christ's command, it is of necessity! Remember, this is not referring to a family vacation, coffee with your buddies, or basketball at the park. It is talking about a retreat to which only you are invited. Such abandonment to the Lord will recharge your faith and empower your vision to serve Jesus with all your might (**Psalm 51:10, 12; 80:7; 85:6**). Then, as you weary and tire from that endeavor...rest again. The cycle is endless, and so is the Lord Jesus.

THE COMMAND ILLUSTRATED:

So, what does "*rest*" look like? By way of an example, turn to **Joshua 1:13**. Following Moses' death on Mount Nebo (**Deuteronomy 34**), the nation of Israel (God's covenant people) was in need of a new leader. God chose for them a man named Joshua. After the Lord God encouraged Joshua in his new role of leadership (**1:8-9**), Joshua in turn exhorted the tribal leaders with **verse 13**. After waiting patiently and wandering for years, they had finally come to the promised land. However, it was not the land itself that was the blessing but the "*rest*" God promised for them to enjoy in that land!

As a disciple of Jesus Christ, learn from Joshua and the nation of Israel. Like the Israelites, there will be pain, hostility, and strife in life all around you, for that is the price we pay for the fruits of sin and a sin-cursed world. Therefore, since there will always be a need for peace, there will always be a need for rest. In the midst of these difficulties that you will face in this world from persecutors, troubled marriages, career conflicts, and relationship issues, just remember to rest in the Lord (**Psalm 37:7**). The children of Israel had not yet entered into the land; they were excited over the promise of rest alone. The same goes for you. Believe God for rest and peace in Him before storms rage against you. Then, when those raging waves of worry, doubt, and fear billow against you, surf those waves in the promised "rest" of your heavenly Father. Give Him praise!

THE COMMAND INITIATED:

To put rest into action in your life as a disciple is the way to the greatest peace and comfort you will ever enjoy with the Father. It is clear thus far that Christ has commanded you to periodically rest from your labors for Him. There is no greater joy to encompass your body, soul, and spirit than true rest and retreat in Christ.

In his book *Jesus for the Rest of Us*, John Selby comments on the meditative aspect of "being still," based on Scripture. He offers an insightful view into what it really means, physically and spiritually, to be at rest with and in God:

> In a direct quote from God in **Psalms 46**, God gives, long before Jesus was born, what for me has always been the primary meditation commandment, and also the driving psychological dictum on how to manage our minds so as to connect directly with the divine...Communing directly with God is another of those ultimate two-word statements: "Be still." In all of the world's most powerful meditation traditions, we must first of all quiet our nonstop mental chatter if we're to shift into a spiritual state of mind in which we're receptive to deep contact with Spirit. As long as the ego is chattering inside our minds, with all its busy comments, judgments, worries, plots, and plans, we simply cannot hear the voice of God. Jesus doesn't push into our consciousness. Spirit patiently waits for us to quiet our minds and tune in to our deeper awareness, before

becoming active in our lives... Is God telling us to "be still," and at the same time delve into deep theological reflection on what it means to be God? Or are we supposed to truly be still and know directly, beyond all words and beliefs, the direct experiential reality of God...The same Hebrew word was used in the statement "Be still, and *know* that I am God" as was used in Genesis in the statement "Adam *knew* Eve, his wife, and she conceived"...In other words, God is inviting us to "know" Him at the same level of intimacy that we experience in our deepest relating—heart to heart. We're being invited to experience God as directly as possible, in a way that, at some spiritual level, could include the creation of a new being, the union of human and divine, and whatever consequences come from that union.[8]

Do you see how Selby's spiritual yet psychological approach to **Psalm 46:10** fits perfectly with Christ's command to rest? True, it is an intimacy with God in the sense of our spirit bearing witness with the Holy Spirit (**Romans 8:16**). There is a communing with God that invigorates your new nature to triumph relentlessly over your mortal nature. When you are still, you can listen, comprehend, and most importantly, respond. Oh, disciple, rest in Christ! Do not allow your life to become so busy that it costs you sweet, intercessory rest with Jesus Christ your Lord. Remember, as the command goes, Christ is calling you to this rest. Answer Him. Come to Him. Rest in Him.

THE COMMAND INTERROGATED:

By now, you can probably see what Satan loves to use against you to keep you from resting in Christ. It is unnecessary business. Let's face it: much of what our modern society endorses has nothing to do with the Kingdom of God. Right? So, how do you think this affects Christianity today? Grossly. The sad result in many Christian communities is much involvement with pleasurable things and little involvement with spiritual things. It is as if the command to fulfill Christ's objectives gets put on the back burner. Do you know what I mean?

Beware of becoming so self-absorbed in what you like and what society and media tell you is important, all to the neglect of what Christ says is important. Satan would love to keep you as busy as Martha, but Jesus wants to see you rest in Him like Mary (**Luke 10:38-42**). Rest in Christ is the good part that lasts forever in the heart of God. Satan has distracted your attention away from Christ if you are too busy to daily meditate in His word, pray to the Father, and evangelize the lost people around you. Watch out for these subtle ways that you can become so busy at your church that, like Martha, you find your worship and communion with God suffering. Beware.

THE COMMAND INDESTRUCTIBLE:

In spite of Satan's deceitful attacks to keep you so busy that you don't rest in Christ, there is good news. God's word contains a swift blow to Satan you can use to remind him that you choose rest. It is the memory verse antidote against busyness, and it is found in **Psalm 116:7**: "*Return to your rest, O my soul, for the Lord has dealt bountifully with you.*" Praise God, hallelujah; that's it! Ponder once more the word *return*. Obviously, you can only return somewhere that you've been before. The Psalmist was away from God and needed that rest in God once again. So, he chose to return to that secret place, the location in his soul where he communed with the Holy God of Israel.

Dear disciple, quote this memory verse every time you see yourself drifting in your rest with Christ in the form of inconsistent quiet times with God and unbalanced prayer. Don't be a victim of Satan's disguises. If you have to cut something out of your schedule, do it. If you have to end a time-consuming relationship, do it. If you have to drop a sport or a hobby, do it. There is nothing more valuable than your fellowship with Christ in rest! You are a disciple, not a pushover whom the devil can easily sway. Stand your ground. Tighten your armor. Position your faith. Unsheathe your sword.

Remember, although we work and labor now during this pilgrimage (**1 Peter 2:11**), we wait for our homecoming where our true citizenship is registered (**Philippians 3:20-21**). That's right, precious disciple; keep on serving Christ with a faithful, unwavering heart of faith, for great is your coming reward (**1 Corinthians 15:58; Hebrews 6:10**) and your eternal rest (**Revelation 14:13**).

THE COMMAND INQUIRED:

What cannot be measured cannot be evaluated. Therefore, it is essential to measure your comprehension of Christ's command in this teaching, or else the devil will snatch away the "seeds" of Scripture sown into your heart (**Matthew 13:19**). To keep this from occurring, write down your answers to the following questions as they correlate with the teaching this week:

In what passage(s) of Scripture do you find Christ's commandment on **rest**?

_____

_____

_____

What is the accurate interpretation of **rest** you have discovered?

_____

_____

_____

_____

_____

In your own words, what are some real-life examples in Scripture of **rest**?

_____

_____

_____

_____

_____

_____

What steps of initiation did you learn to take in order for **rest** to transform your life?

_____

_____

_____

_____

_____

How will Satan attack you to hinder **rest** in your life?

_____

_____

_____

_____

_____

What memory verse will you use to protect Christ's command of **rest** in your life? Write it out.

_____

TEACHING # 2.12: ABIDING

Week 21

This week's objective: To process and identify the details that compose this command, as well as to glean the wonderful benefits that obedience produces through abiding.

THE COMMAND INTRODUCED:

- **John 15:4-8** *"Abide in Me, and I in you. As the branch cannot bear fruit of itself, unless it abides in the vine, neither can you unless you abide in Me. I am the vine, you are the branches. He who abides in Me, and I in him, bears much fruit: for without Me you can do nothing. If anyone does not abide in Me, he is cast out as a branch and is withered: and they gather them and throw them into the fire, and they are burned. If you abide in Me, and My words abide in you, you will ask what you desire, and it shall be done for you. By this My Father is glorified, that you bear much fruit: so you will be My disciples."*

THE COMMAND INTERPRETED:

Well, there is no doubt whatsoever that these commands to *abide* are given with both direct and implicit verbiage. What does it mean to abide? What does it look like? How do you know if you are abiding in Christ or not? These are questions that many people ask when reading this passage because Jesus is so blunt. Therefore, by way of interpretation, such questions deserve an accurate translation so that you effectively grow and abide in Christ as His disciple. Let's break this passage into its components so that the meaning becomes clearer to you.

First of all, abiding is a *permanent* choice (**verse 5**). To give a clear perspective of this choice, Jesus begins by contrasting the vine and the branches. This analogy illustrates that the vine is to the branches what roots are to a tree or what oxygen is to the body. One is completely necessary for the other to function. Likewise, just as the vine extends its life in the form of its branches, so Christ is our life (**Colossians 3:4**), and we are as branches grafted into His nature, His power, His Resurrection! The branches are inseparable from the vine; their life depends on it.

That's why Jesus used the word *abide* to refer to our relationship with Him. The Greek meaning for "abide" (*meno*) is a common word that refers to "staying, remaining, or continually dwelling." Indeed, abiding is a permanent choice, reflected literally as the lasting evidence that salvation has occurred (**1 John 2:3-5, 19; 3:9-10**). The branch comes to the realization that it has no life in itself; apart from the vine, death is the only option. Therefore, such a decision to abide only leads to one thing because of the relationship to the vine: *fruit*.

Hence, abiding has a *productive* goal (**verse 8**). This goal is fruitfulness. And while the goal of abiding is to bear fruit, the goal of bearing fruit is to glorify God. Such a process has a dramatic effect on the world around you: "*so you will be My disciples.*" The chief goal of life in Christ is to glorify the Father (**Psalm 115:1**). Nothing else. Moreover, the productive goal resulting from abiding and glorifying God is the production of spiritual fruit.

What does it mean to *bear much fruit*? Obviously, there is nothing short of an abundant expectation here by Jesus. Not a little fruit. Not some fruit. Much fruit! For understanding, what Jesus means is that your life will overflow with indicators (spiritual fruits) that point to your abiding in Him. "*...As the branch cannot bear fruit of itself,* **unless** *it abides in the vine, neither can you,* **unless** *you abide in Me*" (**verse 4**; emphasis added). Your fruitfulness finds its primary dependency upon the vine. You cannot produce fruit *for* Jesus *without* Jesus! You have been appointed by command (**verse 16**) to this lifestyle of quality, fruitful production.

Also, the fruitfulness of your life is a reflection of your relationship to Christ, just as a pear tree produces pears (not grapes) and a sparrow hatches sparrows (not chickens). The relationship is indicated by what is produced; anything else would be incompatibly unnatural (**Matthew 7:16; James 3:11-12**). So, the meaning is clear: continual abiding results in continual fruit, pointing to one factor—*your identity*.

It's also important to remember that abiding is a *purchased* identity (**verse 6**). While abiding in the vine is expected for believers, there are some who are not. What Christian would dare even attempt to forsake abiding in the vine? Well, that's Jesus' point: none would. You see, choosing to not continually abide in the vine is choosing to spiritually die, for there is no spiritual life apart from Jesus, the vine. Therefore, this creates an identity check, for if anyone doesn't *abide* in the vine, he is not of the vine—in other words, he is an unbeliever.

This sounds judgmental to some people, but the reality of what Jesus is saying is not up for negotiation. In fact, Christ gives you permission to inspect the fruit of people's lives, not to judge them (**Matthew 7:1-5**) but rather to assess their "fruit basket" lifestyles (**Matthew 7:17-20**). Some things are undeniable, such as rotten, useless fruit. In the same manner, Jesus very bluntly makes it clear that a branch (person) who does not abide withers away (perishes in sin). There is only one option for such a useless branch: burn it up (hell). Have you ever been on a camping trip? When you start a fire, do you look for branches attached to a tree? No, because they are of use to the tree, not suited for a fire. Rather, you look for dead branches because they are no use to the tree any longer, and they burn well because the life within them is dried up. By comparison, that's exactly what Jesus is warning in the form of eternal destruction for the non-abiding unbeliever (**Matthew 3:10-12; 7:21-23; Mark 9:43-49; Revelation 20:10-15**).

Therefore, Christ's goal here is not to spend time on identifying an unbeliever, but to use the useless branch as a stepping stone of interpretation for the heart of the passage: a believing, abiding branch. If anything at all, it is a boast to our purchased identity in Christ, that we have been bought with the price of Jesus' blood (**1 Cor. 6:19-20; Ephesians 1:7; 2:13**) and reconciled to God our Father (**2 Corinthians 5:18**). It is in this relationship to the Vinedresser (**verse 1**) that we commune in a beautiful way: *prayer.*

You see, abiding is a *prayerful* journey (**verse 7**). Jesus does not fail to mention the aspect of prayer in its connection to abiding in Him. Did you notice the condition here? Jesus says, "*If you abide in Me, and My words abide in you...*" Interesting. Conditions always precede expectations. The expectation in this verse is that we are given opportunity to ask or pray to the Father, with the promise that He will hear and answer us. Amen! However, the key to properly conversing with the Father is to be in right relationship to Christ and His Word.

Do you see the goal here? It's not merely to make you realize that your prayers are ineffective if you don't abide. Actually, the real issue that Christ addressed is a plea for commitment to His Word. Previously with His disciples, Jesus already discussed this repeatedly as His desire for them (**John 14:15, 21, 23-24**). The result? Fruitful, answered prayer (**John 14:13-14**). Therefore, prayer is conditioned to abiding. Your obedience to Christ's Word reveals His abiding in you, and your answered prayers display God's approval of your abiding in Him. Hallelujah!

THE COMMAND ILLUSTRATED:

Perhaps the best Scriptural example of what abiding looks like is that of the Apostle Peter. This account of abiding is found in **John 6:60-69**. Earlier in this passage Jesus "weeded out" a large quantity of His followers from the multitudes. Many of them had been with Jesus for several days, enjoying front-row seats for the grandeur of the spectacular miracles, but not with the intention of personal surrender (**verses 26-27**). So, Christ tested their inner obedience by making a substantial claim in **verses 41-58**. As a result, what Jesus said offended many of His own followers (**verses 60-65**), and their response was one of the most sobering moments in Jesus' ministry (**verse 66**). They were there for the show, not for the practice. They wanted to cheerlead as spectators, not take up their cross as participators. So, after this mass exodus of His followers, Jesus asked a fitting question in **verse 67**. Simon Peter's answer to the question gives disciples for all generations an example of what true abiding in Christ looks like (**verses 68-69**).

Peter truly was a disciple of Jesus Christ. That was his caliber. That was his quality of faith. As a disciple of Jesus, your abiding in Christ does not continue because of *what* He can do for you. It continues because of *Who* He is! Now that is uncontaminated, pure, holy, God-fearing motivation. You're not choosing to be a disciple because of what you can get out of it, but rather because you understand Who Jesus Christ is and the privilege you have to be His servant. Like Peter, you realize that you have nowhere else to go, nothing else to do, no one else to love when compared to Jesus your Lord. In Christ, there is eternal life— you cannot buy that anywhere! The branch needs the vine! Your devotion is forever a small price to pay (**Romans 12:2**) in comparison to Who Christ is and the redemption He freely gave. Again, like Peter, just the reality alone of Who Jesus is ensures your decision to remain in Christ and His Word. Your mind is made up. Though none go with you, still you will follow. You could not care less about winning the popularity contest with society. Your heart's cry is simply this: "Just give me Jesus" (see **Psalm 84:1-2, 10**).

THE COMMAND INITIATED:

Abiding in Christ is like breathing oxygen: you cannot live without it. In the same manner, we cannot really begin living the "life" we were created for until this abiding becomes as standard to us as breathing. Honestly, regardless of worldly interpretation and opinion, there is no life without Christ, both now and in eternity.

Let's close our examination of this passage with one final summation. In her book *The Power-Filled Life: Abiding in Christ*, Dr. C. S. Jenne gives a dazzlingly accurate picture, second to none, of the command in **John 15**. This description is priceless:

> Jesus is the True Vine, and we are the branches. The Vine and the branches become One Plant as the Father, Vinedresser, does His grafting work. "*You, a wild olive shoot, were grafted in to share the richness [of the root and sap] of the olive tree*" (**Romans 11:17**). Grafting is a joining together of two living portions from two separate plants to form a permanent union. The part of the plant with roots is called the "stock" and the "scion" is a part of another plant that, when properly joined to the stock, draws it life from the stock. The stock and scion must be compatible. Jesus, our Stock, became compatible with us, the scion, when he took on human form. The stock is cut and an incision is made into which the scion is inserted. Our Stock's side was pierced so that we might be grafted in to Him to share the richness

and the sap of His life. The Father has grafted us into the wounded side of His Son so that we might draw from all that He is. The graft is then secured by raffia. The raffia is our faith and trust in His finished work. Sealing wax covers the graft to cement the Stock and the scion together permanently. The sealing wax is the Holy Spirit of God "by Whom you were sealed for the day of redemption" (**Ephesians 4:30**). The scion must give up its old life and be severed from its old roots in order to be grafted into the new stock. We must die to our old life that we might live our new life in Christ Jesus. When we abide in Him, we partake of His death. When He was nailed to the cross, our old self was nailed to the cross with Him in order that we might be freed from the power of sin and death. Since we are abiding in His death, we have crucified the flesh with its passions and appetites and desires. We have been crucified to the world and the world to us. When we abide in Him, we share in His life and we partake of His nature. We draw from His life-sap, and He becomes our food and drink. As His life flows into us, we bear the fruit of His nature and the character of righteousness and holiness. As His life flows out through us, we walk and conduct ourselves in the same way in which He walked and conducted Himself while in His earthly body...We demonstrate His victory over the flesh, the word and the devil. We are living testimonies that His death, burial, and resurrection and ascension were not just events that happened centuries ago. All that He has done for us is being done in and through us today! We declare the reality of His power by our power-filled lives.[9]

THE COMMAND INTERROGATED:

Satan hates abiding disciples because they are virtually untouchable. It is as though they're under a protective shield of Christ's Presence. However, this does not mean that any disciple is exempt from Satan's temptations. Since you have already seen the Apostle Peter faithfully abiding in Christ, it is necessary then to show you how quickly Satan can distract from abiding.

The backslidden state of the Apostle Peter is found in **Luke 22:54-62**. Yes, it is true. In the heat of the moment, Peter denied His relationship with Jesus because he feared for his life. Notice, though, that Peter did not leave Jesus completely, but stood at a distance (**verse 54**). He was keeping His eye on Jesus because He loved the Master, but his voice stammered in denial. This temporary departure from abiding in Christ and His Word is exactly how Satan attacks you as a disciple.

As a disciple of Jesus, beware of this subtle interrogation by the devil. Satan's method for attack is usually in seasons, according to **Luke 4:13**. Abiding, however, is not a season but a lifetime commitment, designed to outlast any fiery trial. Don't abandon ship in a time of temptation or distress. Don't give in to Satan's shining lures of worldly attraction or camouflaged comforts. Protect your abiding relationship in and with Christ by choosing a faithful stance in His Word.

THE COMMAND INDESTRUCTIBLE:

The Word of God is truly your only hope as a disciple. It is so indestructible (**Matthew 24:35**) that nothing can stop it (**1 Peter 1:22-25**). Satan can do a lot of damage, but he gets the "red light" when it comes to a disciple fighting him with Scripture. Therefore, your memory verse to wage war against the devil is **Philippians 1:11**: *"being filled with the fruits of righteousness which are by Jesus Christ, to the glory and praise of God."* When Paul wrote that Scripture to the disciples in Philippi, he must have had **John 15** in mind. Do you see the similarities? Jesus said fruitfulness would be a byproduct of abiding in Him; Paul calls it *"fruits of righteousness."* Jesus said to bear much fruit; Paul calls it *"being filled..."* Jesus said fruit would come by abiding in Him; Paul agrees by saying that this fruit is *"by Jesus Christ..."* Jesus said that such a production of fruitfulness would result in glorifying God the Father; Paul agrees with his statement *"to the praise and glory of God."*

Day by day, examine yourself as a believer by conducting a "harvest inventory" (**2 Corinthians 13:5**). Fruit is what you should find. Claim the Word of God by quoting your memory verse in prayer to the Father. Yield to Him. Repent of any weakness that resulted in sin (**1 John 2:1-2**). Constantly remind yourself of the will of God in your memory verse to display a life "filled" with fruitfulness that comes from abiding in Jesus. Oh, disciple, it is Christ who strengthens you. You can do it! Abide. Abide. Abide.

THE COMMAND INQUIRED:

What cannot be measured cannot be evaluated. Therefore, it is essential to measure your comprehension of Christ's command in this teaching, or else the devil will snatch away the "seeds" of Scripture sown into your heart (**Matthew 13:19**). To keep this from occurring, write down your answers to the following questions as they correlate with the teaching this week:

In what passage(s) of Scripture do you find Christ's commandment on **abiding**?

_____

_____

_____

What is the accurate interpretation of **abiding** you have discovered?

_____

_____

_____

_____

In your own words, what are some real-life examples in Scripture of **abiding**?

_____

_____

_____

_____

_____

_____

What steps of initiation did you learn to take in order for **abiding** to transform your life?

_____

_____

_____

_____

_____

How will Satan attack you to hinder **abiding** in your life?

_____

_____

_____

_____

_____

What memory verse will you use to protect Christ's command of **abiding** in your life? Write it out.

_____

_____

CHAPTER 3: THE *ALLUREMENTS* TO A DISCIPLE

"*And those who are Christ's have crucified the flesh with its passions and desires*" (**Galatians 5:24**). Crucified? That's right. This is a clear identification marker for a disciple, one whose fleshly appetites are daily annihilated (**1 Corinthians 15:31**), thus showcasing the righteousness of Jesus Christ (**Philippians 3:9**). Such a lifestyle is to be the norm for a disciple. However, there is a problem—not primarily with the flesh, but more so with the inward battle to deny its gratifications. Since the beginning of creation, there has been a constant spiritual war on the people of God (**Genesis 3:15; Ephesians 6:12**). The target zone for the enemy's attack is your flesh—that is, your carnal, sinful desires within your heart and mind. As a born-again believer, you experience a tug-of-war between the indwelling Holy Spirit and your inborn fleshly indulgences (**Galatians 5:16-17**). It is through this spiritual, satanic war against you that the devil plots, attracts, and then entraps by his allurements, in the same way that a fisherman would use a shiny lure to snare a fish. The battle, then, is decided by a lifetime of choices.

When disciples give in to their fleshly desires, hypocrisy is born. Tragically, when unbelievers see professing Christians living double lives and broadcasting double standards, they push aside the possibility of a relationship with Jesus. Disciples are the salt of the earth and the light of the world; yet obeying fleshly lusts instead of the Holy Spirit will cause the salt to lose its flavor (**Matthew 5:13**) and the light to be hidden (**2 Corinthians 4:3-4**). The result is a contaminated witness for Christ!

Therefore, the following ten teachings are drawn from Jesus' commands that pinpoint these allurements to a disciple and expose the devil's schemes. Just as the prophet Habakkuk was a watchman for the nation of Judah (**Habakkuk 2:1**), disciples of Jesus must "watch" and discern the crafty ways Satan seeks to entrap them. Remember, you have a choice to make, not just flesh to restrain. Obey the Lord Jesus.

TEACHING # 3.1: LIFESTYLE CHOICES

Week 22

This week's objective: To identify the unholy, attractive paths of the world that pull at a disciple, as well as to discover the underlying conviction that motivates right choosing.

THE COMMAND INTRODUCED:

- **Matthew 7:13-14; Luke 13:24** *"Enter by the narrow gate; for wide is the gate and broad is the way that leads to destruction, and there are many who go in by it. Because narrow is the gate and difficult is the way which leads to life, and there are few who find it."*
- **Matthew 7:24-27; Luke 6:46-49** *"Therefore whoever hears these sayings of Mine, and does them, I will liken him to a wise man who built his house on the rock: and the rain descended, the floods came, and the winds blew and beat on that house; and it did not fall, for it was founded on the rock. But everyone who hears these sayings of Mine, and does not do them, will be like a foolish man who built his house on the sand: and the rain descended, the floods came, and the winds blew and beat on that house; and it fell. And great was its fall."*

THE COMMAND INTERPRETED:

One command is direct; the other is implicit. Both call for a decision, one that is grounded by observing what is portrayed through divine imagery. How is this done? Jesus invites His disciples to imagine two gates and two foundations. He is telling them that they are at a crossroads; a lifestyle choice is to be made. Between the two gates, His followers will need to either choose the broad way and abandon Christ or the narrow, difficult way and follow Christ. Between the two foundations, they will need to choose a lifestyle built upon Christ and His commands (rock) or a lifestyle built without Christ's commands (sand).

To gain an accurate interpretation of these commands, take a look at the one involving the two gates (**Matthew 7:13-14; Luke 13:24**). Notice the obvious contrast that Jesus highlights to clarify this command: narrow versus broad, destruction (death) versus life, many versus few. The purpose of Jesus using a "gate" to make His point is to show entrance into something. By opening a gate to a baseball field, a park, or even your backyard, you are making a choice. By making that choice, you are entering into your destination. You want to play baseball, you want to swing on a playground, or you want to run with your dog.

Therefore, the emphasis for accurate understanding of this "gate" of choice involves the nature of the gate: broad or narrow. The Greek word for "broad" (*euruchoros*) means "wide; spacious." Moreover, the Greek word for "narrow" (*thlibo*) means "to crowd; throng." Do you see the difference? The broad gate in life is very wide, one that many people enter because it is full of pleasure, lust, selfishness, and worldliness, which is why it leads to destruction. However, choosing the narrow gate in life is like being in a crowded elevator: you become a lot thinner than you really are. That's the idea behind this narrow gate. It is thin. It is difficult to enter it. You must "cast off" some spiritual weight (**Hebrews 12:1**) so that only your pliable, contrite heart goes through this narrow gate. Can you see the difficulty in this? That's why only a "few" find this life because "many" are not up for the sacrifice. What a command! What a challenge! A disciple is to choose the narrow, difficult way.

Now, take a look at the command involving two foundations (**Matthew 7: 24-27; Luke 6:46-49**). As with the two gates, there are respective contrasts that Christ makes here as well: wise versus foolish, rock versus sand. The main train of thought that Jesus seeks to implant in His disciples is the understanding of a foundation. If you know anything about the construction of a building, you are already aware that its foundation must be level and suitable for the building. If it is not, the building doesn't stand a chance, all because the foundation is not appropriate.

Therefore, the only foundation for the Christian life is Jesus Christ (**1 Corinthians 3:11**). There is no alternative. It is Jesus or nothing. And as Christ's disciple, you ensure your "building" upon

Him through obedience to His commands. That's why Christ says the one who hears what He commands and *"does"* what He says (obeys) is a *"wise"* man to Him. But the one who hears what He commands and *"does not"* do what He says (disobeys) is a *"foolish"* man to Jesus.

You see, as a disciple, when you build your life on Christ and His Word, you build your life on the *"rock"* (**1 Corinthians 10:4**). Anyone who chooses another foundation is building his life on the *"sand,"* which is destined for disaster. Interestingly, in this analogy, the rain, floods, and wind—representing the trials and tribulations in life—affected both foundations. The difference, though, is in the survival. Life built on the Rock does not fall apart; life built on the sand (worldliness) will eventually endure a *"great"* catastrophic fall into disaster. There's but one life to live, one life to build, so choose Jesus Christ and His commands as the foundation. Any other choice will prove foolish and disastrous (**Psalm 127:1**).

THE COMMAND ILLUSTRATED:

One of the best examples to further explain lifestyle choices involves a situation when Jesus was traveling on the road outside of a Samaritan village. Turn to **Luke 9:57-62**. As Christ went through villages and towns, He attracted followers regularly, but as we have seen, not every follower is a true disciple. Thus, Christ prodded people constantly with questions that unveiled the underlying motive for following him, such as in this passage.

Here you see three people interested in following Jesus, but Christ tested them to see whether they understood that discipleship is a lifestyle choice. Jesus mentioned that following Him meant that animals sleep better than He did, and that family should always be second to service to the Father. By these statements, Jesus weeded out His followers so that He could concentrate on those who really wanted to be His disciples. The same goes for you. For every generation of disciples, the standards do not change. As a disciple, you are enlisted in the army of God, a soldier for Jesus Christ (**2 Timothy 2:3-4**). This is your choice. This is your lifestyle. Focus intently. Fight righteously. Fear God.

THE COMMAND INITIATED:

When we initiate lifestyle choices to follow Jesus, we transition from "knowing what to do" to "doing what we know." By now, in your transformation journey as a disciple of Jesus, you can probably identify numerous changes in your life when comparing your lifestyle before Christ versus after Christ. These changes are not a reflection of legalistic requirements; they are the results of a loving relationship with GOD. The *want* to change is powerfully present in the heart of a disciple because once you've tasted the mercy of God, nothing else besides Jesus will do.

In their book *Discipleship: A Growing Christian's Lifestyle*, James and Martha Reapsome very accurately identify what following Jesus looks like in action:

> In a culture where individuality and "doing your own thing" are considered sacred rights, we still see many people desperately seeking someone or something to follow that will give their life meaning and structure. And there is no shortage of gurus and experts to follow these days: spiritual teachers, indulging therapists, fitness fanatics, political innovators, scientific theorists—take your pick. The choices we make about whom we admire, follow, and wish to emulate reveal much about who we are and who we want to be. Those who follow Jesus and learn His way are called His *disciples*. Both the requirements for and the steps toward discipleship are laid out in various ways in Scripture...Following Jesus is not a matter of simple belief; it is a decision that will affect our worldview, our choices, our relationships, our entire life. Jesus welcomes everyone to follow Him and insists that we seriously consider the cost of being His disciple. His requirements are the same today as they were two thousand years ago...
> The cultural view of greatness in Jesus' day was not much different from ours. But Jesus taught and exemplified an altogether different kind of greatness for His disciples to emulate...It's a tall order: loving God above all else, counting the cost, knowing our identity, leaning on the Scriptures, serving with humility, being an ambassador of

reconciliation, winning the battles against sin and circumstances, setting goals, and renewing our mind. We can easily feel overwhelmed by what it really means to be a disciple of Christ. But underneath all of these requirements for discipleship is simply a desire to follow Christ—to walk with our Lord, to go in His direction. We don't have to do it perfectly, just steadfastly. And as we trust His love and live our lives in the power of the Holy Spirit, we will come to know the joy of remaining in Him.[1]

Your devotion to Jesus Christ is to be unscathed by worldly attraction. That is all Christ wants from His disciple: loving, devoted commitment to Him and His Word. This is not to be an occasional event; it is a lifestyle! This lifestyle must be your choice. There's a Kingdom to build, lost people to reach, and discouraged people to encourage. Until the day Christ calls you to Heaven, this is what your life is all about, because this is what Jesus is all about. Praise the Lord. Serve our Christ unwaveringly!

THE COMMAND INTERROGATED:

There's no doubt at all that Satan will do whatever he can to provide just the right temptations to "redirect" your path of choice. It is a sickening tragedy when disciples of Jesus Christ turn back (**Hebrews 10:38**) to the ways of the world (**2 Timothy 4:10**). This is the primary way Satan will attack you in regard to your lifestyle choice. He sees your devotion to Christ, and it makes him angry. So, his primary tactic is to entrap you in a yoke of bondage, which is nothing more than old habits and old ways. Do you know why Satan does this? Because he knows your weaknesses! He knows those areas in which you served him when you were lost without Christ. So, after you come to Christ, the enemy tries to ensnare you again; and if you abandon Christ, the latter end of your life is worse than the beginning (**2 Peter 2:20-22**). Consider that not only a sobering warning from God's Word but also a reminder to remain steadfast in your commitment to Jesus (**Galatians 5:1**). Beware of Satan's attacks and his ways. I assure you, this is his plan to sway you, to maneuver you off your chosen lifestyle path and onto the one you used to travel before Christ. Don't give in.

THE COMMAND INDESTRUCTIBLE:

Well, praise to the Lamb of God, there's good news for you. Since God's Word is your weapon to fight the devil, there is a memory verse that you can utilize in times of heavy, overwhelming allurements that seek to draw you away from Christ's lifestyle. That verse of Scripture is **Psalm 119:133**: *"Direct my steps by Your word, and let no iniquity have dominion over me."* Hallelujah, that says it all! Between two gates (broad, narrow) and two foundations (rock, sand), your steps must not slip. During your lifestyle choices, you take one step at a time, each ordered by God Himself (**Psalm 37:23**) as you keep His Word.

Therefore, according to your memory verse, the only hope for your steps to be directed divinely is found in your obedience to what God says. This is why you bring your entire body, soul, and spirit into conformity to the living Word of God. All counsel apart from Scripture is futile and misleading. God guards your way, disciple. He cares for you as you allow Him to direct your steps along life's road. Align yourself with Christ and His Word...always. Never let go. Never back up. Stay committed all your days! If you sense your feet are slipping, return to **Psalm 119:133**. Quote it. Believe it. Live it. Your lifestyle depends on it.

THE COMMAND INQUIRED:

What cannot be measured cannot be evaluated. Therefore, it is essential to measure your comprehension of Christ's command in this teaching, or else the devil will snatch away the "seeds" of Scripture sown into your heart (**Matthew 13:19**). To keep this from occurring, write down your answers to the following questions as they correlate with the teaching this week:

In what passage(s) of Scripture do you find Christ's commandment on **lifestyle choices**?

What is the accurate interpretation of **lifestyle choices** you have discovered?

_____

_____

_____

_____

_____

In your own words, what are some real-life examples in Scripture of **lifestyle choices**?

_____

_____

_____

_____

_____

What steps of initiation did you learn to take in order for **lifestyle choices** to transform your life?

_____

_____

_____

_____

_____

_____

How will Satan attack you to hinder **lifestyle choices** in your life?

_____

_____

_____

_____

_____

What memory verse will you use to protect Christ's command of **lifestyle choices** in your life? Write it out.

_____

_____

_____

_____

_____

TEACHING # 3.2: FLESHLY LUSTS

Week 23

This week's objective: To gain a comprehensive understanding of your sinful flesh, as well as to learn the precise ways Christ teaches you to conquer it.

THE COMMAND INTRODUCED:

- **Mark 9:43-50; Matthew 5:29-30; 18:8-9** *"If your hand causes you to sin, cut it off. It is better for you to enter into life maimed, rather than having two hands, to go to hell, into the fire that shall never be quenched—where 'their worm does not die, and the fire is not quenched.' And if your foot causes you to sin, cut it off. It is better for you to enter life lame, rather than having two feet, to be cast into hell, into the fire that shall never be quenched—where 'their worm does not die, and the fire is not quenched.' And if your eye causes you to sin, pluck it out. It is better for you to enter the kingdom of God with one eye, rather than having two eyes, to be cast into hell fire—where 'their worm does not die, and the fire is not quenched.' For everyone will be seasoned with fire, and every sacrifice will be seasoned with salt. Salt is good, but if the salt loses its flavor, how will you season it? Have salt in yourselves, and have peace with one another."*
- **Matthew 5:27-28** *"You have heard that it was said to those of old, 'You shall not commit adultery.' But I say to you that whoever looks at a woman to lust for her has already committed adultery with her in his heart."*

THE COMMAND INTERPRETED:

Jesus Christ cannot be any clearer on His standards regarding fleshly lusts than He is here. These two commands are for the most part direct and are to be categorically interpreted. One

180

command deals with *multiple lusts*, the other with *sexual lusts*.

The first command (**Mark 9:43-50; Matthew 5:29-30; 18:8-9**) addresses multiple lusts, or different avenues people take to fulfill their lustful desires. Upon first encountering this command from Jesus, you may have gasped at the graphic detail and horrific cost you are to endure if you want to go to Heaven. Before you come to any conclusions, it is important to understand that Jesus was speaking in a figurative hyperbole. He was by no means literally advocating self-mutilation! Rather, there is a call for context here and an appreciation for application.

The point Jesus was making for you as His disciple is to not give in to sin just because it invitingly sits in front of you. The idea Jesus was portraying is to rid yourself of the sinfulness that exists within. You see, Christ spotlighted sinning "with" your hand, foot, or eye for the purpose of pointing to that which wars inside you: *sin*! Since you are dealing with what you touch (hand, foot) and what you see (eyes), you must learn to arrest these areas, bringing them under control as you follow Christ (**Romans 6:1-14**). This will be your inward battle (**Galatians 5:16-17**) until the day you die; these areas must be crucified (**Galatians 5:24**). So, it is far better to live only for Christ and neglect fleshly desires than to neglect Christ for the passing pleasures of sin (**Hebrews 11:24-25**) and wake up in Hell for eternity! Every mortal must choose.

While He was on this subject with everybody's attention glued to His words, Christ gave the punch line in **verses 49-50**. Everyone will be seasoned with fire, in the sense of Christ's judgment regarding both believers (**1 Corinthians 3:11-15**) and unbelievers (**Revelation 20:11-15**) alike. However, the sacrifices, which come from disciples alone (**Romans 12:1**), are to be seasoned with salt. Salt? The command is to have "*salt in yourselves.*" Having previously devoted many teachings to fleshly lusts, Jesus was concerned that the "*salt*" inside believers would lose its flavor. How could this happen? If the followers gave in to fleshly desires.

You see, salt is a preservative, and Christians are called and equipped to "preserve" holiness in an unholy world (**Matthew 5:13**). To lose your "*salt*" is to lose your witness and influence in the presence of lost people all around you. For the sake of the gospel and people's eternal separation from God in Hell, you cannot afford to ruin your "*flavor*" among men. You are called to be a preservative that counteracts moral decay. If you give in to the lusts of your flesh, you become useless to Christ (**2 Timothy 2:21**), just as ruined salt is worthless for food.

The second command (**Matthew 5:27-28**) addresses the area of sexual lust, meaning the usage of the eyes to fulfill unholy sexual desires. Granted, sexual intimacy is a gift from God, to be enjoyed only in the context of marriage between a man and a woman (**Genesis 2:22-25; 1 Corinthians 7:1-5; Hebrews 13:4**). Now, while this second command is supplemented by the first command (**Mark 9:47**), it goes into more depth as to how one may sin with his eyes. There are many ways you can sin with your eyes, but here Jesus exposed perhaps the most confining addiction for people regarding sexuality. The problem is not a man looking upon a woman to admire her beauty (**Genesis 29:17; 2 Samuel 11:2; Song of Solomon 6:4; Esther 2:7**). Rather, the problem is when he perverts a woman's beauty (**Proverbs 6:25**) through the sinful wanderings of his mind and heart. That's why Jesus used the Greek word for "lust" (*epithumeo*), which means "to set the heart upon; long for." You see, the sinfulness of the heart is the problem after all (**Jeremiah 17:9-10**)!

An unguarded heart explains why so many men are addicted to pornography. This is why you "see" so much sexuality in magazines, television shows, and movies, because unrestrained sexuality has reached full magnification. It has resulted in an explosion of gross immorality that does nothing but confirm the perverted depravity of the human heart. This rampage mimics the days of Israel's judges (**Judges 21:25**). Sadly, when lusting eyes go unchecked, adultery in the heart solicits the consequence.

In a sense, if a man lusts for a modestly dressed woman, she is not accountable because she has properly clothed herself, and, in his heart, he has raped her. However, in the context of the command, to commit adultery "*with her*" is literally consensual. You know what this means, right? It means a woman has allowed herself to dress in such a way that she advertises her sexuality. She exposes parts and sections of her body, enticing and provoking a man, and thus giving him something to "*lust*" after. This is not rape. It is consensual, flirtatious, carnal adultery in heart. As a disciple of Christ, if you are a woman, dress yourself appropriately in the fear of God. If you are a man, restrain your eyes intentionally (**Psalm**

119:37) in the fear of God. This is your non-negotiable standard.

THE COMMAND ILLUSTRATED:

Perhaps the greatest example of the reality of fleshly desires is what happened to a man in the Corinthian church. Turn to **1 Corinthians 5:1-5**. This was indeed a sexual sin, that a man became sexually involved with his...father's wife? That's right. As impossible and degrading as that sounds, it really happened. Paul's advice to the church was to deliver this man to Satan to destroy his flesh (**verse 5**), which was a type of chastening (**Hebrews 12:5-11**) for the sin committed against God (**Psalm 51:4**). When someone mocks fleshly desires with a "willpower mindset," destruction awaits such an ignoramus.

It seems the subject of sexual lusts is something every human being has struggled with because of sin's presence in our flesh.

To add to the reality of what happened in the Corinthian church, you can also see the devastation that comes in the passages of **Proverbs 2:16-19; 5:1-14; 6:20-29; 7:6-27**. The common thread running through these passages is identified as sexual lusts, but it begins with the eyes and works its way into action through the body. Never think to yourself as a disciple that you can fight your fleshly nature on your own. Prayerfully abandon yourself to the throne of God, and He will give you grace and power in His Spirit to wage war against your desires. Put your trust in the living God!

THE COMMAND INITIATED:

Is it really possible for you as a disciple to win the war against the flesh on a daily basis? Yes, it is (**Philippians 4:13**). The only way to gain a right understanding of this possibility is to realize that you must choose to obey Christ in your areas of weakness, because such obedience does not come naturally to your fleshly desires. Choose whom you will obey, Jesus or your sinful flesh (**John 8:34-36; Romans 6:18**). In Christ Jesus, you are more than a conqueror (**Romans 8:37**)! Gaining the victory over fleshly desires does not have to be merely a dream; it is real through your faith (**1 John 5:4**). Put your faith into action.

Andrew Singletary has one of the best perspectives on this subject that has ever been communicated. In his book *Conquering the Flesh*, Singletary articulately explains the necessary, childlike obedience required to conquer your fleshly nature:

> We must present our bodies as living sacrifices. And we must renew our minds continually. Otherwise, our minds and bodies will disobey God and run haywire. You have to renew your mind. You have to renew it by keeping it exposed to the word of God...The flesh is lusting or warring against the Spirit. And we know that the flesh is the mind and body not obeying God, but functioning on their own. So now I ask another question. Who's controlling you? Before you answer, remember this is an experience that is unique to the Christian. This is not an unbeliever's battle. The unbeliever has no Holy Spirit in him to fight against...But you are a believer. And you have an enemy called the flesh. He is your greatest enemy. You know who and what he is. The flesh is your mind and body not obeying God, but functioning on their own. And **Romans 8:8** says that *"they that are in the flesh cannot please God."* So how do we conquer the flesh?
>
> Walk in the Spirit! **Romans 8:1** says, *"There is therefore now no condemnation to them which are in Christ Jesus, who walk not after the flesh, but after the Spirit."* If you want to conquer the flesh, you have to be led of the Spirit of God. Otherwise, the works of the flesh will eat at you just like a cancer. You can't feel it. There may not be any symptoms. But walking after the flesh will kill you just as dead.[2]

Can you see the peril that will poison your Christian witness like a venomous snake? There is such a risk, such a cost, for a disciple to fail to crucify the flesh every single day (**Luke 9:23**). Put this discipline into practice immediately. If you in any way still have some old habits or ways that have not been crucified with Christ, then you are still gratifying your fleshly desires. Stop! Halt! Such is not Christ's plan for you. Because of Jesus and His mercy on your life, there exists a miraculous distinction between who you are now and who you used to be (**1 Corinthians 6:9-11; Ephesians 2:1-13**). This is true for you, isn't it? Of course it is. Therefore, out of gratitude to Jesus' blood and His righteousness (**Ephesians 1:7**), live like you're saved. Exemplify Christ!

THE COMMAND INTERROGATED:

Since the command from Christ is to fight against the lust of your flesh that rises from what you see and feel, how do you think Satan will try to provide you with opportunity to violate Christ's command? Well, obviously the devil will craftily place objects, people, or both in your path to give you a way of stumbling through your weaknesses. By no means does this give a disciple an excuse to sin (**Romans 6:1-2**), but it does give a disciple an explanation as to how he is tempted to sin (**2 Corinthians 2:11**). Satan is so sly! Beware of his subtle attacks that involve the lust of your flesh, your eyes, and your pride of life (**1 John 2:15-17**).

Your body is the temple of the Holy Spirit (**1 Corinthians 3:16; 6:19-20**). This means the Spirit of God is inside you, fighting your flesh for you as you surrender daily to the Lordship of Jesus Christ and His Word. But if you quench the Spirit's power in exchange for your fleshly desires, you trash your temple. If you do this, Scripture says God will destroy you (**1 Corinthians 3:17**), and I assure you, God is serious because He is never mocked (**Galatians 6:7**). A disciple must destroy completely anything that is harming the temple, such as overeating, drug addictions, smoking, and intoxication by alcoholic beverages (**Ephesians 5:18**). Put away your old life—the old person with the old ways. You're a new person in Christ (**Ephesians 5:8-14**). Conquer your flesh. Stand strong in God's Word against Satan.

THE COMMAND INDESTRUCTIBLE:

Child of God, you are equipped as a disciple in your battle against Satan. If we didn't have the Word of God to fight with, the Body of Christ would be a pitifully weak and wounded army of saints. But we do have the Word of God to fight with and the Spirit of God to empower us as we do so. There are so many Scriptures that you could use in your daily discipline to fight your fleshly desires, but there is one that is universally applicable: **1 Corinthians 9:27**. It says, *"But I discipline my body and bring it into subjection, lest, when I have preached to others, I myself should become disqualified."*

That's your answer, friend. That's your hope. That's your sword. You see, as you live your life on this earth, you have to remember that you are a pilgrim passing through to your upcoming heavenly country. As you journey, you will constantly have to wage the fleshly war in which you are mortally engaged (**1 Peter 2:11**). As you discipline yourself to fight against these hellish urges through your surrender to Christ and His commands, you will beautifully demonstrate to the world sanctification (**2 Corinthians 7:1**) and holiness (**1 Peter 1:13-16**). You can do it! That's what Jesus Christ the Lord wants to see as a product of your life. Serve Him. Love Him. Obey Him. Discipline yourself for Him.

THE COMMAND INQUIRED:

What cannot be measured cannot be evaluated. Therefore, it is essential to measure your comprehension of Christ's command in this teaching, or else the devil will snatch away the "seeds" of Scripture sown into your heart (**Matthew 13:19**). To keep this from occurring, write down your answers to the following questions as they correlate with the teaching this week:

In what passage(s) of Scripture do you find Christ's commandment on **fleshly lusts**?

_____

_____

_____

What is the accurate interpretation of **fleshly lusts** you have discovered?

_____

_____

_____

_____

_____

_____

In your own words, what are some real-life examples in Scripture of **fleshly lusts**?

_____

_____

_____

_____

_____

_____

What steps of initiation did you learn to take in order for the teaching regarding **fleshly lusts** to transform your life?

_____

_____

_____

_____

_____

How will Satan attack you with **fleshly lusts** in your life?

_____

_____

_____

_____

_____

_____

What memory verse will you use to protect Christ's command regarding **fleshly lusts** in your life? Write it out.

_____

_____

_____

_____

_____

_____

TEACHING # 3.3: MATERIALISM

Week 24

This week's objective: To reveal the process of entrapment through over-indulgence of possessions, as well as to teach you the state of contentment.

THE COMMAND INTRODUCED:

- **Matthew 6:19-21** *"Do not lay up for yourselves treasures on earth, where moth and rust destroy and where thieves break in and steal; but lay up for yourselves treasures in heaven, where neither moth nor rust destroys and where thieves do not break in and steal. For where your treasure is, there your heart will be also."*
- **Luke 6:25** *"Woe to you who are full, for you shall hunger..."*

THE COMMAND INTERPRETED:

These commands—one direct, one implicit—are by far some of the most difficult for believers to align with. When Jesus spoke forth His commands addressing materialism, it is important to recall that His disciples and the multitudes surrounding them were a rather impoverished class of people. They did not have much to begin with and were by no means wealthy. So for Jesus to make these claims against materialism was a dagger to some, because they didn't want to stay in their condition.

This is precisely why Jesus clarified His command against being materialistic. At the heart of His concern was forgetfulness. Jesus knows that if His people become wrapped up in materialism, they will engage in a forgetful departure from the Lord just like the children of Israel did (**Deuteronomy 6:10-12**). So please, dear disciple, take the commands of Christ seriously in regards to materialism. View all of Christ's words as nothing more than wise protection of your relationship with Him through your discipline to swat away the alluring, attractive "stuff" that gratifies your pleasure more than it satisfies the demands of Almighty God.

The first command (**Matthew 6:19-21**) is not without identification; Christ specifically brings your attention to the subject of treasures. The Greek word for "treasures" (*thesauros*) translates "to place a deposit; wealthy." Does this mean it is wrong to have money? No. Actually, the issue at hand has absolutely nothing to do with money itself, but rather with the objects in which that money is invested. That is why Jesus referred to the "*moth*" and the "*rust*," for these destroy material items. Our Lord Jesus was commanding a lifestyle that is not saturated with materialism, because such "*treasures*" only waste away, but "*treasures*" in heaven do not! How do you obtain treasures in heaven? You invest your money *more* into meeting the material needs of the poor and needy than you do into clinging to your own (**Matthew 19:21-22**).

Your goal in your life as a disciple is to be richer in God's eyes than you are in the eyes of man (**Luke 12:21**). Jesus reminds you that your heart will always be attached to your treasure. A disciple is to invest his time, money, and resources into the Kingdom of God through a people-focused lifestyle. If he does not, he will become materialistic, living more for the here-and-now than for the hereafter. The command is clear: "deposit" your treasures in Heaven.

The second command (**Luke 6:25**) touches on the idea of over-indulgence. It is interesting to note that the Greek word "full" (*empletho*) means "to fill up or satisfy," an understandable expression considering Jesus's audience—those who focus on satisfying and pleasing themselves instead of pleasing God. Remember, the problem here is the negation and avoidance of moderation, not enjoying a blessing from the Lord Himself. In reality, Christ is not only specifying the command but also predicting the "hunger" or material drought (**Proverbs 21:13**) that will come from filling up on fleshly gratifications. Such a caution is interpreted as a type of judgment or chastening upon a disciple who disobeys the Master. A life of materialistic imbalance tips the scales of your heart, leaving you weighed down so that you are of no use to the Lord and no benefit to needy people. Avoid overt self-consumption. It is more blessed to give (**Acts 20:35**) than to store up treasures that you will not take with you when you die (**1 Timothy 6:7**).

THE COMMAND ILLUSTRATED:

Scripture is by no means silent when it comes to examples of materialistic endeavors. One of the best illustrations of materialism and its effect on the human heart is found in the attitude of the rich young ruler. Turn to **Luke 18:18-23**.

Well, now that you have read that, you can close your awestruck, open mouth. Is that shocking or what? Jesus launches an investigation of this young ruler, for the heart is the "X marks the spot" location for buried treasure. Christ knew the young man was telling the truth. Indeed, he had kept all the commands since his childhood—in all except one area that was no match for Christ's omniscience. Jesus knew the young man's heart was anchored to his material wealth. In fact, Jesus understood that the only real test of the young man's obedience was to hit him where it hurt. That's why Christ nailed him by exposing his heart, revealing his attachment to his material possessions. The young man had no intention of giving his wealth to anyone, much less to the poor. So, when Jesus demanded it as a requirement for following Him, the young ruler *"became very sorrowful."* What a shame. What a tragedy. He missed his opportunity at eternal life (**Ephesians 2:8-9**) because he didn't want to "miss" his material wealth.

As a disciple of Christ, learn a valuable lesson from this rich young ruler: God is focused on what you will *do* with what you have, not what you *have* because of what you do. Jesus doesn't care how materially rich or poor you are. He just wants to use what you have to reach other people for the Kingdom of God! That is exactly why a materialistic attitude will devastate a Christian lifestyle. If you become self-absorbed, you immobilize your faith and stunt your giving. Jesus doesn't want His disciples to get comfortable in this life. You are a pilgrim. You are on a journey; travel as "light" as possible. This world (and its stuff) is not your home.

THE COMMAND INITIATED:

It is of utmost importance to put this teaching into action. So, what does it look like to be materialistic? Where is the balance, and where is the compromise? As a disciple, you are highly accountable to share your blessings instead of hoarding them. Your goal as a Christian is to be like Christ. You want your life to look like His. Therefore, you want to live on and with as little as you need, while giving away your excess to help the poor and reach the lost. This discipline keeps you from storing up treasures on Earth.

Randy Alcorn offers one of the best approaches to both revealing and understanding materialism. In his book *Money, Possessions, and Eternity*, Alcorn takes the teachings of Scripture and parallels them to the modern society in which you live:

> God created us to love people and use things, but materialists love things and use people. Take for example our society's tendency to treat people as objects. In the marketplace we refer to *consumers*—economic units that are of value to a company insofar as they contribute to its profits. Products are marketed to "consumers" without regard to the fact that they may become addicted, depressed, obese, or diseased—taking years off their lives— as a result of consuming those products. We have every reason to be alarmed about our country's materialism but no reason to be surprised by it. We cannot reject the Creator and His truth without rejecting the respect for human dignity that naturally flows from it...
>
> What other values than materialistic ones would we expect from a generation of materialists? As a society, we are reaping exactly what we have sown...Materialism can only be corrected by changing our view of God. This change, in turn, can only come from a belief in and study of the Scriptures, which tell us about God, and which alone give us the context to understand ourselves and the proper place of money and possessions. Materialism results from a failure to realize that we were made for only one person (Jesus) and one place (heaven)...The hardest part of dealing with our materialism is that it has become so much a part of us. Like people who have lived in darkness for years, we have been removed from the light so long that we don't know how dark it really is. Many of us have never known what it is not to be materialistic...If we were to gain God's perspective, even for a moment, and were to look at the way we go through life accumulating and hoarding and displaying our

things, we would have the same feelings of horror and pity that any sane person has when he views people in an asylum endlessly beating their heads against the wall...Seeking fulfillment in money, land, houses, cars, clothes, boats, campers, hot tubs, world travel, and cruises has left us bound and gagged by materialism—and like drug addicts, we pathetically think that our only hope lies in getting more of the same. Meanwhile, the voice of God—unheard amid the clamor of our possessions—is telling us that even if materialism did bring happiness in this life, which it clearly does not, it would leave us woefully unprepared for the next life.[3]

In addition to Alcorn, Richard Foster also has an excellent grasp on the materialistic plague in our culture that has grossly influenced the body of Christ. In his book *Celebration of Discipline*, Foster elaborates on the discipline of simplicity:

Contemporary culture lacks both the inward reality and the outward life-style of simplicity. We must live in the modern world, and we are affected by its fractured and fragmented state. We are trapped in a maze of competing attachments. One moment we make decisions on the basis of sound reason and the next moment out of fear of what others will think of us. We have no unity or focus around which our lives are oriented. Because we lack a divine Center our need for security has led us into an insane attachment to things. We really must understand that the lust for affluence in a contemporary society is psychotic...We are made to feel ashamed to wear clothes or drive cars until they are worn out. The mass media have convinced us that to be out of step with fashion is to be out of step with reality. It is time we awaken to the fact that conformity to a sick society is to be sick. Until we see how unbalanced our culture has become at this point, we will not be able to deal with the mammon spirit within ourselves nor will we desire Christian simplicity.[4]

Wow. There is no room for speculation or debate.

Materialism is wrong; materialistic living is sinful. Now, please remember, you have what are called your "basic necessities" for life as a mortal human being. It is when you leave behind your contentment with these blessings and go after more and more and more that you sin against God. This is materialism! This is the atrocity of being swayed and influenced by others who have been sucked into this hellish vacuum of possessions. The only protection is to give; the only cure is to give. Dear disciple, run from materialism, and build up your treasures heavenward.

THE COMMAND INTERROGATED:

Satan loves blinding God's people with materialistic attitudes; materialism is a harness tightened by Hell. The devil's primary way to attack you in the area of possessions is to pervert the blessings of God through your hoarding them. Hoarding? Exactly. Haven't you ever seen a little child attempt to politely play with another child's toy, only to witness a sudden snatching and the growling, selfish face of the toy's owner? That childish drama seems to have made its way into the everyday lives of adults all over the world. Hoarding is the shelf for "stacking up" your materialism in the barnyard of your heart. This is Satan's delight for you because you become his rag doll to continually dishonor the poor (**James 2:1-6**). Beware of his subtle ways of ensnaring your heart to trust in your materialistic blessings. Do not do this, for the Lord your God will not endorse your behavior; He will hold you accountable (**Proverbs 23:4-5; James 5:1-5**).

At this very moment, I am going to ask you a question, one that demands an answer: are you a materialistic person? If so, based on Christ's command, what are you going to do about it? Whatever you do, do not allow Satan to keep you backed into your materialistic corner. Make extreme adjustments. Have a garage sale and give your profit to a mission project overseas. Pack up your excess and give it to a local homeless shelter or a disaster relief fund. Do you see the point? Choose contentment over materialism.

THE COMMAND INDESTRUCTIBLE:

By now, you more than likely have an overwhelming sense of conviction. Perhaps you are materialistic because you grew up that way. On the contrary, maybe you did in fact grow up relatively poor but attained a level of financial success and have begun purchasing all the "stuff" you and your family never could afford. In either case, this command applies to you. It is a command that calls for a decision, one that tests the sincerity of your heart to follow Christ in total contentment.

You must discipline yourself to transform from a hoarder to a distributor. But this kind of discipline demands motivation and strength. Praise God, there is a Scripture straight from the mouth of the Lord Jesus, one that serves to remind you to focus on contentment in the midst of Satan's materialistic temptations. This great memory verse for you to use is found in **Luke 12:15**: "*Take heed and beware of covetousness, for one's life does not consist in the abundance of the things he possesses.*" Now, that's a sword with which to fight materialism! Oh, disciple, you can do this; you can live this kind of contented lifestyle. It is a mark of godliness (**1 Timothy 6:6**). It is a lifestyle that is learned (**Philippians 4:11-12**). So, if contentment is *learned*, as the Apostle Paul stated, then it is a process of adjustment to living with *less* for you so that you can give *more* to others. You live a life of trusting God for what He knows you need (**Matthew 6:8; Philippians 4:19**).

Always remember to quote your memory verse in defense of your faith to remain content. If an uprising of material wealth overtakes you, praise God out of thanksgiving for His blessing, but then in turn use only what you need of it, and as a faithful steward, distribute your excess to the poor and needy. Equality is the will of God (**2 Corinthians 8:14-15**). Share your blessings (**Acts 2:44-45; 4:32-35**). Such perpetual practices like that will keep you humble and content yet give you avenues to reach people for Christ as well as edify believers through the blessings God has given you. Hallelujah!

THE COMMAND INQUIRED:

What cannot be measured cannot be evaluated. Therefore, it is essential to measure your comprehension of Christ's command in this teaching, or else the devil will snatch away the "seeds" of Scripture sown into your heart (**Matthew 13:19**). To keep this from occurring, write down your answers to the following questions as they correlate with the teaching this week:

In what passage(s) of Scripture do you find Christ's commandment on **materialism**?

_____

_____

_____

What is the accurate interpretation of **materialism** you have discovered?

_____

_____

_____

_____

_____

_____

In your own words, what are some real-life examples in Scripture of **materialism**?

_____

_____

_____

_____

_____

_____

What steps of initiation did you learn to take in order for the teaching regarding **materialism** to transform your life?

_____

_____

_____

_____

_____

_____

How will Satan attack you with **materialism** in your life?

_____

_____

_____

_____

_____

What memory verse will you use to protect Christ's command regarding **materialism** in your life? Write it out.

_____

_____

_____

_____

_____

TEACHING # 3.4: VISUAL EXPOSURE

Week 25

This week's objective: To identify the horrendous visual atrocities that hinder your Christian perspective, as well as to show you how to guard yourself.

THE COMMAND INTRODUCED:

- **Matthew 6:22-23; Luke 11:34-36** *"The lamp of the body is the eye. If therefore your eye is good, your whole body will be full of light. But if your eye is bad, your whole body will be full of darkness. If therefore the light that is in you is darkness, how great is that darkness!"*

THE COMMAND INTERPRETED:

This command from the Lord Jesus is implicit, and its nature is rooted in the soil of visual exposure. Christ identified a truth that affects every mortal to ever live with the ability to see. The heart of the passage surrounding this command is addressing materialism, but in context, Christ is merely concerned for how His people are grossly affected by sensory stimuli. As His disciple, you are commanded by the Lord to be very cautious of what you allow yourself to be exposed to on a daily basis.

This brings you to the interpretation. Using a metaphor to clarify His point, Christ compares the eye to a lamp. This understanding sets the tone for the entire command. Think about what Jesus is saying. He is passionately advocating for *light*, not darkness, and *good*, not bad. The only way that you can physically see anything is because of the light in your environment, which activates the vision processes within your eye! Likewise, you can spiritually see what is pleasing to Christ only when He, the Light of the World, is your environment (**1 John 1:7**).

The goal here is perception. Your entire purpose in life is to be a bright shining light in this darkened world (**Matthew 5:16; Philippians 2:15; 2 Peter 1:19**). Christ commands for your "whole body" to shine, which points to being consumed by the filling power of the Holy Spirit to empower your life, renew your mind, and enlighten your spiritual understanding as you grow in Christ! Wow! The source of this light is through the "lamp," and the position of the lamp is the "eye." Obviously, the "lamp" is Jesus Christ, and praise God, He is the bulb that never burns out (**1 John 1:5**), continuously piercing the darkness. Therefore, this means that your eye is like a window that the light of Christ penetrates, in turn illuminating the whole room (your body) surrounding that window. This gives you, as Christ's disciple, the ability to "see" and perceive with spiritual vision the things of God, as well as to envision the world, the lost, the hurting, and the poor from His point of view.

However, the tragedy comes when the eye is "bad." Jesus used the Greek word *poneros*, which means "hurtful; grudgingly." Christ is wanting you to understand that you are only hurting yourself if your eye is bad, leaving you empty of His light and full of evil darkness. Such potential clouding of your spiritual perception will always be a threat all the days of your life. Jesus even warns that it is a *"great darkness,"* meaning it can consume you and will destroy you. Therefore, the point the Lord Jesus is making to you as His disciple is stay focused on Him, His will, His Kingdom, and His Word. This discipline is the only way that you keep the "shades" up on the window so that His glorious light can shine in daily. Do not allow the lust of your eyes (**1 John 2:16**) for the stimulating, indulgent pleasures of your body to pull the shade down, blocking Christ's light and leaving you in worldly darkness. Do not lose sight of what you have been saved for, redeemed from your sins and bought at a price you could not pay (**1 Corinthians 6:19-20**). Your life is not your own anymore! Glorify God in your body, full of His radiating, penetrating light.

THE COMMAND ILLUSTRATED:

In the Old Testament, there is a disturbing yet necessary example that exemplifies perfectly what it looks like for someone to be visually affected in their service to God. Turn to **Genesis 13:1-13**. This is the incident of Abram and his nephew, Lot. In sum, they were both fairly wealthy people because God blessed them abundantly. The land they were dwelling in was not conducive for both of them in light of their possessions. So, the decision was respectfully made for Abram and Lot to separate in order to solve their crowding problem.

As it turned out, Abram went the way the Lord wanted him to go, but Lot "saw" the beautiful plain of the Jordan valley near the city limits of wicked Sodom and Gomorrah. The issue here is that Lot started in the plain of the Jordan valley but eventually gravitated toward evil and wicked Sodom (**verses 12-13**). To use the verbiage of the command of Jesus, Lot's *"eye"* was evil, and his body was full of darkness. As Christ's disciple, you must guard yourself from the pursuit of the "better" life, the one that the world, culture, and media say you have to live to be happy. It's the one that is driven by lost people with the attitude that says, "You only live once! So have fun and do whatever you want until the day you die." Heresy! That kind of mindset has no room whatsoever for the cross of Christ nor for the keeping of His commands. Dear disciple, don't *"pitch your tent towards Sodom."* Use Lot's abandonment of God for the pleasures of life as your warning. Such a choice only led him into bondage and captivity (**Genesis 14:12**). Do not be deceived. Guard yourself. Keep your *"eye"* open to Christ but closed to the world.

THE COMMAND INITIATED:

Well, the question you might be asking yourself is, "How do I actually apply this command?" The question definitely deserves an explanation. You cannot apply the command until you know how to understand its purpose. While the command has already been interpreted, it is important to know *why* Jesus gave it. The answer is this: temptation. You see, once your *"eye"* sees something that excites your mind and heart towards their fleshly desires, you officially become victimized by temptation. So, it is clear that the purpose of the command from Christ is to help you fight against the temptation so that you can preserve your eye, which in effect only continues His glorious light to shine through your life and speech.

Since you now have an understanding of its purpose, you can properly apply the command in your daily walk with Christ. So, what does it look like to put this command into practice? Since temptation is the opponent, you will have to wage war against it, fighting with your faith in God's Word and your commitment to restrain your eyes from sensual, worldly lusts. Manickam Chandrakumar has an impressively clear understanding of the overwhelming power of Satan's disguises. In his fantastic book *Overcoming Temptation*, Chandrakumar not only labels what temptation looks like but also showcases the way out:

> Our natural inclination, which is both sudden and fierce, is to desire. All at once a secret, smoldering fire is kindled. The flesh burns and is in flames. Whether it is sexual desire, ambition, vanity, the desire for revenge, the greed for money, the love of fame and power, or that strange desire for the beautiful things of the world, the lust thus aroused envelops the mind and will of man in deepest darkness. Our discernment and decision-making abilities are weakened at this point. All kinds of questions come into our minds: "Is what the flesh desires really sin in this case? Is it really not permitted to me to appease my desire?" The tempter puts us in a privileged position as he once tried to urge the hungry Son of God to change stones into bread (see **Lk. 4:1-4**). We boast of our privileges that can sometimes be against God. There is only one reality stronger than our desire and Satan's influence and that is the image and the presence of the Crucified. Against this power, the power of desire dissolves into nothingness, for here it is conquered. Here, the flesh has received its right and reward, namely, death. We read in **James 1:15**, "*When lust has conceived it gives birth to sin; and when sin is accomplished, it brings forth death.*" The lust of the flesh is nothing else than the anguish of the flesh in the face of death. Only the death of Christ rescues us from the temptation of the flesh.[5]

What a fight it is to discipline your fleshly desires,

allurements, and attractions that do nothing more than aggravate and agitate your purity in Christ. Put the command of Christ into action. Face it: you are going to be plagued with temptations daily, but as long as you choose not to yield to them, you will walk in Christ's victory! This is your goal. This is your choice. This is your "*eye.*"

THE COMMAND INTERROGATED:

There is no need to convince you that Satan wants to destroy you by luring you toward ungodly visual images. However, it is important for you to know the actual manner in which he hooks you. This manner is found in **James 1:14**: "*But each one is tempted when he is drawn away by his own desires and enticed.*" Do you see it? You are your own victim. The desires belong to you, not Satan. If you choose to allow yourself to be hooked, then that's your regretful choice.

The Greek word "enticed" (*deleazo*) means "to entrap; delude." The fish goes for the bait only to be hooked, reeled, and grilled! You are that fish. If you bite the attractive, alluring temptations that face you and bombard your imagination, Satan will hook you, trap you, and attempt to destroy you. Beware of this cunning hitman, the devil. He is sly and ruthless. He is bent on your destruction. All it comes down to is *choice*! That's all. Nothing more spiritual. Nothing less. Just choose to obey Christ, and you will defeat the devil. Choose, or you will lose.

THE COMMAND INDESTRUCTIBLE:

God's Word is full of encouraging reminders that illustrate so beautifully the paths of the righteous. But the memory verse that will empower you daily to overcome Satan in the face of visual temptations is **Psalm 119:37**: "*Turn away my eyes from looking at worthless things, and revive me in Your way.*" That's what you need. Every temptation must be seen as worthless, for it does not honor Christ, and it does not profit godliness. You can do this! You can live victoriously for the Lord Jesus Christ. Like Job, you must be willing to make a covenant with your eyes (**Job 31:1**). You become accountability partners with the Holy Spirit within you. Day by day, you steadfastly devote yourself as Christ's disciple to *"set nothing wicked before your eyes"* (**Psalm 101:3**). The key to overcome with God's Word here is to remain focused, and that without exception. As you would avoid looking down while walking a tightrope, so don't look around for sensualities arousing sexuality, greed, fame, and revenge. Just walk the tightrope only—look straight ahead (**Proverbs 4:25**). Look unto Jesus, for He is the blazing light for your *"eye"* (**Hebrews 12:2**).

THE COMMAND INQUIRED:

What cannot be measured cannot be evaluated. Therefore, it is essential to measure your comprehension of Christ's command in this teaching, or else the devil will snatch away the "seeds" of Scripture sown into your heart (**Matthew 13:19**). To keep this from occurring, write down your answers to the following questions as they correlate with the teaching this week:

In what passage(s) of Scripture do you find Christ's commandment on **visual exposure**?

_____

_____

_____

What is the accurate interpretation of **visual exposure** you have discovered?

_____

_____

_____

_____

_____

In your own words, what are some real-life examples in Scripture of **visual exposure**?

_____

_____

_____

_____

_____

What steps of initiation did you learn to take in order for the teaching regarding **visual exposure** to transform your life?

_____

_____

_____

_____

_____

How will Satan attack you with **visual exposure** in your life?

_____

_____

_____

_____

_____

What memory verse will you use to protect Christ's command regarding **visual exposure** in your life? Write it out.

_____

_____

_____

_____

_____

TEACHING # 3.5: MONEY

Week 26

This week's objective: To examine the proper use of finances for a Christian, as well as to address the ways in which money can become an idolatrous god in your life.

THE COMMAND INTRODUCED:

- **Matthew 6:24; Luke 16:13** *"No one can serve two masters; for either he will hate the one and love the other, or else he will be loyal to the one and despise the other. You cannot serve God and mammon."*
- **Luke 6:24** *"But woe to you who are rich, for you have received your consolation."*

THE COMMAND INTERPRETED:

These commands are very insightful regarding the subject of money. One command is direct, and the other is implicit. In spite of their different approaches, the appeal is the same: examine your *relationship* to money. Relationship? That's right. The entire economic system for thousands of years has revolved around currency. The concept of supply and demand is nothing new to the manufacturer and the consumer, to the employer and the employee. It seems that as members of society, all people are inevitably influenced by money. This is precisely why Jesus is concerned. He knows that you and I will be influenced by money, but He is more interested in knowing to what degree we have been affected. It is this concern that gives rise to His commands on money.

The first command (**Matthew 6:24; Luke 16:13**) is direct. The key to interpreting its meaning is found in the word *serve*. The Greek word Jesus used is *douleuo*, which is a root of *doulos*, meaning "bondslave." In Biblical times, a bondslave was by definition a human being, but by legal constraints a piece of property. A master was considered to own a bondslave in the same fashion that he owned a plow, a shovel, or a cart. This meant he could do whatever he wanted to his slave, even kill him or her, and never answer for it to anyone. Basically, bondslaves had no rights whatsoever. Their entire service toward their master was immense, unwavering devotion, with no change in status.

With that being said, now do you see the significance of the word *serve* that Jesus used? It was impossible for a bondslave to have two masters. In fact, it was against the nature of his obedience and the duty of his identification. Based on the standards for a bondslave's commitment, he could not obey one master and rightfully be in service to another master because of his duty to his first master. The second master would not consider him as his bondservant because of his failure to meet the requirement for a bondslave, which was total devotion to him and not another master. Again, this proves how literally impossible it is to "*serve*" two masters.

Using this cultural system of slavery in Biblical times, Jesus emphatically paralleled such undying devotion to Himself and "mammon," a reference to money. In the context of the subject of materialism that He previously addressed, Christ finally narrowed His topic to the money that buys material possessions. Christ was so clear, for either you will love money and hate Him, or you will love Him and hate money. You can be loyal to Him and despise "enslavement" to money, but you cannot be loyal to both Him and money. It is a call for a choice—a surrender to whichever master you want to be a slave to.

The second command (**Luke 6:24**) is implicit. Having just delivered a series of blessings (beatitudes), Christ in the same manner delivered a series of woes, including this command on money as it targets the rich. There are so many stereotypes in the world today of what it means to be rich. The most common ideas include earning a certain income, enjoying a specific size of house, or even driving a particular make and model of car. However, Christ erased the stereotypes with the Greek word *plousios*. This is the word He used when attributing a woe to the rich, and it means "to be copious; abounding in wealth." When someone acts copiously, they try to "keep up with the Joneses" or use whatever amount of wealth they have to copy the materialistic lifestyles of surrounding peers.

So, in literal context, Jesus was not referring to a certain amount of money that classifies you as rich. Rather, Christ was distinguishing *"rich"* as using money, regardless of amount, to copy and abound in materialistic indulgences. The reason Christ has a problem with this is that it takes the focus away from building up His Kingdom and focuses instead on building your own. This is why Christ pronounces a *"woe,"* or dreadful misfortune, to these who are categorically described as *"rich."* It is a blatant and consequential sin to hoard wealth and despise the poor (**James 5:1-5**).

In our world today, these people feel their reward is found in the stuff that their money buys them. Christ humbled such people by saying, *"You have your consolation."* The Greek word for "consolation" (*paraklesis*) means "a type of comfort." Christ was in reality rebuking the rich, for they are more "comforted" by their money which can purchase and exceed their materialistic needs than they are by the rewards that could await them in eternity. The rich want their reward—their comfort and ease—now. They do not desire to build up for what they cannot see, because they have no faith at all in the eternal reward (**2 Corinthians 5:7**). And this is why Christ pronounced a woe upon the money-hungry, rich segment of society, for their heart is infested with a gross indulgence in and love for money. As a disciple of Jesus, run as far as you can from this mindset! Do not waste your time trying to consider otherwise. Be faithful, and Christ will take care of you and provide for you. He is your everything!

THE COMMAND ILLUSTRATED:

Money can be a corrupter to the human heart, enhancing its depravity and maximizing its foolish deceits. An accurate example of this is found in **Acts 8:14-24**. As a sorcerer, Simon was wicked, vile, and manipulative. When the apostles laid their hands on the repentant, the new believers received the Holy Spirit to empower them in their Christian lives. As a spectator, Simon found this intriguing rather than holy. Being a sorcerer, perhaps he thought he could add this "act" to his bag of tricks, and thus, he offered the apostles money (**verses 18-19**). Rightfully so, the Apostle Peter was boiling angry at this offer to buy God's favor and blessing. Outrageous! Peter told Simon the sorcerer what he needed to hear (**verse 20**).

This is a classic case of how money can corrupt the heart and lead it astray. It is safe to say that the heart is not capable of properly handling money. That is why God gives us His Word, for in it are the teaching and instruction that guide us in discovering the proper role finances are to play in our Christian lives. As Christ's disciple, do not fall prey to selfish deceits and misappropriate the money God gives you. Glorify God with your money by investing it more into the lives of others (poor, needy, families in crisis, etc.) than into your own personal gain. Store up your reward in Heaven, not on Earth. Focus.

THE COMMAND INITIATED:

It is possible that you have until today maintained a corrupted worldview of money. If you have had no biblical training or teaching on this subject, that means that years have passed in which you have been taught something else. Anything that is not Scriptural is sure to fail, regardless of its fundamental principles. It is imperative to know how to activate a lifestyle that has as its goal to build up the Kingdom of God through reaching others with God's financial blessings. This is what you need to do with the money God has given you. Learn to become others-focused, not you-focused.

Randy Alcorn has a way of simplifying this subject. In his book *Money, Possessions, and Eternity*, Alcorn gives an exhaustive summary like none other of money's place in the Christian life:

Once we allow money to have lordship over our lives, it becomes Money with a capital *M*, a god that jealously dethrones all else. Money makes a terrible master, yet it makes a good servant to those who have the right master— God. To regard money as evil, and therefore useless for purposes of righteousness, is foolish. To regard it as good and therefore overlook its potential for spiritual disaster is equally foolish. Use it, Jesus said, but don't serve it. The goal, then, is not that money be put to death, but that it be trained and handled with discipline, as a lion we are seeking to tame. Money may be temporarily under our control, but we must always regard it as a wild beast, with power to turn on us and others if we drop our guard. Money must not call the shots. We may have plenty of money to buy a new car, but we must not take our direction from Money. If we serve God, we will buy the car only if we believe He wants us to—and we must base that belief on more than preference. Likewise, if we believe God is leading us to go to the mission field or to help a brother in need, we do not say, "There's no money, so I can't." That also would be serving Money. If God is our master, all money is at His disposal. We must concern ourselves not with what Money says, but with what God says. The need for money may be a factor in our decisions, but it is never *the* factor. God, not Money, is sovereign. Money—whether by its presence or absence—must never rule our lives. Money is neither a disease nor a cure. It is what it is, nothing less and nothing more. We may use it well or poorly. Either way, how we use money is always of critical importance to our spiritual lives. It has a lasting impact on two worlds—this one and the next.[6]

What truth! What reality! Christ's command regarding money's place in your life is what you need to both hear and practice. Either you are money's master, or it is your master. There is no room for neutrality here. Dear disciple, keep close to your heart the true riches of life, which are connecting with people and meeting their needs (**Luke 16:11**). This is how you become rich more in the eyes of God than in your own sight (**Luke 12:21**). If this is difficult for you to accept, that merely indicates the extent to which money is your master. Repent and start over in obedience to Christ's command. Trust the Lord and His Word. He will not fail you.

THE COMMAND INTERROGATED:

There are so many ways Satan wants to destroy you, but the ungodly and unbiblical use of money is at the top of his list. He wants you to be a terrible steward of money, blowing it on unnecessary items and gambling it away to get more wealth, so you can buy more stuff, so you can be more miserable! Satan wants to manipulate your desire for money and for what it can purchase. In fact, he wants your desire for money to outweigh your devotion to Jesus Christ, because he wants money to become your god. He wants you to worship it, serve it, and fall in love with it. By doing so, he can cause you to lose sight of what really matters in life: people. It is the love of money, not having money, that is the taproot of all forms of evil (**1 Timothy 6:10-11**). Be very, very careful to avoid both a love for your money and a desire to spend it more for your selfish gratification than for meeting the needs of others.

Wealth and money are gifts from God as they relate to our provision, but they become a curse to mankind when they are diluted with evil motives. The wealthy in Jesus' day were so blinded that they couldn't see their need for Christ and His salvation, nor could they comprehend their spiritual poverty (**Luke 14:12; 16:1-4, 19-26, 19:1-10**). As a child of God, beware of Satan's assault on you in this area of finances. Every time God blesses you financially, give a tithe of your income to your local church. Whatever is left over, spend only on your basic necessities (groceries, housing expenses, clothing, etc.) and intentionally target the rest toward known needs in your neighborhood, community, church, school, family, or even place of employment. Do not let Satan distract you; remember this is God's money that just happens to be in your pocket. Use it for the glory of Christ, defeating Satan in every way possible.

THE COMMAND INDESTRUCTIBLE:

Thank God for his infallible Word! Oh, how saturated the Scriptures are with verses that govern your heart to stay true to the proper use of money in your discipled life! There is a memory verse that will realign your heart every time you face the temptation to use your money wrongly or pursue more money selfishly. That verse is **1 Timothy 6:17-19**: *"Command those who are rich in this present age not to be haughty, nor to trust in uncertain riches* *but in the living God, who gives us richly all things to enjoy. Let them do good, that they may be rich in good works, ready to give, willing to share, storing up for themselves a good foundation for the time to come, that they may lay hold of eternal life."* Amen! God wants you to be rich, but He specifies in what manner: *good works.* He wants you to be rich and abound in good works, for this is what you are created in Christ Jesus to do anyway (**Ephesians 2:10**).

Choose daily to not hoard what you have but to be ready to give it away, willing to share with those who need what you have more than the dust on your shelf does. Store up for the eternal, not the temporal. Remember, you cannot keep these commands from Christ about money and remain the way you are right now. His Word literally transforms your life, disciple. Avoid heaping up riches (**Psalm 39:6**), bragging on your riches (**Psalm 49:6**), and trusting in your riches (**Psalm 52:7; Proverbs 11:28**). In fact, don't set your heart on your money whatsoever (**Psalm 62:10**). If you receive a promotion at work, praise God and then ask Him how you can use the "extra" income for His Kingdom, not to incur more debt and attract more creditors.

Use your memory verse as often as necessary so that you will be mindful to continuously obey the commands of Christ about money. You can do this! If you've never had this mindset, it will be tough. The deeper the root, the harder the pull. Christ is awaiting your obedience. Give your money to Him, and let Him use it for others through you all the days of your remaining life. Assuredly, your reward will be waiting.

THE COMMAND INQUIRED:

What cannot be measured cannot be evaluated. Therefore, it is essential to measure your comprehension of Christ's command in this teaching, or else the devil will snatch away the "seeds" of Scripture sown into your heart (**Matthew 13:19**). To keep this from occurring, write down your answers to the following questions as they correlate with the teaching this week:

In what passage(s) of Scripture do you find Christ's commandment on **money**?

_____

_____

_____

What is the accurate interpretation of **money** you have discovered?

_____

_____

_____

_____

_____

In your own words, what are some real-life examples in Scripture of the proper and improper uses of **money**?

_____

_____

_____

_____

_____

What steps of initiation did you learn to take in order for **money** to not destroy your life?

_____

_____

_____

_____

_____

_____

How will Satan attack you and tempt you to wrongly use **money** in your life?

_____

_____

_____

_____

_____

What memory verse will you use to protect Christ's command regarding **money** and its proper use in your life? Write it out.

_____

_____

_____

_____

_____

TEACHING # 3.6: WORRY

Week 27

This week's objective: To define what worry is and what it does, and to learn the principles necessary to overcome it on a daily basis.

THE COMMAND INTRODUCED:

- **Matthew 6:25-34; Luke 12:22-34** *"Therefore I say to you, do not **worry** about your life, what you will eat or what you will drink; nor about your body, what you will put on. Is not life more than food and the body more than clothing? Look at the birds of the air, for they neither sow nor reap nor gather into barns; yet your heavenly Father feeds them. Are you not of more value than they? Which of you by **worrying** can add one cubit to his stature? So why do you **worry** about clothing? Consider the lilies of the field, how they grow: they neither toil nor spin; and yet I say to you that even Solomon in all his glory was not arrayed like one of these. Now if God so clothes the grass of the field, which today is, and tomorrow is thrown into the oven, will He not much more clothe you, O you of little faith? Therefore do not **worry**, saying, 'What shall we eat?' or 'What shall we drink?' or 'What shall we wear?' For after all these things the Gentiles seek. For your heavenly Father knows that you need all these things. But seek first the kingdom of God and His righteousness, and all these things shall be added to you. Therefore do not **worry** about tomorrow, for tomorrow will **worry** about its own things. Sufficient for the day is its own trouble."*

THE COMMAND INTERPRETED:

Jesus gives one direct command yet multiple reminders to obey His command. Six different times in just nine verses, Jesus refers to the word *worry*. Have you ever heard of that word before? Of course you have, and you have probably practiced it ten times more than you have heard it! The Greek word "worry" (*merimnao*) actually means "to be anxious about something." However, following this Greek word to its source shows us that it comes from *merimna* (distraction), which attaches to the main root word *merizo* (to part; disunite).

Therefore, the reality of Jesus' command is literally understood as not allowing yourself to be divided, disunited, or distracted through your anxieties in life circumstances. This is so important because if faith is a guest, worry doesn't open the door, and if trust is a vehicle, worry doesn't get behind the wheel. Worry is the paralyzing blow to faith and trust in Almighty God. As a disciple, you are commanded to guard yourself from this cycle of living in a continual state of anxiety.

The point that Jesus wants you to learn is easily understood. The issues at hand involve eating, drinking, and clothing (**verse 25**). These are obviously viewed as necessities, not wants, for food and drink sustains us, while clothing is used to cover and warm us. While these are true needs, Christ commands that "*life*" is about the Kingdom of God (**verse 33**), not food, drink, and clothing. So, Jesus reminds you when you're hungry and thirsty to look at the birds of the air (**verse 26**). Also, when you need to be clothed, Jesus reminds you to view the grass and flowers (**verses 28-30**). The command is still on the table (**verse 31**). Faithlessness is the antagonizing enemy against you. If Christ feeds the birds and clothes the grass, which have no redeeming value by Jesus' blood, how much more will God care for you, His child?

Worrying about things in life is unnecessary because your Father God already knows what you need (**verse 32**). Trust Christ for today in full, contented faith, forsaking to entertain worry about what to eat for supper or what you're going to wear tomorrow. Do not lie in bed at night worrying about the deadline for your test, the meeting with your boss, or the court case that you didn't ask for. Leave "*tomorrow*" for the Lord (**verse 34**), and trust Him today.

THE COMMAND ILLUSTRATED:

There are countless Scriptures that take you into the lives of people in a worried state. However, there is one passage in the Bible that not only addresses worry but also puts into perspective what it hurts the most. Turn to **Luke 10:38-42**. Here you see two sisters, Mary and Martha. Both have been at the feet of Jesus, which means they honor Him as Lord and worship Him. The problem is that Martha is trying to clean house because Jesus is coming over. Can you imagine her frenzy? How would you react to Christ coming to your house for a visit?

What is interesting is that Jesus didn't have a problem with Martha cleaning house in preparation for His coming. Rather, the issue at hand is that once Jesus arrived, Martha kept cleaning, working, and preparing. She never stopped. So, when she came to Christ distraught and upset that Mary was sitting at His feet while she was in the kitchen, Jesus humbled her with His reply. That day Martha leaned that worshiping Christ is more important than working for Him. Granted, there is a balance, but be sure not to justify working for Jesus in place of worshiping Him. The greatest lesson of all is that Martha's stress, worry, and anxieties were totally unnecessary. Martha brought that upon herself, because Jesus was not impressed with a clean house. What Jesus wanted was a stress-less, worry-free believer more concerned about hearing His Word than washing dishes! Never forget this example as long as you live.

THE COMMAND INITIATED:

There is probably a part of you that is thinking, "This is much easier said than done." If you are thinking this way, I want you to remember one thing: your life until now has been completely backwards because you have not allowed Jesus Christ and His Word to renew your mind. Do you know what this means? It means your entire response to life has been based upon your own ability and wisdom in a spiritually lost condition. It means Christ has not been sought after. It means you have handled issues by worrying because that's all you have known how to do. But this is not what you see when you surrender your heart to the commands of Jesus (**Ephesians 4:20-21**). When you do, you choose Christ's Word over your unbearable circumstances. You put your faith into action.

Dr. Robb Thompson understands truth because he writes

from a heart that has practiced it. In his book *Give Up Worry Forever*, Dr. Thompson deliberates whether or not Jesus battled worry. Using the scene of the Lord Jesus in the garden before He was crucified (**Luke 22**), Thompson portrays an accurate snapshot of Christ's humanity in light of worry:

> Because Jesus was the Son of God, we think of Him as being a superman without emotions. But **Hebrews 4:15** says that He was *"touched with the feeling of our infirmities."* And when He prayed for God to "remove this cup," there was a reason. He was not being paranoid about being crucified; He had been looking at the certainty of it from before He was even born in human flesh. Now it was right in front of Him. However you want to categorize what Jesus went through emotionally when He prayed on the Mount of Olives that night, it was so hard that He sweat drops of blood. That means He was experiencing the worst stress a human being can experience. There is no doubt that He went through many emotions, and worry was probably one of them! I mean, if you were facing crucifixion, wouldn't you be worried? What made Jesus different from the rest of the human race was that even though He experienced all the things and all the emotions that we experience, He didn't sin. In the end, He didn't hesitate to say to the Father, *"Not My will, but thine, be done."*...Jesus passed the ultimate test, and He didn't go to the cross being worried about anything. The moment He fully accepted God's will for His life, He had peace about it. It was *"for the joy set before Him"* that He endured the cross. And that's the joy He wants us to walk in every day...believers are not called to live a life of worry. We're called to live a life of joy and peace by walking in God's will. There's something safe and secure when you know that you're in God's will. No matter how bad things get or how awful you might feel, you are okay inside because you know you're right where you're supposed to be. And if you're right where God wants you to be, then you have the confidence and faith to believe that He's going to get you through to the victory.[7]

The only way to experience a life in and with Christ that is not hindered by worry is to exercise your faith (**1 John 5:4**). It is within the parameters of the power of faith that you overcome the temptation to worry about what you cannot control. A disciple of Jesus Christ can be identified by a lifestyle of standing firm in the Word of God, believing the Lord over the negativity of any circumstance. Refuse to stay within the vicious grip of worry. Live empowered by your faith!

THE COMMAND INTERROGATED:

The snares of the devil are always clear and open when it comes to worry. How many times have you caught yourself staring into space with random concerns and questions running through your mind? Do you remember how an entire hour or more passed by, and afterwards you realized you accomplished absolutely nothing by worrying? Furthermore, it seems to be a common problem that your heart is more weighed down with grief and stress after worrying than it was before you started.

This is Satan's trap. He used it with Peter when the disciple superseded the law of gravity by walking on water. Peter's faith was in the Christ Who called him, but when he took his eyes off Jesus and focused on his frightening circumstances (**Matthew 14:30**), he sank into the water in his worry. This is the devil's strategy against you. Be very careful not to allow your most negative situations to hurl your sensitive heart into a panic-driven state of worry. It's when your faith is soaring that Satan wants to pluck your wings! Oh, disciple, be on guard. Be self-controlled and alert for his attack on your heart in the midst of your most uninvited circumstances. Whether it is a phone call conveying news of a death, or the unexpected loss of your job, or an unwanted divorce, stay focused on obeying Jesus Christ and His Word. Do not worry; God is in control.

THE COMMAND INDESTRUCTIBLE:

There's good news to share because of your great and awesome heavenly Father. He provides you with a memory verse that will never fail, one that will conquer Satan's attack. That verse of Scripture is **Philippians 4:6-7**: *"Be anxious for nothing, but in everything by prayer and supplication, with thanksgiving, let your requests be made known to God; and the peace of God, which surpasses all understanding, will guard your hearts and minds through Christ Jesus."* What an unmitigated, indestructible word from God to you! It is full of assurance and promise. According to this Scripture, when you find yourself tempted to worry about uncontrollable obstacles, you should stop and begin to pray to the Father. As you pray, don't attack God immediately with, "Here's what's going on in my life." Rather, first begin to praise Him with thanksgiving, acknowledging and confessing to Him all that you are grateful for in your life. Only after that should you bring your requests to Him.

Once you lay all burdens and worries at His throne, He in exchange promises to give you peace (**Isaiah 26:3**), the kind that literally does not make sense in mortal flesh or by psychological explanation. It is supernatural peace, like a spiritual "Band-Aid" for your worry. This peace is powerful, standing as a mighty fortress to guard your heart and mind from the worries of life, all through the Lord Jesus Christ. Dear disciple, it's not the memory verse alone that will help you overcome worry, but the belief and practice of it in every circumstance. Praise God, His Word is fighting for you, so like a good and faithful soldier (**2 Timothy 2:3-4**), you fight with Him and for Him, too.

THE COMMAND INQUIRED:

What cannot be measured cannot be evaluated. Therefore, it is essential to measure your comprehension of Christ's command in this teaching, or else the devil will snatch away the "seeds" of Scripture sown into your heart (**Matthew 13:19**). To keep this from occurring, write down your answers to the following questions as they correlate with the teaching this week:

In what passage(s) of Scripture do you find Christ's commandment on **worry**?

_____

What is the accurate interpretation of **worry** you have discovered?

_____

_____

_____

_____

_____

In your own words, what are some real-life examples in Scripture of **worry**?

_____

_____

_____

_____

_____

What steps of initiation did you learn to take in order for the teaching regarding **worry** to transform your life?

_____

_____

_____

_____

_____

_____

How will Satan attack you with **worry** in your life?

_____

_____

_____

_____

_____

What memory verse will you use to protect Christ's command regarding **worry** in your life? Write it out.

_____

_____

_____

_____

_____

_____

TEACHING # 3.7: CARNAL-MINDEDNESS

Week 28

This week's objective: To identify the selfishness that promotes carnality in your thinking, as well as to learn the process of renewal through developing a mindset like that of Jesus.

THE COMMAND INTRODUCED:

- **Matthew 16:21-23; Mark 8:33** *"From that time Jesus began to show to His disciples that He must go to Jerusalem, and suffer many things from the elders and chief priests and scribes, and be killed, and be raised the third day. Then Peter took Him aside and began to rebuke Him, saying, 'Far be it from You, Lord: this shall not happen to You!' But He turned and said to Peter, 'Get behind Me, Satan! You are an offense to Me, for you are not mindful of the things of God, but the things of men.'"*
- **John 21:20-22** *"Then Peter, turning around, saw the disciple whom Jesus loved following, who also had leaned on His breast at the supper, and said, 'Lord, who is the one who betrays You?' Peter, seeing him, said to Jesus, 'But Lord, what about this man?' Jesus said to him, 'If I will that he remain till I come, what is that to you? You follow Me.'"*

THE COMMAND INTERPRETED:

Both of these commands from the Lord Jesus are not only implicit in their delivery but also practical in their application. Christ exposes carnal-mindedness for what it really is and how it relates to a disciple. From a biblical view, your *"mind"* is a reference to your way of thinking, which directly parallels your attitude about *everything.* While there are many Scriptures that educate you about the depravity of the human mind, Jesus summarizes the entire scope of the issue in these two commands.

The first command (**Matthew 16:21-23; Mark 8:33**) brings to your attention the *combative* mind. To be combative is to stand in stark, disgruntled, stubborn, argumentative contrast to agreement of any nature. A combative mind stays in "fight mode," always ready to both defend its case and justify its cause against anything or anyone that would dare disagree with it. Unfortunately, such a mindset crept its way into the thinking of one of Christ's disciples: Peter. Usually, Peter is seen as an overachiever, a man who jumped when Jesus says to. But here, you are introduced to another side of Peter. As Christ explained to all His disciples that it was time for Him to die on the cross in Jerusalem and resurrect three days later, it was Peter who had a combative response. Unbelievably, he had the audacity to back Jesus in a corner only to confront Him with resistance.

It was in this moment that Jesus responded to Peter in righteous indignation: "*Get behind Me, Satan! You are an offense to Me, for you are not mindful of the things of God, but the things of men.*" Jesus called Peter "*Satan,*" meaning Satan was attacking Peter's mind in an attempt to keep Jesus from going to the cross. Peter's entire combative thinking was identified as an offense to Jesus. The Greek word for "offense" (*skandalon*) means "stumbling block; snare." In fact, our English word "scandal" is derived from this Greek term. The point is that Satan was plotting a scandal against Christ, hoping to use one of His own disciples to "trip Him up" and stop Him from reaching Jerusalem. As a result, Jesus brought to light the root of the problem in Peter's combative mind: "*you are not **mindful** of the things of God, but the things of men.*" Caught and no doubt humiliated, Peter was forced to realize that his mind was claiming its own rights and defending its own selfish agenda—focusing on the things of men, not the will of God. Christ was on a mission to die for the whole world's sins (**John 3:16**), including Peter's, yet Peter was trying to stop Jesus. A disciple must have his mind set upon things above (**Colossians 3:1-4**), things which are holy and pure (**Philippians 4:8**). Our mindful, heartfelt meditation must be pleasing in the sight of God (**Psalm 19:14**). As a disciple, concentrate your mind on Christ and His Word, for His glory, upon His Kingdom. Such thinking will still be combative, but the fight will be against Satan, not the Lord Jesus.

The second command (**John 21:20-22**) focuses your

attention on the *comparative* mind. To be comparative is to be a judge, measuring and evaluating yourself based on a standard that involves something or someone else. Being comparative is to some degree a self-made bridge that connects to vanity and can lead to a judgmental spirit, envy, disunity, and strife. Such a description is not fitting to be named among disciples. However, take a wild guess regarding whom Jesus had to correct because of his comparative mind. The Apostle Peter...again.

After Jesus predicted to Peter how the disciple would die (**John 21:18-19**), Peter responded by asking, "*But Lord, what about this man?*" What man? This other disciple Peter was comparing himself to was John. This was not the first time Jesus had had to rebuke and correct His disciples for comparing themselves to each other (**Mark 9:33-37**). Peter's stumbling block was his comparative mind. Since Jesus told him how he was going to die, he demanded to know how John would die. Jesus' reply is so insightful for you and me today: "*If I will that he remain till I come, what is that to you? You follow Me.*" Now that will humble you and shut your mouth at the same time!

Do you see the point Christ was making to Peter? Jesus was not advocating an escape from death for John (**John 21:23**). Rather, the punchline of the moment is Christ's question: "*What is that to you?*" Jesus was telling Peter, "Mind your own business!" What a lesson a comparative mind needs to heed! As a disciple, do not compare yourself to any other person based upon physique, appearance, clothing, finances, possessions, or spirituality. If you do, Jesus' reply to you will be no different than it was to Peter. Bloom where you are planted! Grow in Christ just as you are. Refuse to be combative and comparative with your way of thinking. Disciple, surrender your entire mindset and attitude to think like the Lord Jesus Christ (**Philippians 2:5**).

THE COMMAND ILLUSTRATED:

What does it look like to have a carnal mind? An applicable yet horrendous example is found in **Matthew 26:14-16, 47-49**. One of Jesus' twelve disciples, Judas Iscariot, betrayed Jesus for thirty pieces of silver, which was in Bible times the price for a common slave. How degrading! Here you see Judas's combative mind, fighting against the will of Christ to be His disciple, as well as his comparative mind, seeking greed over contentment as a disciple. Carnal-mindedness allows sin to run in your mental faculties like a dog off a leash. However, you are responsible to capture your thoughts in obedience to Christ (**2 Corinthians 10:5**). It is not a disheartening sight to find a disciple with a carnal mind; it is only when a disciple does nothing about it that the heart of God is nauseated. Learn from the example of Judas that Satan will treat your mind like a punching bag if you let him. Occupy your thoughts instead through the filtration of Scripture, allowing God's Word to cleanse your thinking and energize holiness and purity into your mind.

THE COMMAND INITIATED:

I heard it said many years ago that an idle mind is the devil's workshop, and there is strong biblical support for such a statement. Do you know why? Simply because if your mind is not disciplined to replace fleshly, carnal thoughts with Scriptural truth, it idles right into the path of destruction. You see, you are what you think (**Proverbs 23:7**). The idea is that you become what you set your mind on. Your obsession translates into mental possession. Someone who has their mind fixed on the works of the flesh (envy, backbiting, hatred, strife, filthy language, jealousies, ungodliness, murder, adultery, etc.) will become what they concentrate on. Likewise, the same is true for those disciples that place their minds under the control of the Holy Spirit, for they become a product of Spirit-controlled thoughts (**Galatians 5:22-23**). This is what it looks like to abandon carnal-mindedness for the mindset of life and peace (**Romans 8:5-11**). Otherwise, our thoughts can become entrapments that shackle us in unnecessary bondage.

T. W. Hunt offers us liberating insight in his book *The Mind of Christ*, so that we can develop victorious patterns in overcoming carnal-mindedness:

> Many believers have unconscious areas of bondage to sin in their lives. So long as sin has control over any area of our mind, we are in bondage in that area. *"Sin shall not be master*

over you" (**Romans 6:14**). Positionally, the Christian is free from bondage to sin. Because of his position, he need not be enslaved to sin. This is not only a matter of fact (our position in Christ) but of responsibility. Practically though, Satan has certain areas in which he works unceasingly on our thought patterns. Usually we are unconscious of our bondage in these areas. No Christian will become free of sin in this life, but we can be free from bondage.[8]

There is no other way to evict carnal-mindedness except through the Word of God. It is the cleansing that our mind and conscience need (**Psalm 119:9**). This is precisely why you are transforming into a disciple: your obedience to the commands of Jesus is transforming who you are and the way you think, all because God's Word is renewing your mind. Praise to the Lord!

THE COMMAND INTERROGATED:

Have you ever used a big yellow sponge to wash a car? When you place it in the bucket of soap, it soaks up so much water that it seems to increase its weight tenfold. Your mind is just like that sponge: it soaks up whatever you allow it to. So, what evils do you feel Satan sets before people since they will "soak up" his wickedness in their minds? A beginning point of his attack is through the television or movies, for your mind absorbs both what you see and what you hear. You see, there is an inward battle raging inside every human being, and that battle is against the law of our mind (**Romans 7:23**), which stands destitute and oppositional without the Spirit of God (**Romans 8:7**). Satan knows exactly how to ensnare your fleshly, carnal mind.

If you are not on guard with a Spirit-controlled mind that is set on the things of God, the enemy will victimize you! One of the greatest ways Satan tempts you to nurture a carnal mindset is through sexual immorality, through a process of thinking, looking, and then acting upon it. This attack has infiltrated the Body of Christ, even among church leaders. Ungodly, sexually explicit, worldly music soaks into the mind, roots in the heart, and commonly appears in the countenance of an individual. Oh, how tragic if the church looks more like the world than the world looks like the church and ultimately like Jesus Christ! Beware of Satan's battle against your mind. He wants to bring you into captivity to the law of sin, which wars against the Spirit of God Who is pulling for you in this fight. Turn the television channel immediately, don't watch a movie you wouldn't watch in Sunday morning worship service, and throw away wicked CDs that poison your mind through minimizing marital failure, encouraging drug abuse, and bragging about premarital sexual intercourse. Disciple, stand strong for Christ against these subtle attacks of Satan. If you seem to stand all by yourself, then praise to the Lamb of God, for Christ will be standing with you when all forsake you (**2 Timothy 4:16-18**).

THE COMMAND INDESTRUCTIBLE:

Hallelujah to the Lord Jesus, for His Word prevails over any attack of the devil. The memory verse of Scripture for you to fight Satan's attempts to subject you to a carnal mind is found in **2 Corinthians 4:16**: "*Therefore we do not lose heart. Even though our outward man is perishing, yet the inward man is being renewed day by day.*" The distinction here is between the outward and inward man. Your outward man is the fleshly, carnal side of you; your inward man is the Spirit-led, Christ-controlled part of you. The key to dwell on here is the inward man, the person you are now "in" Christ (**2 Corinthians 5:17**), in which Jesus is sanctifying you through a daily maturing process to imitate Him more in your mindset, attitudes, and actions. Since you have crucified your outward man (**Galatians 5:24**), you give way to the new, inward man. Day by day, you are "renewed" in Christ, looking more like Him all the time in your lifestyle and speech. This renewing is through the Word of God (**Colossians 3:10; Ephesians 4:22-24**), which transforms you into a replica of the Lord Jesus in all facets of life. Day by day, examine and evaluate yourself. If your fleshly desires are raging against you, quote your memory verse in faith and for reminder. If Satan is using your friends to invite you back to an old way of life, quote your memory verse in faith and watch them get saved or get lost; Christ will send you new friends. Whatever you do, daily apply yourself to the Scriptures for the renewing of your mind. This is your only hope to become anything like the Christ Who has saved you. Give up the carnal mind, and give way to the mind of Christ.

THE COMMAND INQUIRED:

What cannot be measured cannot be evaluated. Therefore, it is essential to measure your comprehension of Christ's command in this teaching, or else the devil will snatch away the "seeds" of Scripture sown into your heart (**Matthew 13:19**). To keep this from occurring, write down your answers to the following questions as they correlate with the teaching this week:

In what passage(s) of Scripture do you find Christ's commandment on **carnal-mindedness**?

_____

_____

_____

What is the accurate interpretation of **carnal-mindedness** you have discovered?

_____

_____

_____

_____

_____

In your own words, what are some real-life examples in Scripture of **carnal-mindedness**?

_____

_____

_____

_____

_____

_____

What steps of initiation did you learn to take in order for the teaching regarding **carnal-mindedness** to transform your life?

_____

_____

_____

_____

_____

How will Satan attack you with **carnal-mindedness** in your life?

_____

_____

_____

_____

_____

What memory verse will you use to protect Christ's command regarding **carnal-mindedness** in your life? Write it out.

_____

CHAPTER 4: THE DISCIPLE'S TEST IS ISSUED

TEACHING # 3.8: FEAR

Week 29

This week's objective: To gain the right definition of fear from Jesus' perspective, as well as to learn exactly how to keep it from taking root in your heart.

THE COMMAND INTRODUCED:

- **Matthew 10:27-31; Luke 12:4-7** *"Whatever I tell you in the dark, speak in the light; and what you hear in the ear, preach on the housetops. And do not fear those who kill the body but cannot kill the soul. But rather fear Him who is able to destroy both body and soul in hell. Are not two sparrows sold for a copper coin? And not one of them falls to the ground apart from your Father's will. But the very hairs of your head are all numbered. Do not fear therefore; you are of more value than many sparrows."*
- **Matthew 14:26-31; Mark 6:50; John 6:20** *"And when the disciples saw Him walking on the sea, they were troubled, saying, 'It is a ghost!' And they cried out for fear. But immediately Jesus spoke to them, saying, 'Be of good cheer! It is I; do not be afraid.' And Peter answered Him and said, 'Lord, if it is You, command me to come to You on the water.' So He said, 'Come.' And when Peter had come down out of the boat, he walked on the water to go to Jesus. But when he saw that the wind was boisterous, he was afraid; and beginning to sink he cried out, saying, 'Lord, save me!' And immediately Jesus stretched out His hand and caught him, and said to him, 'O you of little faith, why did you doubt?'"*
- **John 14:27** *"Peace I leave with you, My peace I give to you; not as the world gives do I give to you. Let not your heart be troubled, neither let it be afraid."*

THE COMMAND INTERPRETED:

All of Jesus' commands on the subject of fear are direct and to the point. Haven't you ever been afraid of something or someone? It is a terrible, emotional attack. It is like being held prisoner and searching frantically for the keys to release yourself from fear's bondage. The Lord Jesus knows exactly how you and I are plagued by the vicious grip of fear, yet He wants us to know there is a right response to it.

The first command (**Matthew 10:27-31; Luke 12:4-7**) highlights the *voice* to silence fear. Jesus' talk with His disciples about fear was preceded by his cautions about their coming persecution from unbelievers. This explains why Christ discussed such a subject, for indeed they were afraid of what they had not yet encountered. This is where fear makes its mark in your life: causing you to panic about something that has the potential of occurring, yet is not a reality at the time. In the context of this command, Jesus wants you as His disciple to not be afraid to speak up for Him publicly, regardless of the ramifications. What has been spoken in the "*dark*" or in the "*ear*" reflects a type of privacy, such as quiet time with Christ in the secret place of His Presence (**Matthew 6:4, 6, 18**). To go from the dark to the "*light*" and from the ear to the "*housetops*" is to transition from quiet time with Christ to bold proclamation of Christ.

It is while you are proclaiming the Lord Jesus to people you encounter daily that you are to prepare for persecution (**2 Timothy 3:12**). Jesus commands, "*Do not fear.*" The Greek word Christ uses for *fear* (*phobeo*, derived from *phobos*) means "alarmed or frightened." This kind of fear has the idea of being terrified by something, to the point of being controlled by a seemingly hopeless situation. This is where the voice to silence fear is understood—it is the very Word of Jesus, resonating within us. It's this voice that strengthened the disciples. Even though their lives were at risk because of persecution, Christ commands them in this passage to give a reverential fear only to Almighty God, Who can destroy the body and the soul in hell, whereas persecutors can only destroy the body. God alone is just; evil never gets past Him. He vindicates the righteous!

To exemplify just how much He cares for you in the midst of any fear, Christ uses an analogy of sparrows. Interestingly, something so invaluable and inexpensive is treated so well by the Father. If God takes such good care of the sparrow, will He not take care of you? Since the Father knows the number of hairs on your head, He knows all about you, including your fears. You are much more valuable than a sparrow, so do not fear. The point here is that God values you, for He purchased you with the blood of His Son, Jesus Christ, which was so expensive that only death sufficed the payment. That's how much you're worth to the Lord. Fear Him, not man.

The second command (**Matthew 14:26-31; Mark 6:50; John 6:20**) highlights the *volume* of fear. Using the same Greek word as in the first command, Jesus built this example of fear upon a very real-life illustration: stormy water. Early one evening, Jesus sent the disciples by themselves across the sea while He ministered to the multitudes. Within a short time, a storm developed. Hours into the storm, Jesus in His glory began walking on the water to rescue His disciples from the storm.

Here you can see the volume of fear—not necessarily in the water but in the number of lessons that took place on it. In the middle of their storm, the disciples saw Jesus coming for their rescue, and insultingly they called Him a ghost, not the Savior. Even after Jesus spoke out boldly to reassure them, Peter remained uncertain that the figure he saw truly was Jesus. So, Peter moved from insulting Christ to doubting Christ with the phrase *"if it is You."* Patient with Peter even in his fear, Jesus called the disciple to Himself. Miraculously, in the midst of the storm, Peter walked on water to Jesus. Why? Because he trusted the Word of God (*"Come"*) instead of nursing his fear of the storm.

However, when Peter took his eyes off Christ and looked around at the storm, he began to sink into the choppy waters and cried out to Jesus again! Notice this: when did Peter begin to become fearful again? Before or after he sank? Before. You see, it was not the actual sinking that frightened Peter; it was the wind and the waves that pointed to his sinking. Again, fear masks itself in possibilities, not realities! Just because the wind was blowing and the waves were crashing did not mean Peter had to sink, because His eyes were on Jesus. But when His eyes left Christ, they fixed themselves on the circumstances surrounding him, leaving him fearful and sinking. Do you see the volume of lessons that fear teaches through Peter's failure? Fear will always result in doubt, and doubt will always be nothing more than an excuse to neglect faith.

Do not allow fear to take your eyes off Jesus. Focus, don't flounder.

The third command (**John 14:27**) highlights the *victory* over fear. In context here, Jesus was nearing His departure through His death and Resurrection. He not only pointed to the coming of the Holy Spirit to dwell within His disciples but also emphasized His peace to give to them. Christ recognized that without His physical Presence, fear would threaten the hearts of the faithful eleven. They would need something that they could not get in the world—a divine, supernatural transfer. And it was Christ's personal peace that met the need.

The victory over fear in this command is that Christ could not give away such a living, perpetual peace if He Himself had not risen again. Therefore, this peace that eradicates fear hinges upon Christ's Resurrection, which is the victory for all believers. Since Christ lives, we too will live for eternity. In addition to the victory of Christ rising from the dead, there is also victory in the offer of Christ's peace. To help you appreciate it, Jesus exhorted you to "*not be afraid*." The Greek word "afraid" (*deiliao*) means "timidity." It is not a horrific, terrorizing fear, as with the first two commands, but rather a discouraged, depressed type of fear. Christ's peace is your protection from timidly shying away from confidence in Him and proclamation of His gospel. You are a disciple, with the freely bestowed, victorious peace of Jesus Christ. Don't forget it.

THE COMMAND ILLUSTRATED:

A fine example of reverential fear is found in **Hebrews 11:27**. When Moses heard God speak from the burning bush (**Exodus 3**), the mission was on. God had a plan for Moses and the other people of His covenant (Israel). Nothing would stop God's plan regardless of how impossible things seemed. Moses believed and trusted God, and according to this verse in Hebrews, Moses did not "*fear*" the wrath of the king because something else motivated him. What was it? Money? Fame? Property? No, it was simple: he feared God more than he feared the wrath of Pharaoh, the king. The number-one driving force in Moses' heart was his endurance to accomplish God's will and plan, as if God were right in front of him. Now that's faith!

As a disciple, follow Moses' example. Fear and faith do not live together! There's not enough room in your heart for both. You must cling with a holy stubbornness to your faith in Who God is and what He commands. Be bullheaded about your obedience to Christ. Do not allow anything or anyone else to distract you into wavering from His commands. Regardless of the circumstance and its seeming impossibilities, surrender yourself to trust God for His will, His results, and His protection. Fear is against your nature as a disciple and does not deserve to nest in your heart. Give glory to God through a life of obedience that constantly chooses faith and peace over fear.

THE COMMAND INITIATED:

What does it look like to put fear out of business? It is useless to know the commands of Christ about fear without the practice of them. As you initiate obedience to Jesus' commands, you can harness your fear with the muzzle of faith. Gary Whetstone has studied the subject of fear devotedly and has wonderful comments to offer you as a disciple of Christ. In his book *Make Fear Bow*, Whetstone gives a glimpse into the spirit of fear as it relates to sensory stimuli that you and I face daily:

> Biologically, when a stimulus engages any of our senses—sight, hearing, smell, taste, or touch—they react. When one or more of them react to something, it can affect us emotionally, creating fear and inhibitions. Because we are human, every one of us experiences sensory responses. Our senses continually react to natural information, and we often anticipate the worst. If our senses react with doubt or uncertainty, we can become fearful. Unfortunately, most of us have not considered why we experience fears that arise from our senses. In any situation in which your senses react or receive information, you must consider how pessimistic your thoughts and expectations are about what you encounter...For example, if you wake up in the middle of the night and smell smoke, what happens? Does instant panic and fear hit? Are you convinced your house is burning

down?...If you eat something that tastes odd, do you instantly suspect food poisoning?...If your heart palpitates or you have indigestion, do you panic, thinking it is clearly a heart attack? If you feel a small lump under your skin, are you convinced it is the initial stages or cancer, from which your great-grandmother died?...Are you continually affected negatively by what you see, hear, smell, taste, or feel? Do you dread certain sights, sounds, smells, tastes, or touches? When your senses repeatedly react in this manner, you life is riddled with tension. Whatever you encounter, you conclude that the worst-possible scenario is unfolding. If this describes your life, you are living in bondage to fear. Each time you envision the worst because your senses react spontaneously to natural information, fear is the driving force. Your sensory reactions are inducing fear and limiting you.[9]

Knowledge increases sorrow (**Ecclesiastes 1:18**). Can you see, especially after Whetstone's summary, how paralyzing fear can be through the avenue of knowledge? Yes, it is necessary to be informed about anything that is harmful, but information should be only to protect you, never to confine you. Learn this lesson: you become what you think (**Proverbs 23:7**). Regardless of the stimulating affects that come from bad news or sudden tragedy, faith is your defensive shield. Choose faith, not fear. Do not allow yourself to gravitate to the worst thought or worry in your mind.

It's one thing to face the reality of a tragic car accident, yet it is quite another to deal with the potential injuries from that accident. The difference is in what is fact and final versus what is potential and possible. Do not kill someone with your fear if they haven't died! Granted, no matter what, fear will jump all over you in any negative circumstance, but it is what you do with that fear that matters to Christ. You are to exercise your faith and overcome the situation (**1 John 5:4**). This is not a denial of fear's reality but a statement that your faith is the greater force in spite of it.

THE COMMAND INTERROGATED:

If fear were a college degree, Satan would have an exponential number of doctorates. He has mastered the way in which he attacks you—not with fear directly, but with circumstances that arouse it within you. You see, fear is of the fleshly nature, only existing after Adam and Eve sinned (**Genesis 3:9**), not before. You and I were not created to be *in* fear, but only *to* fear God. Satan has brought about a perversion of your fear of God through giving you situations that turn your heart away from its focus on your Creator. This is the devil's agenda—his priority! If you lose your fear of God, not intentionally but ignorantly, you settle for a miserable, defeated Christian life. Your life as a disciple will move from the palace of faith to a prison of fear.

Beware of this subtle plot from Satan in your life. Examine and guard yourself daily. Take all things—all phone calls, all mail, and all relationships—into account as you remember Satan's hidden assassinations that could be embedded against you through these circumstances. Don't be foolish; he's after you. This is not a game of circumstance; it's your life. And if you fail to be ready and steadfast, Jesus Christ and His gospel suffer for your disobedience. Arm yourself with Scripture, and do not allow yourself to be victimized.

THE COMMAND INDESTRUCTIBLE:

No one—no devil, no circumstance, no possibility—can destroy the truth of God's Word. Oh, disciple, if you didn't have the Scriptures to fight against Satan's attacks, you would be a weak, wounded soldier of Christ with no vitality to stand. Thank God, such is not the case for the Body of Christ! You are wonderfully equipped with Scriptures to stand with. Perhaps the greatest verse in the Bible on the subject of fear is the reminder in **2 Timothy 1:7**: *"For God has not given us a spirit of fear, but of power, and of love, and of a sound mind."* This is your memory verse to fight with daily as any fear rises against you. You see, "fear" is a spirit, an attack from Satan against you, a demonic assault through thoughts and circumstances to destroy your faith. God does not give this to you. Rather, He gives you *power* (**Acts 1:8**), *love* (**1 John 4:18**), and a *sound mind* (**2 Corinthians 10:4-5**), all of which are used to keep fear from taking root in your life.

Hallelujah! The beauty of this is that God does not leave you and me to suffer relentless attacks from a spirit of fear. He gives and gives and gives. We are ever supplied with the power to overcome fear, the love to cast it out, and a sound mind to bar it from persuading our thoughts. All of this is possible only because you are a child of God. Raise your hands and shout in victory, for fear has no business holding you captive because the Lord Jesus Christ has set you free.

THE COMMAND INQUIRED:

What cannot be measured cannot be evaluated. Therefore, it is essential to measure your comprehension of Christ's command in this teaching, or else the devil will snatch away the "seeds" of Scripture sown into your heart (**Matthew 13:19**). To keep this from occurring, write down your answers to the following questions as they correlate with the teaching this week:

In what passage(s) of Scripture do you find Christ's commandment on **fear**?

_____

_____

_____

What is the accurate interpretation of **fear** you have discovered?

_____

_____

_____

_____

_____

_____

In your own words, what are some real-life examples in Scripture of **fear**?

_____

_____

_____

_____

_____

What steps of initiation did you learn to take to stop **fear** from destroying your life?

_____

_____

_____

_____

_____

How will Satan attack you to promote **fear** in your life?

_____

_____

_____

_____

_____

_____

What memory verse will you use to protect Christ's command of battling **fear** in your life? Write it out.

_____

_____

_____

_____

_____

_____

TEACHING # 3.9: HYPOCRISY

Week 30

This week's objective: To unveil the truth behind hypocrisy, as well as to learn how Christ expects a disciple to conquer it.

THE COMMAND INTRODUCED:

- **Luke 12:1-2** *"In the meantime, when an innumerable multitude of people had gathered together, so that they trampled one another, He began to say to His disciples first of all, 'Beware of the leaven of the Pharisees, which is hypocrisy. For there is nothing covered that will not be revealed, nor hidden that will not be known.'"*

THE COMMAND INTERPRETED:

This is a direct command from Jesus, signifying to His disciples that hypocrisy was not to be tolerated. It is interesting to note that Christ did not begin teaching on this subject until there was *"an innumerable multitude,"* as if to reach as many hearts as possible with His truth while the masses aggressively gathered. It was at this point that Jesus began to teach, focusing on His disciples first.

Once Jesus had both the disciples and the multitudes in position, He began to expound on the subject of His teaching: *hypocrisy.* The Greek word for "hypocrisy" (*hupokrisis*) means "acting under a mask." This was a common word used in Greek theater to label actors in dramas and other presentations, such as storytelling and comedy. Jesus addressed as His target group the Pharisees, a group of religious leaders that were "acting" out their devotion to God. They were fake, insincere, and deceitful. In fact, Jesus despised their hypocrisy so much that He scolded them at length with righteous indignation (**Matthew 23:1-33**). Christ's command offers this implied plea to His disciples: "Do not fake a relationship with Me. Serve Me, love Me, obey Me, but don't humiliate Me with a superficial, pretend-based, half-committed lifestyle." Christ wants devotion, not an act!

To better explain how hypocrisy penetrates a Christian's life, Jesus used the illustration of *leaven*, a type of yeast that makes bread rise. By process, leaven actually creates air pockets in the dough, evenly distributed throughout the bread. This means that leaven has the ability to spread, thus affecting the entire loaf, not merely a portion of it. Do you see the point Jesus was trying to make? Leaven is a picture of sin in your life.

As His disciple, Christ forbids you to allow "little sins" in your life, for this is hypocrisy. A little sin will spread and ultimately affect you to the degree that your Christian life is a stumbling block to lost people more than it is a stepping stone toward Christ. The warning from Jesus needs no further explanation. He clearly identifies that your "every work" is under examination, for nothing covered or hidden will go unnoticed by the eyes of God. Everything (not sins, but works) will be judged in righteousness by the Righteous Savior one day (**1 Corinthians 3:11-15; 2 Corinthians 5:9-11**). Therefore, obey this command. Repentance is the filter that keeps leaven (sin) from contaminating your life as a disciple. Repent! Be holy as Christ is holy. Live for Him with a clean, committed conscience.

THE COMMAND ILLUSTRATED:

Hypocrisy is by no means a new word in Christian vocabulary. It seems to be that it is mostly exhibited by those who model a seemingly devoted Christian life but have a dark side that reflects a bondage to secret sin. It is this type of double standard that sickens our Lord Jesus (**Revelation 3:15-16**). Sometimes, the godliest of men and women have fallen into Satan's traps because they were weak at the moment and failed to protect themselves with God's armor (**Ephesians 6:10-17**). From a lost man's vantage point, such obvious examples of apostasy validate his mounting excuses to not commit himself to Christ. He says in his heart, "Why should I come to Christ? That Christian doesn't live or talk any differently than I do. Therefore, I will keep living the way I want to and doing what I want to do. Christianity is not for me." Sadly, such a lost man fails to notice the thousands of Christians who *do* live for Christ blamelessly.

Such a committed life was the case for the apostles, except for one particular time when Peter became weak. You find this example of his hypocrisy in **Galatians 2:11-13**. In sum, when Peter came to Antioch, he ate with the Gentiles, which culturally was empowering to the witness of the anti-racist gospel of Christ. But, when the Apostle James arrived with some Jewish friends, Peter *"separated himself"* from the Gentiles because of fear of what his Jewish comrades would say—like a teenager eating with people at a lunch table until his "cooler" friends show up. Likewise, all the Christian Jews joined Peter in his abandonment of the Gentiles, as well as one of the godliest men of them all, Barnabas.

The Apostle Paul wrote the letter to the Galatians to lovingly rebuke Peter for his hypocrisy, in hopes that they would learn to not follow his example. Pay special attention to one phrase: *"carried away."* Again, like leaven, that's what sin does: it carries you away to a place you later regret going, to words you later regret uttering, and to thoughts you later regret thinking. Such is hypocrisy. It is a cursed bondage that webs the believer. It started with Peter, and like leaven, it "spread" to the Jews and finished the whole loaf off with Barnabas. What a lesson: a little leaven (sin) in your life not only affects you but also spreads to other believers, thus causing them to stumble. Flee hypocrisy! Oh, disciple, live surrendered and clean daily before the Lord Jesus Christ.

THE COMMAND INITIATED:

What does a life without hypocrisy look like? Well, it seems the stereotype that is common in many circles of thought is that no hypocrisy means no sin. This is entirely false and is a denial of the reality of our sin nature as it fights against the indwelling Spirit's nature (**Galatians 5:16**). So, what then is the answer? If a lack of hypocrisy does not mean sinlessness, what does it mean?

Tod Bolsinger has a marvelous explanation from Scripture as to what the underlying meaning of hypocrisy is. In his book *Showtime*, Bolsinger liberates many believers who have been held captive by the idea that being perfect is the only outlet from hypocrisy. Here's what he has to say:

> I believe this is a great opportunity for the church, if we have effective faith. Almost fifty years ago, Martin Lloyd-Jones wrote words that are even more accurate today: "If Christianity is what it claims to be, then it should be producing a type and order of life which is quite exceptional. If, therefore, we are to meet the challenge of the modern world we must be living the Christian life; and the question arises how we are to do so." This is exactly the question that **2 Peter** aims to address. The first step for living an effective Christian life is to begin being transformed because we have been saved, not in order to be saved. This is why after recounting the power and promises available to believers so that they might *"escape from the corruption that is in the world,"* Peter charges us to *"make every effort to support your faith with goodness."* Now, if we translate this passage more literally, it reads, *"Express your faith with virtue."* So the first lesson we need to learn if our lives are going to speak to people effectively and make a difference in the real world can be summarized by a concise charge: faith for the real world produces virtue, so be good and live better...Now, before we go any further, a word of caution is in order. When we talk about being good, we are not encouraging either perfectionism or legalism. Both are distortions of biblical virtue. When the Bible speaks of being virtuous, it is not exhorting people to live without flaw or to strictly adhere to a list of rules. But too often in the church today, those are the messages being taught. The result is that far too many of us have struggled far too much with trying to be perfect; and far too many of us have expressed self-righteousness, not virtue. But neither the word nor the implication in the passage is about achieving perfection or keeping rules. Instead, in **verse 8**, Peter sums up the entire list by saying, *"If these things are yours and are increasing among you, they keep you from being ineffective and unfruitful."* (NRSV). He does not challenge us with perfectionism or rule-keeping but instead exhorts us to become people of a character that requires the steady, slow ripening of faith. Virtue requires

not perfection but maturity. Christian virtue is about being declared good and then consequently growing in goodness each day.[10]

Praise the Lord for this clarification! Trying to be perfect is just as hypocritical as sheer disobedience, for perfectionism is not maturity. Of course, this is by no means an excuse to sin, for God's grace is not to be polluted with such thinking (**Romans 6:1-2**). Rather, it is the Scriptural proof that you need room to grow in Christ, which means God's grace through conformity to and transformation by His Word will prove to sift away the chaff from your life daily.

Do you see now how this is a process and not a destination? When a baby is born, it has not arrived at maturity because *time* for development is necessary. In the same manner, when you are "born again," you also do not arrive instantly but go through a process of renewing your mind (**Ephesians 4:23-24**) as you feed on the Word (**1 Peter 2:2**). The inner man is the "new creation" (**2 Corinthians 5:17**) inside you, whom the Spirit of God empowers. Daily, through your obedience to Scripture, you are formed more and more into Christlikeness (**Galatians 4:19**). What a glorious process!

THE COMMAND INTERROGATED:

Satan is to hypocrisy what water is to a glass: he is its volume. You have probably heard the phrase before from unbelievers: "I'm not going to that church. It's full of hypocrites." Why is that such a common phrase among lost people? It obviously has something to do with a failure on behalf of disciples. In defense of an unbeliever making such statements, many professing Christians claim a title without the "deed" (**James 2:17, 26**). Dead faith results in a stinking lifestyle. The devil loves to place every obstacle imaginable before you in hopes of enticing you. And, if you bite his hook, he'll reel you in and display your hypocrisy in front of as many unbelievers as possible. The result? More excuse for them to stay dead in their sins, hell-bound without the Savior. How tragic is this?

Dear disciple, *"to him who knows to do good and does not do it, to him it is sin*" (**James 4:17**). As Christ's disciple, you are accountable for and entrusted with what you *know* to be His commands. Therefore, you are expected to obey what you know, and if you do not, you enter into hypocrisy. Beware of Satan's little "leaven-like" tricks to distract you from your obedience to Jesus. Be on guard, steadfast and watching diligently. Your standard is God's Word, and anything that violates it or causes you to compromise it is potential for hypocrisy. Again I say, beware.

THE COMMAND INDESTRUCTIBLE:

Since hypocrisy is always just a decision away, its nearness is frightening. God's holy, indestructible Word is your only hope to overcome and conquer hypocrisy. There is a Scripture that serves more as a reminder to remain alert than as an encouragement. It is found in **Job 8:13-14**, and this is your memory verse to prevail with in times of attack: "*So are the paths of all who forget God; And the hope of the hypocrite shall perish, whose confidence shall be cut off, and whose trust is a spider's web.*" Ouch. Remember, though, the caution is meant to arm you, not discourage you.

Hypocrisy is interpreted here as forgetting God. This makes sense, for if you disobey, you intentionally "forget" what you know you should do in order to do what you want to do. Consequently, your hope and confidence are taken away, leaving your trust in a frustrated state like a tangled spider's web. So, the application is this: cling to Christ in obedience so that you will not forget His Word. You can do this! In every decision you make, keep Scripture at the forefront. Be very sensitive to the reality of Satan's desire to destroy you and entangle you with his snares, leading you into hypocrisy. Oh, dear disciple, your obedience is the key. Just obey. Just choose to follow Christ and keep His commands. Cultivate your faith, and Christ will produce in you and through you a life of praise to the Father. Whatever you do, avoid choices that lead to hypocrisy, and give God the glory (**1 Corinthians 1:31**).

THE COMMAND INQUIRED:

What cannot be measured cannot be evaluated. Therefore, it

is essential to measure your comprehension of Christ's command in this teaching, or else the devil will snatch away the "seeds" of Scripture sown into your heart (**Matthew 13:19**). To keep this from occurring, write down your answers to the following questions as they correlate with the teaching this week:

In what passage(s) of Scripture do you find Christ's commandment on **hypocrisy**?

_____

_____

_____

What is the accurate interpretation of **hypocrisy** you have discovered?

_____

_____

_____

_____

_____

In your own words, what are some real-life examples in Scripture of **hypocrisy**?

_____

_____

_____

_____

_____

What steps of initiation did you learn to take to keep **hypocrisy** from destroying your life?

_____

_____

_____

_____

_____

How will Satan attack you to promote **hypocrisy** in your life?

_____

_____

_____

_____

_____

What memory verse will you use to protect Christ's command against **hypocrisy** in your life? Write it out.

_____

_____

_____

TEACHING # 3.10: SELF-RIGHTEOUSNESS

Week 31

This week's objective: To expose the malicious components of self-righteousness as well as to learn the discipline necessary to avoid such spiritual egotism.

THE COMMAND INTRODUCED:

- **Matthew 23:1-7; Mark 12:38-40; Luke 20:45-47** *"Then Jesus spoke to the multitudes and to His disciples, saying, 'The scribes and the Pharisees sit in Moses' seat. Therefore whatever they tell you to observe, that observe and do, but do not do according to their works; for they say, and do not do. For they bind heavy burdens, hard to bear, and lay them on men's shoulders; but they themselves will not move them with one of their fingers. But all their works they do to be seen by men. They make their phylacteries broad and enlarge the borders of the garments. They love the best places at feasts, the best seats in the synagogues, greetings in the marketplaces, and to be called by men, 'Rabbi, Rabbi.'"*
- **Matthew 5:20** *"For I say to you, that unless your righteousness exceeds the righteousness of the scribes and Pharisees, you will by no means enter the kingdom of heaven."*

THE COMMAND INTERPRETED:

Jesus' commands against self-righteousness are mixed in format, being both implicit and direct. However, His intent is clear: He did not want His disciples to become corrupted by the practices of the scribes and Pharisees. By definition, what does it mean to be self-righteous? To put it simply, it refers to a lifestyle of idolizing your achievements and elevating your ego, all while covering your heart in a spiritual garment of pride. When someone is self-righteous, they view their own goodness as valuable and attempt to offer it to God. They insist on a lifestyle that boasts itself independent of God's grace, thus insulting Him.

Self-righteous people view their depravity through the lens of their humanity, not the Scriptures. They believe their accomplishments in the name of spirituality are "good enough," and they see no need for God's imputed righteousness (**Romans 4:23-25**) because they are persuaded their righteousness is sufficient, when in fact it is not (**Isaiah 64:6**). To be self-righteous is to be in relationship with yourself, not Jesus Christ. It is this atrocity that Jesus wants His disciples to zealously avoid. His commands clearly convey such conviction.

The first command Jesus gave (**Matthew 23:1-7; Mark 12:38-40; Luke 20:45-47**) is direct. He began by addressing Moses' seat, a reference to the Law of Moses or Scripture. This was God's Word; thus, regardless of who spoke it, the disciples were to obey it. By obeying the commands of Moses, they were obeying God, not the Pharisees who delivered those commands. The command against self-righteousness is birthed here. Jesus wanted His disciples to do what the Pharisees *said*, insofar as it related to Moses, but not what the Pharisees *did*, for they twisted the Law of Moses to form their own religious standard. This was their root of self-righteousness! The Pharisees would load people down with legalistic burdens but never use *"one of their fingers"* to practice what they commanded.

In order to turn their spirituality into a performance, they would *"broaden their phylacteries and enlarge the borders of their garments."* These phylacteries were little scrolls of paper inscribed with four prestigious parts of the Law and bound in leather (**Exodus 13:2-11; 13:11-16; Deut. 6:4-9; 11:13-21**). These scrolls were positioned on the Pharisees' foreheads and left arms. So, by broadening these phylacteries, the Pharisees gained more attention for themselves and gave people an impression of overt zeal for the Law.

The same effect was achieved by the enlarging of their garments. God had ordained the Jewish people to hem their clothing with borders or fringes (**Numbers 15:38**). This was to identify Israel as a peculiar, sanctified, distinguished nation among other pagan nations. To further enlarge these fringes would only attract attention to oneself, which is what the Pharisees loved. In fact, with such noticeable evidences of religiosity, the Pharisees were sure to place themselves in as many public gatherings as possible. Their self-righteous behavior translated into arrogant selfishness in that they maneuvered their way to the *"best"* seats to be noticed by men. They loved the attention, flocking to the *"greetings"* of men and absorbing the title *"Rabbi, Rabbi,"* for they loved to hear their names called.

The scribes and Pharisees were so self-indulged in their own pit of religious affirmation that anyone attempting to steal their attention would be considered an immediate enemy. It is no surprise, then, that our Lord Jesus was hated by them all. This is the self-righteous behavior that Christ does not want you to emulate. Obey the Scriptures as they are; don't twist them to promote exalted spirituality. Align yourself with a childlike observance of Scripture rather than exempting yourself from certain teachings. Draw attention to Christ, not yourself. Prefer others before yourself, instead of selfishly gravitating to the "best" all the time. Fill men's ears with a testimony of Christ, rather than have men tickle your own ears with your titles of conceitedness. You are a disciple, not a Pharisee. You are a contributor, not a consumer.

The second command (**Matthew 5:20**) Jesus gave is implicit, and for better understanding, it is important to take into consideration one important cultural reality. In the large audience, everyone surely froze when He issued this implicit command. Do you know why? It is because, in their minds, no one was more spiritual than the scribes and the Pharisees. So, as you can imagine, everyone listening to Jesus probably thought, "I'll never make it into the Kingdom of God. I'm doomed." Such teaching in effect stirred the people up to one realization: their righteousness was not sufficient.

This explains the interpretation. You and I must have a righteousness that exceeds that of the scribes and Pharisees. Where do we get this righteousness? From Jesus Christ (**Romans 4:24-25**). Praise God! After gaining the understanding of the first command, now you can see how eye-opening this second command is. Do you see it? Do you get it? The scribes and the Pharisees have a *"righteousness"* that originates through the flesh, which is *self*, making this "self"-righteousness. However, the righteousness that comes from Jesus Christ originates from sinlessness (**Hebrews 4:15**), which is perfection, making it "imputed" righteousness. This is salvation.

When you repent in faith and turn to the Lord Jesus Christ, He saves you and imputes to you (covers you with) His righteousness, which the Father accepted the day Jesus rose from the dead.

Therefore, the command of Jesus is to continuously celebrate that your righteousness has vanished and Christ's righteousness stands. It is a rejoicing over an undeserved divine exchange! It is a command to die to your own efforts of righteousness and merits of credibility. You must willingly admit to God, "I have nothing to boast of. I am empty. I am sinful. I receive with thanksgiving and praise Your righteousness, Father. I am complete through Your redemption. I am saved and made the righteousness of God in Christ."

THE COMMAND ILLUSTRATED:

The best example in the Bible on self-righteousness is found in **Luke 18:9-14**. This passage is used to teach the principle of humility as well as the context of the self-righteous person. This entire subject has been exclusively limited to that of Pharisees, so it is no surprise to find Jesus using them once again as examples.

In this parable, Jesus' purpose is clear: to humble the righteous and to exalt the humble. The problem with the Pharisee in this passage was found in his decision to trust in himself and judge others who were not like him. Do you notice how many times the Pharisee uses the pronoun *"I"* when praying, as if trying to impress God? On the contrary, the tax collector had nothing to boast of. He perceived his depraved, sinful condition, whereas the Pharisee was blinded to his because of his self-justification. Well, according to Jesus, who was justified? The tax collector.

The lesson is clear: don't step on others to build yourself up. This example is priceless! Humility is essential to protect you from pride. If you become prideful, you are promised to fall into destruction (**Proverbs 16:18**). Whatever you must do, live daily with a wonder that God has been merciful to you, a sinner. If you lose sight of the appreciation that Christ has saved you, self-righteous behaviors will begin to creep into your walk with Christ. Such a relationship with Him is a stench that He despises. Walk in humility. Love in humility. Serve God, ever mindful that you are

His, not by your merit, but because of His mercy. Amen.

THE COMMAND INITIATED:

By now, you probably have a strong grip on what it takes to avoid a self-righteous attitude. But the real issue at hand is this: do you have some behaviors and attitudes that are self-righteous? If so, it is imperative to learn how to repent of those and let Christ transform you into a humble servant that loves people more than you talk about them.

In his book *12 Steps for the Recovering Pharisee (Like Me)*, John Fischer understands how the devastation of self-righteousness has poisoned the hearts of many people. Fischer sets a goal for the unmasking of hypocritical, self-righteous people, in hopes that you will see the cultural, traditional standard to which "righteousness" has been lowered:

> Sometimes I wonder if we want our spiritual leaders to be perfect so we don't have to be. As long as we believe somebody's perfect, we can go on perpetuating the myth that perfection is possible and keep on shrouding our own sin safely behind the lie of the "almost." We are *almost* there. We have *almost* arrived. We are *almost* holy...That's why when leaders fall, it blows the cover on this charade. Suddenly this elusive spiritual life we are trying to lead is further away than we thought. "Almost" is not even close. If the pastor can fall, what does that say about our chances? If we were honest with ourselves, we would know that the real question is not how someone so high could fall so far, but rather why hasn't it happened sooner in such an atmosphere of denial?...The real problem in this case is not with sin, it is with our false idea of who we think we are. We need to understand that when someone falls, it's not the end; it's just the truth finally being known...I often wonder how a gospel based solely on the merits of one who has died to forgive sin could be perpetuated on the merits of those who don't

seem to need it. If the whole point of the gospel is forgiveness of sin, then why do we insist on continually parading these *almost perfect* lives in front of each other? How has it happened that the people who proclaim forgiveness of sin don't seem to have any sins to be forgiven of themselves? How has a church that once was the happy possession of common fishermen and prostitutes and tax collectors become the home of the spiritually elite?[11]

The mindset you must embrace if you are going to keep self-righteousness from infesting your life is that no one is perfect. Not you. Not me. This does not provide you with a license to sin, but it does explain why Christ is your Advocate in the midst of sin (**1 John 2:1-2**). The goal is to not sin, thereby reflecting total surrender to Jesus Christ and His commands. However, if you do sin, then repent, trust the Christ of **1 John 1:9**, and seek first the Kingdom of God (**Matthew 6:33**). It is not blasphemy to say that you will sin after you have been saved; in fact, such a statement does nothing more than remind you of the struggle against your new nature, like that of the Apostle Paul (**Romans 7: 13-25**). You have been *justified* (purchased), you are being *sanctified* (process), and after you die you will be *glorified* (perfection)! Keep saying "no" to your flesh and "yes" to the commands of Jesus Christ by which you are sanctified (**John 17:17**). Don't give up (**Philippians 1:6**).

THE COMMAND INTERROGATED:

There are really two avenues Satan utilizes to wreck humanity with self-righteousness. One avenue is for *unbelievers*. Satan loves to attack lost people with the element of pride. It is pride that will keep a lost person self-justified. They look at their mistakes, and instead of calling them sins, they excuse them as part of being "human." Everything is morally relative to a lost man swallowed by pride. Satan has blinded his heart to do what he wants, as if everything is acceptable on the grounds of relativism. God will allow Satan to bring him down for his pride (**Daniel 4:37**) in this life and in Hell.

The other avenue is against *believers*, such as you and me. Satan attacks disciples with the element of being judgmental. Ultimately, Jesus Christ the Lord is the *Judge* of the living and the dead (**2 Timothy 4:1**). But it seems to be that one of Satan's greatest assaults on our hearts is the tendency to act in place of Christ. We judge other people based on what their economic standards are, which cars they drive, what clothes they wear, how they look, how they laugh, who their friends are, what kind of job they have, who their spouse is, how their children act, and even what kind of house they live in!

Yes, dear disciple, it seems to be that Satan uses such judgmental attitudes (**Matthew 7:1-5**) against us, distorting our perception of people for whom Christ died. This is a type of self-righteousness, in that we look for something in people's lives to compare to something in our own, and thus permit ourselves to feel more "righteous" in that area than the person we judged. Do you see the hellish fallacy in this? It's more than a distortion; it's a distraction! It keeps us more focused on maintaining our egos than on building up the Lord's Kingdom. Beware of how Satan will use such crafty thoughts and judgment calls against others to entangle you in a self-righteous mindset.

THE COMMAND INDESTRUCTIBLE:

The good news is that Satan must cower to the everlasting Word of God. Oh, how fortunate we are to have a weapon with which to fight Satan! Since you know the maneuvers the devil uses to launch attacks on you, it will be wise for you to know how to overcome him. Those days will come when you begin growing in Christ to such a degree that much fruit of the Holy Spirit (**Galatians 5:22-23**) or characteristics of Christ are abounding in your life. It is during these times that Satan can attack you by putting thoughts like these into your mind: "I'm doing more for Christ than he is. I've helped care for more of the poor and needy in our community than she has all year. I've witnessed to more people about Christ this month than my pastor has in his entire life!" Satan knows how to take what the Lord is doing in your life and twist it to your own self-righteous corruption.

If you ever sense that humility in your heart is beginning to suffocate at the hands of judgmental pride, there is a memory verse that will release its grip every time: **Philippians 3:9**. It declares, "*And be found in Him* [Jesus], *not having my own righteousness, which is from the law, but that which is through faith in Christ, the righteousness which is from God by faith.*" Hallelujah! This is your answer. This is your weapon against self-righteous thoughts so they never are allowed to blossom into actions. You have no righteousness. You never will. Satan is a liar to even attempt to convince you that you and I have anything whatsoever that impresses God. No, no, no!

In those times of attack, claim your memory verse. Your boast is not in yourself or your accomplishments, but rather it is in the Lord Jesus Christ, your Righteousness. He satisfied the demands of the Father with His sacrifice for your sins, and when you were saved by faith, He imputed His righteousness to you (**2 Corinthians 5:21**) because you had none. Now, you stand redeemed before the Father, purchased with the blood of Jesus, covered with His righteousness alone. Praise the Lord God Almighty! You see, you cannot produce righteousness. Christ releases His righteousness as a fragrance to the Father as you abide in His Word, which diffuses the fragrance of His aroma everywhere you go, to everyone you encounter (**2 Corinthians 2:14-15**). Therefore, never legalistically try to "be righteous," but rather devotedly "be obedient" so that Christ's righteousness will be manifested. Praise the Father's Name!

THE COMMAND INQUIRED:

What cannot be measured cannot be evaluated. Therefore, it is essential to measure your comprehension of Christ's command in this teaching, or else the devil will snatch away the "seeds" of Scripture sown into your heart (**Matthew 13:19**). To keep this from occurring, write down your answers to the following questions as they correlate with the teaching this week:

In what passage(s) of Scripture do you find Christ's commandment on **self-righteousness**?

_____

_____

What is the accurate interpretation of **self-righteousness** you have discovered?

_____

_____

_____

_____

_____

_____

In your own words, what are some real-life examples in Scripture of **self-righteousness?**

_____

_____

_____

_____

_____

_____

What steps of initiation did you learn to take to keep **self-righteousness** from destroying your life?

_____

_____

_____

_____

_____

_____

How will Satan attack you to promote **self-righteousness** in your life?

_____

_____

_____

_____

_____

What memory verse will you use to protect Christ's command against **self-righteousness** in your life? Write it out.

_____

_____

_____

_____

_____

SECTION B: CHRIST'S COMMANDS AS THEY RELATE TO THE DISCIPLE *SOCIALLY*

CHAPTER 4: THE DISCIPLE'S *TEST* IS ISSUED

"*And Jesus answered and said to them: 'Take heed that no one deceives you'*" (**Matthew 24:4**). In the Greek New Testament, there are nine different forms for the word "deceive." The Greek word Jesus used in the above text (*planeo*) means "to roam from truth." It carried the idea of someone who would go astray. Clearly, Christ was pleading with His disciples to cling to what He taught them because they would face "deceivers" after His Ascension. He did not want to see His disciples "roam" away from the truth with which He had entrusted them. Jesus is just as concerned for you now as He was for His first disciples, because you hold the same truth they did. Protect it.

What is truth? Jesus Christ is Truth! The Lord Jesus Christ did not merely *claim* to be the Son of God. He *was* and *is* the Son of God, proving Himself to be so with undeniable, undebatable, unshakable realities (**Acts 1:3, 2:22-24; 1 Corinthians 15:3-8**). You see, Christ did not simply know the truth or point to the truth. Dear disciple, He was and is and always will be the TRUTH (**John 14:6**). Do you realize what this means? Christ is the foundation for *all* truth (**1 Corinthians 3:11**). Life can only be lived as a lie against the heavenly Father until we surrender to the truth found in His Son, Jesus (**Ephesians 3:20-21**). How do you surrender? By submitting your entire body, soul, and spirit to the Word of God, not out of obligation, but out of the realization that you were created for relationship with Him.

Therefore, know the "truth" in every sense of the word, for such is your only hope for freedom from false teachers (**John 8:32**).

Your time here on Earth serves as a test, one that determines not how much you know but *Who* you know: Jesus (1 John 2:18-27; 4:1-6). It is not sufficient to know what you believe. Disciple, you need to also know *why* you believe what you believe (1 Peter 3:15); otherwise, you are easy prey for false teachers to capture your undisciplined mind (**Ephesians 4:14**). There is a war in religious society, one that is being fought for the territory of truth. There are many terroristic cults emerging, all empowered by Satan, to suction every ounce of truth from the hearts (**Matthew 13:19**) of pew-sitting churchgoers who sit *near* sound doctrine but not protectively *under* it (**2 Timothy 4:3-4**). Brace yourself. Test yourself (**2 Corinthians 13:5**), for you will be tested.

Avoid getting bogged down by unnecessary arguments with fellow disciples; such is not the will of God (**Philippians 2:14-15; 1 Timothy 1:3-4; 6:3-5; Titus 3:9-11**). Prepare yourself, for false prophets are everywhere in this world, looking for disciples like you. Satan has them lined up, from the television, to the radio, to a pulpit in your town (**2 Corinthians 11:13-15**). The satanic deception is not found in their appearance but in their speech, for it twists the truth of God and opens floodgates for apostasy! Are you ready to face these false teachers? Oh, dear disciple, stand anchored to your belief in Christ and His Word as the Apostle Paul did (**2 Corinthians 11:10-12**). False prophets and teachers are present, leading away professing believers daily. How can you avoid being one of those who receive the grace of God in vain (**1 Corinthians 15:1-2**)? You will be safe, so long as you remain committed to the gospel of Jesus Christ. Be faithful (**Revelation 2:10**).

TEACHING # 4.1: FALSE PROPHETS

Week 32

This week's objective: To distinguish the traits that identify a false teacher as well as to learn how to avoid being deceived by one.

THE COMMAND INTRODUCED:

- **Matthew 7:15-20; Luke 6:43-45** *"Beware of false prophets, who come to you in sheep's clothing, but inwardly they are ravenous wolves. You will know them by their fruits. Do men gather grapes from thorn bushes or figs from thistles? Even so, every good tree bears good fruit, but a bad tree bears bad fruit. A good tree cannot bear bad fruit, nor can a bad tree bear good fruit. Every tree that does not bear good fruit is cut down and thrown into the fire. Therefore by their fruits you will know them."*
- **Matthew 16:5-12; Mark 8:15** *"Now when His disciples had come to the other side, they had forgotten to take bread. Then Jesus said to them, 'Take heed and beware of the leaven of the Pharisees and the Sadducees.' And they reasoned among themselves, saying, 'It is because we have taken no bread.' But Jesus, being aware of it, said to them, 'O you of little faith, why do you reason among yourselves because you have brought no bread? Do you not yet understand, or remember the five loaves of the five thousand and how many baskets you took up? Nor the seven loaves of the four thousand and how many large baskets you took up? How is it you do not understand that I did not speak to you concerning bread?—but to beware of the leaven of the Pharisees and Sadducees.' Then they understood that He did not tell them to beware of the leaven of bread, but of the doctrine of the Pharisees and Sadducees."*

THE COMMAND INTERPRETED:

Both of these commands from Christ are direct, and both

include the word *beware*. The Greek "beware" (*prosecho*) means "to hold the mind toward; caution." In other words, the disciples were not to exercise a flippant attitude toward professing Christian teachers without cautiously guarding what they themselves had first been taught by the Master. The same standard applies for you.

The first command (**Matthew 7:15-20; Luke 6:43-45**) deals with the ***characteristics*** of a false prophet. Jesus predicted that His disciples would be bombarded with false teachers. Culturally speaking, many of the disciples were highly accustomed to sheep and the art of shepherding them. Using the linguistic comparison of "*sheep's clothing*," Christ was immediately able to provide an illustration for His disciples. False teachers disguise themselves! They resemble sheep, but inwardly they are corrupt wolves, ready to destroy and devour you with their heretical teaching. False-teaching Pharisees fit this description well (**Matthew 23:27**).

So, as you can imagine, the dilemma for the disciples was the obvious question: *how will we be able to recognize these false teachers?* Jesus provided the answer: fruitfulness. What did Christ mean when He said, "*By their fruits you will know them*"? In biblical terms, fruitfulness refers to the factual proof of your inward commitment, whether it be to Christ or to Satan and this world. So, to illustrate this, Christ referenced grapes and figs. Think about this: every fruit tree looks the same until it produces its fruit, such as peaches, pears, and apples. Clearly, the fruit distinguishes the tree; for example, an apple tree does not produce peaches.

Likewise, a false prophet, regardless of his appearance (**2 Corinthians 11:13**), cannot produce the "*fruit*" of the Holy Spirit (**Galatians 5:22-23**) because the Holy Spirit does not indwell him. This is precisely why Christ adamantly uses the absolute form of "*cannot*." A false teacher *cannot* produce what he, without the Spirit, is incapable of producing. This makes him a masquerading deceiver, ignorant of his own eternal destruction. He will attempt to take as many to Hell with him as he possibly can (**Matthew 23:15**), for indeed he will be "*cut down and thrown into the fire*."

As Christ's disciple, you are expected to be a fruit inspector. Just as some fruit from a tree may rotting with fungi from the inside out, so it is with the spiritual fruit of false teachings. In the same way you learn how to discern bad fruit from a tree, you learn how to detect bad spiritual fruit from a false teacher.

For another example, consider the task force of a bomb squad. If a bomb threat is reported, the bomb squad comes to the rescue. They are trained to inspect suspicious objects that may or may not be actual bombs. Dear disciple, you are the bomb squad! You are to be trained in the commands of Jesus Christ and the sound doctrine of the Scriptures. Studying the Word of God is your training, so that you will be able to distinguish the characteristic teaching of false prophets.

The second command (**Matthew 16:5-12; Mark 8:15**) deals with the *content* of a false prophet. Do you see the progression? First, Jesus dealt with the characteristics of their lifestyles. Next, He addressed the content of their teaching. In other words, Christ transitioned from what false teachers look like to what they sound like. Interestingly, the last time you heard the phrase, *"Beware of the leaven of the Pharisees,"* you learned it to relate to hypocrisy (Teaching 3.9), which was correct for that context. However, in this scenario, Christ intended to teach His disciples that the leaven also represented the false *doctrine* of the Pharisees. If you think about it, hypocrisy is a byproduct of false doctrine, linking both of these allusions to leaven.

Now, to establish the most accurate interpretation, Christ referred to the leaven here as *doctrine*. The Greek word Jesus used for "doctrine" (*didache*) means "instruction." Information enlightens your awareness, but instruction anticipates reaction. Do you see the difference? I can *inform* you that there is a hurricane coming, making you aware of the danger. But, if I *instruct* you in regards to escaping the hurricane, I naturally expect you to act upon my advice for your safety. Therefore, the fact that the *"doctrine"* of the Pharisees was not information but instruction is paramount! It served as the breeding ground for apostasy, which is the *action* of turning away from the gospel of Jesus Christ. False doctrine was the outlet for the Pharisees to trample Christ's teaching and replace it with that of their own.

The disciples were in danger because they were truly newborn babes in Christ. They were new Christians, just like you. In fact, you can see that their spiritual maturity was incredibly low when they misunderstand Jesus' statement about the leaven, interpreting it as a reference to their mistake of not taking bread with them. After He explained and explained, Christ finally said,

"How is it that you don't understand..." It was after this statement that the disciples finally comprehended that Jesus was tackling false doctrine and not physical leaven. As Christ's disciple, you are in the same boat with those disciples. You will learn many commands that stimulate your thinking and solidify your spiritual maturity. Keep your faith in Christ and His Word, even when it does not really make sense at first to you. Trust the Lord; He will give you understanding (**Luke 24:45**) as long as you remain faithful to sit at His feet and hear His Word. Stay away from false doctrine.

THE COMMAND ILLUSTRATED:

A good example for you to see is found in **Acts 13:4-12**. Barnabas and the Apostle Paul found themselves in a situation exactly as Jesus described. As they were preaching the gospel, the proconsul Sergius Paulus—a reputable man—was eager to hear the Word of God personally. So, he called for Paul and Barnabas. Elymas, a sorcerer and Jewish false prophet (**verse 6**), decided to be the contender against the men of God, diligently attempting to turn the proconsul away from faith in Christ. Therefore, the scene was turned into a divine tug-of-war, as Paul and Barnabas tried to pull the eager lost man from the hellish grip of the false prophet (**Jude 23**). Ultimately, the Spirit of God filled Paul, and he rebuked the false prophet boldly and witnessed God's blinding judgment come upon him. And, praise God, the Lord Jesus saved the proconsul!

Do you see the underlying issue at hand in this passage? The issue is truth. The false prophet, using the proconsul's intelligence (**verse 7**), was trying to distort his intellectual faculties with false teaching. As a disciple of Jesus, learn from this and remember that you are sanctified by the truth of Scripture (**John 17:17**) so that you are equipped and ready if you are put into position at times to battle false doctrine. Stand up boldly for Jesus Christ to defend truth when you see or hear it being manipulated. Be very aware of this reality. A false prophet may prey on a family member of yours even during seemingly innocent situations, such as a conversation with a fellow employee during a lunch break. Be ready, not to argue and debate, but to rescue and invite your loved one back into the shelter of Holy Scripture. Be on guard, both for yourself and for your family and friends.

THE COMMAND INITIATED:

Indeed, the battle against false doctrine is a very realistic one that you as a disciple must face. However, as you live your life for Jesus Christ, it is not sufficient to merely know that you are to guard against false doctrine. You must also know how to encounter false doctrine in such a way that you're able to both identify and avoid false teachers. Identifying does not mean debating with them, and avoiding does not necessarily mean ignoring them. Instead, by identifying a false teacher, you are prepared for the encounter as you gently yet firmly use Scripture to engage them, and if they will not listen to Scripture, you avoid them by walking away.

In his book *Deceivers and False Prophets Among Us*, Todd Tomasella Scripturally equips the disciple with holy ammunition to use when detecting false teachers:

> "Mark them which cause divisions and offences contrary to the doctrine which ye have learned; and avoid them" (**Romans 16:17**). Identifying and marking "them which cause divisions and offences contrary to the doctrine" of the LORD is to be a regular part of the Christian life. In an hour when the proliferation of false teaching is mutating at an increasingly exponential rate, those who love the LORD must view and test everything against the final authority of the recorded oracles of God. The following warning underscores this: "Beware lest any man spoil you through philosophy and vain deceit, after the tradition of men, after the rudiments of the world, and not after Christ" (**Colossians 2:8**)...People can be spoiled (derailed, made shipwreck of) through false doctrines and philosophies, which, without fail, elevate men and demote Christ (**Col. 2:8-9; 18-19**). These derailment elements are designed to steal glory form Christ. If we love Him, we are to "heareth God's words' and 'hate every false way" (**Jn. 8:47; Ps. 119:104, 128; Amos 5:14-15**)...All human sediments, reasonings, excuses must be crucified. "Mark them"—the Greek word here for "mark" is

skopeo, which means "to scope out; to take aim at, consider, watch." Believers are here mandated to wisely scope out closely, observe and scrutinize all teachings and spiritual leaders under the lamp of God's holy Word. We are to closely discern between true and false doctrines and leaders and sound the alarm on that which is found to be inconsistent with holy Writ. This is to be done especially when dealing with foundational, essential truths (which are a salvation issue)...Disciples are to examine every teaching, philosophy, and notion encountered in the light of His holy oracles. In such, the disciple is to identify deceivers, false teachings and practices and "mark them," that is, watch out for and take aim at them, while warning others. The Holy Spirit also says we are to "avoid them" (**Romans 16:17**)...Disciples of Christ are held accountable for progressively learning and proclaiming the whole will and counsel of God, as well as warning others of false teachings and those responsible for them (see also **Is. 58:1; Ez. 33:7-9; 34:1-10; Acts 20:26-32; Gal. 1, 6-9; 2 Tim. 2:17-18**). Christ's true representatives are known by their purity of character and doctrine (**Tit. 1:5-9; 2:6-8**).[1]

THE COMMAND INTERROGATED:

Well, it is quite obvious that the greatest way Satan interrogates the command of Christ regarding false prophets is through persuasive deception. The devil and those through whom he works seek to convince people to believe a lie. That is what the enemy is known for (**John 8:44**). Satan loves to turn your attention to an unbelievable heresy or to dress up certain Scriptures in garments of twisted perversion. Beware!

In light of this reality for you and all other believers, there are two different value systems that false prophets will always attack. The first has to do with the *value of God*. This is the number-one determination to identify a false prophet. The greatest value with which God has invested Himself regarding the demonstration of His merciful love for sinners is through His Son, Jesus Christ (**John 3:16-17**). The very fact that God accepted Christ's sacrifice indicates that Jesus was indeed His Son, the sinless Lamb of God! Therefore, Christ is deity, meaning Jesus is God in the flesh.

A false prophet will debate the deity of Jesus Christ, by saying either that He did not exist or that He did exist but was only a prophet. Jesus Christ was God (**John 1:1, 14**). That settles it. There is no other way to God the Father except through His Son, Jesus (**John 14:6**). This means no human being can ever live in Heaven with God without coming first in repentance through Christ. A false prophet will renounce Jesus' claim to divinity (**1 John 4:1-3**), and therefore, you must count him accursed by you (**Galatians 1:6-9**) for the polluted gospel he teaches. There's nothing else to discuss beyond this point. If Christ is not acknowledged as God, the conversation is over!

The second value system that false prophets will always assault is the *value of money*. What do people really value the most in life? Is it their houses? Cars? Clothes? Hobbies? Believe it or not, none of these things answer the question. What people really value is the money with which they buy their lifestyles. Seriously, think about it for a moment. Our entire economic system has always been governed by currency. Supply and demand, manufacturer and consumer, banking and investing—these are terms with which humanity is familiar. In fact, we as a people cannot function without money, can we? We use it to buy groceries so we do not hunger. We use it to pay utility bills to stabilize our livelihood. Do you see that money has a place in our lives?

But there's a problem: the love of money (**1 Timothy 6:9-10**). It is not wrong to have money or spend money wisely, but it is evil in the sight of God to *love* money. To do so is the root of all kinds of evil. To do so is to fall into a snare, to drown in destruction and perdition. To do so is to abandon faith in Christ through greediness and to be pierced through with sorrow! Who in the world would so knowingly welcome such personal destruction? That's just it. While no one would consciously choose this, many believers become victimized through the craftiness of Satan working through false prophets. Beware of their ways, and mark them (**Jude 4, 10-15**), for their description is easy to identify (**2 Peter 2:1-3, 12-17**).

This is not a subject new under the sun. It even happened in Bible times with false teachers in the Corinthian church (**2**

Corinthians 2:17). The method of choice was through peddling the Word of God. The Greek word "peddling" (*kapeleuo*) means "to retail; adulterate." In context, it refers to a huckster, someone who deceives you by ripping you off. False teachers take the most valuable commodity to mankind (money) because of their greed for gain at the expense of people's gullible minds. This is taking advantage of people in the name of religion, misleading them to believe a lie (**Jude 16-19; 2 Peter 2:18-19**). These kinds of false teachers seek to build a kingdom of their own, not the Kingdom of God. Such heresy has turned into a gospel of wealth, not a gospel of repentance and salvation. The focus of many hearts is an over-indulgence in prosperity, not a burning passion for seeing people saved, baptized, and discipled. Behavior always reflects attitude.

Dear disciple, beware! These false teachers are diverse, in many denominations and religious sects, from social media platforms to radio programs to television broadcasts. Yes, it's true, God desires to bless you financially, materially, and spiritually (**Luke 6:38; Ecclesiastes 11:1**), but only within the parameters of contentment (**1 Timothy 6:6-8**). Contentment does not mean you take a vow of poverty. It means you use what God gives you financially and materially to meet your most basic needs, and then use the excess to meet the needs of the poor. You live a life for Christ that is more marked by giving than receiving (**Acts 20:35**). That is God's will. Therefore, beware of any blasphemous, heretical false teaching that tries to persuade you in any other direction. Give thanks to God for how He blesses you, but don't hoard it and keep asking for more. Use it to invest in the lives of the poor and needy, to reach the lost for Christ, and to build the Kingdom of God.

THE COMMAND INDESTRUCTIBLE:

Oh, praise the Lord God Almighty, His Word prevails forevermore! You are a disciple of Christ, equipped with the Holy Spirit's power (**Acts 1:8**) to shun false prophets and honor Jesus Christ. The memory verse that you can use each time you will deal with false teaching is **Colossians 2:8**. It says, "*Beware lest anyone cheat you through philosophy and empty deceit, according to the tradition of men, according to the basic principles of the world, and not according to Christ.*"

That says it all. In other words, your standard is Jesus and His Word. Period. Therefore, if someone dares to teach you an idea or doctrine that Christ Himself does not support in the Scriptures, rebuke them lovingly (not brutally) and exhort them in the truth. Use that verse of Scripture everywhere, whenever necessary. Triumph in the grace of Jesus. God's Word, regardless of the assaults of false prophets, will never know defeat. It is your sword with which to fight! Be on guard, disciple; you are in a spiritual war against false teaching in society. Be a faithful soldier of Christ and endure to the end (**2 Timothy 2:3-4**). The Lord Jesus will honor your faithfulness.

THE COMMAND INQUIRED:

What cannot be measured cannot be evaluated. Therefore, it is essential to measure your comprehension of Christ's command in this teaching, or else the devil will snatch away the "seeds" of Scripture sown into your heart (**Matthew 13:19**). To keep this from occurring, write down your answers to the following questions as they correlate with the teaching this week:

In what passage(s) of Scripture do you find Christ's commandment on **false teaching**?

_____

_____

_____

What is the accurate interpretation of **false teaching** you have discovered?

_____

_____

_____

_____

_____

_____

In your own words, what are some real-life examples in Scripture of **false teaching**?

_____

_____

_____

_____

_____

_____

What steps of initiation did you learn to take to be better prepared to unmask **false teaching**?

_____

_____

_____

_____

_____

_____

How will Satan attack you with **false teaching** in your life?

_____

_____

_____

_____

_____

_____

What memory verse will you use to protect Christ's command against **false teaching** in your life? Write it out.

_____

_____

_____

_____

_____

_____

CHAPTER 5: THE DISCIPLE'S *TREATMENT* IS INTERACTIVE

"*And just as you want men to do to you, you also do to them likewise*" (**Luke 6:31**). The "golden rule" idea is to be credited to Jesus. What an integral standard of operation this is for all humanity, especially for a disciple! Treating others the way you want to be treated radiates healthy socialization at the highest degree imaginable. As His disciple, Jesus expects you to set the pace for others to follow such a standard. In fact, shoulder to shoulder with the greatest commandment, Jesus admonished, "*You shall love your neighbor as yourself*" (**Matthew 22:39**). It is so clear: first, love God, and second, love people. Loving God generates His love for people through you. The order is never reversed.

Ultimately, your social influence is on the line. For the last thirty-two weeks, you have focused on a deep, intense, inward examination of Christ's commands as they relate to you personally. This means your "personal" relationship with Christ has begun. Now, Christ wants to put you in social waters, to see how well you can swim. You see, you are expected to love other Christians sacrificially. By doing so, you identify yourself as a disciple of Christ (**John 13:34-35**). The glorious result is that outsiders notice your loving actions toward other Christians, which has nothing but a positive impact on them, creating a response unknown to you but known to the Father.

However, the even greater test for you is not how effectively you love other Christians but how well you love outsiders. I'm talking about the annoying coworker, the impatient customer, and the hateful boss. Daily, you are put in situations in which you not only can observe difficult people but also must interact with them. What do you say? How do you say it? Obviously, some people are going to be easier to love than others. Christ is not asking you to *like* everything about everyone you are around each day. But He does ask you to *love* everyone regardless of everything you don't like about them. Do not allow what you like or don't like about people to dictate your love for them; that would be the cart leading the horse! Remember, your treatment of these people may be the determining factor that stimulates their interest in Jesus Christ.

You are called to this, disciple. This is all a part of your "package deal" received when you committed your life to Christ. Yes, you are to love Christ personally and worship Christ corporately with other believers, but you must move forward in your service to Christ socially. You are called to be a rescuer, not a recluse. You are designed to be a witness to lost people, not a waste of blood-bought property. Dear disciple, people's lives are hanging in the balance. Step up. Speak up. The Lord your God is with you wherever you go and will speak for you to whomever you love (**Matthew 10:19-20**). Trust God, not your nerves (**Proverbs 3:5-6**). There's a lost, confused, hurting society waiting for you.

TEACHING # 5.1: ENEMIES

Week 33

This week's objective: To determine the criteria that constitute an enemy as well as to learn the Christ-like love needed to reconcile such a damaged relationship.

THE COMMAND INTRODUCED:

- **Matthew 5:38-48; Luke 6:27-35** *"You have heard that it was said, 'An eye for an eye and a tooth for a tooth.' But I tell you not to resist an evil person. But whoever slaps you on your right cheek, turn the other to him also. If anyone wants to sue you and take away your tunic, let him have your cloak also. And whoever compels you to go one mile, go with him two. Give to him who asks you, and from him who wants to borrow from you do not turn away. You have heard that it was said, 'You shall love your neighbor and hate your enemy.' But I say to you, love your enemies, bless those who curse you, do good to those who hate you, and pray for those who spitefully use you and persecute you, that you may be sons of your Father in heaven; for He makes His sun rise on the evil and on the good, and sends rain on the just and on the unjust. For if you love those who love you, what reward have you? Do not even the tax collectors do the same? And if you greet your brethren only, what do you do more than others? Do not even the tax collectors do so? Therefore you shall be perfect, just as your Father in heaven is perfect."*

THE COMMAND INTERPRETED:

Direct—that is the best way to describe this command from the Lord Jesus. This command is overflowing with multiple principles to be applied toward enemies; in fact, the volume of those principles is so immense that it is necessary to dissect each one individually so that you may gain an accurate interpretation.

Pay close attention to protect yourself from misunderstanding what Christ is really teaching.

The entire context of this command (**Matthew 5:38-48; Luke 6:27-35**) has to do with retaliation, which is the angry reaction of taking vengeance, either vocally or physically, upon someone who has offended you. Where do you draw the line? Biblically, what are you supposed to do? Christ answered those questions for you.

First of all, the entire passage is broken down into two categories: when you have *oppressors* who retaliate against you (**verses 38-42**), and when you yourself have *opportunity* to retaliate (**verses 43-48**). Do you see the difference?

In dealing with those who oppress you through their retaliation against you, there is a *response* Jesus wants to see (**verses 38-39a**). That response is to *"not resist an evil person."* The Greek word "resist" (*anthistemi*) means "to stand against; oppose." For clarification, the context refers to personal retaliation, not legal authorities. Every law official, regardless of the position, has the ordained right by Almighty God to "resist" evil people so that society is protected (**Romans 13:1-5**).

But in non-law-enforcement situations, such is not the case. According to Christ, you are to replace *resisting* with praise (**Matthew 5:12**) and prayer (**Matthew 5:44**)! Therefore, when there is persecution against your *dignity* (**verses 39b, 41**), remind yourself of **1 Corinthians 9:22-23**. When there is persecution against your *possessions* (**verses 40, 42**), encourage yourself in **Luke 12:15** and **Acts 20:35**. Dear disciple, this is your mandate. It may sound impossible, but it's not (**Luke 1:37**). The oppressor expects you to retaliate, which does nothing more than fan the flames of vengeance. But when he sees you bite your tongue and release your clenched fists, he knows there's something different about you. He doesn't think you are a coward; rather, he knows you must be a real disciple.

Such heated moments serve to introduce to you the second category: when you have opportunity to retaliate. This is where a lot of people, perhaps including you, slip up. You see, enduring the oppression from angry people is only half the battle! If you are going to obey Christ command in full, then you must not only control yourself until you have the opportunity to react. Your feelings in such heated moments will want to disobey, so you must obey on the premise of choice. Discipline yourself (**1 Corinthians**

9:27).

Therefore, when you have opportunity to retaliate, again, there is a *reaction* that Jesus wants to see (**verses 43-44a**). Love? That's right, LOVE. There is no greater weapon to silence retaliation than love (**1 Corinthians 13:13**). Interestingly, when Jesus commanded to "*love*" your enemies, He used the Greek word *agapao*, which refers to a social, moral love, thus fitting the context for the passage. The actual manner in which you express this kind of love is not without explanation.

When you are cursed out or slandered, "*bless*" or say something kind back in response. When you are hated and despised, go out of your way to "*do good*" through a charitable deed or an encouraging card in the mail. When you are persecuted or taken advantage of, be sure to "*pray*" for your enemy with a heart of reconciliation. As a disciple, this is what Christ expects from you, for by doing so His righteousness through your reaction exposes your enemy's wickedness (**verse 44b**). Dear disciple, let God fight your battle for you (**Romans 12:17, 21**), just as Jesus Christ our Lord exemplified (**1 Peter 2:23**).

Furthermore, treating your enemy in such a way is God's will because you are displaying the *relationship* that is pleasing to Christ (**verses 45a, 48**). Your entire resistance of and reaction to your enemy results in being a "*son of your Father.*" Wow. That means you are demonstrating that you really do belong to God the Father because you are exhibiting His qualities (**Ephesians 5:1-2; Colossians 2:6**). Thus, God is getting the glory because your responses are pointing to Him. The only conclusion to such behavior is that you are "*perfect,*" just as God is perfect. This word "*perfect*" has a Greek meaning of maturity, not sinlessness. It is an indicator of your growth in Christ, one that shows you are not a baby Christian but that you have transitioned from the bottle (**1 Peter 2:2**) to the meat of Scripture (**Hebrews 6:1**). Such maturity is commendable!

Finally, there is a *reminder* Jesus wants you to recall (**verses 45a, 48**). Do you see what that reminder is? Well, it is the same concept that **James 2:4-5** addresses. We measure a person's outer moral value (the caliber of their observable actions), but God measures a person's inner spiritual value (their unseen souls). Therefore, how valuable are your enemies? To us, there are conditions; but to Christ, there are no limits. As a disciple, allow Christ's command toward your enemies the freedom to renew your mind. Honestly, you must measure your enemy's worth by the same standard Christ uses to measure your worth. That measuring stick is the limitless, incomprehensible love of God! He sends rain to your house just as He does to the drunkard's house. His mercy will not allow Him to do otherwise. This is a reminder to go beyond a cliquish Christian life in which you only affiliate yourself with those who *"love"* and *"greet"* you. Christ is reminding you to also love and greet the outcasts, those enemies, in spite of their rude and arrogant attitudes. Enlist, dear disciple! You were once an enemy, too (**James 4:4**). You and I were the abandoned orphans kicking in our own blood before the Lord Jesus saved us (**Ezekiel 16:1-14**). Don't forget where you spiritually came from.

To bring this full circle, what is the contextual point Christ is trying to make? The answer is simple: *salvation.* Christ wants you to not resist, but love, an evil person because He desires for that person to see His love through you. Is that clear, or what? Jesus Christ wants to save the lost (**Luke 19:10**)! Your overall reaction to your enemies is not intended to get you a better reward in Heaven or to see if Christ will play favorites with you compared to some other disciple. No, again, the purpose is more than clear: to see your enemy saved by Christ and/or reconciled to you. Christ needs you to humble yourself for this to take place. Put your emotions and feelings on the chopping block for the gospel's sake. This is the call of Christ.

THE COMMAND ILLUSTRATED:

There is a great example in **1 Samuel 24:1-7** that illustrates how you should treat enemies. King Saul was chosen by God to reign and rule over the children of Israel. During the course of his reign, something happened. Do you remember the story of David and Goliath, found in **1 Samuel 17**? After he killed Goliath, David's popularity began to soar, with people chanting this phrase: *"Saul has slain his thousands, and David his ten thousands"* (**1 Samuel 18:7**). This was a paradigm shift for King Saul because from this point forward he became jealous and bitter toward David. The result? King Saul tried to kill David, chasing him through miles of desert land.

This illustrative text of **1 Samuel 24** finds us in the middle of this chase. David and his men sneaked up on King Saul while he was off guard and unaware that David was also in the cave. Although David could have killed King Saul, he chose to cut a piece of the king's clothes to show proof to Saul that he could have killed him but refrained (**1 Samuel 24:18**). Why did he choose such an act of mercy towards King Saul? The reason is found in **verse 6**. Although Saul was an enemy, David valued Saul's anointed calling from God as king of Israel (**1 Samuel 10:1**). This means David's anger took a backseat to the precedence of God's plan for Saul's life and Israel's future. David recognized that his feelings were getting in the way and that if he killed Saul, he would interfere with God's plan.

Learn from this story. God also has a plan for your enemies—one that you are not capable of understanding. If you retaliate against your enemies, you will only damage God's plan in their lives, resulting in more hostility and no change of heart. This is why it is so important to restrain yourself as David did and instead let God work through your obedience. Did you see how God rewarded David? Amazed at David's mercy, Saul entered a state of repentance and brokenness, which ushered in reconciliation for the two men (**1 Samuel 24: 19-22**). Dear disciple, emulate the character of David. You never know what God has planned for your enemy, so don't interfere. Obey Christ's command.

THE COMMAND INITIATED:

By now, you have a firm grip on the nature of your relationship toward enemies. But the question for the moment is how to put what you now know into practice. As a disciple, you need to be ready for such inevitable resistance to form. The world hated Christ, and count on it, it will hate you, too (**John 15:18-19**). However, there is more to obeying this command than merely plunging forward in blind faith. It is to your advantage to know the proper attitude needed when seeking peace with an enemy. Donald Posterski identifies this attitude and calls the people who possess it "collaborators." In his book *Enemies with Smiling Faces*, Posterski beautifully explains the balance you will need during enemy encounters:

> There are ditches on both sides of the road. Conviction and
> compassion are the guardrails that keep us from veering off
> the road and traveling in the ditch. Truth that nurtures
> conviction protects us from mindless permissiveness. Love
> that motivates compassion protects us from judgmental
> arrogance. Balancing conviction and compassion in our
> attitudes and behaviors brings together the virtues of truth
> and love. It is the coexistence and counterbalance of
> conviction and compassion that protects us from excesses
> that turn these virtues into vices.
> *Collaborators* are people who embrace both the virtue of
> conviction and the virtue of compassion. They are neither
> permissive with themselves nor judgmental towards others.
> Collaborators live in the tension of seeking to influence
> others without either apologizing for their convictions or
> denigrating the conviction of others. They are committed to
> mutuality. Collaborators are "us" people. They collaborate,
> not to be in collusion like traitors but in order to cooperate
> with people around them...Christian collaborators affirm
> their spiritual self-definition and respect the spiritual self-
> definition of others. They perceive that the Christian life is
> offered in diverse packages but what is inside is often the
> same: newness of life in Christ. They believe the activity of
> God's Spirit transcends the human limits inherent in all
> church structures. They are ready to *"speak the truth in love"*
> inside the Christian family and in the world (**Eph. 4:15**).[1]

THE COMMAND INTERROGATED:

Christ's command provides you with a process to bring
repair to an enemy relationship. But while Christ advocates repair,
Satan administrates resentment. Satan attacks Christ's command in
your life by attacking your fleshly mind, tempting you to harbor
bitterness against an enemy. Be very careful and keenly aware of
the devil's cunning ways to poison your relationships. He'll ignite
conflict with a best friend. He'll bring division between you and

your family members. He will blow a harmless issue into a balloon of adversity between you and a coworker. Satan delights in confusion and division!

Beware of his crafty, manipulative attacks on your relationships. In fact, if you sense any resentment or bitterness between you and someone else, first repent for your grudge. Then, go to your enemy and settle the dispute between both of you. If you refuse, you are disobeying Christ's command and giving Satan a foothold in your life. This will be a true test for you, because it is impossible to be right with God and wrong with men at the same time (**Matthew 5:23-24**). You are a disciple, not a coward. If you have an enemy, go.

THE COMMAND INDESTRUCTIBLE:

Reconciling with an enemy is much easier said than done. However, when you obey Him, God gives you power to do and say things you never could in your natural ability. And the only way to obey is to first know what He says in His written Word. Praise God that His Word is your triumphant, victorious, invincible weapon to claim amidst Satan's attempted assassinations. When dealing with potential enemies in your life as a disciple, there is a memory verse of Scripture that will both humble your anger and refocus your disappointment. The Scripture you will need to use is **Romans 12:20**: *"Therefore, 'If your enemy is hungry, feed him; if he is thirsty, give him a drink; for in so doing, you will heap coals of fire on his head.'"* Do not allow any situation, regardless of its intensity, to fester in your heart. Deal with it immediately. Stop Satan from getting a victory in your life and that of anyone else. Fast and pray, seek the will of God through His Word, and go lovingly after any enemy coming to your mind. Whether they reconcile with you or not, the point for you is simply to obey Jesus. That's your first priority.

THE COMMAND INQUIRED:

What cannot be measured cannot be evaluated. Therefore, it is essential to measure your comprehension of Christ's command in this teaching, or else the devil will snatch away the "seeds" of

Scripture sown into your heart (**Matthew 13:19**). To keep this from occurring, write down your answers to the following questions as they correlate with the teaching this week:

In what passage(s) of Scripture do you find Christ's commandment on **enemies**?

_____

_____

_____

What is the accurate interpretation of **enemies** you have discovered?

_____

_____

_____

_____

_____

_____

In your own words, what are some real-life examples in Scripture of **enemies**?

_____

_____

_____

_____

_____

_____

What steps of initiation did you learn to take to develop a proper love for **enemies**?

_____

_____

_____

_____

_____

_____

How will Satan attack you with **enemies** in your life?

_____

_____

_____

_____

_____

_____

What memory verse will you use to protect Christ's command regarding **enemies** in your life? Write it out.

_____

_____

_____

_____

_____

_____

TEACHING # 5.2: JUDGING

Week 34

This week's objective: To expose the ingredients of a judgmental attitude as well as to learn the discipline needed to overcome judgmentalism.

THE COMMAND INTRODUCED:

- **Matthew 7:1-5; Luke 6:37, 41-42** *"Judge not, that you be not judged. For with what judgment you judge, you will be judged; and with the measure you use, it will be measured back to you. And why do you look at the speck in your brother's eye, but do not consider the plank in your own eye? Or how can you say to your brother, 'Let me remove the speck from your eye'; and look, a plank is in your own eye? Hypocrite! First remove the plank from your own eye, and then you will see clearly to remove the speck from your brother's eye."*
- **Mark 9:38-40; Luke 9:49-50** *"Now John answered Him, saying, 'Teacher, we saw someone who does not follow us casting out demons in Your name, and we forbade him because he does not follow us.' But Jesus said, 'Do not forbid him, for no one who works a miracle in My name can soon afterward speak evil of Me. For he who is not against us is on our side.'"*

THE COMMAND INTERPRETED:

The nature of these two commands is direct and to the point. The Lord Jesus has as His concern the perilous assumptions His disciples might make when trying to reach people with the gospel. The old phrase "Don't judge a book by its cover" seems to fit here. This temptation to make judgment calls regarding other people is a runaway train for our sinful nature. We look, we listen, and we judge—whether we have all the information or not! Jesus cannot tolerate such behavior and attitudes from His people.

The first command (**Matthew 7:1-5; Luke 6:37, 41-42**) addresses ***comparative*** judgments. Jesus begins with this clear command: *"Judge not."* If you do not comply in obedience, your every judgment will actually become the standard by which you are judged in like manner. It is an inevitable boomerang effect, for what you say about others has potential to root itself in your own life. This is why Jesus said, *"And with the measure you use, it will be measured back to you."* That's a promise, not a possibility.

Years ago, a young teenage girl did exactly what Christ commanded not to do. She noticed another teenage girl at school who had a scar on her face in the shape of the letter *L*. In the presence of her friends, she began to point, whisper, and make fun of the scarred young lady. A few days later, this judgmental teenage girl went water skiing. As she jumped out of the boat, the propeller on the motor mysteriously clipped her foot, cutting her terribly. After she returned to the boat and bandaged her foot, the bleeding finally stopped. When she removed the bandage to look at the cut, she was in awe to find it was in the exact shape of the letter *L*. Immediately, she realized her judgment call was *"measured back"* to her that day. I assure you that Christ is not mocked.

You see, as a disciple you must be very careful to not form comparative judgments of other people. To do so is to operate in a spirit of faultfinding criticism. Strangely, the behaviors that upset us in others are so often the very traits we dislike in ourselves! It is like trying to change in others what you actually want to change in yourself. To counteract such behavior from His disciples, Jesus exhorts you to remove the *"plank from your own eye"* before you judgmentally reach for the *"speck"* in your brother's eye.

Notice the contrast between *"plank"* and *"speck."* The Greek word for "plank" (*dokos*) means "a stick of timber" and "speck" (*karphos*) translates as "a twig or straw." The difference in size is obvious; a piece of timber would do far more damage to the eye than a piece of straw would. The point is that you cannot accurately help your brother with his speck until you first remove your plank. This is a call for self-examination (**2 Corinthians 13:5**). Judgment must begin with yourself first before it ever dares to reach the premises of another person's life (**1 Corinthians 11:31-32; 1 Peter 4:17**).

This provides you with a pathway to avoid hypocrisy. To judge yourself (remove your own plank) actually empowers you to properly discern your brother, not judgmentally criticize him. Do you see the beautiful difference? Instead of judging your brother's sins and thus elevating yourself, you judge your own sins and are able to help your brother. Basically, by not becoming judgmental, you put yourself in a position to minister to your brother by helping him conquer a sin with which he struggles. Rather than judging him, you are able to encourage him to overcome a certain weakness, because you also overcame the same weakness by assessing your own "*plank*" first. Help your brother instead of judging him (**Galatians 6:2**).

The second command (**Mark 9:38-41; Luke 9:49-50**) addresses *doctrinal* judgments. John, the beloved disciple, brought the discussion of sectarianism to the table. Sectarianism is spiritual racism toward other denominational groups. Jesus' disciples were acting in such a manner when they saw a man who was casting out demons in Jesus' Name but was not one of the twelve disciples. Because of their boxed-in faith and spiritual immaturity, they rebuked the man.

This did not set well with Christ. It was a doctrinal issue, and it deserved to be settled. After hearing how His disciples treated the man, Jesus commanded them, "*Do not forbid him...*" The entire understanding of this command hinges upon that word *forbid*. Its Greek meaning (*koluo*) is interpreted as "prevent or hinder." This means the disciples went beyond merely voicing any concern regarding the man to actually taking action to halt his ministry entirely.

To explain His rebuke, Jesus pointed out two groups: those who speak for Him, and those who are not against Him. These were to be the building blocks of maturity and clarification for the disciples. It was impossible for those speaking for Christ to speak evil of Him (**1 Corinthians 12:3**), as well as for those standing for Christ to stand against Him (**Matthew 12:30**). Does this mean Christ endorses all religions? Absolutely not, for many religions and denominations do not adhere to the deity of Jesus Christ, and therefore, they must be rebuked and avoided, for they are false teachers.

However, any denomination that preaches Jesus Christ's death, burial, and Resurrection and that affirms that He alone offers salvation by His grace indeed has the foundation laid (**1 Corinthians 3:11**). Just as every house differs from each other, so will Christian denominations differ doctrinally as well. But just as every house has the same foundation, regardless of its building structure, so

Christian denominations also have the same foundation (Jesus Christ) regardless of their doctrinal structure. The point is to not become so doctrinally judgmental of others that we divide ourselves, resulting in stunted Kingdom growth. Such division in the Body of Christ goes against the unity that Jesus prayed for His people, the Church (**John 17:11, 21-23**). Be the answer to His prayer by seeking unity.

THE COMMAND ILLUSTRATED:

Believe it or not, a judgmental attitude plagued the people of Israel at one time. The account of this situation is found in **Numbers 11:24-29**. What a revival! What an awakening! The same Holy Spirit of God that rested upon Moses, God Himself, put His Spirit upon seventy chosen elders in Israel. They prophesied and preached under His anointing. Since Israel was an eyewitness to this scene, they knew all the elders. Among those elders were two men, Eldad and Medad. For a reason not recorded in Scripture, these two men remained in their camp in Israel rather than joining the other sixty-eight elders back at the Tabernacle to prophesy to the people of Israel. The Holy Spirit of God rested upon and prophesied through these two men no differently than with the others, regardless of their absence from the tabernacle.

Immediately, a young tattletale came to Moses complaining against the two men, and even Joshua, Moses' assistant, raised concerns. What was Moses to do? Were these two men out of line? As Jesus did with His disciples, Moses rebuked the young man and Joshua with clear explanation (**verse 29**). The point is conveyed: Do not frustrate God's working by His Spirit through the vessels He so chooses. Be careful to focus only on what Christ has called you to do, not on being a busybody in other people's matters (**John 21:20-22**). The manner in which Christ is at work in others' lives is dispensationally congruent with His sovereign plan for those people. He has His own plan for you (**Jeremiah 29:11**). Don't become so judgmentally distracted by peering into God's workings in others' lives that you miss His movement in yours. Instead of judging and making assumptions, focus and remain faithful.

THE COMMAND INITIATED:

The very process by which you apply what Christ has commanded is crucial to your social maturity as a disciple. Wherever you go and whatever you do, people will always be a part of your life, and this social environment will serve as continuous practice for these commands. You goal is to initiate these commands into reality. It is so easy, for example, to judge a waitress as rude and arrogant, without realizing that her attitude is actually reflective of her broken heart over her mother's death the week before. In sensitive moments like that, the Father wants you to pray and love instead of judge and criticize.

Your life as a disciple is in the balance. How do you really live day after day, regardless of the difficult people you face, and keep from making judgments about them? In his book *Making Judgments without Being Judgmental*, Terry Cooper answers that question. His desire is for you as a disciple to collect an appropriate understanding of judgmentalism so that you can know how to correct it:

> The first step in dealing effectively with judgmentalism is fully recognizing how slippery, conniving and insidious it can be. We may become *less* judgmental, but it is doubtful that that we'll ever be completely *nonjudgmental*. Therefore, humility is needed. My suggestion, as we explore the topic of judgmentalism, is to begin with the assumption that we *are* judgmental. Let's move away from an "us" and "them" mentality that focuses on the judgmentalism out there...Judgmentalism involves two forms of superiority. First is moral superiority. This is one of the primary reasons that Jesus tell us in **Matthew 7:1** to "*Judge not*." As we judge another person, we are acting as a condescending spectator, not as a player. We are pushing aside our own shortcomings, faults, limits and finitude while we assess another. But once we get off the bleachers and into the game, we may find that life is much more complex than our spectator position had realized. Second, judgmentalism also involves a deep sense of intellectual superiority insofar as we believe we are capable of evaluating the entire context of another's life,

with all its variables. It is an arrogant illusion that we can size up someone's entire life; we simply don't know the whole story. We don't know how others have been hurt, the struggles of their lives or the overall context out of which they have lived. Some may think this sounds dangerously close to excusing another's behavior, but this is not at all what I am suggesting. I am simply saying that we, coming out of our own set of assumptions, viewpoints, limitations and cognitive finitude, cannot possibly deliver a "final verdict" about another's entire life. We may have very definite judgments about specific *acts* this person has committed, but we don't have the intellectual resources to determine the nature of his or her entire existence. Perhaps one of the reasons Jesus warned so vigorously against judgmentalism is that it makes a god or idol of our own viewpoint.[2]

THE COMMAND INTERROGATED:

Satan loves to attack a disciple with an unguarded mind and heart. How? What process does the devil take? Believe it or not, he will do so primarily when you remove the plank from your eye and attempt to help your brother who is struggling with the speck in his own eye. Read **Galatians 6:1**. Satan loves to twist God's Word in our lives. Clearly, when you help a brother or sister in Christ who has fallen into one of Satan's traps, in gentleness and meekness you reach them, but do not be blinded to the temptation Satan has waiting for you, too.

You see, it is no different from the way a doctor can also catch the illness that has plagued his patient. Likewise, be very cautious when you have successfully refrained from judging your brother or sister and instead helped them through their bondage of sin. Satan will be waiting. Protect yourself with Scripture, *"considering yourself lest you also be tempted."* Do not allow the enemy to bring you down as he did the one you are helping up. This is not a matter of willpower; it's a matter of the Holy Spirit's power. Depend upon the living God (**Proverbs 3:5**).

THE COMMAND INDESTRUCTIBLE:

Hallelujah—the Word of the Lord is the true, overcoming, devil-chasing power you need for victory in the area of judgmentalism. Thankfully, the Word of God is full of Scriptures that encourage you to overcome and to keep your mind from entertaining judgmental thoughts. Your memory verse to cling to daily as you live and interact with people is **James 4:11-12**. It says, *"Do not speak evil of one another, brethren. He who speaks evil of a brother and judges his brother, speaks evil of the law and judges the law. But if you judge the law, you are not a doer of the law but a judge. There is one Lawgiver, who is able to save and to destroy. Who are you to judge another?"*

Can God's Word be any clearer than that? Dear disciple, remember, the only judgment you and I are permitted to give is righteous judgment (**John 7:24**), which means rebuke against blasphemous, heretical false teaching. However, this will only take place a fraction of the time. Most of your time in life will be spent around people whom you are tempted to judge without even knowing them. Use your memory verse to fight against such an inward judgmental temptation.

Overcome in this area. Talk with people and love them with Christ's love. Make no apologies or compromises for your commitment to Christ, but at least give people a chance before you write them off your heart. You are a disciple and therefore equipped with the right factory-installed spiritual "machinery" to fulfill Christ's commands. Every person deserves a chance. Christ is counting on you, so obey Him faithfully.

THE COMMAND INQUIRED:

What cannot be measured cannot be evaluated. Therefore, it is essential to measure your comprehension of Christ's command in this teaching, or else the devil will snatch away the "seeds" of Scripture sown into your heart (**Matthew 13:19**). To keep this from occurring, write down your answers to the following questions as they correlate with the teaching this week:

In what passage(s) of Scripture do you find Christ's

commandment on being **judgmental**?

_____

_____

_____

What is the accurate interpretation of being **judgmental** you have discovered?

_____

_____

_____

_____

_____

In your own words, what are some real-life examples in Scripture of **judgmentalism**?

_____

_____

_____

_____

What steps of initiation did you learn to take to keep **judgmentalism** from destroying your life?

_____

_____

_____

_____

_____

_____

How will Satan attack you to promote **judgmentalism** in your life?

_____

_____

_____

_____

_____

What memory verse will you use to protect Christ's command against **judgmentalism** in your life? Write it out.

_____

_____

_____

_____

_____

TEACHING # 5.3: RECONCILIATION

Week 35

This week's objective: To determine the process of reconciliation, as well as to examine your damaged relationships in need of it.

THE COMMAND INTRODUCED:

- **Matthew 5:21-26** *"You have heard that it was said to those of old, 'You shall not murder, and whoever murders will be in danger of the judgment.' But I say to you that whoever is angry with his brother without a cause shall be in danger of the judgment. And whoever says to his brother, 'Raca!' shall be in danger of the council. But whoever says, 'You fool!' shall be in danger of hell fire. Therefore if you bring your gift to the altar, and there remember that your brother has something against you, leave your gift there before the altar, and go your way. First be reconciled to your brother, and then come and offer your gift. Agree with your adversary quickly, while you are on the way with him, lest your adversary deliver you to the judge, the judge hand you over to the officer, and you be thrown into prison. Assuredly, I say to you, you will by no means get out of there till you have paid the last penny."*
- **Matthew 18:15-17** *"Moreover if your brother sins against you, go and tell him his fault between you and him alone. If he hears you, you have gained your brother. But if he will not hear, take with you one or two more, that 'by the mouth of two or three witnesses every word may be established.' And if he refuses to hear them, tell it to the church. But if he refuses even to hear the church, let him be to you like a heathen and a tax collector."*

THE COMMAND INTERPRETED:

This is a subject that may very well be sensitive for you, especially considering your relationships before becoming a

Christian. Both of these commands on reconciliation are direct, and neither leaves room for debate. Jesus specifically addressed the issue in such a clear, concise way that all people have the exact blueprint to reconstruct a new relationship with those they have offended. Do you have any relationships that are in need of divine reconciliation? Pay close attention to Christ's words.

The first command (**Matthew 5:21-26**) provides the *gateway* to reconciliation. Based on the context of the passage, it is as if Jesus was cautioning His disciples to be alert for certain attitudes and behaviors that hinder reconciliation. First of all, you must *look out* for causeless anger (**verses 21-22**). Plainly, Jesus equated anger with murder. When anger is stored in the heart, it callouses the conscience and causes a person to become inwardly murderous in tone toward an offender (**1 John 3:15**). This evil will destroy a believer; it is a bitter, raging beast that violates God's command to love (**1 John 4:7**). Cain refused God's merciful option to rule over his anger (**Genesis 4:7**). Don't repeat his mistake in your relationships. It is permissible to have a righteous anger *toward* sin and yet *not* sin (**Ephesians 4:26**), but it is not acceptable to be angry *in* sin, because the fleshly nature runs rampant. Therefore, beware of anger that has no biblically justifiable cause. If it is not dealt with, anger will provoke irrational, harmful decisions.

If a disciple does not get his or her anger under control, he or she must secondly *look in* for damaged relationships (**verses 23-24**). In Bible times, the Temple altar was used for people to leave their purchased gifts for consecration to the Lord. Such an action was intended to exemplify devotional service on behalf of the individual. However, such outward commitment was never an accepted replacement for inward sin—in this case, unrestrained anger and the shattered pieces of broken relationships because of that anger. To even dare to offer a sacrificial gift to God in light of these inward conditions would be an evil cover-up for one's sin. Jesus Christ cannot be bought out with a gift. The only hope for clearing the conscience is reconciliation between the individual and the offended person.

The Greek word for "reconcile" (*diallasso*) means "to change thoroughly." It carries the idea of being brought back into fellowship with your brother. Therefore, it is unthinkable to offer your sacrificial service to God while knowingly suppressing a guilty conscience of offense toward someone you have hurt. First, be reconciled; then give God your sacrificial service. This order is never reversed! Your relationship with the Father can only be as healthy as your relationships with others. You have a ministry of reconciliation (**2 Corinthians 5:19-20**). Don't forsake it.

However, if you do neglect to make peace with your brother, dreadful consequences can invade your life. This is why Jesus warned thirdly to *look ahead* for harmful ramifications (**verses 25-26**). You see, unrepentant sin leads to destruction. Can this really happen? Dear disciple, this is no joke or game. If you don't control your anger and reconcile with those whom you may have offended, you increase your risks of backfire from those whom you hurt with your anger. Pleadingly, Jesus advises you as His disciple, *"Agree with your adversary quickly..."* The Greek word "agree" (*eunoeo*) translates "to be well-minded." It means you do whatever is necessary to build a bridge of unity, to even agree to disagree if you must (**1 Corinthians 6:7**). Do not be stubborn (**Acts 7:51**).

If you do not seek peace and forgiveness, then heed the expected promise of **verse 26**! Your justice will come full circle as your offender transforms into your enemy and "delivers" you to hardship. The Greek "deliver" (*paradidomi*) interprets "yield up; betray." An enemy bent on revenge that you could have reversed will seek to ruin you (**Proverbs 25:8-10**). Obey the Lord Jesus in this area and avoid unnecessary chastening from disobedience (**Hebrews 12:5-11; Revelation 3:19**).

What are you supposed to do if the scenario is just the opposite? How are you to react if you are the one who has been offended, not doing the offending? Well, such questions bring you to the second command (**Matthew 18:15-17**), which provides the *guidelines* for reconciliation. In contrast with the first command, this command begins with this phrase: *"If your brother sins against you..."* In the context of the passage, please note that this principle was designed for Christians within a congregation, not unbelievers within a community. Therefore, as a disciple, if this happens to you, obey the guidelines that serve to make a way for reconciliation.

First of all, Jesus commanded for you to lovingly confront your offender. You are not supposed to talk *about* the person who has hurt you (gossip) but rather *to* them. What a wonderful design for conflict resolution! However, if your offender resists you, your second step is to find one or two more people to seek reconciliation with your brother again. The purpose here is so that they can witness and report anything necessary about the conversation. Ultimately, if you still have resistance from your offender, take the matter then to your local church leadership (pastors, elders, deacons) so that the church can deliberate the matter and, as a congregation, reach out in love to the offender with you. Regrettably, if the offender doesn't respond to the local church, he is then viewed as a disobedient *"heathen and tax collector."* This is a form of church discipline that keeps the congregation healthy and unified (**1 Corinthians 5:11-12; 2 Thessalonians 3:5, 14-15**). As a disciple, be prepared for this to happen. I do not say that as a faithless comment but rather as a grim reality because people are not to be trusted. Therefore, get ready, and pray that Christ would give you wisdom in practicing this command.

THE COMMAND ILLUSTRATED:

A great example of reconciliation in the Bible is found in **Acts 15:36-41**. As you can tell from the reading, there are four men in view: Paul, Barnabas, John Mark, and Silas. Notice that Barnabas was not in disagreement with Paul's idea to check on new disciples. He merely wanted John Mark to join them on their journey. Paul disagreed with that decision because, for an unknown reason, John Mark had abandoned Paul on a missionary journey in **Acts 13:13**. Paul had never forgotten it.

Sadly, the tension increased and caused a split between the four men. The beauty of this passage is that eventually, reconciliation did take place between Paul and John Mark, evidenced by Paul's comment in **2 Timothy 4:11**. In fact, such an attitude continued in Paul's ministry (**Philemon 8-18**). Somewhere in his heart, Paul had to choose forgiveness for John Mark's offensive abandonment. Likewise, since John Mark was in the wrong for abandoning the apostle and leaving him in distress, he had to choose to reconcile with Paul. Their focus was back on the Kingdom of God, and never again in Scripture did it suffer division (**Matthew 12:25**) over their personal differences. Dear disciple, learn this lesson: if you have need of reconciliation in your life, blatant refusal is harmful to you and the other person. Repent and reconcile for the Kingdom's sake alone.

THE COMMAND INITIATED:

It's a miserable feeling to be at odds with someone you care about. Can you really reconcile, or is that something you only dream about because of how long it has been? Well, Jesus gave the command to reconcile because He knew it would be needed. Furthermore, Christ would not give a command if it could not be obeyed, so there is hope for you. It's time to put reconciliation into action in your life.

John De Gruchy has a fascinating understanding of reconciliation from both a contextual and theological viewpoint based on his study of the Pauline letters. In his book *Reconciliation*, De Gruchy draws from his insights into the Apostle Paul's writings and establishes the parameters that will help you activate a reconciled attitude in any damaged relationship:

> Reconciliation in Paul, as in the Sermon on the Mont, always has to do with personal relationships, but Paul's understanding of its meaning is particularly rich in texture and character, and it is from him that we discover both its range of meaning, and the reason for its appeal. Arguably the most remarkable aspect of Paul's teaching on reconciliation is that in virtually every instance in which he uses the word or its cognates, God is the subject or agent of reconciliation. In speaking of God in this way, Paul becomes the first Greek author to speak of the person offended as the one who initiates the act or process of reconciliation. This not only distinguishes Paul's use of the term "reconciliation" from other Hellenistic sources, but also from other cultures and languages. For in the latter it is normally the case that reconciliation has to be initiated by the person responsible for the alienation and hostility, hence acknowledgment of guilt becomes the precondition for reconciliation. But, for Paul, the gospel is precisely that God is the one who takes the initiative in seeking an end to hostility. Thus

reconciliation in Pauline theology refers to the way in which the love of God in Jesus Christ turns enemies into friends thereby creating peace. Significantly, then, reconciliation tells us something about the personal and relational character of God, namely, that God is love. This understanding is embodied in the way in which Christian tradition understands the triune nature of God in whom difference is not the cause of division but the enrichment of unity...Thus there is an interaction between the divine act of reconciliation in Christ and human appropriation of that act in relating in a new way to each other...As a result, Christians have no need to engage in vain speculation, but rather to live a life that matches up to their reconciliation in Christ.[3]

THE COMMAND INTERROGATED:

Well, what do you believe Satan uses against believers when confronted with the command to reconcile? In essence, what is the greatest tool the devil utilizes to hinder a reconciled relationship in your life? The answer is found in **James 3:6, 8** and may surprise you: it is your *tongue*. You're probably thinking, "How does my tongue hinder reconciliation?" Think about this for a moment: when you are angry or offended, what is the first thing you want to do? Blow off your steam! You are designed to express your emotions, preferably in a prayer closet with the Lord first.

However, if you don't go to the Lord, you will ultimately go to someone else. If you bottle all your offenses up inside, what happens? You blow up on somebody, right? Do you see the point? The greatest way Satan attacks you is through your unrestrained, wagging tongue. When you're offended, he does not want you to go *to* your brother, as Jesus commanded. He wants you to go to someone else so that you can gossip *about* your brother, allowing your hearer to tell you what you want to hear, thus fanning the fire of resentment and bitterness in your heart! This kind of reaction with the tongue does nothing for reconciliation. It only stabilizes confusion and division, which are both devoid of love.

Beware of a gossiping tongue in the midst of relational differences. It is a lion that you cannot tame! Therefore, as you choose to obey Christ's commands, you will mature and grow in Christ, allowing Jesus to tame your tongue for you (**James 3:2**), because no human being can. Trust the Lord and give Him glory! Do not allow Satan to gain victory over you. It will be very difficult for you to bite your tongue and go to your brother, but it will be worth it in the end. You are blood-bought and Spirit-led, so do not allow Satan to have any victory in your life (**1 John 5:18**).

THE COMMAND INDESTRUCTIBLE:

You need a memory verse that will enhance your comprehension of Christ's commandment to always reconcile your relationships. What is the Scripture? Where is it found? Praise God, it is this: **Romans 5:9-10**. It says, *"Having now been justified by His blood, we shall be saved from wrath through Him. For if when we were enemies we were reconciled to God through the death of His Son, much more, having been reconciled, we shall be saved by His life."*

Do you see the significance? You and I were once alienated enemies to God (**1 John 4:4; Ephesians 2:12-13; 4:18-19; Colossians 1:21-23**). We were children of the devil, terminally infected with sin, eternally stained with the blemish of hopelessness...until the Lord Jesus Christ saved us, washed us, and set us free. Now, we are children of God (**1 John 3:1**)—we have been adopted by our heavenly Father, praise the Lord! The point is clear: If this is what God did for us, reconciling us to Himself by His dreadful sacrifice of Christ for our sins, then it is by far not too much to ask or expect that we too would seek parallel reconciliation with our enemies and offenders. Since Christ has reconciled you to the Father, you also must use your ministry of reconciliation (**2 Corinthians 5:18-20**) to do the same for others. Live your entire life just as Christ did (**Colossians 2:6**).

THE COMMAND INQUIRED:

What cannot be measured cannot be evaluated. Therefore, it is essential to measure your comprehension of Christ's command in this teaching, or else the devil will snatch away the "seeds" of Scripture sown into your heart (**Matthew 13:19**). To keep this from occurring, write down your answers to the following questions as they correlate with the teaching this week:

In what passage(s) of Scripture do you find Christ's commandment on **reconciliation**?

_____

_____

_____

What is the accurate interpretation of **reconciliation** you have discovered?

_____

_____

_____

_____

_____

_____

In your own words, what are some real-life examples in Scripture of **reconciliation**?

_____

_____

_____

_____

_____

_____

What steps of initiation did you learn to take in order for **reconciliation** to transform your life?

_____

_____

_____

_____

_____

_____

How will Satan attack you to hinder **reconciliation** in your life?

_____

_____

_____

_____

_____

_____

What memory verse will you use to protect Christ's command of **reconciliation** in your life? Write it out.

_____

_____

_____

_____

_____

_____

TEACHING # 5.4: MERCY

Week 36

This week's objective: To discover the beauty of mercy, as well as to learn the different approaches you should take to display it.

THE COMMAND INTRODUCED:

- **Matthew 5:7** *"Blessed are the merciful, for they shall obtain mercy."*
- **Luke 6:36** *"Therefore, be merciful, just as your Father is merciful."*

THE COMMAND INTERPRETED:

One command is implicit; the other is direct. When you think of the word *mercy*, what is your first thought? It has been said that the difference between grace and mercy is that *grace* is getting what you do not deserve, and *mercy* is not getting what you do deserve. There's a lot of truth in that statement. There is no better spokesman on the subject of mercy than Jesus Christ, for He is the embodiment of mercy to the world. Moreover, He wants you to not simply receive His mercy but also dispense it abroad, for there are many hurting hearts that need God's mercy.

The first command (**Matthew 5:7**) conveys the ***promise*** of mercy. Just as in the other Beatitudes, "blessedness" is referring to true spiritual happiness and joy. Using this as His platform, Jesus introduces two words, grammatical relations to one another: *merciful* and *mercy*. The Greek word "merciful" (*eleemon*) means "compassionate" and "mercy" (*eleeo*) means to "have compassion on." Linguistically, it is a cause-and-effect relationship. To be merciful means to exercise compassion toward another, whereas to obtain mercy means to experience compassion from another. What a beautiful relationship!

The Lord Jesus Christ strongly desires that your heart reflect such a pattern of mercy. His command is to be merciful, but His promise is that you will receive mercy, too. God ultimately glorifies Himself through your *"merciful"* actions towards the poor, needy, and destitute (**Psalm 18:25**). Mercy cannot be purchased or obtained except at the price of mercy itself! God wants to awake within you a compassion for those whom the world has forgotten, society has rejected, and unconcerned churches have ignored.

The second command (**Luke 6:36**) introduces the *practice* of mercy. This command proves that Jesus wants you to model the Father's mercy. What a task! Using the same Greek words as in the first command, Jesus stated one objective: *"Be merciful."* You are to practice mercy, emulating the Father and showing the same compassion that He has shown to you. In what ways has the Father shown mercy? Well, such a pursuit would be inexhaustible, for no mortal man can ever adequately explain the mercy of God. However, while we cannot *explain*, we most certainly *experience* constantly because God delights to show mercy (**Exodus 34:6; Ezekiel 33:11; 1 Timothy 2:4; 2 Peter 3:9**).

In like manner, this is where your practice comes in. Just as your guilty sins and their stains have been forgiven, show the same mercy to others that your Heavenly Father has shown to you (**Colossians 3:13; Ephesians 4:32**). To the man who scolded you, be merciful as your Father is. To the son who disobeyed you, be merciful as your Father is. To the employee that cheated you, be merciful as your Father is. You get the picture. Practice, practice, practice.

THE COMMAND ILLUSTRATED:

There is perhaps no greater story in the Bible to illustrate mercy than that of the Good Samaritan in **Luke 10:30-37**. Imagine this: a man traveling down the Jericho road was horrifically met by a band of robbers who beat him down, stole his goods, and left him for dead! As he was lying in the middle of the road, both a priest and a Levite passed by him. Being religious leaders, these men could have been expected to harbor the compassion of God in their hearts, but neither man helped the injured traveler. Then, a Samaritan also came by the man. The difference is that the Samaritan actually stopped. When he looked upon the man, beaten down and hurting, he responded with merciful compassion (**verse 33**), and the compassion in his heart resulted in action from his body. He bandaged the man, transported him, housed him, and paid his bills!

I have a question for you: which one are you—the priest, the Levite, or the Samaritan? Dear disciple, this is what mercy looks like. It is love in work clothes. It views inconvenience as a luxury. It didn't matter if the Samaritan was on his way to a meeting at work, heading home for supper, or involved in a project across town. He stopped. He looked. He had compassion. The call and demand for mercy must exceed cheap talk; it needs to see some Samaritan action (1 John 3:17-18). Do you know someone struggling? Do you know someone who is in trouble, who has wrecked their life and needs someone to talk to? If you do, have mercy on them. If you don't, be ready for Christ to channel His mercy through you to those whom He knows need it the most.

THE COMMAND INITIATED:

Perhaps you have done a good deed or two to help someone. Maybe you clothed a little orphan boy or fed a hungry family. While this is commendable in the sight of God, there is a need to take it a step further. With the power of Jesus, you want to move into a merciful attitude day by day, not just in seasons. You want mercy to live in your heart, not visit it like a tourist. Truly, you want to be known for Christ-centered compassion among the hurting and the dying. The real question is *how*?

Terry Rush has a good grasp on mercy's involvement in our lives. He wrote a book called *The Miracle of Mercy* and has filled its pages with answers to many of your questions. The only way mercy will ever become a vital part of your life is if you comprehend its true, transforming power:

> Can you imagine having the assignment of describing the Pacific Ocean by examining a quart jar full of sea water? Or how about trying to gather comprehensive information about the Rocky Mountains with a camera and a roll of film? When astronauts gather research from outer space with the

"technologically advanced" robot, what percentage of God's vast universe do they really reveal to us? How much more overwhelming to attempt to explain the meaning of mercy—an essential spiritual element of God—in one chapter? Efforts to capture the completeness of any given particle of God are inadequate...

Mercy is grace with a twist. Where grace applies to our lives regarding the ability to do things we can't do on our own (like endure hardship or grow spiritually or gain eternal salvation), mercy applies to our relationships with other people. It provides power for restoring and maintaining relationships—power that we don't possess on our own. Both mercy and grace are gifts from God. Grace applies His arm to the labor required of us when we are weak. Mercy applies His strength to relationships required of us when we can't make them work. Each enables us to do what we could not do on our own. Mercy, like grace, is divine participation in human weakness. But mercy's emphasis is on *not* giving us the "justice" we deserve. Rather than cutting us off from His continued blessings—as we deserve—God gives us another chance...and another...and another. Mercy, however, is a double-edged sword, and with its blessings come responsibilities. Mercy calls upon us to bless others in ways they do not deserve—just as our heavenly Father blesses us, though we are undeserving.[4]

THE COMMAND INTERROGATED:

To be unmerciful is to receive no mercy. How tragic that would be for you! Satan is on a rampage to destroy you and your new life with Christ as a disciple. You must be prepared. The greatest way to uncover Satan's plot against you is to see how exactly he wants to eradicate mercy from your life. The Apostle Paul gives us a glimpse into the way Satan will render you powerless in **Romans 12:1.**

Do you see it? *"By the mercies of God,"* the Apostle Paul admonished the believers to present their bodies a *"living sacrifice."* This meant that a total surrender to the Lord was a byproduct of personally appropriating God's mercy. In other words, because of God's mercy, your *"reasonable service"* is to be a living, bold, sold-out disciple for Jesus Christ. This kind of life is only reflective of a proper understanding of God's mercy.

However, Satan wants to see you give up your surrender. If he can tempt you and distract you enough to do so, do you see what will happen? You will lose appreciation of God's mercy, which in turn affects drastically the mercy you show to others. This means you will become judgmental, selfish, and prideful because a life wrapped up in yourself is no life at all! Do not allow Satan to get a foothold in your life of surrender to Jesus. Stay firm. Remain steadfast. Mercy is on the line.

THE COMMAND INDESTRUCTIBLE:

Satan is a liar, but Jesus is *the* Truth. And since you are sanctified by His truth (**John 17:17**), you can trust it and hold on to it. Your only hope is the Word of God! You are not to be a cowardly, confused believer that Satan manipulates. You have manna, dear friend. You have Scripture that will know no end. So, do you believe it? Of course you do. Today, implant your memory verse deep into the contours of your mind and heart, because you will need to humble yourself with this reminder: **James 2:13**. It says, *"For judgment is without mercy to the one who has shown no mercy. Mercy triumphs over judgment."*

Live that verse of Scripture. Anytime you exercise mercy, regardless of the situation, Christ takes note of it, for judgment becomes a cancellation policy. The Lord will not require a judgment from you that you have not earned. Oh, dear disciple, do not lose sight of the mercy you have received from Christ the Lord (**Titus 3:4-6**). Some people will be easy to show mercy to, for they will be hurting and needy. Others will be more challenging to give mercy to, for they will be rude and vindictive. Remember, mercy is not ever going to be something you generate in feeling; it will be something you appropriate with gratitude. May the love of Christ compel you! May the Spirit of God empower you! May the Word of God sustain you!

THE COMMAND INQUIRED:

What cannot be measured cannot be evaluated. Therefore, it is essential to measure your comprehension of Christ's command in this teaching, or else the devil will snatch away the "seeds" of Scripture sown into your heart (**Matthew 13:19**). To keep this from occurring, write down your answers to the following questions as they correlate with the teaching this week:

In what passage(s) of Scripture do you find Christ's commandment on **mercy**?

_____

_____

_____

What is the accurate interpretation of **mercy** you have discovered?

_____

_____

_____

_____

_____

In your own words, what are some real-life examples in Scripture of **mercy**?

_____

_____

_____

_____

_____

_____

What steps of initiation did you learn to take in order for **mercy** to transform your life?

_____

_____

_____

_____

_____

How will Satan attack you to hinder **mercy** in your life?

_____

_____

_____

_____

_____

What memory verse will you use to protect Christ's command of **mercy** in your life? Write it out.

_____

_____

_____

TEACHING # 5.5: PEACEMAKING

Week 37

<u>This week's objective</u>: *To assess the biblical art of peacemaking, as well as to imitate its principles to put into practice in your daily life.*

THE COMMAND INTRODUCED:

- **Matthew 5:9** *"Blessed are the peacemakers, for they shall be called sons of God."*
- **Matthew 26:51-54** *"And suddenly, one of those who were with Jesus stretched out his hand and drew his sword, struck the servant of the high priest, and cut off his ear. But Jesus said to him, 'Put your sword in its place, for all who take the sword will perish by the sword. Or do you think that I cannot now pray to My Father, and He will provide Me with more than twelve legions of angels? How then could the Scriptures be fulfilled, that it must happen thus?'"*
- **Luke 6:26** *"Woe to you when all men speak well of you, for so did their fathers to the false prophets."*

THE COMMAND INTERPRETED:

All three of these commands are clearly implicit and can be arranged into two categories: *retaliation* and *compromise*. The first two commands highlight retaliation; the third command focuses on compromise. The Lord Jesus Christ does not want you to overlook what true peacemaking is all about. Your surrender to these commands will revolutionize your entire social structure.

As mentioned, retaliation governs the first two commands from Jesus. The first command (**Matthew 5:9**) addresses the ***display*** against retaliation. As with the other beatitudes, Jesus uses the word *blessed*, which means "happy." His focus is on the "*peacemakers*." The Greek word He used to refer to such people is *eirenopoios*, which translates "to make peace; peaceable." Only one more time in the Greek New Testament is this exact form of the word used (**Romans**

12:18), in an instance regarding social peace.

You see, the point is not to be at peace with yourself but to trigger peace socially through your active obedience to Christ's command to be a peacemaker. This results in a display against retaliation because Jesus says you *"shall be called sons of God."* In other words, such action can be connected to the way God's *"sons,"* or children, conduct themselves in the presence of enemies (**Matthew 5:44-45**). By making peace with so-called enemies, you are treating them the same way that your heavenly Father treated you. Never forget it: you used to be an enemy of the cross of Christ (**Philippians 3:18**), but now you have made "peace" through the blood of that same cross (**Colossians 1:20**)! Dear disciple, do not retaliate. Display that you're one of God's kids.

The second command (**Matthew 26:51-54**) addresses the *devastation* from retaliation. Can you imagine the scene? Matthew does not give as many details in his Gospel as do John (**18:10**) and Luke (**22:51**). Naturally, the Apostle Peter loved Jesus and had grown extremely attached to Him. So, when the angry mob came against the Lord to arrest Him, Peter acted defensively. It's one thing to say, "Leave Him alone," but it's quite another to cut a man's ear off his head.

This is the devastation of what happens when undue retaliation takes place. Did Peter really think Christ, the Son of God, the commander of all legions of angels in Heaven, could not defend Himself? No, that's just it: Peter didn't think at all! That is what happens when we react impulsively before we think rationally about what we're going to say or do amidst enemy forces in our daily lives.

The only solution to avoid devastation is to obey Jesus' command: *"Put your sword in its place, for all who take the sword will perish by the sword."* This may be one area of your new life in Christ that will require time and patience. When you "put away your sword" during seasons of testing, you grow spiritually each time to be that much more like Jesus. The sword with which you can do the most damage is your tongue (**Psalm 57:4; Proverbs 18:21; James 3: 6, 8**). It is the fuel for the fire in the midst of retaliation! Spouting vengeful words is worse than cutting off a man's ear, because these words enter the ears and cut deep into the emotions of the heart. Restrain your tongue when retaliation is tempting. Put away your sword. Obey Christ, your Lord and Master.

Lastly, the third command (**Luke 6:26**) shifts into a different gear, one that is governed by compromise. Christ cut right to the point. With cautionary warning, Jesus said, *"Woe to you."* As a disciple, pay close attention to the idea the Lord conveys. If everybody everywhere speaks good about you all the time, your life as a believer is one of compromise. Sure, that sounds accusatory, but please remember what Jesus said in **Matthew 10:34-39**. You, like anyone else, must choose which side of the fence you want to be on. No lukewarm, shallow indecisiveness is allowed.

If you side with Jesus, your very obedience to His commands will sanctify you so much that people will tell you apart from the corruption of this world and its ways. You will look different and act different because you *are* different. You are saved. Your nature is reflective of Christ's nature and worthy of maturing. You are not called to be a spineless coward; you're a disciple! Persecution comes to people like you who follow Christ's commands wholeheartedly (**2 Timothy 3:12**), as it came to those "true" prophets before you (**Luke 6:22-23**). But these false prophets are always looking ways to blur the lines of truth. People speak so well of them all the time because they are people pleasers (**John 12:43**), seeking the wrong kind of "peace"-making among men, the kind that doesn't want to offend people or hurt their feelings.

When the Word of God is at stake, it is better to offend people with the truth than to compromise the truth and offend the Lord Almighty (**Matthew 13:57; Matthew 15:10-14; John 6:61**). Oh, disciple, whatever you do, stand for what you know the Word of God teaches, even if you stand alone. Know what you believe and *why* you believe it (**1 Peter 3:15**). Above all, seek to please the Lord (**Ephesians 6:6; Galatians 1:10**), not men. Never, ever apologize for the truth of Scripture. It is what it is. Don't seek peace with men at the cost of compromising the Scriptures.

THE COMMAND ILLUSTRATED:

A good example in the Bible of peacemaking is the incident of Joseph and his brothers (**Genesis 37:1-11**). As the passage opens, you can tell that Joseph was the "baby" of all the children. Due to the abundant love that Israel (Jacob) showed toward Joseph, his brothers became envious and enraged, resulting in **verse 4**. Their indignation led to their inability to live "*peaceably*" near Joseph. So, when he told them about his dream, they were even more furious; this time, even Joseph's parents were angry. Amazingly, Joseph's brothers sold him into slavery to get rid of him and then lied to their dad about his disappearance. How evil! However, as for Joseph's vision, what was called a dream was actually prophecy in the making.

Look at **Genesis 47**. After years of separation, Joseph and his brothers prophetically reunited, just as Joseph's dream had vividly portrayed. Isn't that amazing! However, it is even more incredible to see Joseph's response. He was second in command in all the land of Egypt, which means he could have used his authority to have his brothers killed, but he chose to not retaliate. Joseph's example is the perfect way to illustrate the principle of Christ's command to be a peacemaker—not a pushover, a peacemaker. In fact, the way that Joseph ended the hostility between him and his brothers is literally breathtaking (**Genesis 50:15-21**). What a picture of grace and mercy! Peacemaking does not seek revenge (**Romans 12:17-21**). Rather, it seeks unified, forgiven results that produce peace.

THE COMMAND INITIATED:

Honestly, isn't real peace what you long for? If you have enemies because of their stubbornness to receive the gospel, that's normal and expected (**Romans 10:16**). But if you have enemies because of your stubbornness to seek peace, that's wrong and in need of correction. Humble yourself. Your relationship with Christ is only as strong as your relationships with people. Christ is calling you not only to obey this command but also to exemplify it to a society that doesn't see it in action enough.

In his book *Seeking Peace*, Johann C. Arnold has nothing but pure motives in trying to unveil some underlying truths about peace. His goal is to help you appropriate this authentic, Biblical peace in all your relationships. Moreover, he emphasizes the reality of spiritual warfare and its damaging effects on peace in your relationships:

Many Christians today disdain the idea of spiritual warfare. For one thing, they feel it is a figment of the imagination; for another, they feel the language used to describe it is too confrontational, too in-your-face and, worst of all, too old-fashioned. Yet the cosmic fight between the angels of God and the hosts of Satan continues to this day, despite dwindling belief in its reality. Why should we presume it is an abstraction just because we don't see it? I believe that the invisible powers of good and evil are every bit as real as the physical forces that make up our universe, and unless we are able to discern them, we cannot enter into the vital battle that takes place between them. As light cannot share space with darkness, so good and evil cannot coexist, and we must, therefore, decide which side we will take...One of the greatest risks in taking up arms against evil is to mistake the battle for something that must be fought on a human level, between opposing camps of "good" people and "evil" ones. We may speak of God and the church in contrast to Satan and the world, but the reality is that the dividing line between good and evil runs through every human heart. And who are we to judge anyone but ourselves?...Each of us creates an atmosphere around himself. As we "fight the good fight," let us not forget to pause, now and then, and ask ourselves whether this atmosphere is one of fear, or of the love that casts out fear. It is tempting to carry out the fight in others rather than in ourselves. Horrified at the state of the world or at other people's lives, we may become filled with a righteous (if not self-righteous) zeal. But rather than winning others over to a new life, or finding their hearts, we may end up distancing ourselves from them. The battle must be waged in our own hearts first.[5]

THE COMMAND INTERROGATED:

Fear. Doubt. Panic. These are the ways Satan attempts to uproot the peace that Christ has given you (**John 14:27**). It's the same situation you see in **Mark 4:35-41**. The storm was raging. The peace was fleeing. Fear gripped the disciple's hearts, to the point that the thought of peace would have been the joke of the day. "*Peace, be still.*" That's all you hear from Jesus. No rebuke. No lecture. Just *peace*. He wanted to use the ocean to speak to the disciples' hearts. Christ desired to "*calm*" the fear and cover it with His peace. Satan doesn't want this for you! Beware of his multiple attacks to provide you with countless situations, possibilities, circumstances, and health scares to plant fear and doubt in your heart, in hopes of destroying peace.

It is a sly move on the devil's part to ruin you in this manner. Think about how clever it is: how can you seek peace with another human being if you are not at peace within yourself? That's like trying to offer someone a drink of water with an empty glass. You cannot give what you do not have. You cannot make peace with others if you are not abiding in peace with Christ and His Word over your fears and doubts. Do not let Satan prevail. Christ's command is at stake.

THE COMMAND INDESTRUCTIBLE:

Realistically, you are going to encounter many people whom you will offend with the gospel. They may not like the Jesus you preach or teach. They may very well hate that you give thanks for your meal in the lunchroom. So, what are you going to do? If you choose to obey Christ's command and not let the air out of their tires or otherwise seek revenge, you will be victorious, and their hearts will stand amazed. When people hurt you, they expect you to fight back. To seek peace with them is not an option because it is against your nature. But when you show them the "new nature" as it comes alive within you, hallelujah! Praise God that this does not make you a coward; it makes you a conqueror. You need a memory verse to hold you accountable, one that you can recall in every circumstance through which Satan tries to tempt you away from peace: **James 3:18**. It says, "*Now the fruit of righteousness is sown in peace by those who make peace.*"

The *"fruit of righteousness"* is simply the byproduct of any work through faith that you do to glorify God. Any fruit of righteousness comes from the Righteous One, Jesus, because of your relationship with Him. Fruit of righteousness is *"sown."* You cannot sow what you do not have, which explains why Christ says your hunger for His righteousness (**Matthew 5:6**) results in being filled with it. Before all men, you sow, and sow, and sow peace. Not resentment. Not bitterness. Not unforgiveness.

Dear disciple, filling up with Christ's righteousness through your love for and obedience to Him is what brings Him glory and praise (**Philippians 1:11**). With anyone, regardless of the nature of the situation, seek peace. Sow it deep into the ground of their heart, and do so with a love like that of Jesus. You can sow peace into people's lives! View this not as an obligation but as a privilege to brag on Jesus and the peace He's given you and guarding you with (**Philippians 4:6-7**). You are a peacemaker. Give Him praise and give Him glory!

THE COMMAND INQUIRED:

What cannot be measured cannot be evaluated. Therefore, it is essential to measure your comprehension of Christ's command in this teaching, or else the devil will snatch away the "seeds" of Scripture sown into your heart (**Matthew 13:19**). To keep this from occurring, write down your answers to the following questions as they correlate with the teaching this week:

In what passage(s) of Scripture do you find Christ's commandment on **peacemaking**?

_____

_____

_____

What is the accurate interpretation of **peacemaking** you have discovered?

_____

_____

_____

_____

_____

_____

In your own words, what are some real-life examples in Scripture of **peacemaking**?

_____

_____

_____

_____

_____

What steps of initiation did you learn to take in order for **peacemaking** to transform your life?

_____

_____

_____

_____

_____

How will Satan attack you to hinder **peacemaking** in your life?

_____

_____

_____

_____

_____

_____

What memory verse will you use to protect Christ's command of **peacemaking** in your life? Write it out.

_____

_____

_____

_____

_____

_____

TEACHING # 5.6: BENEVOLENCE

Week 38

This week's objective: To discover the true meaning of a benevolent lifestyle, as well as to learn how to engage in the disciplines necessary for such a life.

THE COMMAND INTRODUCED:

- **Matthew 6:1-4** *"Take heed that you do not do your charitable deeds before men, to be seen by them. Otherwise you have no reward from your Father in heaven. Therefore, when you do a charitable deed, do not sound a trumpet before you as the hypocrites do in the synagogues and in the streets, that they may have glory from men. Assuredly, I say to you, they have their reward. But when you do a charitable deed, do not let your left hand know what your right hand is doing, that your charitable deed may be in secret; and your Father who sees in secret will Himself reward you openly."*
- **Matthew 14:14-18; Mark 6:37-40; Luke 9:13-15; John 6:9-13** *"And when Jesus went out He saw a great multitude; and He was moved with compassion for them, and healed their sick. When it was evening, His disciples came to Him, saying, 'This is a deserted place, and the hour is already late. Send the multitudes away, that they may go into the villages and buy themselves food.' But Jesus said to them, 'They do not need to go away. You give them something to eat.' And they said to Him, 'We have here only five loaves and two fish.' He said, 'Bring them here to Me.'"*

THE COMMAND INTERPRETED:

These two commands could not be any more direct. Jesus did not stutter! He eagerly desired for His disciples to learn His heart toward the needy. Though the term *benevolence* is not used, its principle saturates the commands. Benevolence is a sacrificial deed that is done to benefit someone in need. To put it plainly, it is love in work clothes. Pay close attention to the idea that Christ wants to embed in your heart.

The first command (**Matthew 6:1-4**) reveals the *goal* of benevolence. The path of Christ's command paves the way to understanding the chief goal. Jesus started by *cautioning* of the motive of your benevolent deeds (**verses 1-2**). All *"charitable deeds"* refer to acts of benevolence. The concern Jesus has addresses the attention-seeking behavior involved in helping people—*"to be seen by men."* If such is the case, motive is exposed. To illustrate, Christ said the Pharisees acted this way by sounding *"a trumpet in the synagogues and in the streets."* The sin of *"man praise"* is insidious and subtle. Benevolence done for recognition indicates the evil motive of the heart, and it robs God of His glory (**Psalm 115:1**).

You must discipline yourself to reject the prideful egotism that may come from your sacrificial deeds. Be careful not to become attention-seeking, always wanting an applause for your hard work and travail. Sure, it is kind and courteous for others to recognize what you've done for them. But if they should choose not to, your real motive will surface. Whatever you do, do not emulate benevolence only to be seen (**verse 1**) and heard (**verse 2**). Everything you do or say is produced from motive, and it is your motive that will come under full examination one day at the Judgment Seat of Christ (**1 Corinthians 3:13; 2 Corinthians 5:9-10**). Your *"deeds"* will be exposed here, and it will become *"clear"* why you *really* helped others, whether for your own glory or for God's.

Immediately after Jesus cautioned of the motive of your benevolent deeds, He *conditioned* the means for such deeds (**verses 3-4**). How do you give of yourself to help others? Why do you do so? What is the balance in demonstrating the benevolence of Christ? The idea in mind here is so simple yet requires such discipline to obey. Jesus confirmed the goal of true benevolence: secrecy! Are you any good at keeping a secret—you know, the kind that someone whispers in your ear when they say, "I'm pregnant" or "You'll never believe what happened yesterday..."? The ability to keep a secret is important in everyday life, but it's even more paramount when you are helping people in your Christian walk.

The ultimate goal of benevolence that Jesus was trying to teach is *privacy*. If at all possible, do your *"charitable deeds"* privately, to the degree that metaphorically, your *"left hand doesn't know what your right hand is doing.*" Why? Reward! You see, God delights in rewarding you Himself, in whichever way He so chooses. You discipline yourself to help others privately and quietly. Your mind and heart are more committed to how you can meet the need than to what you can receive. Avoiding recognition means God gets the praise. Therefore, again, the condition for your deeds is clear: secrecy is *expected* (**verses 3-4a**), and then it becomes *exposed* (**verse 4b**). Position yourself in God's secret place (**Jeremiah 23:24; Psalm 91:1**), and I assure you, He Himself will reward your faith (**Hebrews 6:10; 11:6**) as it shows up in benevolent deeds. But remember, until then, *shhhhhhhh.*

The second command (**Matthew 14:14-18; Mark 6:37-40; Luke 9:13-15; John 6:9-13**) reveals the *gem* in benevolence. A gem is something of tangible value, and on the same scale, you find something of spiritual value in this command. Just after Christ finished healing all the sick among a multitude, He and the disciples found that the crowd did not leave. In fact, collectively the Gospel accounts indicate that there were thousands of people. Exhausted from the day's work with Christ, the disciples requested to send the multitude away to seek their own meals in the city. However, Jesus was appalled. Why? The disciples had food with them! Therefore, the command "*You give them something to eat*" was not a surprise.

Jesus has not changed His command or His tone. Five loaves of bread and two fishes was insufficient to feed several thousand growling stomachs in the natural, but in the supernatural, it fed and exceeded, with abundance left over. Jesus was proving a point to teach His disciples, just as He is teaching you right now through His command: when you bring to Him what little you've got, He'll multiply it, moving Heaven and Earth to reach the poor and needy with His love. This is the gem in benevolence, the diamond in the dust when it comes to ministering to the poor. Little is much when God is in it!

God forbid that you ever turn anyone away who is cold, hungry, hurting, and poor. How could the love of God abide in you if you ever did (**1 John 3:17-18**)? As long as you obey Christ's command, this will not be an issue with you. Love, love, love. Reach, reach, reach. Give, give, give. Your "little" is not as little as you think (**Proverbs 15:16; 16:8**). If you don't believe me, just take another look at the widow in **Mark 12:41-44**. Never forget this, you precious disciple. If all you have is a piece of bread to help a homeless man, amen! If all you have is twelve dollars to clothe a cold and frightened woman, amen! Trust God for His multiplying power, whether you see it or not (**2 Corinthians 5:7**). Put this gem in the treasure box of your faith. Don't lose it...use it.

THE COMMAND ILLUSTRATED:

Oh, there are so many places in Scripture where you could go to unravel story after story of benevolent deeds. One of the best ones you will find, however, has absolutely nothing to do with benevolence from a monetary, tangible standpoint. To illustrate this, turn to **Acts 3:1-10**. Now, after reading the story, do you see the benevolence of Peter? Think about it for a moment: Peter gave the lame man what he needed, not what he wanted. You see, all this man's life he had been a beggar. Yet all his daily begging at the gate of the Temple had done nothing for him except keep him in his same miserable condition. Why would Peter want to add to that? That would hold no value for that poor man. Therefore, Peter took it a step further.

"Silver and gold I do not have, but what I do have I give you: In the name of Jesus Christ of Nazareth, rise up and walk." All the silver in the world would not help the man walk. Every ounce of gold imaginable would do nothing for his real need. But now, never would this man be the same! Peter, with authorized, apostolic healing power, witnessed that day the miraculous use of "what he did have." Dear disciple, what do you have? Use it; don't hoard it. If a drunk corners you to buy him whiskey, don't give him more whiskey—that's not what he really wants. He's trapped, alone, and afraid, and he only seeks alcohol to cover up and hide from who he has become. Instead, give him Jesus, give him hope, give him praying faith. Give him what you have in Jesus Christ our Lord! Until Jesus has people, they have nothing. Your benevolent acts are limitless in Christ.

THE COMMAND INITIATED:

It might seem that the picture of benevolence has been

applied and exhausted. Well, while this is true so far for these commands, it does not replace your actual practice of such commands. Are you benevolent? Do you find yourself doing things for people only as they do things for you, or are you serving others with nothing expected in return (**Matthew 5:46**)?

Alexander Strauch excavates the meaning of benevolence in a way that will leave you in awe. He focuses on where benevolence must first begin: not in the world, but among Christians. In his book *The Hospitality Commands,* Strauch bridges the entire concept of benevolence into your life by addressing its identical twin, hospitality. Embrace this teaching:

> The Christians to whom Peter is writing were facing bitter persecution (**1 Peter 4: 12-19**). In the face of pagan hostility, Peter knows that fervent love and unity among the Christians are essential in keeping them safe during the rough storms of persecution. So Peter urges his brothers and sisters to *"keep fervent in your love for one another"* (**verse 8**). The Greek word for "fervent" conveys the idea of earnestness, persistent effort, or resolve. Cranfield warns, "Fervently gives perhaps a wrong nuance; for it might suggest that the emphasis is on warmth of emotion, whereas the Greek word it represents suggests rather the taut muscle of strenuous and sustained effort, as of an athlete. It suggests a certain toughness of love, love which endures." As Christians, therefore, we should press ourselves to the full extent in loving one another. One very practical way to exert our love is to show hospitality. Hospitality fuels the flames of love. It promotes and preserves love. It enriches and deepens *agape* love. It renews love. Hence, Peter naturally follows his exhortation to love fervently with the command to practice hospitality gladly. It is important that we observe the kind of command Peter delivers here. The command to practice hospitality (**verse 8**) is a "one-another command," one of many such commands in the New Testament. Christians are instructed to love

one another, pray for one another, serve one another, admonish one another, edify one another, care for one another, bear one another's burdens, and here, to be hospitable to one another...Since we are all *"members of one another"* (**Romans 12:5**), we all are to minister the love and care of Jesus Christ to one another. This is part of life in the body of Christ. This is part of the dynamic interdependence that exists between members of Christ's body. So, members of the Christian community are to mutually exercise hospitality.[6]

THE COMMAND INTERROGATED:

You can probably identify many ways in which Satan loves to hinder benevolence and hospitality in your life. But what is his greatest move, his chief tactic to silence your deeds to help others? I'll tell you what it is: *greed*. Greed is the mother of hoarding, the kind that nursed the rich young ruler (**Luke 18:22-23**). Greed is an untamed beast, one that devours you from the inside out (**1 Timothy 6:10**). It mimics the ways of Balaam (**Jude 11**) and brings destruction to families that play with its venom (**Proverbs 15:27; 21:26**). This is Satan's primary target of attack against the confines of your heart. Be very, very alert of this. Greed's breaking blow will paralyze benevolence in your lifestyle. Satan tempts you to worry about something you value and to hoard it in spite of your awareness of a needy man who needs it more than you do! Satan tempts you to support a bad habit, to the point that you invest more into feeding your addiction than you do into feeding needy children. Do you see the point? Greed! Beware of Satan's assault on you, for he would love for you to build a wall against hospitality and meeting the needs of others. May this not be named among you.

THE COMMAND INDESTRUCTIBLE:

The living Word of God comes to the rescue! Satan cannot stop the power of a disciple when he or she is living by faith in belief of the Scriptures. Day by day, you will be surrounded by needs. The poor will always be with us (**Matthew 26:11**), and indeed, you and I may be in that position at times in our lives because of Satan's devouring attack (**Malachi 3:11**). To protect yourself from becoming either defiant or spiritually numb to opportunities for benevolence, you *must* use Scripture to fight for you as well as remind you of your responsibility.

Therefore, your memory verse is **Proverbs 21:13**. It says, *"Whoever shuts his ears to the cry of the poor will also cry himself and not be heard."* Wow. What goes around comes around. You reap what you sow. To help the poor and needy is to minister unto the Lord our God Himself (**Proverbs 19:17**). It is shameful to hide your eyes from the cry of the needy, because by doing so you will bring chastening curses into your life (**Proverbs 28:27**).

You can overcome every obstacle of greed by faith in Christ's command to be benevolent. In spite of how little you may have, trust God to multiply it. You are called to and equipped for this; as a believer, "benevolence" is your middle name! Bless the poor, enrich the needy, feed the hungry, clothe the ragged, and pray for the sick, being as quiet about it as possible. Use your memory verse day by day, opportunity by opportunity. Attention: report for duty.

THE COMMAND INQUIRED:

What cannot be measured cannot be evaluated. Therefore, it is essential to measure your comprehension of Christ's command in this teaching, or else the devil will snatch away the "seeds" of Scripture sown into your heart (**Matthew 13:19**). To keep this from occurring, write down your answers to the following questions as they correlate with the teaching this week:

In what passage(s) of Scripture do you find Christ's commandment on **benevolence**?

_____

_____

_____

What is the accurate interpretation of **benevolence** you have discovered?

_____

_____

_____

_____

_____

In your own words, what are some real-life examples in Scripture of **benevolence**?

_____

_____

_____

_____

_____

What steps of initiation did you learn to take in order for **benevolence** to transform your life?

_____

_____

_____

_____

_____

How will Satan attack you to hinder **benevolence** in your life?

_____

_____

_____

_____

_____

_____

What memory verse will you use to protect Christ's command of **benevolence** in your life? Write it out.

_____

_____

_____

_____

_____

_____

TEACHING # 5.7: KINDNESS

Week 39

This week's objective: To unravel the true, undiluted meaning of kindness, as well as to learn how to practice it day-to-day.

THE COMMAND INTRODUCED:

- **Matthew 7:12** *"Therefore, whatever you want men to do to you, do also to them, for this is the Law and the Prophets."*

THE COMMAND INTERPRETED:

This command from Christ is direct and easily comprehended. Although the term *kindness* is not used, it is more than obvious in the linguistic tone of Jesus' words. Before you examine this command in its context, there is an essential observation to make about kindness. *Kindness*, in the biblical sense, is different from that in the moral sense. Think about it for a moment: both a lost man and a Christian can be kind. What's the difference? Jesus Christ!

You see, Christ is not asking for a degree of kindness that you can produce in your lost state. If you could be just as kind in your lost state as you can be when you are born again, why be saved to begin with? Therefore, the "kindness" that you are to produce behaviorally towards others is a result of your new nature in Christ (**2 Corinthians 5:17**). Dead leaves fall from a tree, not because the tree died, but because *new* life emerged! Likewise, Christ-like kindness exceeds the kindness you produced as a lost person, for it roots from your *new* life in Christ (**Romans 6:4**). The sanctified difference is Jesus.

Now, back to the command. The "golden rule" idea has surfaced once again. "Treat others the way you want to be treated" is definitely a modern-day paraphrase of what Christ is teaching here. The general idea being portrayed by Jesus is that you seek to establish your own social system. Do you see it? Jesus is not asking for your vocal obedience but your behavioral obedience. Christ says, *"Whatever you want men to do to you..."* He is giving you a platform on which to build your entire life! Nobody, including you, enjoys being lied to, cheated, or pushed around by people. Why? Because you are designed to be a channel of kindness. Love is not found in a critical, mean-spirited heart. So, again, talk is cheap; Jesus is interested in what you *do* to, for, and with people (**1 John 3:18**).

    To conduct yourself this way is to reflect the Old Testament Law and prophets. The Law was centered on valuing human dignity and preferring others before yourself. The prophets pleaded for people to seek unity in Israel through loving and serving one another. Kindness fits here. It is made to be an extension of the *"Law and the Prophets,"* one of the two greatest commandments to mankind (**Matthew 22:37-40**). Therefore, while you can say a kind word, the true test of your sacrifice and inconvenience is in displaying your kindness as Jesus said. Make your social environment what Christ wants it to be. Kindness shines through good works (**Ephesians 2:10; Titus 3:8**). You were created for this. Open your eyes. Get to work.

THE COMMAND ILLUSTRATED:

    Among the top examples of kindness in the Bible is the story of Ruth and Boaz (**Ruth 2**). If you have never read all four chapters of the Book of Ruth, you need to do so before you go any further in this teaching. If you have read this story before, allow me to stir your memory. Since there was a famine in Bethlehem, a man named Elimelech journeyed to the land of Moab, along with his wife, Naomi, and their two sons. During their ten years of living there, Elimelech's sons married. Then, for unexplained reasons, both Elimelech and his sons died. This left Naomi widowed, along with her two daughters-in-law, Ruth and Orpah. When the moment of decision came, Orpah left, but Ruth stayed with Naomi. Ruth's loyalty was remarkable, and her kindness to Naomi in such a time of need was not forgotten by the Lord. One day Ruth left in search of food, for she and Naomi had no husband to support them financially. That's when a wealthy man named Boaz—interestingly, a relative of Elimelech—came into the picture. Divinely, yet unintentionally, Ruth found herself in Boaz's field (**verse 3**).

This is where kindness is introduced. Boaz took notice of Ruth and inquired about her (**verse 5-6**). He approached Ruth and discovered what was on her heart (**verse7**). Finally, after getting to know Ruth, Boaz showed a surpassing measure of kindness to Ruth (**verse 8-10**). In fact, he even explained why he acted so kindly towards her (**verse 11-12**). Ruth was in awe (**verse 13**).

But notice an interesting point of observation. Ruth did unto Naomi what she wanted done unto herself. Now, in a reciprocating fashion, Ruth's kindness intricately backfired, not from Naomi, but from someone totally different! What does this tell you? It means that as you follow Christ's command of kindness toward others, He takes notice and will repay. While it is expected that you will be treated kindly from someone you ministered to, your reward is not limited to coming from that same individual.

You may treat a homeless man kindly by doing something for him yet never see the man again to receive his kindness back to you. But the kindness you receive from someone else the next week, possibly even a total stranger, demonstrates the principle here. The Lord is the one watching (**Proverbs 15:3**). He knows when His kindness through your obedience to His Word prevails. Give Jesus what He deserves. When you show kindness to people, you do it unto the Lord Himself (**Matthew 25:40**).

THE COMMAND INITIATED:

It is my hope that you now have a good grip on the type of kindness Jesus expects. He saved you, and He loves you, and your obedience is everything to Him. Christ would have no greater joy than to see His command in action in your daily life. An atheist can show kindness by greeting you politely. A lost man can do a kind deed by helping you in an emergency. But this is not the standard; Jesus is. What does it look like to exceed human morals? Well, it looks like Jesus. You see, an atheist being kind and a lost man acting kind have their limitations if you are not kind to them in return. Christ, however, is kind regardless of your treatment of Him. In like manner, He calls you to follow Him and operate in the same capacity of kindness. That's the real, undeniable difference.

Are you practicing this manner of kindness? You are not if you are only kind to those who are kind to you. Christ's command indicates the hope that people will respond to you with the same kindness, but this is not guaranteed. Sure, you want others to treat you as kindly as you treat them, but be prepared if they don't. Affirm your commitment to Jesus' command by choosing, in the midst of unkindness, to obey Him instead of your hurt feelings.

In her book *Kindness*, Phyllis J. Le Peau does a beautiful job of explaining and illustrating kindness in its biblical form. As a disciple, take her advice and put devotional acts of kindness into practice daily:

> Several years ago some seminary students were asked to preach on the story of the Good Samaritan. When the hour arrived for their sermon, each one was deliberately delayed en route to class. As the students raced across campus, they encountered a person who pretended to be in need. Ironically, not one of the students stopped to help. After all, they had an important sermon to preach!
> It's easy to laugh at the hypocrisy of those students. Yet every day in various ways we reenact Christ's parable. Whether it's a family on the side of the road with car trouble, a homeless person sleeping over an outdoor heating vent, or a panhandler asking for spare change—we either pass by or reach out in kindness...The Bible tells us that God's kindness is freely given, that it preserves us, that it is "better than life." It involves the warmth of God's fellowship as well as the security of His goodness and faithfulness. It certainly follows that if we experience God's kindness, we will be transformed by it and reach out in kindness to others...[7]

THE COMMAND INTERROGATED:

There is no doubt about the exact way Satan seeks to corrupt kindness in your life. It all comes down to the very storehouse of kindness in your life: the indwelling Holy Spirit of God (**Galatians 5:22-23**). Did you notice *"kindness"* among the byproducts of fruitfulness in your Christian life? The obvious battle against the Holy Spirit comes from the flesh (**Galatians 5:16-17**). There is a war, a fight for your obedience. Biblical kindness threatens Satan, because the love of God and His kindness to you is a reminder of the enemy's eternal defeat. He hated you and wanted you hell-bound, but God loved you through Jesus and wanted you saved.

Therefore, when you are walking in the Spirit, you are producing God's kindness in your life. Satan's only option is to get you in the flesh. How? To sway you into acting unkind. It may come when someone makes you really mad, and instead of letting kindness show forth, you harbor resentment against them, which eventually comes out in the form of anger. Unkindness may come from a boss that is seemingly trying to get you fired, or a sibling that has a vendetta against you, or even perhaps from a best friend that has always been so kind to you until recently. Do you see how Satan cannot make you unkind (that's your choice), but he can provide you with tempting circumstances to see if you'll budge from the Spirit's power? If you do, you are defeated. Beware of the devil's tactics. Do not allow him to overwhelm you with his limited powers of darkness. You are a child of the living God. Act like it. Fight Scripturally!

THE COMMAND INDESTRUCTIBLE:

The Word of God is full of so many Scriptures that involve kindness. If Satan is going to be defeated, it will not come merely by your quoting of these Scriptures, but by your belief in and practice of them. Among them, one verse seems to say it all, in the form of a mandate: **2 Peter 3:12**. It says, *"Therefore, as the elect of God, holy and beloved, put on tender mercies, kindness, humility, meekness, longsuffering."* This is your memory verse. As the *"elect of God,"* you are a part of the family of God, which means you are one of His children now. Haven't you heard the phrase, "You act just like your daddy"?

Well, that's exactly what your heavenly Father is wanting people to say about you. He wants you to be holy. And, as His tender mercy has been shown to you (**Titus 2:4-7**), so you also are to "*put on*" the same like a garment. You are to not only act like Him but also dress like Him (**Romans 13:14**). The point is this: do unto others what Christ has done unto you. He saved you from sin. He forgave your past. He healed your broken heart. Did you deserve it? Of course not—who does? Did you get what you didn't deserve? Yes—who hasn't? Therefore, be a river of kindness, flowing into the parched, arid hearts that thirst for the substance of Jesus Christ. Your kindness in the form of deeds and sacrifices, regardless of their costliness, is fully recognized by the Omniscient Father who's watching you. Give Christ obedience so that you can give this world His kindness. Glory to the Lamb of God!

THE COMMAND INQUIRED:

What cannot be measured cannot be evaluated. Therefore, it is essential to measure your comprehension of Christ's command in this teaching, or else the devil will snatch away the "seeds" of Scripture sown into your heart (**Matthew 13:19**). To keep this from occurring, write down your answers to the following questions as they correlate with the teaching this week:

In what passage(s) of Scripture do you find Christ's commandment on **kindness**?

_____

_____

_____

What is the accurate interpretation of **kindness** you have discovered?

_____

_____

_____

_____

_____

_____

In your own words, what are some real-life examples in Scripture of **kindness**?

_____

_____

_____

_____

_____

_____

What steps of initiation did you learn to take in order for **kindness** to transform your life?

_____

_____

_____

_____

_____

_____

How will Satan attack you to hinder **kindness** in your life?

_____

_____

_____

_____

_____

_____

What memory verse will you use to protect Christ's command of **kindness** in your life? Write it out.

_____

_____

_____

_____

_____

_____

TEACHING # 5.8: FORGIVENESS

Week 40

This week's objective: To define what authentic forgiveness is and what it looks like, as well as to learn how to apply its power in broken relationships.

THE COMMAND INTRODUCED:

- **Matthew 18:21-35; Luke 17:3-4** *"Then Peter came to Him and said, 'Lord, how often shall my brother sin against me, and I forgive him? Up to seven times?' Jesus said to him, 'I do not say to you, up to seven times, but up to seventy times seven. Therefore the kingdom of heaven is like a certain king who wanted to settle accounts with his servants. And when he had begun to settle accounts, one was brought to him who owed him ten thousand talents. But as he was not able to pay, his master commanded that he be sold, with his wife and children and all that he had, and that payment be made. The servant therefore fell down before him, saying, 'Master, have patience with me, and I will pay you all.' Then the master of that servant was moved with compassion, released him, and forgave him the debt. But that servant went out and found one of his fellow servants who owed him a hundred denarii; and he laid hands on him by the throat, saying, 'Pay me what you owe!' So his fellow servant fell down at his feet and begged him, saying, 'Have patience with me, and I will pay you all.' And he would not, but went and threw him into prison till he should pay the debt. So when his fellow servants saw what had been done, they were very grieved, and came and told their master all that had been done. Then his master, after he had called him, said to him, 'You wicked servant! I forgave you all that debt because you begged me. Should you not also have had compassion on your fellow servant, just as I had pity on you? And his master was angry, and delivered him to the torturers until he should pay all that was due him. So My heavenly Father also will do to you if each of you, from his heart, does not forgive his brother his trespasses.'"*

THE COMMAND INTERPRETED:

Direct—that's it. This command is not only direct but also captivating because of its needed potential in your relationships. It is extremely rare for Jesus to issue a command by introducing it through a parable. The fact that He did so in this case points to the sensitivity of the teaching. In fact, the very nature of forgiveness is against our sinful, human nature. In the flesh, forgiveness is not an option. In the Spirit, it is the only option. So, depending on which side you choose in each instance of relational dysfunction, you will receive back what you put out. This means the quality of your relationship with Christ will never exceed the quality of your relationships with people. This principle is the point of Christ's command.

First of all, a relatively good question from Peter actually birthed the command of Jesus. *"Lord, how often shall my brother sin against me, and I forgive him? Up to seven times?"* Peter was so honest and simple in his question, willing to voice what everybody else would not. His real dilemma was *how often* we should forgive an offender. In other words, is there a point in a relationship where you draw the line of forgiveness? Can there be a boundary line, a parameter beyond which unforgiveness is allowed to occupy? Jesus answered Peter's question: *"Seventy times seven."* Wow. This means there is no boundary; a parameter does not exist. Christ's forgiveness of sin is unlimited! Jesus forgives patiently (**2 Peter 3:9**). He expects the same from you.

Just to make sure Peter understood His point, Jesus taught the parable to give the command a visual presence. Can you believe what happened? It is absolutely shocking. Rightfully so, the master was obliged to collect what was his, for the servant owed it to him. When the servant did not have it, the master's compassion translated into his forgiveness of the servant's debt. The servant was free and forgiven! However, the servant himself had a coworker (*"fellow servant"*) that worked for the same master. His coworker was in the exact same position with him as he had been in with the master, except the debt was substantially lower than what he had owed.

Surprisingly, he reacted wickedly by imprisoning his servant, showing no forgiveness of the debt, contrary to the way his master had treated him. When his master found out, the servant himself was rebuked and also thrown into a prison of torturers for his wickedness. The master had only one question: *"Should you not also have had compassion on your fellow servant, just as I had pity on you?"*

If he had been forgiven the greater debt (*"ten thousand talents"*) from his master, how could he dare be unforgiving toward a smaller debt (*"five hundred denarii"*) from his servant? Are you the unforgiving servant? Who do you harbor unforgiveness toward? If you have been forgiven the *great* debt of all your sins, then how can you, by contrast, not forgive the smaller debt of your brother's sins? It is this question that Christ's command forces you to answer. In fact, the punchline of Jesus' command is governed by a warning to you, His disciple (**verse 35**).

Can you sense God's intolerance of unforgiveness? If you choose not to *really* forgive, God the Father involves Himself in your chastening by *"doing to you"* what you have done through unforgiveness (**Hebrews 12:5-11**). Jesus commanded your forgiveness to be *"from the heart."* This means it must be real, not fake. It must be inwardly experienced, not outwardly voiced. If your brother repents, forgive him. If he does not, forgive him. There are no exceptions. Meet God at His demands, on His terms.

THE COMMAND ILLUSTRATED:

A fabulous example in the Bible of administering forgiveness is found in **2 Corinthians 2:3-11**. In his second letter to the church at Corinth, the Apostle Paul addresses the issue of forgiveness. Although not specified, he mentions channeling forgiveness to a *"man"* in the Corinthian church that needed to be forgiven, not forgotten (**verses 6-8**). Paul commented that he himself forgave the offender, too (**verse 10**). This man in the Corinthian church is presumably the man Paul rebuked in his first letter (**1 Corinthians 5:1-5**) because of the man's sexual immorality.

By no means was Paul apologizing for his rebuke, but he wanted to give the sinning brother a chance to repent and be reconciled with the fellowship of the church (**Luke 17:3-4**). Forgiveness was the springboard for this to happen. If forgiveness was not offered, unforgiveness would then be enthroned in the

Corinthian church, allowing Satan to *"take advantage"* of the congregation through such an open door (**verse 11**). If the man refused to repent, it was his loss, but the forgiveness remained nevertheless.

You see, God is not as interested in your thoughts about forgiveness as He is in your practice of it. Forgiveness, then, is properly illustrated when you stop thinking about it and start doing something about it. Gently but firmly, rescue your sinning brother with a lasso of forgiveness (**Galatians 6:1**). Quit talking about him and "what happened" between you, for it only fuels your rage and handicaps the hearts of your listeners. Dear disciple, go get him! Flood him with forgiveness. May he never be the same. May *you* never be the same.

THE COMMAND INITIATED:

Through Christ, you are forgiven exhaustively. Does that excite you or what? *"As far as the east is from the west, so far has He removed our transgressions from us"* (**Psalm 103:12**). Amen! Just as there is unending scope from east to west, so there are no limits to the Lord's forgiveness. In like manner, as you have learned thus far, you are to forgive. But, on a serious note, *how* do you really do it? What does it look like to truly forgive from the heart?

In his book *Total Forgiveness*, R.T. Kendall offers a fascinating grasp of what forgiveness looks like. Listen very carefully to the Spirit-empowered wisdom from this man of God. He wants you to learn how you can truly forgive someone even though you remain fully aware of what they did to you or someone you love:

> Total forgiveness is not being oblivious to what an offender did; it is not covering up, excusing or refusing to acknowledge what happened. That would be living in denial. Some people choose to live in denial as a way of dealing with pain; this often happens during the time of grief when a loved one dies. But sooner or later the grieving person must come to terms with reality...It is no spiritual victory to think we are forgiving people when we are only avoiding

facing up to their wrong behavior. It is, if anything, evading true forgiveness. It is as though we are saying to ourselves, "I want to forgive them, but I don't think I really could if they actually did what it seems they did." So we postpone recognizing the true offense in order to keep from experiencing the pain, and we let them carry on as though nothing happened. Total forgiveness is achieved only when we acknowledge what was done without any denial or covering up—and still refuse to make the offender pay for their crime. Total forgiveness is painful. It hurts when we kiss revenge good-bye. It hurts to think that the person is getting away with what they did and nobody else will ever find out. But when we know fully what they did, and accept in our hearts that they will be blessed without any consequences for their wrong, we cross over into a supernatural realm. We begin to be a little more like Jesus, to change into the image of Christ.[8]

THE COMMAND INTERROGATED:

As the rival of forgiveness, unforgiveness is the dagger with which Satan comes at you. See if you can answer this question: How does the devil interrogate forgiveness? Your answer should be one word: *bitterness*. To be bitter is to be enslaved by the shackles of your own unforgiveness. To be bitter is to nurse your grudge, evading forgiveness's healing power and settling for infectious hostility. Bitterness is a beast, an untamed lion that has the potential to destroy everything in the heart in which it has freedom to roam.

Satan would love to grow a root of bitterness in you (Hebrews 12:15), and if you have any unresolved unforgiveness, he will. Be very aware of your relationships. Assume nothing. The devil is seeking ways to provide you with damaged relationships, hoping that you will respond with the sword of unforgiveness. Do not allow him to conquer you! You are created and saved by Christ to dispense His forgiveness, not to shamefully bow to its enemy. Again, beware of Satan's traps with people. Daily, be ready to forgive.

THE COMMAND INDESTRUCTIBLE:

Regardless of your hurt and in spite of your disappointment, there is hope. There is healing. There is a way to deal with it all. God's way is and always will be through the pathway of His Word. Scripture is invincible. It is the guardrail that protects your runaway feelings from nosediving off a cliff of vengeance. Forgiveness is your answer and your victory!

True forgiveness first finds its wings in your life when you learn its process. First, you *appreciate* the opportunity for God's forgiveness (**2 Chronicles 7:14; Psalms 86:5; 130:4; Acts 13:38-39; 1 John 1:9; 2:12**). Then, you can *appropriate* the depth of God's forgiveness (**Psalm 103:3-4; Micah 7:19; Mark 2:6-12; Luke 7:41-43, 47-48; Acts 26:18; Colossians 2:13-14; Ephesians 1:7**). Finally, once God's forgiveness is appreciated and appropriated, then it can be activated. *Activate* the model of God's forgiveness (**Matthew 6:12; John 20:23; Ephesians 4:32; Colossians 3:13**).

Since modeling forgiveness is your goal, Jesus gives you a memory verse to always help you attain it: **Matthew 6:14-15**. It says, *"For if you forgive men their trespasses, your heavenly Father will also forgive you. But if you do not forgive men their trespasses, neither will your Father forgive your trespasses."* Now that says it all. You can only be forgiven as much as you are willing to forgive. This is the memory verse you need to use...daily. Every encounter with anger needs it. Every relationship must apply it. Every annoying individual that offends you must receive it. Needs what? Applies what? Receives what? Your forgiveness. Use the Word of God to determine your standard of forgiveness for all people. It will not be easy, but it will be necessary. Remember, the standard by which you forgive determines the standard by which Christ forgives you. Forgive always; love much.

THE COMMAND INQUIRED:

What cannot be measured cannot be evaluated. Therefore, it is essential to measure your comprehension of Christ's command in this teaching, or else the devil will snatch away the "seeds" of Scripture sown into your heart (**Matthew 13:19**). To keep this from occurring, write down your answers to the following questions as they correlate with the teaching this week:

In what passage(s) of Scripture do you find Christ's commandment on **forgiveness**?

_____

_____

_____

What is the accurate interpretation of **forgiveness** you have discovered?

_____

_____

_____

_____

_____

_____

In your own words, what are some real-life examples in Scripture of **forgiveness**?

_____

_____

_____

_____

_____

What steps of initiation did you learn to take in order for

forgiveness to transform your life?

_____

_____

_____

_____

_____

_____

How will Satan attack you to hinder **forgiveness** in your life?

_____

_____

_____

_____

_____

What memory verse will you use to protect Christ's command of **forgiveness** in your life? Write it out.

_____

_____

_____

_____

_____

CHAPTER 6: THE DISCIPLE'S *TARGET* IS IDENTIFIED

"*Looking unto Jesus, the author and finisher of our faith, who for the joy that was set before Him endured the cross, despising the shame, and has sat down at the right hand of the throne of God*" (**Hebrews 12:2**). What courage! What divine stamina! How did Jesus maintain such a "joy" while going to the cross? His joy provided Him with strength (**Nehemiah 8:10**), a strength that God alone can supply (**Isaiah 40:29**), a strength that we possess through Christ (**Philippians 4:13**). Jesus endured shame and crucifixion because there was value in the path, and that value was redemption for you and me. Salvation came! Eternal life still is free to all!

Christ referred to this targeted pathway as "His hour" that was set before Him. Jesus' very purpose for coming to earth (**John 1:14**) was for this "hour" of trial (**John 12:27**). It is a figurative "hour," meaning a time of testing, not a chronological sixty-minute period. His hour was constantly set before Him (**John 2:4; 7:30; 8:20**), like a target for which He was aiming. Then one day, during the Passover, Jesus knew that His "hour," His time of crucifixion, had finally arrived (**John 13:1; 17:1**). His bullseye was the cross, on which He poured down His sacrificial love. No more miracles. No more multitudes. No more sermons. His hour had come, and it was time for Him to die for your sins.

As Christ's disciple, you are to "look unto Jesus" just as He looked unto His Father (**John 5:19-20**). As Christ was only focused on what His Father directed Him to accomplish, so you also must only focus on what Christ has pointed you toward. What is your target? What is your bullseye? The Lord Jesus Christ distinctly guides your aim in this direction: loving children, serving people, evangelizing unbelievers. Loving. Serving. Witnessing. This is your target! This is your aim! From the social arena of your daily life, you will have no other goal in your effort of reaching people for Jesus. Treat the following commands as what you are created for in Christ. Your target is identified. Aim, release, and glorify the Name of Almighty God.

TEACHING # 6.1: LOVING CHILDREN (PART 1)

Week 41

This week's objective: To properly identify the avenue of ministry that reaches all children, as well as to discover why Jesus wants you intentionally involved in their lives.

THE COMMAND INTRODUCED:

- **Matthew 18:1-4** *"At that time the disciples came to Jesus, saying, 'Who then is greatest in the kingdom of heaven?' Then Jesus called a little child to Him, set him in the midst of them, and said, 'Assuredly, I say to you, unless you are converted and become as little children, you will by no means enter the kingdom of heaven. Therefore whoever humbles himself as this little child is the greatest in the kingdom of heaven.'"*
- **Matthew 18:10-14** *"Take heed that you do not despise one of these little ones, for I say to you that in heaven their angels always see the face of My Father who is in heaven. For the Son of Man has come to save that which was lost. What do you think? If a man has a hundred sheep, and one of them goes astray, does he not leave the ninety-nine and go to the mountains to seek the one that is straying? And if he should find it, assuredly, I say to you, he rejoices more over that sheep than over the ninety-nine that did not go astray. Even so it is not the will of your Father who is in heaven that one of these little ones should perish."*
- **Matthew 18:5-7; Mark 9:36-37, 42** *"Whoever receives one little child like this in My name receives Me. Whoever causes one of these little ones who believe in Me to sin, it would be better for him if a millstone were hung around his neck, and he were drowned in the depth of the sea. Woe to the world because of offenses! For offenses must come, but woe to that man by whom the offense comes!"*
- **Matthew 19:13-15; Mark 10:13-16; Luke 18:16-17** *"Then little children were brought to Him that He might put His hands on*

them and pray, but the disciples rebuked them. But Jesus said, 'Let the little children come to Me, and do not forbid them; for of such is the kingdom of heaven.' And He laid His hands on them and departed from there."

THE COMMAND INTERPRETED:

All of Jesus' commands involving children are direct and to the point. Personally, my wife and I have been blessed with children. Do you have children? If so, you have also been uniquely blessed by Almighty God (**Psalm 127:3-5**). Yes, they can be messy, fussy, and of course whiny, but that does not change the fact that they were ordained to be born by the sovereign plan of the Lord (**Psalm 139:13-18**). A child is never a mistake—never. The Lord Jesus validated this truth in His commands to His disciples. Oh, how Christ loved children! Jesus highlighted the innocence, brilliance, and resiliency of children, and He wants you, as His disciple, to see every child from His vantage point, not your own.

The first command (**Matthew 18:1-4**) emphasizes the *attitude* of a child. The disciple's question of "greatness" indicated the condition of their heart: *pride*. They were zealous to know their rank in Heaven, desiring to compare their placements in the Kingdom with each other. God is unmistakably clear with His feelings about pride (**1 Peter 5:5**).

It was our Lord's appeal for humility that drove Him to call a little child to His side as a "show-and-tell" exemplification of His command. Visually, Jesus set the child *"in the midst of them."* Vocally, Christ commanded, *"Unless you are converted..."* The Greek word "converted" (*strepho*) means "to turn around; twist." This idea of a change in direction was followed by Jesus' mandate to *"become as little children."* This means the change of direction would inevitably result in a change of attitude.

Can you imagine how insulted the disciples felt at first mention of this? Can't you hear them say, "Become like an immature, silly kid to be in right standing with Christ? That doesn't make any sense!" Sure, they were more intelligent than children, but Christ wasn't after their intelligence; He wanted their humility. It was time for them to lose their dignity in exchange for devotion.

The disciple's attitude is to mirror that of a little child through humility, not pride. If pride is east, then humility is west! Anyone not willing to humble himself *"will by no means enter the Kingdom of heaven."* However, whoever does humble himself will not only enter the Kingdom but also be considered the greatest in it.

Do you see the point now? Using a child as the example, Jesus wants your entire lifestyle to be clothed in humility. Christ wants you, as His disciple, to learn from the children you love. Glean their humility and reap its benefits with the Lord. Naturally, you desire to be all you can be as Christ's disciple. Your goal is to please Him, and your aim is to follow Him. However, if all you do for Christ is not done out of humility, then all is in vain. When coming to Christ, humble yourself as a little child does. Such is the key to following Him as well as to love children well.

The second command (**Matthew 18: 10-14**) emphasizes the *atonement* for a child. Jesus opened this command with these words: *"Take heed that you do not despise one of these little ones..."* Interestingly, the Greek word "despise" (*katagelao*) means "laughing down; scorning." So, to despise a child is to make comical mockery of their innocence, to scorn their character. Christ gave warning to anyone mistreating a child that their angels *"continually behold God's face"* as He sees everything. Angels have a very real presence and ministry in our lives (**Hebrews 1:14**), especially in the lives of children.

Perhaps one of the greatest reasons that Jesus exhibits such caution and protection for the *"little ones"* is because they don't need any stumbling blocks to hinder them from experiencing salvation from Jesus (verse 11). The urgency is understood because we all (including children) are sinners in need of the Savior. King David expressed it (**Psalm 51:5**). King Solomon expounded on it (**Proverbs 22:15**). Jesus wants you to see that children need His salvation just as much as you do. They need their sin atoned for, forgiven, and washed in His blood (**Ephesians 1:7**).

To further convince His disciples, Jesus contextually demonstrated the value of a lost child by comparing the little one to a lost sheep. One hundred sheep are all equal in value to the shepherd. If one gets away, that's one too many. So when the shepherd retrieves the sheep, he rejoices. Why? Because of its value! Using a lost sheep as His model, Christ passionately advocates,

"Even so it is not the will of your Father who is in heaven that one of these little ones should perish." God's will is evident. Jesus wants children to be saved from sin's penalty and biblically to overcome sin's power (**Proverbs 22:6**).

This is your motivation to love a child: because he or she needs the Savior. Whether children are adorably cute or rebelliously mean, remember their lost condition before God. You are responsible for giving them the love of Jesus Christ. You are the evangelist! Be an instrument, not an instigator, in your relationship with all children. They need to be reached and saved. Be patient, and be faithful, because they must receive Christ's atonement to be born again.

The third command (**Matthew 18:5-7; Mark 9:36-37, 42**) emphasizes the *atrocities* to a child. By definition, an *atrocity* is a wicked, cruel act against another human being. Jesus tackled this unfortunate reality by setting the reception of a little child as equivalent to the reception of Christ. To invest your time and influence into the life of a child is like doing so for Jesus Himself, and the concept of this is elsewhere reinforced (**Matthew 25:34-40**). However, to provide circumstances for a child that would cause him or her to sin is what Christ called an "*offense.*"

The Greek word "offense" (*skandalon*) means "to set a snare; stumbling block." Jesus warned that this kind of evil towards children "*must come,*" meaning Satan is on the prowl (**1 Peter 5:8**). The greater warning is to the individual who bows to Satan's temptation and delivers the "*offense*" to a child. For anyone who dares to trample on the innocent territory of a child's heart, Jesus said, "*It would be better for him if a millstone were hung around his neck, and he were drowned in the depth of the sea.*"

In biblical times, a millstone was used for grinding and was so heavy that people depended on mules to move it. It would be better to die a millstone death than to cause a little child to sin. To sexually abuse a child is an abominable perversion, prematurely exposing them to a realm of sexuality they're not ready to enter. To abuse children, either physically or emotionally, is to cause them to sin, for their anger becomes a time bomb ready to explode. To under-discipline children is to cause them to sin, for their foolish hearts grow continually more invincible, disrespectful, and selfish. To welcome children to a local church and then ignore them is to cause them to sin, for it gives them no place to serve Christ, thus discouraging them and tempting them to turn back to the world of Satan's vices for fulfillment.

Dear disciple, the goal here is not only to protect yourself from such actions but also to be very sensitive to their realities in the lives of children. Remember, children to some degree can be products of their environments. If a child's behavior is not congruent with your standards and convictions, don't gripe and turn the child back over to Satan's path of destruction. Rather, influence the child through the love of our Lord Jesus, displaying to him or her what it's like to love and be loved. With all children, if they've been ignored, spend time with them. If they feel inferior, show them their superior value. If they are hyper and out of control...pray and take medication (I'm *"kid"*-ding)! Just remember that in the lives of many children, atrocities are realities, not mere possibilities. Children need you, and you need them. Invest and love. Their angels are watching.

The fourth command (**Matthew 19:13-15; Mark 10:13-16; Luke 18:16-17**) emphasizes the *acceptance* of a child. Sometimes it is difficult to listen to children, because they can be, well, irritating. However, this will never by any means be grounds for not accepting them. Accepting the little children was a problem for the disciples. Though it was normal in Jewish culture for people to bring children to rabbis, the disciples didn't see it that way.

In context, on the day that the children were brought to Jesus, the disciples, not Jesus, *"rebuked"* the children. Based on their rebuke, they probably used statements such as, "Get out of here. Leave the Master alone. Go play somewhere. Jesus has more important matters to tend to!" The value they placed on children was extremely low compared to Jesus' view. Children were a liability to them, like leeches sucking away precious time from Christ and His ministry to save the lost, heal the sick, and raise the dead! Firmly, the Lord Jesus corrected the malicious behavior of His disciples by exhorting them, *"Let the little children come to Me, and do not forbid them..."*

The Greek word "forbid" (*koluo*) means "to prevent, hinder." Clearly, the disciples were hindering precious children from coming to Jesus, for He wanted to lay hands on them and pray for them. How special and valuable is that? There's nothing in the world more important than you, the disciple, being personally involved in positioning children at the feet of Jesus. If prominent Jonathan would allow a child to be involved in his ministry to King David (**1 Samuel 20:17-24, 35-42**), you can bring children to Christ, too. You do not know what exactly Christ has planned for a child, but you do know that He wants the child. Never look at a child and say, "There's no hope for him. He's a spoiled brat and beyond help." Don't make that child pay the consequence for your lack of faith. Rather, accept that child with his snotty nose, failing grades, and terrible behavior, but don't passively stop at mere acceptance. Instead, get that child to the feet of Jesus, and then let Christ take it from there.

Attitude. Atonement. Atrocities. Acceptance. As you learn from a child, pay close attention to his or her humility and apply it in your own life. As you love a child, do so on the basis that he or she is lost and in need of the Savior. Do so with sensitivity to the circumstances that the child may be facing. Do so with a heart of acceptance and belief that the child in your path is entrusted to your influence. As a disciple of the Lord Jesus Christ, always be found loving children with the love of Christ. Children need the Savior.

THE COMMAND ILLUSTRATED:

One of the best examples in the Bible of loving a child is found in **Genesis 22:1-14**. This would be the greatest test of Abraham's faith. At this time in Abraham's life, he had only one son, Isaac. After Abraham had waited years and years for the promise of Isaac's birth, his patience had been rewarded with the gift of a son. Now, however, that father-son attachment would seemingly come to an end. God commanded Abraham to sacrifice his son on a mountain called Moriah, near the ultimate place of Christ's death. Sacrifice? Kill? Why would God give Abraham a child only to command him to kill the child? Rather than questioning God on the matter, Abraham faithfully obeyed God.

When the time came, Abraham readied the altar, positioned Isaac, and took the knife in his hand. Suddenly the angel of the Lord spoke: "*Do not lay your hand on the lad, or do anything to him; for now I know that you fear God, since you have not withheld your son, your only son, from Me.*" So that was God's purpose! The encounter was to be a litmus test indicating a fear of God, a love for Him, and a devotion to Him. And the Lord still provided a ram to show His faithfulness to Abraham. Amen!

You see, Abraham's love for his child was only meant to be a pathway toward his love for Jehovah God. Abraham loved Isaac so much that he refused to let him interrupt his love for Jehovah, for that would only hurt both Abraham and Isaac. That day, the Lord knew that Isaac was not more important to Abraham than He was. If you are a parent, how do you measure up to Abraham? Do you see your child rightly as a blessing from God or as an idol with whom you're obsessed?

Yes, parents love their children, but the Lord God Almighty who gives them to parents must be adored above all. As a disciple, your love for children should always teach you God's love for you. When you can learn to appropriate the Lord's love and desire for fellowship with you, it will radically transform your perception of how you display the same devotion to children that Christ does to you. Love like Abraham.

TEACHING # 6.2: LOVING CHILDREN (PART 2)

Week 42

This week's objective: *To properly identify the avenue of ministry that reaches all children, as well as to discover why Jesus wants you intentionally involved in their lives.*

THE COMMAND INITIATED:

Children are much smarter than what most adults recognize. It seems to be that when you don't think they're listening, you later drill them with questions and find out they were. A child's mind is a diamond in the rough. It has the potential to be shaped and developed in the fear of God, if only given the opportunity through parental and role model training. However, disaster strikes when a child is left to himself, allowed to wallow in the sinful faculties of his "own way," unrestricted and unguarded from the devices of the devil.

This is where many children can be found, and this is not acceptable! Whether you are a parent or not, the children in your life have been placed there by God, not by accident. In obedience to Christ's commands, initiate your involvement and make a Kingdom difference in the life of a child. Perhaps those seeds of Scripture you plant in his or her little heart will sprout one day, transforming the child into a mighty man or woman of God.

Is there anyone out there who believes in God's plan in a child's life, someone who is willing to stand up and speak up for a child? David Walters is a voice heard around the country when it comes to fighting for the faith of our children in both families and communities. In his book *Kids in Combat*, Walters adamantly preaches that children should be trained to be powerhouses for Christ. His comments are worth applying, piercing the heart and exposing a deteriorating, morally fearless society:

Our children are being influenced by peer pressure

outside the home, and the parents are losing the children to the system. Children who spend unlimited time among their own peers will be adversely affected. As **Proverbs 22:15** says, *"Foolishness is bound in the heart of a child."* The sin nature is like the law of gravity; it has a downward tendency. If we simply leave our children to their own devices, they will naturally develop in their sin. Children are not born innocent. The Adamic nature is their inheritance. They may be innocent about the different ways of sinning, but you can be sure that their nature is to sin. **Psalm 51:5** says, *"Behold, I was shapen in iniquity; and in sin did my mother conceive me."* I have yet to meet a parent who is frustrated because his or her child refuses to disobey. It is always the other way around! We invest all our energy in training them to obey. We never have to train them to disobey. That comes naturally...Are our children too young for us to expect much from them? Do we have to wait a number of years for them to have their own relationship with God? If children do not possess real faith in Christ for themselves but just an inherited belief from their parents and teachers, then you can be sure that they will eventually be influenced by other modes of thought in the world...Our children and teens need to know God in such a way that if their parents stopped believing or if their friends stopped believing or even if their pastor became backslidden, their faith would stay strong. Their confession and experience must be: *"I know whom I have believed, and am persuaded that He is able to keep that which I have committed unto Him against that day"* (**2 Timothy 1:12**).[1]

THE COMMAND INTERROGATED:

By now you know how much Jesus expects you as His disciple to love the children He places in your life. Obviously, the devil hates any command of Christ, so your obedience to love a child will not be without attack from a devil who is flagrantly careless of children. There are two primary ways by which Satan will attempt to shake your obedience to Christ's command: parentally and publicly.

If you are not yet a parent, let's agree by faith that one day you will be. Parentally, the mother has a responsibility as well as the father. The mother is a teacher to her children, guiding them with the Law of God's Word (**Proverbs 1:8; 2 Timothy 1:5**). The father is a disciplinarian, a leader that maintains order in his home through the correction of his children (**Ephesians 6:4; 1 Timothy 3:4**).

A mother teaches and a father disciplines out of love for the child, because through teaching, the child is trained, and through correction, the child is guided. When a mother fails to teach and a father over- or under-disciplines, the child is more hurt than loved by the parents. Satan triumphs in this parental disobedience, because the child is left open to Satan's attacks since the Scriptural canopy of parental protection has been disobediently removed.

Publicly, you will always be around children. Always. They are everywhere! There will be times that Christ places a certain child in your path to nurture because he or she has parents that don't. Such a child may be hungry, or perhaps hurting emotionally and needing loving counsel. Publicly, the command of Christ to love and accept a child is clear, but Satan may distract you with thoughts such as these: "I'm already late for my meeting," or "I can't afford to give this child anything to eat," or "I'm tired and don't feel good."

Also, the devil may shift your mind to judgmental thinking: maybe the child smells bad, and you don't want to mess with him. Or perhaps you may be tempted to think, "He deserves the mess he got himself into. He's not my responsibility." Publicly, you will find that Satan will be waiting for you, to fight against the compassion of your heart to reach a child with Christ's love. Don't judge that child unfairly (**Matthew 7:1-2**). Love that child just as he is, and then help that child. Beware of Satan's ploys.

THE COMMAND INDESTRUCTIBLE:

Scripture is not silent when it comes to standing up for children. You know the command of Christ very well by now. You know what Jesus expects from you regarding your love for children. When Satan strongly assaults you, either as a parent or in public or both, have this memory verse ready in your heart to defend Christ's command: **John 21:15**. It says, "*So when they had eaten breakfast, Jesus said to Simon Peter, 'Simon, son of Jonah, do you love Me more than these?' He said to Him, 'Yes, Lord; You know that I love You.' He said to him, 'Feed My lambs.'*"

Throughout the next several verses, Jesus gave an additional command to "*tend*" and "*feed*" His sheep. A lamb is a sheep that is less than one year old. A sheep can be several years old. Do you see the point Christ is making? A lamb is to a child as a sheep is to an adult. "*Feed My lambs*" is the command to memorize! Jesus wanted Peter to not forget nor neglect the little children, for they were to be fed His Word, His teachings, and His commands. As a disciple, never, ever forget that. The Word of God should have priority and prominence in your ministry as a disciple among all children (**2 Timothy 3:15**). Use your position and opportunities to reach as many children for Christ as possible. Feed His lambs. Distribute His Word. As you walk with the resurrected Christ, love and feed His precious little lambs. Hallelujah for children!

THE COMMAND INQUIRED:

What cannot be measured cannot be evaluated. Therefore, it is essential to measure your comprehension of Christ's command in this teaching, or else the devil will snatch away the "seeds" of Scripture sown into your heart (**Matthew 13:19**). To keep this from occurring, write down your answers to the following questions as they correlate with the teaching this week:

In what passage(s) of Scripture do you find Christ's commandment on **loving children**?

_____

_____

_____

What is the accurate interpretation of **loving children** you have discovered?

_____

_____

_____

_____

_____

_____

In your own words, what are some real-life examples in Scripture of **loving children**?

_____

_____

_____

_____

_____

What steps of initiation did you learn to take in order for **loving children** to transform your life?

_____

_____

_____

_____

_____

_____

How will Satan attack you to hinder your **love for children**?

_____

_____

_____

_____

_____

_____

What memory verse will you use to protect Christ's command of **loving children** in your life? Write it out.

_____

_____

_____

_____

_____

_____

TEACHING # 6.3: SERVING PEOPLE (PART 1)

Week 43

This week's objective: *To see the purpose behind servanthood, as well as to learn the attitude required to serve others as Christ did.*

THE COMMAND INTRODUCED:

- **Matthew 20:25-28; Mark 10:42-45; Luke 22:24-27** *"But Jesus called them to Himself and said, 'You know that the rulers of the Gentiles lord it over them, and those who are great exercise authority over them. Yet it shall not be so among you; but whoever desires to become great among you, let him be your servant. And whoever desires to be first among you, let him be your slave— just as the Son of Man did not come to be served, but to serve, and to give His life a ransom for many.'"*
- **Mark 9:33-35** *"Then He came to Capernaum. And when He was in the house He asked them, 'What was it you disputed among yourselves on the road?' But they kept silent, for on the road they had disputed among themselves who would be the greatest. And He sat down, called the twelve, and said to them, 'If anyone desires to be first, he shall be last of all and servant of all.'"*
- **John 13:12-17** *"So when He had washed their feet, taken His garments, and sat down again, He said to them, 'Do you know what I have done to you? You call Me Teacher and Lord, and you say well, for so I am. If I then, your Lord and Teacher, have washed your feet, you also ought to wash one another's feet. For I have given you an example, that you should do as I have done to you. Most assuredly, I say to you, a servant is not greater than his master; nor is he who is sent greater than he who sent him. If you know these things, blessed are you if you do them.'"*
- **Luke 17:7-10** *"And which of you, having a servant plowing or tending sheep, will say to him when he has come in from the field, 'Come at once and sit down to eat'? But will he not rather say to*

him, 'Prepare something for my supper, and gird yourself and serve me till I have eaten and drunk, and afterward you will eat and drink'? Does he thank that servant because he did the things that were commanded him? I think not. So likewise you, when you have done all those things which you are commanded, say, 'We are unprofitable servants. We have done what was our duty to do.'"

THE COMMAND INTERPRETED:

Out of these four commands from the Lord Jesus, three are direct, and one is implicit. In the social atmosphere of your life, the attitude of *servanthood* will be the key to implanting the gospel in the hearts of men. Being a servant breaks down barriers and opens windows of opportunity for quality relationships. Servanthood is a blazing fire, providing warmth to a cold unbeliever and zeal to a lukewarm believer. Because of its potency, servanthood is highly endorsed by Christ. In fact, Jesus establishes it as the entirety of your social life! His call to servanthood is clearly heard, so do more than listen; obey.

The first command (**Matthew 20:25-28; Mark 10:42-45; Luke 22:24-27**) is direct, issued by Jesus to **renovate** the idea of servanthood. It seems to be that the disciples were concerned with greatness. The problem with such a concern is that they had the wrong interpretation because they had been examining the wrong model. You see, the only pattern of greatness with which they were familiar was that of "*the rulers of the Gentiles.*" These rulers did not govern with the love of God in their hearts; they were ruthless dictators, eager for power and control at the expense of people's emotions. What a poisoned model! What a decaying, ungodly, terrible pattern by which to interpret greatness! This cultural influence contaminated the disciples.

Christ came to their rescue by remodeling and renovating their mindset for a correct and more valuable understanding of greatness. Pointing to the malicious cultural model of the Gentiles, Jesus commanded, "*Yet it shall not be so among you...*" Christ used the Greek word *megas*, which means "big; exceedingly." In context, this is a reference to spiritual rank, not physical stature. The disciples did not want to be the janitors, but rather the CEOs of the company.

To counteract this cultural infection of servanthood, Jesus then turned the tables and defined what it means to be *"great"* in His eyes. He commanded His disciples, *"But whoever desires to become great among you, let him be your servant. And whoever desires to be first among you, let him be your slave..."* Servant. Slave. These are synonymous in meaning, for both involve lowering yourself to minister to another. Such a standard was intended to produce leaders who would give their lives away. Jesus was trying to cultivate a servant's heart within each of these rugged disciples. He was raising up an army of servants, those who valued the worth of another human being made in the image of God (**James 3:9**).

This is where cockiness dies and arrogance is assassinated. The true measure of greatness is not in your power, position, or prestige. It is not found in how many men serve you but in how many men *you* serve. This was the driving motivation of Christ (**verse 28**); let it be yours as well. As His disciple, roll up your sleeves and set the example among your family and friends. Shun the cultural model of greatness and lower yourself down to the floors of humanity. You will only be as *"big"* as you are willing to be small. Serve your heart out!

The second command (**Mark 9:33-35**) is implicit, and Jesus issued it to **reinforce** the meaning of servanthood. This second command at first looks almost identical to the first; however, if you read it closely, you will see that Jesus was attempting to further reinforce the idea of greatness by introducing the concept of "first and last." Boldly, Jesus affirmed, *"If anyone desires to be first, he shall be last of all and servant of all."* First, last, and servant.

In the previous command, the idea of *servant* was already explained, but not the idea of *"first"* and *"last."* The Greek word "first" (*protos*) means "foremost; in front of." Also, the Greek word "last" (*eschatos*) translates "farthest; final." It's like waiting in a line with a group of people: the closer you are to the front, the easier it is to be seen. The farther you are to the back, the more difficult it is to be seen. In the front, you are seen, but in the back, you are hidden. Likewise, the attitude of the *"first"* is to be seen and receive the credit (**Matthew 6:1-2**), but the attitude of the *"last"* is to be hidden so Christ can receive the glory (**Matthew 6:3-4**).

As Christ's disciple, your attitude must be that of the *"last."* Humbly serve others in the fear of God. You act the way you think, so you can only be as *"last"* as you treat others as *"first"* (**Romans 12:10**). Cast off the attitude that says, "I deserve this" and put on the attitude daily that says, "Christ deserves my service to others whether their gratitude is present or not" (**Matthew 5:46**). This kind of servanthood puts Jesus in the spotlight! To both the stranger and to your enemy, serve by the rule of last, last, last (**Matthew 20:16**).

The third command (**John 13:12-17**) is direct. Jesus issues it to *reposition* the conduct in servanthood. This command is unique among these four because it is the only one in which you see Christ exemplifying servanthood. Granted, Jesus' entire life was an act of service as the Son of Man, but here it was especially obvious as a teachable moment for His disciples. He did what no rabbi would have done and truly lowered Himself (**Philippians 2:6-7**) by acting as a slave (**John 13:4-5**). In Jewish culture, a slave would gird himself to wash the dirty feet of the occupants in a household. Never were the occupants to wash the slaves' feet. For Christ to humble Himself like this was truly an act of devotional love toward His disciples. Through His example, Jesus set the stage for the conduct of service.

Once Christ finished washing their feet, He asked, *"Do you know what I have done to you?"* Jesus desired to see comprehension. He wanted the disciples to see the meaning, not the method. If His foot-washing service to them is only seen as a method, it will become ritualistic. Jesus positioned His title as Teacher and Lord, using it as His platform to explain humility in service. If He, Who is everything, can be a servant, then we, who are nothing, can certainly follow suit. Christ's example is the momentum for that of our own.

As a fellow disciple with you, this idea of servanthood and foot-washing transformed even my marriage relationship. The night I proposed to my lovely bride along a beautiful lakeside, I invited her to sit in a chair. With marriage on my mind, I read this Scripture to my dearest Jillian: *"Husbands, love your wives, just as Christ also loved the church and gave Himself for her"* (**Ephesians 5:25**). Having said this, I decided to express the sincerity of my devotion to her by washing her feet. So, I poured the water into a basin I had brought with me, girded myself, and began to wash. As I did so, I gazed into her eyes, and said, "Jillian, I commit myself to you as your servant. If you give me the privilege of being your husband, I will devote myself to love and serve you like Christ did His

Church." Already on my knees, I then finished with, "Will you be my wife?"

Perhaps that sounds radical to you, but I can honestly say that after many years of marriage, it has held me accountable to my commitment to her. By no means have I arrived or perfected being a servant, but, like you, I press on (**Philippians 3:12**). Overall, why do I share my marriage relationship with you? To show you that being a servant is like being married: it's a lifelong commitment. Your commitment is to the Lord Jesus. When you serve others, you serve Him (**Matthew 25:40**). Therefore, servanthood is not something you *say*. Servanthood is something you *do*.

This is why Jesus commands *"that you should do as I have done to you."* Do you realize how culturally unacceptable this was for the disciples? It is equivalent to eating at a restaurant and asking your waiter to sit down in your place as you serve him. Unthinkable, right? Well, that's what it was like for the disciples. Wash each other's feet? You can only imagine what they were thinking.

Appropriately, Jesus reminded them that washing each other's feet would never amount to a great standing in relationship to each other (**verse 16**). This "greatness" factor was implied again so that the disciples would understand that Jesus will never be impressed by how much you do for Him. Rather, He is attracted to servanthood that results in much done for others. Your love for Him will never be permitted to separate from your love for others (**Matthew 22:37-39**). Your love for God is always connected to your love for people. Servanthood is the greatest expression of your love!

Whether foot-washing is seen as an ordinance in the local church you attend or a private devotion toward selected people, Jesus does not stutter: *"If you know these things, blessed are you if you do them."* You are not blessed if you *know* Christ's command; you are blessed if you *do* what you know. This is a test of obedience and a call to surrender. As Christ's disciple, engage! Christ introduced this to you not so that you would idolize foot-washing but so that your practice of it would produce humility within your heart and unity with your brethren. Gird and serve.

The fourth command (**Luke 17:7-10**) is direct. Jesus issued it to *reinstate* the attitude in servanthood. When something is *reinstated*, it is brought back into use and thus restored to its previous condition. This is exactly what Christ had in mind with this fourth command. Due to the negative, corruptive influence of the world, your attitude as a disciple can become flawed. Jesus wants to protect you by restoring inside you an attitude that will overcome, bolstered by your every act of service.

Once again using the idea of a servant, Jesus taught the importance of *duty*. As you have already seen, servants were hired in biblical times much as a butler or a maid would be today. These hired servants are seen in this fourth command as *"plowing or tending sheep."* After the servant would cease working in the field, he would come home and prepare supper for the master of the house. This is where Jesus made His point.

Servants would be asked not to sit at the table but to serve food. It was culturally ludicrous to imagine a servant doing anything less. He was not equal with the master, and his position was to serve, not be served. Jesus finished this unimaginable way of viewing a servant by saying, *"Does he [the master] thank that servant because he did the things that were commanded him? I think not."* So, what is the point?

Using this question, Christ's point is vividly clear: "So likewise you, when you have done all those things which you are commanded, say, 'We are unprofitable servants. We have done what was our duty to do.'" The true understanding of "unprofitable" is necessary to understand this command. The Greek word for "unprofitable" (bathmos) literally means "a step toward dignity." It is properly understood as worth, degree. "Unprofitable," then, is the recognition of bestowed status, not earned status.

The command from Christ is to reinstate the right attitude in your heart for servanthood. He wants you to remember that He, the Master, bestowed upon you the status of servanthood. Your self-righteousness did not earn it. Your obedience to God is normal, and in light of His sacrifice for your sins, *"reasonable service"* (**Romans 12:1-2**). Your entire lifestyle of servanthood is an obedient act of thanksgiving to God.

Therefore, when you serve, you are only doing your *"duty"*—that is, what is already expected of you. There is no extra credit or "climbing the ladder of success" with Jesus. Servanthood is a privilege, not a promotion! A professor's status is to teach. A soldier's status is to fight. A disciple's status is to serve. Duty demands discipline. Sure, you will be rewarded, but that alone should not dictate your service. A "thank you" does not determine your service, nor does a pat on the back. A professor teaches, a soldier fights, and a disciple serves because they are discharging their duty. Serve the Lord!

THE COMMAND ILLUSTRATED:

One of the clearest examples in Scripture of incredible servanthood is found in **Luke 7:36-50**. While there are multiple concepts and topics found in this passage, we will focus now only on the area of servanthood. As Jesus was eating at a Pharisee's house, He was sought out by a very sinful woman who had an alabaster box full of expensive oil Then, the service began (**verse 38**). This sinful yet repentant woman was weeping, washing, and wiping. She bowed down to Jesus, washed His feet, anointed them, and kissed His feet out of adoration. Wow! What a servant! Jesus quickly commented on her servanthood because she blessed His heart with her devotion (**verses 44-46**).

As Christ's disciple, there is an aspect of this you must remember in your cross-carrying life: *her alabaster box*. This box was not cheap! It was full of very high-priced imported oil called spikenard. This oil was expensive, costing approximately three hundred denarii (**John 12:5**). For comparison, in Bible times, one denarius was roughly equivalent to a single day's earnings (**Matthew 20:2**).

Therefore, if you could earn up to a denarius per day, how long would it take you to purchase an alabaster flask of fragrant oil? Three hundred days of work! This sinful woman's servanthood cost her something. Likewise, your acts of service will never be without cost. A life of servanthood is not a life of convenience. When you "signed up" to follow Christ, your social perspective took a shift. Day by day, intentionally keep your eyes open for the ways that Christ has positioned you in the paths of people to be their servant. These opportunities are divinely designed by the Master. Like this woman, never allow any money you have, possession you own, or time you are given to keep you from biblical, Christ-commanded servanthood. The mission is yours. The Master is watching.

TEACHING # 6.4: SERVING PEOPLE (PART 2)

Week 44

This week's objective: To see the purpose behind servanthood, as well as to learn the attitude required to serve others as Christ did.

THE COMMAND INITIATED:

Servanthood is not intended to be easy, but it is necessary. The social component of your Christian life should always be an overflow of your private pursuit of Christ. This means your prayer life will reciprocate your public life (**Matthew 7:7-12**). Always keep in mind that serving people is not something you master; rather, it is a product of what you've learned from the Master. The Lord Jesus wants to see you in action! As a student, learn from Christ, and then apply what He teaches you. Initiate your obedience.

A reputable voice on this subject of servanthood is Dr. T.W. Hunt. In his book *The Mind of Christ*, he very adequately explains servanthood from Jesus' perspective. His comments encourage you to actively follow in Jesus' footsteps:

> To have the mind of Christ is to be a servant. The entire Christ story is the story of a servant. The great Messianic passages predicted Him as a servant: *"Behold, My Servant, whom I uphold; My chosen one in whom My soul delights"* (**Isa. 42:1**). The suffering servant of **Isaiah 53** was a "righteous servant": *"As a result of the anguish of His soul, He will see it and be satisfied; By His knowledge the Righteous One, My Servant, will justify the many, as he will bear their iniquities"* (**Isa. 53:11**). Unlike the world system, in Christ's kingdom, servant hood, not position, is the key to greatness. Here spiritual stature is implicit in servant hood...In such a world, joy would come from the privilege of service, and that is available only to the lowly. The last, astonishingly, are first, and the least really

are the greatest. Such a society would have only one supreme authority, and Jesus tells us, *"No servant can serve two masters; for either he will hate the one, and love the other, or else he will hold to one, and despise the other"* (**Luke 16:13**). God is supreme. We can please only one Master—Jesus...We do serve Christ supremely, but we are also to serve one another. *"You were called to freedom, brethren; only do not turn your freedom into an opportunity for the flesh, but through love serve one another"* (**Gal. 5:13**). If this appears contradictory—we are to serve only Christ and yet we also are to serve one another—the solution is that we are not to serve each other as master...Our obedience is to Christ while we serve one another. The two commands—serve Christ as master and serve one another in love—follow the order in the command to love God above all else and to love our neighbor as ourself.[2]

THE COMMAND INTERROGATED:

You know by now that serving creates an atmosphere of love and unity. Since it accomplishes such wonderful qualities in your life and in the life of the one being served, it is no surprise that Satan despises it. The devil has a very cunning way of destroying servanthood in your life. Destroying? Yes, destroying, not merely hindering. If you allow him a foothold, he can fit you into the mold of a conceited, compromising, casual Christian. To degrade into that would be an insult to Christ's command.

Satan wants to turn your service into filth. But how does he attack to bring about such terrible results? Take a look at Mary and Martha to see the picture (**Luke 10:38-42**). Contextually, this passage really addresses the issue of worry—which is also connected to Satan, who uses negative circumstances to attempt to arouse anxiety within us. However, that's not all you see. Look at little closer, especially at **verse 40**. There are two principles that you must never forget, for by these two elements Satan does his damage in your life as a disciple.

The first principle is *distraction*. Martha was *"distracted with much serving..."* Servanthood did not distract her. Rather, it was her "*much*" serving. This means she was serving so much, trying to impress her finest guest ever (Jesus), that she lost sight of her first priority (**verse 42**). Martha was out of balance. Sure, it was great that she was serving Jesus, but not when it caused her to neglect "sitting" at Jesus' feet like Mary. Sitting is first; serving is second. And Satan will try to destroy you by reversing these. If serving ever replaces sitting, you're sunk. Dear disciple, sit at Jesus' feet, grow in His Word, learn His commands, praise His Name, adore His majesty. Only then should come the servanthood of your life. Beware of engaging in a lifestyle that is distracted by more serving than sitting.

This very reality explains the second principle as well. It is called *loneliness*. Martha's words were, "*Do You not care that my sister has left me to serve alone?*" Guess what? She was right. Martha was actually telling truth. In every sense of the word, she was serving *alone*. Think about it: Jesus was with Mary, not Martha. Had Jesus been in the kitchen, He would have been with Martha. But that was not the case. You see, Martha's distraction with "*much*" serving led to her being "*alone.*" Why? Because she was doing everything out of the power of her flesh and not in the power of the Holy Spirit (**Acts 1:8**). You cannot live in the Spirit's power and worry at the same time! No wonder Martha was alone—she was trying to do something *for* Jesus but *without* Jesus.

Beware, because Satan will try to bring about the same results in your life. The amount of your service for God will never qualify His Presence in your life. You can't earn Him. You don't deserve Him. Sitting at His feet will always result in the serving of His people. Never is that reversed. Be careful that you do not allow Satan to pull you into so much busyness that you neglect sitting at Jesus' feet. If you do give in to the devil, the command of Christ to serve will be corrupted, and you will be miserable.

THE COMMAND INDESTRUCTIBLE:

You are not a rag doll for Satan to throw around. You are the blood-bought possession of the Lord Jesus Christ. The Word of God only needs to be believed and spoken forth to keep Satan from destroying servanthood in your life. The Holy Scriptures are loaded with many verses on service, but in light of what Jesus commanded, this is the memory verse with which to fight Satan: **Colossians 3:23-24**. It says, *"And whatever you do, do it heartily, as to the Lord and not to men, knowing that from the Lord you will receive the reward of the inheritance; for you serve the Lord Christ."*

Unlike Martha's service, yours is always portrayed as if you are serving Christ Himself—every time, to everyone. Christ delights in rewarding you for your service, for this is congruent with the honor of the Father (**John 12:26**). Again unlike Martha, you commit yourself to serve in the Spirit's power (**Romans 7:6**), which you only can do as you sit as Jesus' feet and hear His Word. You always serve out of devotion to the living God (**Hebrews 9:14; 12:28; 1 Thessalonians 1:9**). Your life is His life. Your service is to be a complement to His command. In all the power of the Holy Spirit and with all the faith in Christ's command, live a life of servanthood. Steady yourself constantly to serve others with and for Jesus. Oh, dear disciple, you are free to go. Sit first. Serve last.

THE COMMAND INQUIRED:

What cannot be measured cannot be evaluated. Therefore, it is essential to measure your comprehension of Christ's command in this teaching, or else the devil will snatch away the "seeds" of Scripture sown into your heart (**Matthew 13:19**). To keep this from occurring, write down your answers to the following questions as they correlate with the teaching this week:

In what passage(s) of Scripture do you find Christ's commandment on **serving people**?

_____

_____

_____

What is the accurate interpretation of **serving people** that you have discovered?

In your own words, what are some real-life examples in Scripture of **serving people**?

What steps of initiation did you learn to take in order for **servanthood** to transform your life?

How will Satan attack you to hinder you from **serving people**?

_____

_____

_____

_____

_____

_____

What memory verse will you use to protect Christ's command of **serving people** in your life? Write it out.

_____

_____

_____

_____

_____

_____

TEACHING # 6.5: WITNESSING TO THE LOST (PART 1)

Week 45

<u>*This week's objective:*</u> *To learn to share the gospel of Jesus Christ purposely and passionately.*

THE COMMAND INTRODUCED:

- The *Model* for Witnessing—**Matthew 4:19; Mark 1:17; Luke 5:27; John 1:43** *"Then He said to them, 'Follow Me, and I will make you fishers of men.'"*
- The *Commitment* for Witnessing—**Luke 5:10-11** *"...And Jesus said to Simon, 'Do not be afraid. From now on you will catch men.' So when they had brought their boats to land, they forsook all and followed Him."*
- The *Instruction* for Witnessing—**Matthew 10:5-15; Mark 6:7-13; Luke 9:1-6; 10:3-12, 16** *"These twelve Jesus sent out and commanded them, saying: 'Do not go into the way of the Gentiles, and do not enter a city of the Samaritans. But go rather to the lost sheep of the house of Israel. And as you go, preach, saying, 'The kingdom of heaven is at hand.' Heal the sick, cleanse the lepers, raise the dead, cast out demons. Freely you have received, freely give. Provide neither gold nor silver nor copper in your money belts, nor bag for your journey, nor two tunics, nor sandals, nor staffs; for a worker is worthy of his food. Now whatever city or town you enter, inquire who in it is worthy, and stay there till you go out. And when you go into a household, greet it. If the household is worthy, let your peace come upon it. But if it is not worthy, let your peace return to you. And whoever will not receive you nor hear your words, when you depart from that house or city, shake off the dust from your feet. Assuredly, I say to you, it will be more tolerable for the land of Sodom and Gomorrah in the day of judgment than for that city!'"*

- The *Arguments* from Witnessing—**Matthew 15:12-14** *"Then His disciples came and said to Him, 'Do You know that the Pharisees were offended when they heard this saying?' But He answered and said, 'Every plant which My heavenly Father has not planted will be uprooted. Let them alone. They are blind leaders of the blind. And if the blind leads the blind, both will fall into a ditch.'"*

- The *Warning* from Witnessing—**Matthew 7:6** *"Do not give what is holy to the dogs, nor cast your pearls before swine, lest they trample them under their feet, and turn and tear you in pieces."*

- The *Wealth* in Witnessing—**Luke 16:9-11** *"And I say to you, make friends for yourselves by unrighteous mammon, that when you fail, they may receive you into an everlasting home. He who is faithful in what is least is faithful also in much; and he who is unjust in what is least is unjust also in much. Therefore if you have not been faithful in the unrighteous mammon, who will commit to your trust the true riches?"*

- The *Prayer* of Witnessing—**Matthew 9:37-38; Luke 10:1-2** *"Then He said to His disciples, 'The harvest truly is plentiful, but the laborers are few. Therefore pray the Lord of the harvest to send out laborers into His harvest.'"*

- The *Cooperation* with Witnessing—**John 4:35-38** *"Do you not say, 'There are still four months and then comes the harvest'? Behold, I say to you, lift up your eyes and look at the fields, for they are already white for harvest! And he who reaps receives wages, and gathers fruit for eternal life, that both he who sows and he who reaps may rejoice together. For in this the saying is true: 'One sows and another reaps.' I sent you to reap that for which you have not labored; others have labored, and you have entered into their labors."*

- The *Product* from Witnessing—**Matthew 28:18-20; Mark 16:15** *"And Jesus came and spoke to them, saying, 'All authority has been given to Me in heaven and on earth. Go therefore and make disciples of all the nations, baptizing them in the name of the Father and of the Son and of the Holy Spirit, teaching them to observe all things that I have commanded you; and lo, I am with you always, even to the end of the age.' Amen."*

THE COMMAND INTERPRETED:

Wow! The subject of *witnessing* is emphasized more than any other command of Christ you have learned so far. For Christ to spend so much time on this topic obviously means it has great importance. Do you know why? Because every human being is born into sin (**Psalm 51:5**), and unless people repent from their sin (**2 Corinthians 7:10**), they will die in their sins (**John 8:24**) and be lost forever in Hell. Sin has corrupted man's mind and heart (**Jeremiah 17:9-10**), which gives Satan ammunition to blind unbelievers from seeing the gospel (**2 Corinthians 4:4**), just as you and I *once* were blinded (**Ephesians 2:2-3**).

This reality is what drove Jesus to die on the cross for sin; He didn't want people to leave this world the same way they came into it (**Luke 19:10**). Therefore, every disciple is entrusted with the gospel (**1 Thessalonians 2:4**), to share this "good news" with sinful humanity: through Christ you are saved (**Romans 10:9**), and your sins are forgiven (**Ephesians 1:7**)! This is *why* you share and *what* you share, and Jesus Christ is *Who* you share. The gospel of Christ needs to be spread, and you are the disciple for such a task.

Therefore, Jesus introduced His disciples to nine different approaches of witnessing; all of the commands are direct as well as distinguished in principle and intent. The enormity of Christ's commands on evangelism are more easily comprehended when they are categorized into three sections: *Foundation*, *Friction*, and *Focus*. The sections are in order of importance, meaning one follows another intentionally. This week, you will study the first two sections; next week, you will finish with the third. As a disciple of Jesus, give Him your undivided attention, for the dynamics He needs you to learn are in vain if they are not practiced. Christ's goal is to transform you into an effective witness to grow His Kingdom. Be His witness.

The *first* section of commands addresses evangelism's **foundation**: the *model* of witnessing and the *commitment* for witnessing. First of all, the ***model*** of witnessing (**Matthew 4:19; Mark 1:17; Luke 5:27; John 1:43**) is the Lord Jesus Christ Himself. He commanded His new disciples with the phrase, "*Follow Me.*" The Greek word "follow" (*deute*) is the imperative "Come hither!" It is not used as a demand, but as an invitation. Jesus recognized that the disciples were investing all their time in the wrong type of fishing. There is a more valuable catch, the kind that is mounted in the Kingdom of God, not on a wall. Would the disciples listen? Would they believe Him?

In context, you can sense the zeal and enthusiasm in Jesus' voice. His interest was to *"make"* these dirty fishermen into something for His glory. The Greek word "make" (*poieo*) means "abiding; banding together" in this context. Using this word in a future active tense, Jesus was promising to continually transform the disciples as long as they followed behind Him, abiding in His Word (**John 15:4**). Amen! Thus, Jesus interpreted the *what* of His promise as *"fishers of men."* He wanted the disciples to try a new fishing hole altogether: people! They had never fished for *"men"* before, so they had to be trained. Jesus Christ is the model. He has the wisdom required to "fish" for this type of catch. Follow.

Secondly, the **commitment** for witnessing (**Luke 5:10-11**) is nonnegotiable and conditional. After a long, miserable night of unsuccessful fishing, Peter watched Jesus miraculously direct him to so many fish that both boats were beginning to sink. Peter was silenced, for he had never seen anything like that in all his life. Who was this Man Who had power over the laws of nature? When Jesus looked at Peter, He said, *"Do not be afraid."* Before He could get commitment out of Peter, He had to give him comfort (**2 Corinthians 1:3**). From this, Peter then learned to trust Jesus by faith, believing in His deity, and to *"catch men"* the rest of his life.

Once Peter's heart was comforted, His life was committed. Scripture says, *"...they forsook all and followed Him."* The Greek word "forsook" (*aphiemi*) means "sent away; laid aside." In order to follow Jesus, the requirement was clear and conditional. The disciples were sent away with Christ, following Him, because they laid aside *"all"* (pride, egos, agendas, priorities, relationships, materials) to do so. They embraced their crosses devotedly (**Luke 9:23**) and followed Christ without regret (**Luke 9:62**). Nothing was more valuable than the Master! Christ was the fulfillment, the missing piece, of their lives, just as He is in yours. Jesus Christ the Lord is *the* foundation in life and witness (**1 Corinthians 3:11**). You have no other model. You have no other commitment. This is the foundation for evangelism.

The *second* section of commands addresses evangelism's **friction**: the *instruction* for witnessing, the *arguments* from witnessing, and the *warning* from witnessing. First of all, the *instruction* for witnessing (**Matthew 10:5-15; Mark 6:7-13; Luke 9:1-6; 10:3-12, 16**) is given to provide clear direction for sharing the gospel. Once you have committed your all to Christ, He guides you in what He wants you to do when you are witnessing. There are many applicable principles to glean from the first disciples so that you can become the effective witness for Jesus that they were.

First is the *mission*. The disciples were not to go to "*Gentiles*" and "*Samaritans*" but to the "*lost sheep*" of Israel. Granted, Gentiles and Samaritans were important and valuable to Christ, but at that time, He needed His disciples to go specifically to whom He directed them to reach. The most important word of mission Jesus used was "*lost*." As Christ's disciple, you, too, must realize that witnessing is to *lost* people. You can encourage a Christian, but you can't witness to one. They're not lost—they've been found (**John 15:16**). Don't spend all your time in holy huddles with fellow believers. Disband daily to target the lost, faithfully sharing the gospel of the Lord Jesus.

Next is the *message*. As the disciples were on their mission, they had a message to preach: "*the Kingdom of heaven*." That was all. They were not to fill men's ears with anything else. They were not to be people pleasers, telling audiences only what they wanted to hear. They were to be bold, passionate, and assertive on behalf of the Kingdom of God. For the Jew, to hear such words meant the Messiah (Christ) had come. Likewise, regardless of culture or class, that is your message too (**1 Corinthians 15:1-4**). Relentlessly direct men's hearts to Christ and His Kingdom (**Matthew 6:33**). Tell them the story of Jesus and share with them *why* they need the Savior. Proclaim your message!

The next step is the *ministry*. Clearly, after Jesus empowered His disciples (**Matthew 10:1**), He commissioned them to act upon the message they preached to people. This would be their ministry. Christ wanted His disciples to know that everyone to whom they witnessed would be in different spiritual conditions. "*Heal the sick, cleanse the lepers, raise the dead, cast out demons...*" Some people to whom they witnessed were not healthy, but sick and diseased. Some of the families were not happy, but grieving because a loved one had died. Some people were not at peace but tormented by demonic possession. Christ wanted His disciples not to merely acknowledge these afflictions but to do something about them!

Dear disciple, you too are empowered by the Holy Spirit (**Acts 1:8**) to be Christ's witness. You are entrusted with the ministry of reconciliation (**2 Corinthians 5:18**)—that is, to reconcile people to Christ as you have been mercifully reconciled. With that same mercy, you show mercy, using it as a way to bridge people's hardships and reach them with the gospel. Prayerfully involve yourself with the sick and diseased (**James 5:13-15**). Minister to the grieving families who are staring death in the face (**John 11:32-35**). By Christ's delivering power, reach out to those who are possessed or oppressed by demonic attack, and do so by the greatest Name (**Acts 4:12**), that of Jesus Christ the Lord! Your ministry is to embrace hurting people with the gospel of Christ (**Luke 14:21**). Yield to Christ as a vessel for His power (**Philippians 2:13**). *"Freely"* you've received God's grace, so *"freely"* give it away as you labor for the gospel (**1 Corinthians 15:10**).

We can't overlook the *materials*. The disciples were not to allow basic necessities to be a factor when evangelizing. Their money, bags, extra clothes, shoes, and staffs were not to influence their obedience. Christ clearly said, *"...a worker is worthy of his food."* The same goes for you. Never allow basic needs to distract you from your command to witness. Christ will be sure that your needs are met (**Matthew 6:8**) as you are faithful to meet His for the Kingdom! Materials and resources indeed assist in witnessing but should never determine it. Do not allow materialistic excess to have a place in your life, for it will be baggage for the journey. You need Jesus, not stuff, to witness.

Lastly, we see the *measure*. The disciples were to measure each *"city"* and *"household"* by its receptivity to the gospel of Jesus. If the message was received, the city or household was considered *"worthy,"* and therefore the disciple's *"peace"* (approval) of the city or house was welcomed. But if there was resistance, the opposite was true. In this case, the disciples were to *"shake off the dust"* from their feet, which showed their consecration and uncompromised stance for Christ's gospel. Like *"Sodom and Gomorrah,"* wicked resistance such as that, without repentance, will be accounted for in eternity (**Romans 2:16**). The Lord God Almighty is not mocked. No one is the exception. When you share the gospel, always measure your selection by the same standard.

Secondly, the *arguments* from witnessing (**Matthew 15:12-14**) should have no place in our conversations. The Pharisees insulted Jesus and His disciples by accusing them of breaking a manmade tradition (**verse 2**). Jesus responded to them, not for debate, but out of explanation. After Jesus expounded on the real meaning of *"defilement,"* His disciples informed Him that He had offended the Pharisees with His words. This is the evidence of friction that may develop as you share the gospel.

It is here that Jesus seized a teachable moment with His disciples. His command is clear: *"Let them alone."* Christ commanded His disciples to distance themselves from the Pharisees. They were *"blind"* leaders of the spiritually ignorant, and both they and the people they were deceiving were going to *"fall into a ditch"* of destruction. Jesus knew that His Father had not *"planted"* them (**Isaiah 60:21**), for they were not of Him, the Vine, since they would not abide in His Word (**John 15:6**).

Therefore, Christ did not make any apologies for offending the Pharisees, because they had perverted Holy Scripture with their *"traditions"* (**verse 6**). As a disciple, you too must never apologize for standing confidently on the Word of God. You are called to defend the gospel (**1 Peter 3:15**) but never to debate the gospel (**1 Timothy 1:4; Titus 3:9**). If unbelievers want to argue with you over whether Jesus wore long hair or if Adam and Eve had belly buttons, don't oblige them. Steer clear of arguments when witnessing. They only breed further division and contempt of faith.

Last of all, the *warning* from witnessing (**Matthew 7:6**) is a protective shield to avoid unnecessary confrontation. *"Dogs"* and *"swine"* (hogs) were unclean animals in Jewish culture. It would be unthinkable to give something *"holy"* to a dog that was incapable of comprehending it, or to cast something as valuable as *"pearls"* before pigs that were unable to appreciate it. Do you see Jesus' point? You don't give something away until you are convinced your recipient is able to properly use it.

The gospel of Jesus is no different. Witnessing is giving away the gospel. But not everyone wants to hear the story of Christ's love for them. In fact, some people are vehemently offended and violently resistant to His message. That's why Jesus warns you *"Do not give..."*, because He knows that your safety is at stake (**Acts 22:18**). You don't have to be martyred to be persecuted. Sharing the gospel will welcome persecution (**2 Timothy 3:12**), but when it comes, you must discern those who rage against you and peacefully shake the dust off your feet. If you don't, Jesus says they will *"trample"* His Word under their feet and *"turn and tear you in pieces."* Remember, Christ will give you grace to handle unwarranted persecution. But if you stubbornly and unnecessarily invite it, you disobey this command and suffer the consequences (**Acts 19:13-16**)! Be wise.

TEACHING # 6.6: WITNESSING TO THE LOST (PART 2)

Week 46

<u>*This week's objective*</u>: *To learn to share the gospel of Jesus Christ, purposely and passionately.*

THE COMMAND INTERPRETED (CONTINUED):

Last week, you diligently studied the first two sections of Jesus' commands about evangelism—its **foundation** and its **friction**. The *third* section of Christ's commands addresses evangelism's **focus**: the *wealth* of witnessing, the *prayer* of witnessing, the *cooperation* with witnessing, and the *product* from witnessing. Each of these commands complements specific focal areas of evangelization. Do more than memorize them...practice them.

First of all, the ***wealth*** of witnessing (**Luke 16:9-11**) is designed to balance your use of money and resources for evangelism. Jesus' command here actually hinges upon the posing of a question (**verse 11**). Christ was testing the disciples' dedication to Kingdom priorities. Could He *"commit to their trust the true riches?"* The "test substance" in this passage is identified as *"unrighteous mammon."* This command is a call to determine who will be *"faithful"* or *"unjust"* with the mammon; to do either even with *"least"* is paralleled as doing so with *"much."*

So, what does all this mean? How does it relate to witnessing? Well, the mammon represents money and is thus properly labeled as *"unrighteous"* because it has the power to be an idol in your life (**1 Timothy 6:10**). Yet, Jesus wants you to discipline yourself by *"making friends"* with it! Why? Because when you *"fail"* (that is, die), the friends you made will *"receive you into an everlasting home"* (that is, Heaven). Therefore, the *"friends"* you make with money are people, the *"true riches"* of the Kingdom of God!

Don't miss the point Jesus is making. Your use of money is a reciprocal test of your lordship to Christ. People for whom Christ died are the true riches. You are commanded to use your money and possessions to invest more in reaching people for Christ than in any other earthly endeavor. This is the only type of earthly investment that will compound in eternity (**Matthew 6:19-21**). To hoard material wealth is to be disqualified by Christ to handle the vast riches (people) that build His Kingdom. You become dangerously rich in your own eyes and not in those of God (**Luke 12:21**). As a disciple of Christ, do not covet your possessions selfishly (**Luke 12:15**), but rather use your wealth in witnessing by sacrificing it as necessary to reach people for Jesus Christ.

Secondly, the *prayer* of witnessing (**Matthew 9:37-38; Luke 10:1-2**) is uniquely connected to the evangelism process. Jesus was previously expressing His compassion for the multitudes following Him through preaching, teaching, and healing. In the context of a harvest of people, Jesus issued this command. He identified the harvest as "*plentiful,*" meaning abundant and ready. The only problem is that there is a shortage of "*workers*" to harvest the crops of the souls of men.

The only solution that Jesus commanded is to "*pray.*" Christ is the "*Lord of the harvest,*" and as you pray, you ask Him to "*send out laborers into His harvest.*" What would happen if every disciple of Jesus always waited for another disciple to go witness? How much witnessing would be done by the body of Christ? None. Therefore, since you are to be praying, witnessing starts with you. As you are faithful to share the gospel, it is then that you pray for Christ to "*send out*" other laborers to water the seeds of Scripture that you've planted (**1 Corinthians 3:5-6**). Immediately, when you finish sharing the gospel with an uninterested lost person, pray, pray, pray. The command here clarifies and channels exactly *what* it is for which you are praying (**1 John 5:14-15**). There's nothing that moves the heart of God more than His people burdened for the lost.

Thirdly, the *cooperation* with witnessing (**John 4:35-38**) is meant to encourage you in your partnership with other believers. Using the terminology of the "*harvest*" again, Jesus took it to another level by focusing on reaping. In the previous command, you prayed for it; and in this command, you find it. There's no better joy than hearing of someone born again into the Kingdom of God (**Luke 15:10**).

In the secular world, it would be unlikely for someone to "*rejoice*" in watching another "*reap*" what they had "*sown*." You work hard at your job to earn a paycheck, not give it away. Well, in the Christian's world, such a mentality is not accepted. Jesus said that the one sowing and the one reaping "*rejoice together*." Why? It is because they are not in competition with each other. That's the difference! When people have been praying for the Lord of the harvest to send out laborers, He does, and that means you "*enter into their labors*" and "*reap*" what you have not sown (**1 Corinthians 3:7-10; Psalm 126:5-6**). You see, you are cooperating with brothers and sisters in Christ to see the Kingdom grow. Every person won to Christ is always a result of someone working that field before you did. They sowed, and you reaped, but you both rejoice together. Hallelujah!

Lastly, the ***product*** from witnessing (**Matthew 28:18-20; Mark 16:15**) is structured to be the end of the beginning of evangelism. Does this command sound familiar? It is called the Great Commission and was established to be a perpetual model to build Christ's church (**Matthew 16:18**) on Earth until His Second Coming. The dynamic behind it is duplication. Jesus commanded His disciples to go "*make disciples*"; that is, to cultivate in others what Jesus had produced in them.

Once people have been saved, witnessing to them has reached its end, for they are the product. However, witnessing then transforms into the beginning of discipleship, which begins with being baptized by immersion as Jesus was (**Matthew 3:16**). Remember, Christ *commanded* baptism, allowing the new disciple to identify with His death, burial, and Resurrection (**Romans 6:3-6**). Now the disciple is ready to be "*taught to observe all things*" Christ has commanded, which is found verbatim in the volume of this book. Discipleship leads to witnessing from the new believer, which results in someone else being born again, which creates another disciple. Do you see the duplication? Witnessing indeed is the end of the beginning. Therefore, discipled believers are the intended product that Christ fashioned for establishing a healthy local church.

THE COMMAND ILLUSTRATED:

Evangelism is found throughout the Bible, but one of the clearest examples is that of Philip and the Ethiopian eunuch. Turn to **Acts 8:26-40**. The eunuch was a man of great authority, holding the position of treasurer for Queen Candace of Ethiopia. After leaving Jerusalem after a time of worship, the eunuch was reading Isaiah the prophet, yet he did not understand what he was reading. Thus, the Holy Spirit directed Philip to "*overtake*" the chariot of the eunuch and witness to him. Divinely, the eunuch was reading **Isaiah 53:7-8**, which points to Jesus Christ and His death on the cross. Seeing that the eunuch was genuinely interested in the meaning of Isaiah's passage, Philip "*opened his mouth, and beginning at this Scripture, preached Jesus to him.*"

At this point, the eunuch professed his faith in Christ as God's Son and was baptized in a water hole in the middle of the Gaza desert. Miraculous! Glory be to God the Father, for He reconciled the eunuch to Himself that day, and you will meet him in the Kingdom of God. As Christ's disciple, learn from Philip's example. His primary focus was not on *what* to do but on *Who* He listened to: the Holy Spirit (**verse 29**). Philip's witnessing was first preceded by His listening. God the Father; God the Son (Word, **John 1:1**); and God the Holy Spirit—these Three are *One* (**1 John 5:7**). The Holy Spirit is the anointing power of God, dedicated to teaching you (**1 John 2:20, 27**) the very Scriptures that He wrote and inspired (**2 Timothy 3:16; 2 Peter 1:20-21**).

Jesus Christ sent the Holy Spirit after He ascended into Heaven (**John 16:7, 13-14**). He did this to indwell you as His disciple (**1 Corinthians 3:16; 6:19-20**) and empower you as His evangelistic spokesman (**Acts 1:8**). Therefore, like Philip, you are led by the Holy Spirit (**Romans 8:14**) into the pathways of divine appointments to "*eunuchs*" who need to hear the gospel.

That's why it is critical that you deny yourself daily (**Luke 9:23**) and crucify your fleshly desires (**Galatians 5:24**) so that you can walk in the power of the Holy Spirit (**Galatians 5:16-17**). Being filled with the Holy Spirit is essential to showcasing His power through your obedience (**Ephesians 5:18**). Like Philip, a Spirit-filled witness is effective and precise, so follow the Spirit's promptings as you harvest the fields of your daily environment. Share the gospel!

THE COMMAND INITIATED:

There is nothing more exuberating than acting upon the commands of Christ by faith. When it comes to witnessing, the excitement of such obedience is multiplied because it is public and personal. Up to this point, you have learned much about witnessing, but now it is time to initiate what you have learned. So, one of the best ways to put evangelism into action is to see it in action.

O.S. Hawkins has a very good concept of this. In his book *Drawing the Net*, Hawkins elaborates on the necessity of using Scripture when witnessing. He writes from the standpoint that you, the disciple, must invest Scripture into your hearers so as to penetrate with it, not pacify:

> Peter's Pentecostal appeal resulted in his hearers' hearts being "*cut*" (**Acts 2:37**). The next phrase indicates that they asked, "*What shall we do?*" What happened when Peter issued this prophetic, plain, positive, personal appeal? It had a penetrating effect. Their hearts were "*cut.*" We have a word for that in our Christian vocabulary. We call it *conviction.* Modern day appeals are superficial or designed to make our hearers feel good...Simon Peter's appeal did not have that effect. It cut and pierced his hearers to the heart. Perhaps that is the reason 3,000 were saved and baptized that day, but also the reason one out of four churches in today's great missionary-sending denomination cannot even baptize one new convert in an entire year! Until a person recognizes there is no hope within himself to satisfy the righteous demands of God's law, the cross is simply a farce to him. Yet, when our hearts are cut, when conviction of sin becomes a personal matter, we become aware that our only hope of being right with God is through the cross of Christ...One must take personal responsibility for the death of Jesus Christ. He died in our place! When the men and women at Pentecost realized what they had done in crucifying the Lord, their hearts were broken (**vv. 23-37**). In attempting to draw the net today, too few of us attempt to lead our hearers to assume personal responsibility for their sins. Consequently, many appeals are not penetrating and

are left without conviction, resulting in few conversions. Conviction always precedes conversion. The process is referred to as spiritual birth (see **John 3: 1-10; Titus 3:5; 1 Peter 1:23**). It is appropriately illustrated in physical birth. There must be birth pains before the child is born and so it is with spiritual birth. We can no more experience the supernatural new birth without godly sorrow over sin, than we can experience natural physical birth without experiencing labor pains...Many of us who make appeals for Christ wonder why we seldom experience a harvest. Could it be the ground has not been broken? The Word of God, like a sharp, two-edged sword, is the only tool that can cut to the heart. Our appeals need to penetrate, to break the ground of the heart. It doesn't matter how much seed is sown, or how much time is spent in cultivation—if the ground is not broken there will be no harvest. When we issue Christ's appeal, publicly or privately, one of the most important things we can do is...make it penetrating![3]

Very well put. *Sharing* the gospel cannot be separated from *using* Scripture. It is a biblical impossibility because the Word of God is the actual "seed" that is sown (**Luke 8:11**). It nurtures sprouting faith from those who "hear" the Word (**Romans 10:17**), which leads to a lost person being born again (**1 Peter 1:23**). Praise God! This is the pattern that Jesus used. As His disciple, you are to follow in His footsteps, faithfully sharing the gospel and defending (not debating—**1 Timothy 1:4; Titus 3:9**) its integrity (**1 Peter 3:15**) as His gospel is set ablaze in your heart!

Robert Coleman wants you to follow Christ's example, too. In his book *The Master Plan of Evangelism*, Coleman so beautifully captures Jesus in action, all for the purpose of motivating your heart to witness because of the model you find in Christ:

That is why He lost no opportunity to impress on His followers the deep compulsion of His own soul aflame with the love of God for a lost world. Everything He did and said was motivated by this consuming passion. His life was simply the revelation in time of God's eternal purpose to save for Himself a people. Supremely this is what the disciples needed to learn, not in theory, but in practice. And they saw it practiced before them in many ways every day. Though the demonstrations were often painfully hard to accept, as when He washed their feet (**John 13: 1-20**), they could not miss what He meant. They saw how their Master denied himself many of the comforts and pleasures of the world and became a servant among them. They saw how the things which they cherished—physical satisfaction, popular acclaim, prestige—He refused; while the things which they sought to escape—poverty, humiliation, sorrow, and even death—He accepted willingly for their sake. As they watched Him minister to the sick, comfort the sorrowing, and preach the Gospel to the poor, it was clear that the Master considered no service too small nor sacrifice too great when it was rendered for the glory of God. They may not have always understood it, and certainly could not explain it, but they cold never mistake it.[4]

Oh, how I pray that the fire of the Holy Spirit will consume you and propel you toward lost people daily. Dear disciple, are you willing to follow Jesus Christ, the Master, in His pattern of witnessing? Remember, sharing the gospel is not a talent or a calling reserved for certain personality types; it is a command for all! The message of Jesus on your lips will always be a product of your perception of Him (**1 John 1:1-4**). You are redeemed from Hell and the penalty of sin, so talk like it joyfully (**Psalm 107:2**). Salvation has come.

TEACHING # 6.7: WITNESSING TO THE LOST (PART 3)

Week 47

This week's objective: To learn to share the gospel of Jesus Christ, purposely and passionately

THE COMMAND INTERROGATED:

Evangelism is perhaps a greater threat to Satan than any other task of a disciple. A heart on fire for Christ, zealous to obey Him, sends the devil into a panic. The very people whom he has tempted, tried, and led into bondage are the ones you reach for Jesus, snatching them away (**Jude 23**). Evangelism, then, is a tug-of-war for the souls of men. So, it is no surprise that the devil will do whatever he can to keep you from witnessing. You must identify his interrogation.

How does Satan attack you? Fear. This is the devil's greatest weapon against you when you faithfully commit to sharing the gospel. One prime example of fear's reality is found in **Luke 22:54-62**. Just after King Jesus was arrested in the Garden of Gethsemane, all the disciples abandoned Jesus for "fear" they would be arrested, too (**Mark 14:50**). This left Jesus all by Himself, in the hands of murderous men. After this arrest, as Christ was taken to the "*high priest's house,*" Peter "*followed at a distance.*" For years of ministry, Peter had been at Jesus' feet, learning and growing in His grace. And now, he was at a distance. Why? Fear.

Peter was concerned that people would affiliate him with Jesus, which would lead to his arrest. That's why, when he was questioned on three different occasions, Peter denied any connection to Christ whatsoever. When the rooster crowed, just as Christ had predicted (**Luke 22:34**), Peter caught a glimpse of Jesus as he "*turned and looked at Peter.*" Can you imagine the piercing gaze of the Son of God, looking intently at Peter, affirming His prediction? Wow. Naturally, Peter quickly left the courtyard and *"wept bitterly."* He never forgot that day.

Do you see how debilitating fear is to your faith? Peter's faith was completely paralyzed by fear. He did anything but witness to the people in the courtyard, even though the opportunity was there. It's easy to witness when your hearer is receptive, but when you face resistance to the gospel, that's the greatest test. Be careful not to condition your willingness to witness for Christ. Be faithful whether it's easy or tough.

Over all, beware of Satan's attack of fear in your heart. Fear begins with thoughts such as, "How will he respond?" or "What will I do if he says...?" or "What if she gets angry when..." Don't fear and fret over what you do not know. Even if the response of your hearers is vehement, is Christ going to be scared and abandon you? Of course not! Maintain your faith. Do not allow Satan to destroy it (**Luke 22:32**), for it is the mountain-moving power to conquer fears, not be conquered by them. As a child of God, you know Who's in charge (**Matthew 10:28; Psalm 27:1**). Have no fear, just faith, for this is the pattern for all persevering saints (**Hebrews 11:32-40**).

THE COMMAND INDESTRUCTIBLE:

The attitude you must take every day is that witnessing is an honor, not an obligation. Daily, when you leave your home, you are entering a mission field, and you are entrusted with the precious gospel of Jesus. God watches and waits. The conversations in which you may find yourself were set up by Him. Will you witness to these people? Will you share the price paid for their sin? You speak to people as an ambassador, representing your Lord Jesus Christ, pleading with people, *"Be reconciled to God"* (**2 Corinthians 5:20**). This is your ministry. This is your duty.

No matter how much Satan may try to attack you, the power of Scripture will always defeat him—always. The Bible has more power in one syllable than the devil has had since the beginning of time! When you wake up each day, you need a Scripture that reminds you of what God expects evangelistically from you. While there are so many verses on this topic in the Bible, there is one that is especially clear and holds you accountable: **Psalm 71:15**. It is to be your memory verse: *"My mouth shall tell of Your righteousness and Your* *salvation all the day, for I do not know their limits."*

As you wage war against Satan for the souls of men, quote this verse in faith. In it is found the will of God—His utmost desire to save men and women from the devil's grasp and enlist them in His army of discipleship (**2 Timothy 2:3-4**). Do not flap your gums over idle chatter (**Matthew 12:36**). Use your *"mouth"* (not just your lifestyle) to witness for Christ, for this is His chosen method to communicate His gospel with the lost. Be the witness that Christ died for you to be. Be *His* witness.

THE COMMAND INQUIRED:

What cannot be measured cannot be evaluated. Therefore, it is essential to measure your comprehension of Christ's command in this teaching, or else the devil will snatch away the "seeds" of Scripture sown into your heart (**Matthew 13:19**). To keep this from occurring, write down your answers to the following questions as they correlate with the teaching this week:

In what passage(s) of Scripture do you find Christ's commandment on **witnessing**?

_____

_____

_____

What is the accurate interpretation of **witnessing** you have discovered?

_____

_____

_____

_____

_____

In your own words, what are some real-life examples in Scripture of **witnessing**?

_____

_____

_____

_____

_____

_____

What steps of initiation did you learn to take in order for **witnessing** to transform your life?

_____

_____

_____

_____

_____

_____

How will Satan attack you to hinder your obedience to **witness**?

_____

_____

_____

_____

_____

_____

What memory verse will you use to protect Christ's command of **witnessing** in your life? Write it out.

_____

_____

_____

SECTION C: CHRIST'S COMMANDS AS THEY RELATE TO THE DISCIPLE *ETERNALLY*

CHAPTER 7: *REIGN* IS THE DISCIPLE'S ANTICIPATION

"Then the mother of Zebedee's sons came to Him with her sons, kneeling down and asking something from Him. And He said to her, 'What do you wish?' She said to Him, 'Grant that these two sons of mine may sit, one on Your right hand and the other on Your left, in Your kingdom.' But Jesus answered and said, 'You do not know what you ask...to sit on My right hand and on My left is not Mine to give, but it is for those for whom it is prepared by My Father" (**Matthew 20:20-23**).

All authority belongs to Jesus Christ (**Matthew 28:18**). He is Savior, Lord, and King. And as the King, Jesus has a Kingdom that will know no end (**Luke 1:33**) and a throne to occupy to which every knee will bow (**Philippians 3:9-11**). King Jesus saves every repenting sinner, supernaturally securing them "in Christ" (**2 Corinthians 5:17**), which makes them "joint heirs" with Christ (**Romans 8:17**). Could it be better than this? I was that sinner, and you were too. Now, what Christ has, we have, for we are "heirs" of the inheritance with Him. Oh, what unspeakable joy we have in Jesus!

Like Zebedee's two sons, aggressively anticipate your reality of reigning with Christ in His Kingdom. When will you reign with Jesus? How long will it take before then? The joyful impatience is intense. Your only comfort is to know one fact: Jesus Christ is coming back! In the same manner that He ascended to Heaven, He will descend back to Earth (**Acts 1:9-11**). Why? Because you, His body (**1 Corinthians 12:27**), are left here on earth, and God's covenant people, Israel, are not saved. You are to labor faithfully as you wait for Christ's Second Coming. Do not delay and disobey. There will come a day in which you will reign with Christ (**Revelation 20:6**).

Be faithful and steadfast.

TEACHING # 7.1: SECOND COMING OF JESUS CHRIST (PART 1)

Week 48

This week's objective: To identify what the Second Coming of Christ will be like, as well as to learn what your responsibilities are while awaiting His return.

THE COMMAND INTRODUCED:

- 1) His Coming Will Bring *Comfort*—John 14:1-3 *"Let not your heart be troubled; you believe in God, believe also in Me. In My Father's house are many mansions; if it were not so, I would have told you. I go to prepare a place for you. And if I go and prepare a place for you, I will come again and receive you to Myself; that where I am, there you may be also."*

- 2) His Coming Will Bring *Chaos*—Matthew 24:3-25:46; Mark 13:3-37; Luke 12:35-48; 17:22-37; 21:7-36 *"Now as He sat on the Mount of Olives, the disciples came to Him privately, saying, 'Tell us, when will these things be? And what will be the sign of Your coming, and of the end of the age?' And Jesus answered and said to them: 'Take heed that no one deceives you. For many will come in My name, saying, 'I am the Christ,' and will deceive many. And you will hear of wars and rumors of wars. See that you are not troubled; for all these things must come to pass, but the end is not yet. For nation will rise against nation, and kingdom against kingdom. And there will be famines, pestilences, and earthquakes in various places. All these are the beginning of sorrows. Then they will deliver you up to tribulation and kill you, and you will be hated by all nations for My name's sake. And then many will be offended, will betray one another, and will hate one another. Then many false prophets will rise up and deceive many. And because lawlessness will abound, the love of many will grow cold. But he who endures to the end shall be saved. And this gospel of the kingdom will be preached in all the world as a witness to all the nations, and then the end will come. Therefore when you see the 'abomination of desolation,' spoken of by Daniel the prophet, standing in the holy place' (whoever reads, let him understand), 'then let those who are in Judea flee to the mountains. Let him who is on the housetop not go down to take anything out of his house. And let him who is in the field not go back to get his clothes. But woe to those who are pregnant and to those who are nursing babies in those days! And pray that your flight may not be in winter or on the Sabbath. For then there will be great tribulation, such as has not been since the beginning of the world until this time, no, nor ever shall be. And unless those days were shortened, no flesh would be saved; but for the elect's sake those days will be shortened. Then if anyone says to you, 'Look, here is the Christ!' or 'There!' do not believe it. For false christs and false prophets will rise and show great signs and wonders to deceive, if possible, even the elect. See, I have told you beforehand. Therefore if they say to you, 'Look, He is in the desert!' do not go out; or 'Look, He is in the inner rooms!' do not believe it. For as the lightning comes from the east and flashes to the west, so also will the coming of the Son of Man be. For wherever the carcass is, there the eagles will be gathered together. Immediately after the tribulation of those days the sun will be darkened, and the moon will not give its light; the stars will fall from heaven, and the powers of the heavens will be shaken. Then the sign of the Son of Man will appear in heaven, and then all the tribes of the earth will mourn, and they will see the Son of Man coming on the clouds of heaven with power and great glory. And He will send His angels with a great sound of a trumpet, and they will gather together His elect from the four winds, from one end of heaven to the other. Now learn this parable from the fig tree: When its branch has already become tender and puts forth leaves, you know that summer is near. So you also, when you see all these things, know that it is near—at the doors! Assuredly, I say to you, this generation will by no means pass away till all these things take place. Heaven and earth will pass away, but My words will by no means pass away. But of that day and hour no one knows, not even the angels of heaven, but My Father only. But as the days of Noah were, so also will the coming of the Son of Man be. For as in the days before the flood, they were eating and drinking, marrying and giving in marriage, until the day that Noah entered the ark, and did not know until the flood came and took them all away, so also will the coming of the Son of Man be. Then two men will be in the field: one will be taken and the other left. Two women will be grinding at the mill: one will be taken and the other left. Watch therefore, for you do not know what hour your Lord is coming. But know this, that if the master of the house had known what hour the thief would come, he would have watched and not allowed his house to be broken into. Therefore you also be ready, for the Son of Man is coming at an hour you do not expect. Who then is a faithful and wise servant, whom his master made ruler over his household, to give them food in due season? Blessed is that servant whom his master, when he comes, will find so doing. Assuredly, I say to you that he will make him ruler over all his goods. But if that evil servant says in his heart, 'My master is delaying his coming,' and begins to beat his fellow servants, and to eat and drink with the drunkards, the master of that servant will come on a day when he is not looking for him and at an hour that he is not aware of, and will cut him in two and appoint him his portion with the hypocrites. There shall be weeping and gnashing of teeth. Then the kingdom of heaven shall be likened to ten virgins who took their lamps and went out to meet the bridegroom. Now five of them were wise, and five were foolish. Those who were foolish took their lamps and took no oil with them, but the wise took oil in their vessels with their lamps. But while the bridegroom was delayed, they all slumbered and slept. And at midnight a cry was heard: 'Behold, the bridegroom is coming; go out to meet him!' Then all those virgins arose and trimmed their lamps. And the foolish said to the wise, 'Give us some of your oil, for our lamps are going out.' But the wise answered, saying, 'No, lest there should not be enough for us and you; but go rather to those who sell, and buy for yourselves.' And while they went to buy, the bridegroom came, and those who were ready went in with him to the wedding; and the door was shut. Afterward the other virgins came also, saying, 'Lord, Lord, open to us!' But he answered and said, 'Assuredly, I say to you, I do not know you.' Watch therefore, for you know neither the day nor the hour in which the Son of Man is coming. For the kingdom of heaven is like a man traveling to a far country, who called his own servants and delivered his goods to them. And to one he gave five talents, to another two, and to another one, to each according to his own ability; and immediately he went on a journey. Then he who had received the five talents went and traded with them, and made another five talents. And likewise he who had received two gained two more also. But he who had received one went and dug in the ground, and hid his lord's money. After a long time the lord of those servants came and settled accounts with them. So he who had received five talents came and brought five other talents, saying, 'Lord, you delivered to me five talents; look, I have gained five more talents besides them.' His lord said to him, 'Well done, good and faithful servant; you were faithful over a few things, I will make you ruler over many things. Enter into the joy of your lord.' He also who had received two talents came and said, 'Lord, you delivered to me two talents; look, I have gained two more talents besides them.' His lord said to him, 'Well done, good and faithful servant; you have been faithful over a few things, I will make you ruler over many things. Enter into the joy of your lord.' Then he who had received the one talent came and said, 'Lord, I knew you to be a hard man, reaping where you have not sown, and gathering where you have not scattered seed. And I was afraid, and went and hid your talent in the ground. Look, there you have what is yours.' But his lord answered and said to him, 'You wicked and lazy servant, you knew that I reap where I have not sown, and gather where I have not scattered seed. So you ought to have deposited my money with the bankers, and at my coming I would have received back my own with interest. So take the talent from him, and give it to him who has ten talents. For to everyone who has, more will be given, and he will have abundance; but from him who does not have, even what he has will be taken away. And cast the unprofitable servant into the outer darkness. There will be weeping and gnashing of teeth.' When the Son of Man comes in His glory, and all the holy angels with Him, then He will sit on the throne of His glory. All the nations will be gathered before Him, and He will separate them one from another, as a shepherd divides his sheep from the goats. And He will set the sheep on His right hand, but the goats on the left. Then the King will say to those on His right hand, 'Come, you blessed of My Father, inherit the kingdom prepared for you from the foundation of the world: for I was hungry and you gave Me food; I was thirsty and you gave Me drink; I was a stranger and you took Me in; I was naked and you clothed Me; I was sick and you visited Me; I was in prison and you came to Me.' Then the righteous will answer Him, saying, 'Lord, when did we see You hungry and feed You, or thirsty and give You drink? When did we see You a stranger and take You in, or naked and clothe You? Or when did we see You sick, or in prison, and come to You?' And the King will answer and say to them, 'Assuredly, I say to you, inasmuch as you did it to one of the least of these My brethren, you did it to Me.' Then He will also say to those on the left hand, 'Depart from Me, you cursed, into the everlasting fire prepared for the devil and his angels: for I was hungry and you gave Me no food; I was thirsty and you gave Me no drink; I was a stranger and you did not take Me in, naked and you did not clothe Me, sick and in prison and you did not visit Me.' Then they also will answer Him, saying, 'Lord, when did we see You hungry or thirsty or a stranger or naked or sick or in prison, and did not minister to You?' Then He will answer them, saying, 'Assuredly, I say to you, inasmuch as you did not do it to one of the least of these, you did not do it to Me.' And these will go away into everlasting punishment, but the righteous into eternal life.'"*

THE COMMAND INTERPRETED:

The Second Coming of Jesus Christ is more emphasized than any other command He gave, surpassing even that of witnessing. Jesus explained, taught, and exhorted about His Second Coming more so than any other topic! Therefore, this teaching covers more content in greater depth than any other command in this book. For your own recall, read **Acts 1:9-11** again. In the same manner that Christ ascended, He shall yet again descend for His Church—bodily, in the clouds, and upon the Mount of Olives.

We are left here until Jesus returns to faithfully labor for Him by giving to the poor, feeding the hungry, clothing the naked, ministering to the sick, and using these opportunities to implant the gospel of salvation into people's fractured lives. This is our co-mission with Christ! Until His appearing, we labor, watch, and wait, for He promised to come again. Now, it's time to learn what you can expect from the Second Coming of Jesus.

The first command (**John 14:1-3**) indicates that Christ's coming will bring ***comfort***. Considering the context of this command, the disciples are emotionally hurt that Jesus will be leaving. They do not understand why He is leaving (through His death) or where He is going (to Heaven), so He bears them up with this direct command: "*Let not your heart be troubled...*" The Greek *troubled* (*tarasso*) means "to stir; agitate." Literally, the disciples were vehemently frustrated by Jesus' mention of departing because they couldn't make Him stay. Little did they know it was far worse for Christ to stay than to go. Do you know why?

It is because Jesus' ascension back to Heaven was necessary for the sending of the Holy Spirit (**John 16:5-7**)! As a disciple of Jesus, you cannot live in readiness for the return of Jesus Christ without the communing walk with God through the Holy Spirit. We are indwelled (*sealed*) with the Holy Spirit (**John 7:37-39; John 14:16-17, 26; John 15:26; John 20:21-22**). We are to be filled (*empowered*) by the Holy Spirit so that we may imitate Jesus (**Luke 4:1, 18; John 6:63**) and live victoriously in prayer and patience (**Luke 11:13; Luke 24:46-44; Acts 1:4-5, 8; Acts 2:4; Mark 1:8; Matthew 3:11; Luke 3:16; John 1:33**). Praise God, the filling power of the Holy Spirit in our lives also emboldens us to speak in times of persecution (**Luke 12:11-12; Matthew 10:19-20; Mark 13:11**).

Day by day, as we yield to the Holy Spirit of God, Jesus affirms that we will be guided by the Holy Spirit (**John 16:13-14**). The Spirit is our "*Comforter*" who "comforts" our troubled hearts and empowers our witness (**Acts 1:8**) to maximize our lives for Christ while we await His return. Even while He is gone "*preparing a place for us,*" Jesus has not left us (**Matthew 28:20**), for He indwells us by His Holy Spirit (**1 Corinthians 6: 19-20**). He, the Father, and the Spirit are all ONE (**1 John 5:7**)! Until the day we see Christ, we are "*sealed*" with the Holy Spirit (**Ephesians 4:30**).

It is ironic, but the very comfort we receive from the Holy Spirit while waiting on Christ to return points to the comfort we'll receive when He does return. What is that comfort? "*I will come again and receive you to Myself; that where I am, there you may be also.*" To the disciples, that promise melted their hearts and fueled their passion to keep working and waiting. Their bodily separation from Jesus was only temporary, for His Second Coming would initiate a great reunion day. To disciples who left houses and lands and careers to follow Jesus, the *"many mansions"* would be a reward worth waiting for. Christ will come back for you. Remember, He's *"preparing a place"* for you. He cares for you. He remembers your labors for His Kingdom. You are not forgotten! Serve Christ with all your might until He returns.

Now, it's time to examine the nature of Jesus' second command about His coming. As His Second Coming is addressed, please know that there are many interpretive views from theological and eschatological circles about the meaning and timing of Jesus' return. No matter what view you come to understand regarding the Second Coming, the most important principle is that you live your life with gospel witness out of readiness for Jesus' return. While this is your focus, every follower of Jesus needs to be grounded in their basic understanding of the origins for Bible prophecy and the Second Coming. It all begins with **Genesis 3:15**.

This is the first prophecy in the Bible, explaining that Satan began a war against the *"Seed"* of the *"woman."* The woman is Israel, and her seed is Jesus Christ, the *"male"* child of her womb (**Revelation 12:5**). From the stock of Jewish roots came a man named Abraham. He was a man of faith (**Hebrews 11:8-12, 17-19**), which was *"accounted for righteousness"* (**Romans 4:13-25**). Abraham's remarkable faith in and obedience to God was rewarded when the Lord chose to make a covenant with him and his descendants for eternity (**Genesis 12:1-3; 15:17-21**).

From Abraham would descend Isaac, Jacob, Joseph, and eventually Moses. It was Moses who received God's call to deliver the Lord's Jewish covenant people from Egypt (**Exodus 3:1-10**). Moses boldly proclaimed that there was a Prophet that God would raise up to redeem Israel (**Deuteronomy 18:15-19**). This was a prophecy of the Messiah, Jesus Christ, who would come to deliver God's covenant people. Well, that day came (**Luke 2:1-14**), and the Lord Jesus grew in *"wisdom and stature"* (**Luke 2:51-52**) as He approached the beginning of His earthly ministry (**Matthew 3:13-17**).

Calling His twelve disciples to His side, Jesus taught them and trained them (**Matthew 10:1-4**). Although Jesus still loved and ministered to non-Jewish people, the priority of His mission was crystal clear: *"the lost sheep of the house of Israel"* (**Matthew 10:6; 15:24; Luke 19:9-10**). The majority of the people Jesus reached out to did not want Him, yet even this was entirely in God's sovereign plan. With His mind on His Father's covenant with the Jewish people, Christ continued to preach and minister to them, but still, *"His own did not receive Him"* (**John 1:11**).

The religious leaders of that day were called scribes and Pharisees, and they hated Jesus because of His claim to *"fulfill the Law"* of Moses (**Matthew 5:17**). These scribes and Pharisees were blinded to the fact that the Law was the bridge to faith in Christ (**Galatians 3:19-25**). They despised Christ for His claims, and Jesus responded to their retaliation as the Son of God should have (**Matthew 23:1-33**). Knowing that Israel as a whole would not repent and accept Him by faith as their Messiah, Jesus broke down, and oh, you can hear the pain in this verse: **Matthew 23:37-39**. Soon after this, Christ our Lord was arrested (**John 18:12**), beaten (**John 19:1-3**), sentenced (**John 19:5-16**), and crucified (**John 19:17-30**). His own people, Israel, had murdered the very One who came to give them life (**Romans 6:23**)!

But I assure you, Jesus did not die in vain. His precious blood was not wasted because "as many as received Him, to them He gave the right to become children of God, to those who believe in His name" (**John 1:12**). You see, "...whoever calls on the name of the Lord will be saved" (**Romans 10:13**)! Salvation was first offered to the nation of Israel, but it is by no means limited to them (**Romans 1:16**), because salvation is globally extended to the whole world. Since the Jewish people did not receive Christ, His gospel was then spread to non-Jewish people, better known as Gentiles.

The apostle Paul can validate that statement better than anyone else in the New Testament (**Acts 9:15**). To reach *"Gentiles, kings, and the children of Israel"* was Paul's commission from Jesus. However, Paul had the same continuous conflict with Jewish people that Christ did, enduring hardships and persecutions for it, until Jesus narrowed Paul's mission to Gentiles only (**Acts 22:17-21**). This change in mission away from the Jews and toward the Gentiles is understood more clearly through Paul's discourse on the subject to the church at Rome in **Romans 11:1-32**. This is one of the finest explanations of why *"salvation has come to the Gentiles."* Dear disciple, if you are of *Jewish* descent, you are considered a Messianic Jew since you believe Christ was the Messiah. If you are not a Jew, you are classified as a *Gentile* and have received salvation through Christ at the expense of Israel's rejection of Him.

Gentiles are compared to *"wild olive trees"* that are miraculously *"grafted in among them* [Israel]" by the grace of God. All born-again Gentiles (non-Jews) are *"partakers of the root,"* and the *"root"* is Israel's Jesus Christ the Messiah. No Gentile should ever scorn Israel for their disobedience and brag at his *"grafting in"*; as Paul says, *"Remember that you do not support the root, but the root supports you"* (**Romans 11:18**). Jews are *"the branches,"* and had they not been *"broken off"* (through unbelief in Christ), no Gentile could be *"grafted in."* Why? Because the covenant was ordained through Abraham for Israel, not Gentiles. That's why all believing Gentiles are *"grafted in."*

Do you know how this is possible? Look for the explanation in **Galatians 3:6-9, 14-18, 29** and **Ephesians 3:6**: *"...only those who are of faith are blessed with believing Abraham."* Faith. That's it. Just faith, real faith, saving faith in Christ (**Galatians 2:16**). Jesus is the *"cornerstone"* of His Church (**Ephesians 2:20**), having united both Jew and Gentile through faith in Him, in parallel to God's promise to Abraham. This extension of the mission to include both Jews and Gentiles has resulted in the "Church Age" that has co-existed with Abraham's promise since Christ's Ascension and includes our mission to preach His gospel and build His Church until His return.

The age of the Church finds its prophetic foothold somewhere between the sixty-ninth and seventieth *"weeks"* in the prophecy recorded in the Book of Daniel (**Daniel 9:24-27**). Although this is an era marked by the spread of the gospel of Jesus Christ to all nations, it is simultaneously a time met with ever-increasing wickedness within society (**2 Timothy 3:1-5; 2 Peter 3:3-7**). Jesus warned that culture and society would be in this kind of immoral shape when He returned, using the *"days of Noah"* (**Genesis 6: 5-8**) as an example of just how drastically people will rebel against God (**Matthew 26:36-44**). Compare our world today and Noah's world in the Book of Genesis—we're living in the last days that eventually merge into what the Bible refers to as the time of *"Tribulation."*

This tribulation period is identified during the seventieth week of Daniel's prophecy (**Daniel 9:27**) and described with seal-trumpet-bowl judgments in **Revelation 4-19**. Regardless, the gospel is still spreading during such a time of tribulation as people are being saved and persevering (**Revelation 14:6-7, 12-13**), and God is also fulfilling His covenant with Israel when the *"fullness of the Gentiles has come"* (**Romans 11:25-27**). It's at this point, known only to the mind of the Father (**Mark 13:32**), that it will be time for the Second Coming of our Lord Jesus Christ! Jesus will return with great power and glory, coming on the clouds of Heaven both physically and visibly (**Acts 1:9-11**) for His Bride, the Church, just as He said He would (**John 14:3**).

With a shout, He will call the Church—Jew and Gentile—to Himself in glorious marital *"rapture"* (**Revelation 19:7-9; 1 Corinthians 15:51-57; Philippians 3:20**), when both the dead in Christ and the surviving Christians of the Tribulation rise to meet Jesus in the air! Instead of an Ark with a flood, there will be a white horse with the King! This *rapture* of the saints is believed to happen at the end of the Tribulation, rather than at the beginning or middle, because of Jesus' teaching in **Matthew 24:29-31** compared with Paul's instruction in **1 Thessalonians 4:16-18**. Both passages linguistically share the same meaning through similar elements: *"heaven, clouds, trumpets, angels," "coming/descending," "gathering the elect/caught up,"* and most importantly, *"Son of Man / Lord Himself."* This means the rapture of the saints is understood to be synonymous with the Second Coming of Jesus, rather than there being two *"Comings"* of Jesus for His saints and then with His saints.

Rather than leaving our "seed of Abraham" (**Galatians 3:14-18; Romans 11:11-24; 15:26-27**) remnant to suffer alone since we are grafted into the new covenant of Christ with them, we as the Church stand strong in the Lord during the tribulation era, preaching the gospel no matter the cost. At no time in history has the Church been free from suffering persecution, and so it should be of no surprise that during the culmination of the last days of tribulation, when the Church is needed more than ever, she will be anything less than present to finish the good fight of faith to the end.

Upon Christ's return, and with His Bride, the Church, by His side, the Abrahamic and Davidic covenants with Israel will be fulfilled (**Genesis 15:18; 2 Samuel 7:12-16; Revelation 20:1-3**). Jesus will reign on the throne of David (**Acts 2:29-30; Matthew 25:31**) and establish His Millennial Kingdom (**Revelation 20:1-7**). Christ will banish Satan to the Lake of Fire forever (**Revelation 20:7-10**) and issue the Great White Throne Judgment ("Judgment Day") for every unredeemed, spiritually lost human being that has ever lived to be cast into the Lake of Fire forever (**Rev. 20:11-15**). While there are certainly differing perspectives for the meaning and order of these Second Coming events— premillennial, postmillennial, and amillennial—what matters most is that we are with Christ! A new era that began as salvation on earth goes to another level as our faith becomes sight in Heaven. The new era is finally here: *eternity*! A new heaven, new earth, the very dwelling place of God face to face with Him, where the curse of sin is no more (**Revelation 21; 22:1-9**). We are at peace with God eternally, never to be separated from Him again. Hallelujah! There's no place like HOME!

While in the first command, Christ's return brought comfort, the second command (**Matthew 24:3-25:46; Mark 13:3-37; Luke 12:35-48; 17:22-37; 21:7-36**) indicates that Christ's coming will bring *chaos*. The context for this second command is fashioned around the chaotic tribulation period for Israel. When studying it, remember to be chronologically sensitive to the phrase "*this generation.*" It is a reference to the generation of Jews alive at the time that the tribulation events take place. Furthermore, the entirety of this second command has a twofold command for its audience: *listen* and *learn*. Here is the breakdown of what Christ warned His hearers.

First of all, **listen** to the chaos (**24:3-31; 25:31-46**). It is important to notice what *prepares* the onslaught (v. 3-8). Like a world news reporter, Christ says that people "*will hear of wars and rumors of wars...*" and that "*nation will rise against nation, and kingdom against kingdom. And there will be famines, pestilences, and earthquakes in various places.*" In addition, Jesus issues a direct command, saying, "*Take heed that no one deceives you.*" He says this because many people will exclaim, "*I am the Christ,*" out of confusion and deception. Jesus makes it clear that all these chaotic events are merely "*the beginning of sorrows.*" The Greek word *sorrows* (*odin*) means "birth pains; travail," like contractions that will shake the face of the world spiritually, politically, physically, and economically.

As you continue to listen to the chaos, you also notice what *promotes* it (**v. 9-31; 25:31-46**). As the tribulation era begins, murder, hatred, betrayal, deception, and lawlessness will be intensified to the extreme. The "*gospel of the Kingdom*" will still be preached during the Tribulation, and the people who respond to it will "*endure to the end.*" In the middle of this tribulation period, the Antichrist will break his treaty with Israel and fulfill Daniel's prophecy of "*the abomination of desolation*" (**Daniel 9:27**), desecrating the Temple in Jerusalem and establishing worldwide worship of himself as God!

Jesus commands those who "*see*" this event to "*flee to the mountains*" and to leave everything behind, valuing nothing but their lives. This marks the middle of the Tribulation (three and a half years), and therefore this next period is labeled by Jesus as the "*great tribulation.*" To capture its hellacious events, Jesus gives a frightening figure: "*And unless those days were shortened, no flesh would be saved.*" This time will be horrific. Satan will roam the earth (**Revelation 12:7-9**) intensely during the time of tribulation, just like the roaring lion he is now (**1 Peter 5:8**). Deceptions will reach an unimaginable magnitude! Yet Jesus reaffirms that His coming is only a "*lightning flash*" away.

Suddenly, as the Great Tribulation nears its end, the "*powers of the heavens will be shaken,*" resulting in the sun, moon, and stars abandoning the very nature of their existence. With all these cataclysmic events taking place, "*the sign of the Son of Man will appear in heaven...*" This is the second coming of Jesus Christ, which will terminate the Battle of Armageddon (**Revelation 16:12-16; 19:19-21**), thus annihilating the Antichrist and false prophet and ultimately binding Satan. Christ will come back to the very Mount of Olives from which He ascended (**Zechariah 14:4-5**) and will "*send His angels*" to gather His "*elect*"—that is, the redeemed of Jesus Christ (Jew and Gentile).

"*When the Son of Man comes in His glory, and all the holy angels with Him, then He will sit on the throne of His glory*" (**Matthew 25:31**). Christ's Second Coming has two significant objectives: to establish His Millennial Kingdom (**Revelation 20:6**) and to rule on the throne of King David (**Zechariah 6:12-13; Luke 1:31-32**). Jesus declared that "*all the nations will be gathered before Him, and He will separate them one from another, as a shepherd divides his sheep from the goats.*" The righteous redeemed of Christ on His "*right hand*" hear, "*Come, you blessed of My Father, inherit the kingdom prepared for you...*" The wicked rebels on Christ's "*left hand*" hear, "*Depart from Me, you cursed, into the everlasting fire prepared for the devil and his angels.*" Clearly, this is a judgment of all the nations following the tribulation era. Jesus' standard for His judgment of the nations will be this: "*Inasmuch as you did it to one of the least of these My brethren, you did it to Me.*" Feeding the hungry, clothing the naked, housing the stranger, refreshing the thirsty, and visiting the sick and imprisoned will all be measurements by which He reaches His judgment. These actions do not produce salvation, for by grace are you saved (**Ephesians 2:8-9**); rather, they are the products of salvation, evidencing a lifestyle fully committed to Christ.

Second, **learn** from the chaos (**Matthew 24:32-51; 25:1-30**). So far, the Second Coming of Christ has primarily been merely informative for you as a disciple. But as Christ relates His coming to commands, Jesus transitions from informing you to examining you as His disciple. The exam involves your commitment to stay faithful to His commands until He returns for His Church. Therefore, Christ has something very important for you to *learn* from the chaos.

You must *watch* (v. 32-44; 25:1-13). From a natural standpoint, Jesus commands to "*learn this parable from the fig tree.*" Anyone could tell that "*summer*" was near when the tree's leaves changed. In the same manner, you should have the same readiness about you to watch attentively for Christ's coming. From a historical standpoint, Jesus also uses ancient Noah to teach you a valuable lesson about watching. Christ says, "*But as the days of Noah were, so also will the coming of the Son of Man be.*" The comparison that Jesus is making is not only in the cultural decline but also in the fact that the people of that day "*did not know until the flood came.*" When Christ returns for His Church, people can be working in a "*field*" or "*grinding at the mill.*" Some will be taken from the field, while others are left. Some will be caught up to meet the glorious Christ, while others remain at the mill. Christ's command to you as His disciple is so clear: "*Watch therefore, for you do not know what hour your Lord is coming.*" As if preparing for a thief in the night, "*be ready*" for Jesus Christ to break in the sky! Keep Christ's return fixated in your thoughts daily, always prepared for His appearing.

To further plead for your watchfulness, Jesus compares the response to His coming to that of wise and foolish virgins. They actually "*went out to meet the bridegroom,*" meaning all ten had interest in him. However, Jesus said, "*While the bridegroom was delayed, they all slumbered and slept.*" Suddenly, a "*cry*" was heard at midnight, announcing the Bridegroom's arrival. All the virgins jumped up and began to "*trim their lamps*," but there was a problem. Five of the virgins foolishly did not put oil in their lamps—they couldn't see the Bridegroom. And by the time they returned with new oil, He was gone. Christ made His point again: *watch*. Dear disciple, whatever you do, don't get distracted by the leisure of this world and forsake a ready, watchful spirit for Christ's return. Be faithful and watch daily (**Mark 14:38**).

You also must *work* (**25:14-30; 24:45-51**). Jesus tells a story full of application about a "*master*," a man with servants. This master "*traveled to a far country*," but not without first "*delivering his goods*" to his servants. These servants were officially stewards of their master's possessions and were expected to use it, not hoard it. Two servants doubled their "*goods*"; one servant did nothing. The master was gone for a "*long time*" but eventually came back to "*settle accounts*" with his servants. The two faithful servants received reward. The "*wicked and lazy*" servant received rebuke.

I have two questions for you: which servant do you want to be, and which servant do you actually favor? Jesus is like that master: He's been gone for a long time, but He's coming back to settle accounts with you. He has left you with His gospel, and He intends to see if you've used it to reach people for His Kingdom, for that is the greatest investment "*with interest*" you can make! So, His question is worth repeating: "*Who then is a faithful and wise servant, whom his master made ruler over his house, to give them food in due season*" (**24:45**)? Because of his worldly agendas, the "*evil servant*" lives a life of delayed obedience to Christ, not taking His imminent return seriously. The evil servant will be caught off guard by Christ's return and will experience horrific judgment.

Your pattern is to be like the "*wise servant*," who was blessed because He was found working when his master returns. Christ will reward a servant like that by making him "*ruler over all His goods*." As a disciple of Jesus, you are to live like the "*wise servant*" as you serve Jesus while waiting for His return. Before the foundation of the world, you were ordained to "*walk*" in "*good works*," all as an overflow of your "*workmanship*" in Christ (**Ephesians 2:10**). Therefore, "*be careful to maintain good works*" (**Titus 3:8**) until you see Christ Jesus. Labor for your master, letting your lifestyle express a "thank you" to Jesus for how He's changed your life. Praise God!

TEACHING # 7.2: SECOND COMING OF JESUS CHRIST (PART 2)

Week 49

This week's objective: To identify what the Second Coming of Christ will be like, as well as to learn what your responsibilities are while awaiting His return.

THE COMMAND ILLUSTRATED:

There is no other passage in Scripture that offers more clarity on Christ's Second Coming than **Revelation 19:11-16**. This glorious appearing will be the most thrilling event in all of human history! However, it is necessary to recall some important events that will help you correctly interpret and appreciate Christ's return. When you can understand the order and timeframe of happenings preceding Christ's return, you are able to properly interpret the necessity of His return.

The last three and a half years of the tribulation era will be the most horrific time mankind has ever seen. Satan and his demonic arsenal will wreak havoc upon the earth as never before. The devil will totally empower the Antichrist (**Revelation 13:2**), allowing him to rule world nations in pompous cruelty. Due to the Antichrist's relentless rage and God's wrath, two thirds of mankind shall die, but one third (a remnant) shall be spared (**Zechariah 13:8-9**). Satan's own hatred for God's people will ignite within the Antichrist's heart. This hatred will ultimately translate into the attempted obliteration of God's people in a war effort called the *Battle of Armageddon* (**Revelation 16:16; Zechariah 12:1-9; 14:1-3, 12-15**). Just as the pressure and fright reaches its peak from the Antichrist and his international armies, God steps in for His people (**1 Corinthians 10:13**) through the Second Coming of His Son, Jesus.

Amidst the cosmic disturbances in the sky (**Matthew 24:29; Revelation 16:17-21**), the heavens open with Jesus (**Matthew 24:30;**

Revelation 1:7; 19:11). His eyes are *"like a flame of fire,"* He has *"many crowns,"* He wears a *"robe dipped in blood,"* and *"His name is called The Word of God."* Dear disciple, are you shouting yet? Hallelujah! You see Him descending on His *"white horse"* with all the *"armies of heaven"* (saints and angels) as He touches down upon the Mount of Olives (**Zechariah 14:4-5**), causing a valley-opening earthquake to deliver the remnant. Christ's Second Coming will be for the purpose of delivering His remnant and reigning with His people in His Millennial Kingdom (**Revelation 13:8-9; 14:2**) by conquering the Antichrist and his armies, for *"in righteousness He judges and makes war."* Jesus will do this by the *"sharp sword"* that proceeds out of His mouth to *"strike the nations."* This sword is His Word (**Hebrews 4:12**)!

This battle will be the bloodiest war that the world has ever seen, evidenced by the aftermath: two hundred miles of blood (**Revelation 14:19-20**). Scripture gives graphically detailed images of this battle, all as a result from the glory of Christ's appearing. The astonishing glory of Christ descending in the sky will produce a trembling demoralization of the Antichrist's armies. In a manner similar to the devastation from an atomic bomb, both they and their animals will be plagued with the disintegration of their flesh (**Zechariah 14:12, 15**), resulting in a rotting stench (**Isaiah 34:1-3**), all of which will be devoured by *"birds that fly in the midst of heaven"* (**Revelation 19:17-18**).

Jesus Christ captures the Antichrist and the false prophet, casting them *"alive"* into the Lake of Fire (**Revelation 19:19-20**). Satan is also captured and bound in solitary confinement for one thousand years (**Revelation 20:1-3**) so that Christ can establish His Millennial Kingdom. At this point, the remnant of God's people will finally recognize Jesus Christ as their Messiah for the first time (**Zechariah 12:10**), exclaiming, *"Blessed is He who comes in the name of the Lord!"* (**Matthew 23:39**). Praise God, the covenant people of the Lord will be *"grafted in again"* (**Romans 11:23**) and spiritually cleansed with the forgiveness of Almighty God (**Zechariah 13:1; Romans 11:26-27**).

Finally, God's people will be able to settle *"peacefully"* in their homeland with Christ their Messiah (**Zechariah 8:7-8; 14:11**). Christ will then officially establish His Millennial Kingdom (**Zechariah 6:12-13**) and reign one thousand years (**Zechariah 9:10; Revelation 20:4**), as His Church, now Jew and Gentile, unite. When the thousand years have expired, Satan will be released and will once again seek to "*deceive the nations*" (**Revelation 20:7-9**), surrounding the Millennium's "*beloved city*" of Jerusalem again, only to be met by the final blow of the wrath of God, for Satan will be cast into the "*lake of fire*" (**Revelation 20:10**) for eternity.

Judgment Day then comes for all unbelievers as they stand before God's "*great white throne*" (**Revelation 20:11**), from there being "*cast into the lake of fire*" (**Revelation 20:15**), eternally doomed with Satan, the Antichrist, and the false prophet. With all evil eradicated from humanity, God creates a "*new heaven and a new earth, for the first heaven and the first earth had passed away*" (**Revelation 21:1**). We shall live forever in the visible presence of God (**Revelation 21:3**), inhabiting the New Jerusalem with Him (**Revelation 21:10**) as the promised "*place*" with "*many mansions*" prepared for us (**John 14:2-3**). Glory, hallelujah! Come, Lord Jesus!

THE COMMAND INITIATED:

Christ's Second Coming must have precedence in your life as His disciple. If it does not, it will have only intellectual meaning to you, not practical value. When you sincerely value Christ's return, you initiate obedience to faithfully work while you wait for His coming. This initiation is rooted in your belief in the prophecies pointing to it (**Psalm 98:9; Daniel 7:13; Matthew 26:64; Hebrews 9:28; 2 Peter 3:10**). Every day that passes brings you closer to the Day of Christ. Its nearness should propel your obedience to Christ's Word, for He will come quickly (**Philippians 4:5; Hebrews 10:37; James 5:8; Revelation 3:11; 22:7, 20**).

Clarence Larkin further emphasizes Jesus' Second Coming by comparing it with His First Coming. In his book, *The Second Coming of Christ*, Larkin biblically balances the comings of Christ so as to personally relate to the prophecies that keep us watching for His return:

> There is no fact in history more clearly established than the fact of the "First Coming" of Christ. But as His "First Coming" did not fulfill all the prophecies associated with His "Coming," it is evident that there must be another "Coming"

to completely fulfill them. It was because the religious leaders of Christ's day failed to distinguish between the prophesies that related to His "First Coming," and those that related to His "Second Coming" that they rejected Him. Peter tells us (**1 Peter 1:10-11**) that the prophets themselves did not clearly perceive the difference between the "Sufferings" and "Glory" of Christ. That is, they did not see that there was a "time space" between the "Cross" and the "Crown," and that the "Cross" would precede the "Crown." But we have no such excuse. We live on this side of the "Cross," and we can readily pick out all the prophesies that were fulfilled at Christ's "First Coming," and apply the remainder to His "Second Coming." It is clear then that Christ's "First Coming," important as it was, is not the "doctrinal center" of the Scriptures, that is, Christ's "First Coming" was not the center of a circle that contains all doctrine, but was one of the foci of an ellipse of which the other is the "Second Coming."...While the First and Second Comings of Christ are separated by this Dispensation they are nevertheless not complete in themselves, the Second necessitated the First, and the First demands the Second....[1]

THE COMMAND INTERROGATED:

One of the greatest assaults Satan can render in your life as Christ's disciple is to cause you to secretly harbor this thought: *"My Master is delaying His coming"* (**Matthew 24:48**). Because thoughts influence behavior, thoughts about Christ's delay will result in neglect of your duty. Satan wants to hinder your effective influence through the gospel, just as he did with Christ's disciples (**Matthew 17:14-21**). They were distracted and regretfully decreased in their faith while Jesus was away for a short time. The devil did it to them, and he wants to do the same with you.

Satan will be sure to place scoffers in your life who say, *"Where is the promise of His coming?"* (**2 Peter 3:3-4**) While these hellish agents mock you for your perseverance to wait on Christ's return, strengthen yourself by remembering that with the Lord, *"one day is as a thousand years, and a thousand years as one day"* (**2 Peter**

3:8). Jesus Christ is not delaying His Second Coming; instead, He is giving people time to repent and be saved (**2 Peter 3:9**), depending on you as His disciple to warn the wicked of His return (**Mark 8:38; 2 Thessalonians 1:8**) and their certain judgment (**Jude 14-15; 2 Timothy 4:1; Acts 17:30-31**) unless they repent.

Do not slouch lazily in your walk with Christ. You have a gospel to carry as a trustee of the souls of men! Beware of Satan's attack on your faith to cause you to slack off in your fervency to reach men and women for Christ, because Christ's coming will be swift and final. Keep waiting and working. Do not give place to the devil (**Ephesians 4:27**).

THE COMMAND INDESTRUCTIBLE:

Oh, precious disciple, you are not Satan's punching bag. The Word of God speaks for you (**Romans 8:37**). With your trust in the Scripture, there is a memory verse that you must use to steady yourself against Satan's attack, thus protecting your readiness for the Second Coming. **Titus 2:11-13** says, *"For the grace of God that brings salvation has appeared to all men, teaching us that, denying ungodliness and worldly lusts, we should live soberly, righteously, and godly in the present age, looking for the blessed hope and glorious appearing of our great God and Savior Jesus Christ."*

You are not only saved by the grace of God; you are also taught by it to *"deny"* the worldly lusts of Satan's attractions around you and to live *"soberly, righteously, and godly."* This is your lifestyle as you await the *"blessed hope"* of Christ's return. You see, preparation is the key to *"eagerly waiting"* for Jesus to return (**1 Corinthians 1:7**). You are eager, not passive. You are diligent, not neglectful. You are evangelistically committed to handling the Lord's *"business"* until He comes (**Luke 19:13**). You put away bickering and judgmentalism, because you know that Christ's coming will silence your enemies (**1 Corinthians 4:5**). Until the coming of the Lord Jesus, you surrender your lifestyle as blameless (**1 Thessalonians 5:23; 1Timothy 6:14; 2 Peter 3:11**), joyfully anticipating the reward of glorious transformation in His holy Presence (**1 John 2:28; 3:2; Philippians 3:20-21; Colossians 3:4**)! This is your life. This is your call. Jesus Christ is counting on you as

His disciple. When He comes, be found faithful.

THE COMMAND INQUIRED:

What cannot be measured cannot be evaluated. Therefore, it is essential to measure your comprehension of Christ's command in this teaching, or else the devil will snatch away the "seeds" of Scripture sown into your heart (**Matthew 13:19**). To keep this from occurring, write down your answers to the following questions as they correlate with the teaching this week:

In what passage(s) of Scripture do you find Christ's commandment on His **Second Coming**?

_____

_____

_____

What is the accurate interpretation of **Christ's Second Coming** you have discovered?

_____

_____

_____

_____

_____

In your own words, what are some real-life examples in Scripture of **Christ's Second Coming**?

_____

_____

_____

_____

_____

_____

What steps of initiation did you learn to take in order for **Christ's Second Coming** to transform your life?

_____

_____

_____

_____

_____

_____

How will Satan attack you to hinder your anticipation for **Christ's Second Coming**?

_____

_____

_____

_____

_____

_____

What memory verse will you use to protect Christ's command of watching for His **Second Coming** in your life? Write it out.

_____

CHAPTER 8:
RESURRECTION IS THE
DISCIPLE'S JUBILATION

"Now after the Sabbath, as the first day of the week began to dawn, Mary Magdalene and the other Mary came to see the tomb. And behold, there was a great earthquake; for an angel of the Lord descended from heaven, and came and rolled back the stone from the door, and sat on it...But the angel answered and said to the women, 'Do not be afraid, for I know that you seek Jesus who was crucified. He is not here; for He is risen, as He said...And go quickly and tell His disciples that He is risen from the dead...'" (**Matthew 28:1-2, 5-7**).

Hallelujah! Do you know why Jesus Christ rose from the dead? Because it is impossible for Christ to be held captive by death when He Himself is Life (**Acts 2:24**)! Oh, what a glorious Savior, all-conquering and all-powerful! It is no wonder the Apostle Paul exclaimed, "O death, where is your sting? O Hades, where is your victory?" (**1 Corinthians 15:55**). The Resurrection of Jesus Christ is the invincible, divine factor upon which Christianity exists! Do you know why? Because if Jesus Christ did not rise from the dead, all of your sins would not be forgiven (**1 Corinthians 15:17**). The Resurrection validates that Christ was truly the Son of God. He is Lord of all.

Yes, Jesus rose, and yes, over five hundred people testified to it (**1 Corinthians 15:6**). But as glorious and eternal as it may be, Christ's Resurrection means much more than rising from the dead. What more is there to know? The Resurrection of Christ has personal involvement in your life as a Christian. The purpose that Christ's Resurrection serves will change your entire perspective on death. Well, what is the purpose? What value does the Resurrection offer for a disciple? Transfiguration will give you the answer.

TEACHING # 8.1: TRANSFIGURATION OF JESUS CHRIST

Week 50

This week's objective: To examine the meaning of the Resurrection, as well as to learn to appropriate its value in your life as a disciple.

THE COMMAND INTRODUCED:

- **Matthew 17:9; Mark 9:9** *"Now as they came down from the mountain, Jesus commanded them, saying, 'Tell the vision to no one until the Son of Man is risen from the dead.'"*

THE COMMAND INTERPRETED:

The best way to accurately interpret this command is to read the entire passage (**Matthew 17:1-8**). Six days before Jesus took His disciples upon a *"high mountain,"* He told them confidently, *"There are some standing here who shall not taste death till they see the Son of Man coming in His kingdom"* (**Matthew 16:28**). Coming *"in"* (present tense) His Kingdom is differentiated from Jesus coming *"from"* (future tense) His Kingdom (**Matthew 16:27**). Mysterious as it may be, *"some"* (Peter, James, John) were given front-row seats to watch Christ come *"into"* His Kingdom. How would this be? Transfiguration.

On the mountain, Jesus was *"transfigured before them."* The Greek word "transfigured" (*metamorphoo*) means "transform; change." This same Greek word is issued in the command to *"be transformed by the renewing of your mind"* (**Romans 12:2**). Therefore, to be transfigured is to be changed from the inside out, as a cocooned larva is metamorphosed into an elegant butterfly. The evidence for Christ's Transfiguration is expressed as this: *"His face shone like the sun, and His clothes became as white as the light"* (**verse 2**). This sounds very familiar, doesn't it?

Resurrection! Such a description of Christ's physical "change" parallels exactly the imagery of His Resurrection glory in **Revelation 1:16**. You see, the Transfiguration of Christ is the explanation for how Peter, James, and John saw Him *"coming in His kingdom"* before they experienced death. It was a "dress rehearsal" for Christ personally as well as a lesson for His disciples to learn about the Resurrection. Peter saw Jesus in His glory even though Christ had not yet been glorified (**John 7:39**)! He even saw Moses and Elijah *"talking with"* Jesus about His soon-to-be death on the cross (**Luke 9:31**). Peter mistakenly tried to relish the moment by building *"tabernacles"* for Jesus, Moses, and Elijah and was quickly rebuked by God in heaven as He said, *"This is My beloved Son, in whom I am well pleased. Hear Him!"* (**verse 5**). Through it all, it was an experience that Peter would never forget (**2 Peter 1:16-18**).

Therefore, as difficult as it may have been to suppress their excited awe, the disciples were not allowed to speak of the *"vision"* or glimpse they received of Christ *"transfigured."* When could they tell? After Jesus was *"risen from the dead,"* for He would then look just as glorious as He did on the mountain. There would be nothing to hide! The Resurrection is something with which you need to become very familiar. It has personal appeal for you, because in the same manner that Christ is resurrected in a glorified body, so you will be too one day. After Christ ascended to Heaven, *"with great power the apostles gave witness to the resurrection of the Lord Jesus..."* (**Acts 4:33**). They waited; they told! With God's grace, you shall tell as well.

You see, the very concept of a *"resurrection from the dead"* hinges upon the fact that Christ rose from the dead (**1 Corinthians 15:12-13; 20**). In fact, when Jesus rose from the dead on the third day, His Resurrection power shook the graves of dead saints in Jerusalem and released *"many"* (**Matthew 27:52-53**). This supernatural occurrence validated the fact that not only did more than five hundred people eyewitness Christ's Resurrection (**1 Corinthians 15:5-8; Acts 1:3; 10:40-41**), but that Jesus truly has power over death itself (**Acts 2:23-24; Romans 1:4; 6:9; Revelation 1:18**)! It's no wonder, then, why Jesus boldly proclaimed, *"I am the resurrection and the life. He who believes in Me, though he may die, he shall live"* (**John 11:25**). In this promise your hope abides.

Therefore, the Lord's Transfiguration was more than a

mysterious event. It was a powerful lesson on the wonder and beauty of resurrection immortality that comes first and foremost through the death-conquering, grave-stomping Lord and Savior Jesus Christ (**Job 14:14; Psalm 49:15; Hosea 13:14; John 5:25; 1 Corinthians 15:50-57; 1 Thessalonians 4:16**). Praise God, your physical body with all its ailments and weaknesses and limitations will one day be like Christ's glorified body, all because He rose from the dead. As His disciple, your hope is in Him and His transforming power to make this happen. By His promise through His Word, He will. What a change it will be, suitable for abiding in His Presence forever! Christ is risen, so tell the *"vision"* to all. Tell them there will be a resurrection of the dead!

THE COMMAND ILLUSTRATED:

There is a fascinating story in Scripture that gives you a foretaste of what your resurrection will be like. This story is found in **John 11:1-44**. Jesus had a close friend named Lazarus who was *"sick."* Eventually, Lazarus died from his sickness, and after four long days, Jesus finally arrived to minister to the grieving family. Clearly, Jesus' involvement in coming to Lazarus was for one purpose: *"that the Son of God may be glorified through it"* (**verse 4**). Jesus affirmed to the hurting heart of Lazarus's sister, Martha, *"Your brother will rise again"* (**John 11:23**). After crying Himself with the family (**verse 35**), Jesus went to the tomb of Lazarus and commanded, *"Take away the stone"* (**verse 39**). Jesus prayed to the Father; then He shouted, *"Lazarus, come forth!"* (**verse 43**) From the grave Lazarus arose, resurrected by the power of Jesus. That day, many of the Jews *"believed in Him"* because of the miraculous resurrection, which was exactly what Christ had prayed for (**verse 42**). Jesus was glorified.

The story accomplishes more than merely fascinating you. It grips your heart and strengthens your faith that you too will be resurrected by Jesus Christ at your appointed time. The promises of God are sure and steadfast. Like Lazarus, you have a *"living hope"* through the Resurrection of Christ your Lord (**1 Peter 1:3**). Hope? Yes, because if Christ had not risen from the dead, you would *hopelessly* be lost in your sins (**1 Corinthians 15:14-19**). But we know that Jesus is risen from the dead, making your eternal status before God Almighty "*justified*" from your sins (**Romans 4:25; 1 Peter 3:18**). Your *hope* in the resurrection is just as alive as the risen Christ!

THE COMMAND INITIATED:

Obviously, you cannot initiate your resurrection, but you can initiate obedience to "*tell the vision*" that points to it. Your faithfulness to *tell* is the key to obeying this command from the Transfiguration of Christ. However, you cannot speak accurately about this "*redemption of the body*" (**Romans 8:23**) without knowing how to assimilate its resurrection placement in Scripture. A clear and concise explanation is found in **1 Corinthians 15:22-24**. Christ's Resurrection sets the stage for the two types of resurrections in Scripture: the *just* and the *unjust* (**Acts 24:15; Daniel 12:2; John 5:28-29**). The "*just*" refers to righteous believers; the "*unjust*" refers to wicked unbelievers. As for the nature of these two resurrections, the righteous go into eternal "*life*" and the wicked into eternal "*condemnation*."

Furthermore, there is a gap of time between both resurrections of one thousand years. The "*resurrection unto eternal life*" is associated with the Second Coming of Christ, during which He will orderly resurrect "*the dead in Christ*" (**1 Thessalonians 4:16**) first. Then, seven years later, Jesus will resurrect the Old Testament (**Daniel 12:1-2**) and Tribulation saints (**Revelation 20:4**) at the beginning of the Millennium. After the one thousand years have finished, Christ will resurrect the unbelievers from Hell (**Revelation 20:5, 11-14**) to be cast into the Lake of Fire.

Therefore, the reality of the "*resurrection from the dead*" is a driving force in your Christian witness. It is your hope affiliated with the Second Coming of Christ, for "*everyone who has this hope in Him purifies himself, just as He is pure*" (**1 John 3:3**). What a dramatic effect the resurrection hope of Christ's return has on your lifestyle: *purity*. You live in a pure and holy way (**2 Corinthians 7:1**) so that as you give witness to unbelievers of the Resurrection, you do so untainted by impure hypocrisy.

Incredibly, the resurrection of the dead necessitates such purity of lifestyle. E.W. Bullinger connects this purity principle clearly and passionately. In his book *The Resurrection of the Body*, Bullinger so adequately fuses the purity of a sanctified lifestyle with unquestionable focus on the motivating power behind it. His observation is clear:

> As Christ is the blessed object and center of our hope, so He is presented to us in this great subject. *"He that hath this hope in Him"*—not in himself—*"He that hath this hope in Christ."* What hope? Why the hope of being like Him at His appearing, when we shall see Him as He is. He that hath this hope fixed upon Him, what does he do? What is the effect of it? *"Everyone that hath this hope in Him purifieth himself, even as He is pure."* Yes, it is a *purifying* hope. And why is the low standard of walk among Christians at the present day so much deplored? Why are so many efforts put forth for raising the standard of this walk? *Because that standard has been changed*! And why? Because this purifying hope is not held. Why are other methods tried and sought after for the promotion of purity of life, and this great divine *advent method* not tried? Here is God's method to secure our purity of life and walk. *"He that hath this hope"* (of the transformation of His people)—he that hath this blessed hope fixed upon Him—*"purifieth himself."* And this Divine method cannot be carried too far.[1]

THE COMMAND INTERROGATED:

The resurrection of the dead is an eternal slap in the face to Satan because death has been conquered. Although Jesus Christ has defeated Satan's power over the grave (**1 Corinthians 15:55**), the devil finds an avenue to attack you by grieving your heart when a fellow disciple you love has died. Grief and mourning are nothing new in the Bible (**Ecclesiastes 3:4; Matthew 5:4**). While it is normal and expected to grieve the fellowship you had with someone you love, it is more necessary to release them into their long-awaited eternal fellowship with Christ. If you don't, you will idolize your memories.

Idolatry of any nature is not God's will for you. Satan is very vicious in this area of your life as a disciple. Through the death of fellow believers (family or friends), Satan wants to discourage and depress you to the uttermost. He did just this to the Thessalonian believers, delivering such a staggering blow to their faith that Paul said, "*But I do not want you to be ignorant, brethren, concerning those who have fallen asleep, lest you sorrow as others who have no hope*" (**1 Thessalonians 4:13**). You see, there are people who die without Christ, lost into Hell forever. They die with no hope, and their Christian family and friends understandably grieve intensely because all "*hope*" is lost.

Therefore, the grief in these cases is horrendous! But not so with a Christian's death. It is a celebration, "*for if we believe that Jesus died and rose again, even so God will bring with Him those who sleep in Jesus*" (**1 Thessalonians 4:14**). In this same passage, Paul affirms that the "*dead in Christ will rise first*," referring to the bodily resurrection (**verse 16**). Ultimately, Paul exhorts the purpose of his writing as this: "*Therefore comfort one another with these words*" (**verse 18**). *Comfort* is the needed antidote.

Furthermore, do not allow Satan to trample your faith when a fellow believer dies, "*lest you sorrow as others who have no hope*." You *do* have hope through Jesus Christ, and so do the believers you love. Every disciple that dies should celebrate death (as morbid as that sounds) because it is their release from the corruption of this earthly body (**2 Corinthians 5:1-8; Philippians 1:20-23**). Death for the Christian is welcomed, not feared. It is summoned, not sanctioned. Do not allow Satan to steal (**John 10:10**) your joy in the promise of the resurrection for your loved one. Your grief and mourning are only for a season, because your departure is only temporary from those who die in Christ. Praise God, Satan just cannot win, can he? The victory belongs to Christ and all who are in Him.

THE COMMAND INDESTRUCTIBLE:

There will be a resurrection of the dead, and Satan can't stop it. It is ordained by the promise of Christ. The authority of God's Word to set doctrinal truth into motion is the victory of your life. You have cause to celebrate in spite of death, for "*you have passed from death to life*" (**1 John 3:14**). Jesus took the sting out of death for you and me. This changes your whole perspective on those who die in Christ...always. It produces a victory shout from within your heart, an anthem of praise for eternal life and redemption of the body.

When the devil attacks and wars against your mind in the event of a believing loved one's death, use this memory verse every time to fight him away: **Romans 8:11**. It says, "*But if the Spirit of Him who raised Jesus from the dead dwells in you, He who raised Christ from the dead will also give life to your mortal bodies through His Spirit who dwells in you.*" God promised you a resurrection body, Jesus rose from the dead to ensure it, and the Holy Spirit by His power will energize it. Hallelujah!

Oh, the depth and wonder of this glorified, resurrected, incorruptible body! How happy the day when you shall put on the undying glory of the resurrected body! "*Therefore we do not lose heart. Even though our outward man is perishing, yet the inward man is being renewed day by day*" (**2 Corinthians 4:16**). Bless the Lord, O my soul! As Christ's disciple, speak of the Resurrection to others as He commanded, and cling tightly to your hope in it, too. As you and I eagerly await Christ's return, just remember that Christ will "*transform our lowly body that it may be conformed to His glorious body, according to the working by which He is able even to subdue all things to Himself*" (**Philippians 3:21**). Praise God, your change is coming!

THE COMMAND INQUIRED:

What cannot be measured cannot be evaluated. Therefore, it is essential to measure your comprehension of Christ's command in this teaching, or else the devil will snatch away the "seeds" of Scripture sown into your heart (**Matthew 13:19**). To keep this from occurring, write down your answers to the following questions as they correlate with the teaching this week:

In what passage(s) of Scripture do you find Christ's commandment on His **transfiguration**?

_____

_____

_____

_____

_____

What is the accurate interpretation of Christ's **transfiguration** you have discovered?

_____

_____

_____

_____

_____

In your own words, what are some real-life examples in Scripture of Christ's **transfiguration**?

_____

_____

_____

_____

What steps of initiation did you learn to take in order for Christ's **transfiguration** to transform your life?

_____

_____

_____

_____

_____

_____

How will Satan attack you to hinder your application of Christ's **transfiguration**?

_____

_____

_____

_____

_____

What memory verse will you use to protect Christ's command about His **transfiguration** in your life? Write it out.

_____

_____

_____

_____

_____

CHAPTER 9:
REDEMPTION IS THE DISCIPLE'S FASCINATION

"*And according to the law almost all things are purified with blood, and without shedding of blood there is no remission*" (**Hebrews 9:22**). Remission of what? *Sin* (**Acts 10:43**). Ever since sin entered the human race, it has always been an offense toward God. The only atonement for sin must come through the shedding of blood. Yes, it's gruesome, but that's how much sin costs. This is evident in God's interaction with the children of Israel during the plagues on Egypt, when He informed them, "*When I see the blood, I will pass over you...*" (**Exodus 12:13**). His wrath was dispensed, and all who did not have the "*blood*" of slaughtered animals on their doorpost experienced death in their families. This principle is also evident through the sacrificial system in the Book of Leviticus, where we find that not even the blood of bulls and goats can atone for sin (**Hebrews 10:4**). This leaves a gap—an uncompleted account for the sins of mankind.

It is for this purpose that Jesus Christ came from Heaven to Earth. All have sinned (**Romans 3:23**) and are in eternal need of a Savior. No human could die for another's sin, because of their own sin within. Someone who had no sin would have to die, making the sacrifice for sin pure, holy, and spotless and satisfying the demand of our Holy God. Only Jesus could meet that demand, for He "*knew no sin*" (**2 Corinthians 5:21**). Therefore, for you and for me, Christ was tortured, butchered, cursed, ridiculed, mocked, spat upon, beaten, scourged, pierced, and ultimately crucified for the sins of the world (**Isaiah 53:4-8**). The offering for sin has been satisfied!

Therefore, Jesus Christ literally substituted your place on the cross (**Romans 3:25; Hebrews 2:17; 1 John 2:2; 4:10**), taking the heat of the wrath of God for your sin. What amazing love! To be sure you never forget it, He commands Communion.

TEACHING # 9.1: COMMUNION WITH JESUS CHRIST

Week 51

This week's objective: To gain insight into the meaning of the Lord's Supper, as well as to learn how you proclaim Christ's death through your observance.

THE COMMAND INTRODUCED:

- **Matthew 26:26-30; Mark 14:22-26; Luke 22:14-20** *"And as they were eating, Jesus took bread, blessed and broke it, and gave it to the disciples and said, 'Take, eat; this is My body.' Then He took the cup, and gave thanks, and gave it to them, saying, 'Drink from it, all of you. For this is My blood of the new covenant, which is shed for many for the remission of sins. But I say to you, I will not drink of this fruit of the vine from now on until that day when I drink it new with you in My Father's kingdom.' And when they had sung a hymn, they went out to the Mount of Olives."*

THE COMMAND INTERPRETED:

The Lord Jesus Christ gave this instruction as a direct command. Uniquely, it is the only command that intentionally perpetuates the Crucifixion of Christ. This command revolves around the body and the blood of Jesus. Christ has established Communion as a time for you as His disciple to "commune" with Him by humble reflection upon the forgiveness of your sins at the expense of His death. You do more than memorialize Christ; you worship Him with thanksgiving and tears, full of gratitude and surrender.

The interpretation of this command is clear and concise. First of all, the atmosphere of Communion with Christ was saturated in prayer, for it says that Jesus *"blessed"* the bread and *"gave thanks"* for the fruit of the vine. Prayer cultivates your heart to humbly appropriate the sacraments of the Lord's Supper. Furthermore, notice that Christ *"gave"* the bread and the cup to His disciples. In both instances of observance, Christ attached a command. With the unleavened bread, He said, *"Take, eat; this is My body."* With the cup, He urged, *"Drink from it, all of you..."*

The actual purpose for observing Communion with Christ in this manner is twofold. To begin with, the Apostle Paul reminded you that Jesus commanded to observe *"in remembrance of Me"* (**1 Corinthians 11:24-25**). By keeping Jesus Christ as the focal point, the disciple is protected from legalistic ritualism and overindulgent formality.

Another factor is the intake of the bread and the cup. Since Jesus said that the bread paralleled His *"body"* and the cup His *"blood,"* the disciples finally comprehended what Christ meant in **John 6:47-58**. Figuratively, then, Communion for you as Christ's disciple is a complement to abiding in Him in every sense of the word. What unity!

Interestingly, His blood established a *"new covenant."* Under the old covenant (Old Testament), people depended on both a priest and an animal sacrifice to approach God. That's why Christ's blood is a *"new"* covenant, because we can now approach God through Jesus, our Great High Priest (**Hebrews 4:14-16**). The *old* covenant was a shadow of Christ's *new* covenant to come by way of His death (**Hebrews 8:1-13**). What a perfect picture this is of Christ *"fulfilling the Law"* as He promised (**Matthew 5:17**).

From this picture you see yet another: the Second Coming of Jesus Christ. "But I say to you, I will not drink of this fruit of the vine from now on until that day when I drink it new with you in My Father's kingdom." Since Jesus had just expounded upon His foreshadowed Crucifixion, the disciples were strengthened and encouraged when He remarked, "Until that day." What "day"? The Day of Christ (**Philippians 1:6, 10**), His Second Coming, which is why this Communion command has eternal value to you. That's why Jesus will be able to drink the fruit of the vine "new" with them because it will be in His "Father's kingdom" as He reigns one thousand years (**Revelation 20:6**). Such an assuring promise from Christ propelled Him and the disciples to "sing a hymn" of praise and worship to God, thanking Him from the Mount of Olives for His victorious plan. So, when you observe the Lord's Supper with your local church brethren, remember that you "proclaim the Lord's death till He comes" (**1 Corinthians 11:26**). Praise God!

THE COMMAND ILLUSTRATED:

There is no better example in all of Scripture for the Lord's Supper than its predecessor, the Passover (**Exodus 12:3-13; Numbers 9:12**). The *Passover* meal was a Jewish feast day that commemorated how God miraculously delivered the children of Israel from Egyptian slavery. God instituted the Passover with certain requirements that were nonnegotiable. Each of the requirements beautifully pointed to Christ.

Based on **Exodus 12**, the center of attention was a lamb. Conditionally, the lamb had to be a young male without blemish. It was thoroughly examined (for fourteen days) and publicly executed with no broken bones. Lastly, its blood was applied to Jewish doorposts so that God's judgment would "*pass over*" the inhabitants. This Passover meal, with all its requirements, was incredibly prophetic in the sense that it pointed intriguingly to Christ.

The Passover required a lamb. Jesus Christ is the "*Lamb of God who takes away the sin of the world*" (**John 1:29**). The Passover sacrifice occurred during the first night of the Feast of Unleavened Bread. Jesus Christ, the Lamb, began His Passover meal during the exact timeframe (**Matthew 26:17, 20**). The Passover lamb was a young male without blemish. Jesus Christ was also a young male without blemish (**1 Peter 1:19**). Like the Passover lamb of the Old Testament, Jesus Christ was publicly rejected and killed outside the city of Jerusalem (**Matthew 27:27-31; 45-50**), and none of His bones were broken (**John 19:32-36**). Finally, like the children of Israel, when the blood of the "*Lamb*" is applied to your sin, God's judgment "*passes over*" you, too (**Romans 5:9; Colossians 1:14; Hebrews 10:19-22; Revelation 1:5**). Christ is your Passover Lamb (**1 Corinthians 5:7**). Blessed be the Name of the Lord!

THE COMMAND INITIATED:

By its very nature, observing the Lord's Supper allows you to initiate its value in your life personally. However, before any participation in Communion takes place, you are exhorted to examine yourself first. This truthful reminder is found in **1 Corinthians 11:27-29**. The Greek translations are necessary to properly place these words in their context. The word "examine" (*dokimazo*) means "to test; prove." You examine the most evil storehouse of your body—the heart and mind (**Jeremiah 17:9-10**). Anything that is offensive to the blood of Christ is to be confessed and repented of (**1 John 1:9**) before you proceed with Communion.

To neglect this kind of attitude is to observe the Lord's Supper in an "unworthy manner" (*anaxios*), which means "irreverently." This kind of attitude cheapens the body and the blood of Christ. It is a failure to appreciate Christ's sacrifice. The result is horrendous, for you will become "guilty" (*enochos*) of Christ's body and blood; the word used is a Greek legal term meaning "liable to a charge." In other words, the evidence of an apathetic mindset toward Christ's body and blood stacks against you. Ultimately, it is a failure to be "discerning" (*diakrino*) of the Lord's body; that is, "to separate; discriminate." You must distinguish Communion with Christ as anything but common. Your reverence, repentance, and thanksgiving serve as an offering of worship at the Lord's Table. Communion, then, is not a lighthearted matter, but a reverential, zealous approach to God with thanksgiving and worship.

Jim Henry has as good a grasp on the understanding of Communion as you may find. In fact, he has written a book expressing his discoveries, entitled *In Remembrance of Me*. In addition to what you have learned thus far, Henry makes an appeal to you personally to both refresh and celebrate Communion's meaning:

> Far too often, the church has made the Lord's Supper a stepchild in the faith, a tag-on at the end of a service, a snapshot in the corner of a larger portrait…
> "*The Lord's Supper*" is the title given by Paul (**1 Cor. 11:20**). It bears other names. Luke used the phrase "*breaking of bread*" (**Acts 2:42-46; 20:11; Luke 24:35**). Paul employed the term *communion*, which referred to believers' relationship with the Lord (vertically) and with fellow believers (horizontally). *Eucharist*, another designation for the Lord's Supper, is

derived from the Greek word *eucharistia*, "giving of thanks," as it implies the thanksgiving over the bread and wine (**1 Cor. 11:24**). Paul referred to it as *"the Lord's table"* (**1 Cor. 10:21**)...The celebration of Communion also carries eschatological significance. As it commemorates a past event, it also anticipates a future consummation in His coming (**1 Cor. 11:26**). Thus, a feast of love, a memorial of faith, becomes a prophecy of hope. I invite you to join me in celebrating the Table, a dynamic symbol of the faith which foreshadows a future celebration when we will join Him at the wedding supper of the Lamb (**Rev. 19:9**). Celebrate the Table—and all its profound meaning—with zeal and creative effort in your church.[1]

THE COMMAND INTERROGATED:

Satan has attacked continually throughout the ages, but when Jesus Christ died for your sins and rose again, He defeated Satan forever (**Hebrews 2:14-15; 1 John 3:8**). The Lamb of God has prevailed (**Revelation 1:18**)! However, Satan is a sore loser, and he has set into motion vicious assaults, deceptions, and plots against you in your walk as Christ's disciple. How do you suppose Satan attacks you regarding the Lord's Supper? Just look at Judas Iscariot.

When you read **Matthew 26:14-16, 21-25**, you see that Judas, one of Christ's very own disciples, betrayed Him for *"thirty pieces of silver"* before Jesus observed Communion with His disciples. This means that Judas came to that upper room (**Luke 22:12**) with the bitter unconfessed sin of betrayal. Yet, Judas proceeded to observe without examining Himself first, and thus he became guilty of the body and blood of the Lord.

This is exactly the manner in which Satan wants to deceive you. Satan entered Judas and destroyed him (**Luke 22:3**). Hiding sin from God is foolish, for He knows all things (**Proverbs 15:3; Romans 2:16**). Yet secret, unconfessed sin is Satan's battleground in your life. As you have learned in **1 Corinthians 11**, to observe the Lord's Supper without examining yourself is to do so in an unworthy manner, pronouncing you guilty for not discerning the body and blood of the Lord.

Furthermore, the Apostle Paul interpreted what the consequences are for such neglectful examination (**1 Corinthians 11:30-31**). That's shocking, isn't it? For the very *"reason"* of observing in an unworthy manner, *"many are weak and sick among you, and many sleep."* Consequently, you can become weak and sickly because of giving Satan an open door to oppress you. Moreover, many *"sleep"* as well. The Greek "sleep" (*koimesis*) means "dead; reposed." Death? That's what it says. Satan is like a thief out to *"steal, kill, and destroy"* (**John 10:10**).

Dear disciple, do not underestimate the devil's cunning, crafty ways to deceive you into utter oblivion. These words in Scripture are intended to guide you, not hinder you. They merely remind you of God's holy standard. It is a standard by which you call sin what God calls it, and in such agreement, confess and repent from it (**Proverbs 28:13**) out of reverential fear for His Holy Name. As long as you honor that standard, you may proceed and worship Christ for His sacrifice. But whatever you do, beware of Satan's malicious whispers in your mind, the kind that make you treat lightly the death of Christ. Capture those whispers (**2 Corinthians 10:5**), examine your heart thoroughly, and rise up in adoring worship reflecting on the body and the blood of Jesus Christ. Amen.

THE COMMAND INDESTRUCTIBLE:

Praise God, Satan is defeated by the blood of the Lamb of God (**Revelation 12:11**). As Christ's disciple, you are eternally guarded by the blood of Christ. Satan cannot have you because Jesus Christ has bought you (**Revelation 5:9**). Oh, there is power in His blood! Day by day, you will need a memory verse to use, not only in your warfare with Satan, but also as a reminder of the value God has placed on you by purchasing you from the slave market of sin. The perfect memory verse is **Ephesians 1:7**: *"In Him we have redemption through His blood, the forgiveness of sins, according to the riches of His grace."*

As the old song says, "What can wash away my sin? Nothing but the blood of Jesus." Hallelujah, you and I are rescued with His blood (**Ephesians 2:13**), sanctified through His blood (**Hebrews 13:12**), and cleansed by His blood (**1 John 1:7**)! Oh, how fascinating it is, that you have been redeemed by the blood of the Lamb! Daily, rekindle this burning flame in your heart by your passionate celebration of the death of Christ that brought redemption. You should never "get over" the blood of Jesus. In honor of Christ every day, thank Him for His redeeming blood; and as the redeemed, speak out how you've been saved (**Psalm 107:2**). Praise the Lamb!

THE COMMAND INQUIRED:

What cannot be measured cannot be evaluated. Therefore, it is essential to measure your comprehension of Christ's command in this teaching, or else the devil will snatch away the "seeds" of Scripture sown into your heart (**Matthew 13:19**). To keep this from occurring, write down your answers to the following questions as they correlate with the teaching this week:

In what passage(s) of Scripture do you find Christ's commandment on His **Communion**?

_____

_____

_____

What is the accurate interpretation of **Communion** you have discovered?

_____

_____

_____

_____

_____

_____

In your own words, what are some real-life examples in

Scripture of Christ's **Communion**?

_____

_____

_____

_____

_____

_____

What steps of initiation did you learn to take in order for Christ's **Communion** to transform your life?

_____

_____

_____

_____

_____

How will Satan attack you to hinder your participation in Christ's **Communion**?

_____

_____

_____

_____

_____

What memory verse will you use to protect Christ's command about His **Communion** in your life? Write it out.

_____

_____

_____

_____

_____

_____

CHAPTER 10: *REWARD* IS THE DISCIPLE'S MOTIVATION

"After these things the word of the LORD came to Abram in a vision, saying, 'Do not be afraid, Abram. I am your shield, your exceedingly great reward'" (**Genesis 15:1**). There is an undiscovered treasure within the concept of motivation. Real motivation is authentic, not rehearsed. It is driven by reward, not by obligation. Interestingly, you can only be as motivated to serve Christ as you are persuaded that His Word is truth (**John 17:17**). However, when you commit yourself to serving Christ as His disciple, the road is *"narrow and difficult"* (**Matthew 7:13-14**). How long are you to keep going?

Till the day you die, and even then, your tombstone could well say, "To be continued." As a disciple of Christ, reward will always be on your mind—always. To serve Christ merely to get a reward will distract you with conditional motivation. But to serve Christ out of love for Him (**John 14:15**) strengthens your service into unconditional motivation. While reward is not a primary motivation for us to follow Christ, it is a promised result that can be joyfully anticipated. Then the assurance of this reward helps us overcome the challenges we face daily.

What it comes down to is this: you die daily (**1 Corinthians 15:31**). Die? Yes, you crucify your fleshly nature to remain focused on your service. All you know to live for is Jesus (**Philippians 1:21**) as you confidently affirm (**Hebrews 10:35**) that your labor for the Kingdom is not in vain (**1 Corinthians 15:58**). The Father wants you to be reminded that He believes in rewarding you for your works

(**Hebrews 11:6**).

Day after day, you serve the Christ, who is the King eternal (**1 Timothy 1:17**). There will come a day when your life on earth is complete, and everything you did or did not do for Christ will be brought to attention. You will be judged; everything will be examined. The more you serve Christ with a pure conscience, the more you look to the reward. Jesus Christ will judge the living and the dead.

TEACHING # 10.1: JUDGMENT FROM JESUS CHRIST

Week 52

This week's objective: To discover the purpose of Christ's judgment, as well as to learn why a disciple should anticipate it with excitement.

THE COMMAND INTRODUCED:

- **Matthew 7:21-23; Luke 13:25-27** "*Not everyone who says to Me, 'Lord, Lord,' shall enter the kingdom of heaven, but he who does the will of My Father in heaven. Many will say to Me in that day, 'Lord, Lord, have we not prophesied in Your name, cast out demons in Your name, and done many wonders in Your name?' And then I will declare to them, 'I never knew you; depart from Me, you who practice lawlessness!'*"

THE COMMAND INTERPRETED:

In this highly implicit command, Christ is vividly portrayed as the "*Judge*" of the living and the dead (**2 Timothy 4:1**). Truly, "*every knee shall bow*" to King Jesus (**Philippians 2:9-11**). From this command, you notice that Christ draws your attention to those who enter "*the kingdom of heaven.*" The command is born out of this reality because Jesus associates "*doing*" the will of His Father with those who enter into His Kingdom. Therefore, Jesus is not only commanding you to remain devoted to God's will but also warning of the eternal ramifications for those who do not.

The most effective way to appropriate this command is to break it down. Death is the bridge for every person to cross and face God (**Hebrews 9:27**). All believers will face this path until the Lord Jesus Christ returns for His Church. Some people go to *Heaven* when they die (**2 Corinthians 5:8**), and some people go to *Hell* (**Luke 16:24**). Inevitably, every person who dies reaches one of these two destinations. Christ addresses this awkward topic not to frighten, but to explain why people arrive at the destination they do. It is from this understanding that you can see the dividing contrast.

First of all, Heaven is for salvation *recipients*. People who enter the "*Kingdom of Heaven*" when they die exhibit a *validated* faith in Christ because they "*do the will of the Father*" in Heaven. This fits your profile. You "*do*" the will of God, not to meritoriously gain admittance into Heaven, but because you have been graciously saved! All that you do for Christ is merely a product of your faith in Him as a joyful recipient who understands the awe and magnitude of being born again.

Salvation is deliverance from sin's penalty—Hell. It begins by recognizing your sin (**Romans 3:10, 23**). Then, out of panic to find approval with God, you try to "work" for your salvation, and in that process, you realize you cannot because of **Ephesians 2:8-9**. Exhausted, you cry out, "If I can't save myself from Hell, who can?" But standing before you in your deepest consciousness is Jesus Christ, the sacrificial substitute of **Romans 5:8**, and He says the words of **Revelation 1:18** to you. He is offering to you for free in **Romans 6:23** the gift that you cannot earn. For the first time in your life, you realize the depth of God's love for you, and by *faith*, you cry out **Romans 10:9** desperately, expressing your gratitude by permanent surrender to the Lordship of Jesus Christ.

Now, as a recipient of this grace and salvation, you have one objective: to do the will of God (**Romans 12:1-2**). Obedience to God's Word is the test of true, born-again faith in Christ, because your belief will match your behavior. Your faith is now just as much alive as Christ is resurrected from the dead (**James 2:17**). As a born-again Christian, you are assured that the Holy Spirit of God abides within you (**Romans 5:5; 8:9**). The Spirit enables and empowers you to both know and do the Father's will. You do so by listening to Scripture through study and then practicing it according to **James 1:22-25**. By divine transformation, your love for God (**1 Corinthians 8:3**) motivates you to faithfully obey Christ out of privilege, not obligation. It's a joy, not a burden (**1 John 5:3**).

By contrast, Hell is for self-righteous *participants*. People who die and spend eternity in Hell exhibit a *volumized* faith. As the Judge, Jesus affirmed that "*many will say*" or try to explain why they deserve to enter the Kingdom of Heaven, having placed their faith in works, not in God's grace. This kind of attitude declares a person to be self-righteous, because their faith is really in the volume of their works, not in the Christ Who saves. This is detestable, and every malicious deed will be accounted for (**Romans 2:16**).

Jesus echoed the report in the Day of Judgment as being *"Have we not..."* Lost people will try to justify what does not satisfy (**Titus 3:5**). Christ will boldly proclaim to the lost in that Day, *"I never knew you..."* By divine authority, Jesus will ultimately say to the lost, *"Depart from Me, you who practice lawlessness."* To volumize faith in works is an eternal death sentence for the lost (**1 John 2:4; 3:4; John 8:24**).

Indeed, Jesus is not *"Lord"* of a person's life merely because of what they *"say"* they have done for Christ. The true, authentic, Kingdom-entering boast is nowhere near the parameters of self-righteous bragging, but rather in proximity of self-denying, cross-carrying crucifixion to this ungodly world (**Galatians 6:14**). That, my friend, is a lifestyle of doing the *"will of the Father"* (**Luke 22:42; Hebrews 13:21; Philippians 2:13; Ephesians 6:6**). Herein is costly persecution now, but oh, how glorious the reward!

THE COMMAND ILLUSTRATED:

By now, you can clearly see that Jesus Christ is the Judge of your life on Earth. Your mandate as a disciple is to obey His command by doing the will of God. However, there is something else you need to know, something that kindles excitement and zeal within. What is it? Reward. You see, the lost will be recompensed with God's judgment, but the saved will be rewarded with God's blessings for eternity. God delights in rewarding His children as they faithfully obey, doing His will unconditionally.

In the Bible, there is a fine example of how this reward is intended to influence and inspire your service to Christ. Turn to **2 Timothy 4:6-8**. The Apostle Paul compared his life to that of a *"drink offering."* What does that mean? This expression actually has Old Testament roots and is best described as the wine that the Jews poured out on an altar when they sacrificed to Jehovah God (**Exodus 29:41**). The requirement was *"strong wine"* (**Numbers 28:7**), meaning it was not to be watered down, but offered to God in its purest form. Therefore, when the sacrifice was officially performed, the fragrant aroma would ascend heavenward, pleasing God by faith.

This is precisely why Paul referred to his life as a *"drink offering"* because he truly presented himself to God as a *"living sacrifice"* (**Romans 12:1**). Paul offered himself in the purest form of a consecrated (**2 Corinthians 7:1**), disciplined (**1 Corinthians 9:27**) lifestyle. He copied this exact pattern from the Lord Jesus (**Ephesians 5:1-2**). With steadfast hope, Paul told Timothy, *"I have fought the good fight, I have finished the race, I have kept the faith."*

In an anthem of praise at the end of his life, Paul was overwhelmed with joy, motivated to die for his faith in Christ because his mission was accomplished. His conscience was without offense; his heart did not condemn him. Although persecuted, Paul kept fighting. Although wearied, Paul kept racing. Although seemingly abandoned, Paul kept believing. Why? Because he knew God would bring **Philippians 1:6** to pass. Therefore, with godly confidence in Christ's promise, Paul anticipated his reward of the *"crown of righteousness, which the Lord, the righteous Judge"* would delight in giving to him. As Christ's disciple, may your motivation parallel with that of the Apostle Paul. Serve the Lord Jesus Christ without compromise, sacrificing yourself daily, awaiting your reward.

THE COMMAND INITIATED:

The only way you can put the judgment of Christ into practice in your life is to prepare for it. It helps to discern between two eternal judgments in Scripture, for both of which Christ is the Judge. One of these judgments is called the *Great White Throne judgment*, which will only consist of all unbelievers (**Revelation 20:11-15**). They will be judged according to their works that resulted from their sin. The other judgment is called *the Judgment Seat of Christ*, which will only consist of all believers (**2 Corinthians 5:9-11**). Here, you will be judged according to your works that resulted from faith, not sin, because your sin was paid in full by Jesus Christ.

Moreover, the purpose for a disciple standing before the Judgment Seat of Christ is to *"receive the things done in the body, according to what he has done, whether good or bad.*" Everything you do with your body will come under the microscope of God's refining fire to determine the motive and purity of what you've done for Christ (**1 Corinthians 3:11-13**). That is why you will "*receive*" what you have done with your body; that is, either your reward (**1 Corinthians 3:14**) or loss of reward (**1 Corinthians 3:15**). As a disciple, "*make it your aim*" to please Christ. By doing so, you will joyfully anticipate reward at His Judgment Seat, not dread loss.

Erwin Lutzer offers a fantastic understanding of the Judgment Seat of Christ in his book *Your Eternal Reward*. Lutzer combines the principles of this judgment with incredible imagery of what you will experience:

> Imagine staring into the face of Christ! Just the two of you, one-on-one! Your entire life is present before you. In a flash you see what He sees. No hiding. No opportunity to put a better spin on what you did. No attorney to represent you. The look in His eyes says it all. Like it or not, that is precisely where you and I shall someday be...The judgment seat of Christ is often called the *Bema* (the Greek word for judgment seat used by Paul in **2 Corinthians 5:10**...). Literally, the *Bema* refers to a raised platform that was used for the assembly where speeches were given and crowns were awarded to the winners...Think this through: God gives us the faith by which we believe in Christ, and yet for this faith He gives us the gift of eternal life. God then works within us to that we might serve Him, and for our service He honors us with eternal rewards or *privileges*...We do not desire rewards for the reward itself, but because rewards are a reflection of Christ's approval of us.[1]

THE COMMAND INTERROGATED:

In his cunning trickery, Satan realizes that he needs to attack by tempting your body into displeasing Christ. Obviously, he knows this is his primary way to ruin your "big day" with Jesus at the Bema. Perhaps the frontal attack you can expect from Satan is found in the simplicity of **James 4:17**: "*Therefore, to him who knows to* *do good and does not do it, to him it is sin."* This is the devil's battlefield with you, where he cleverly tempts you to neglect obedience to Scriptures by rationalizing and compromising your devotion to them. The more you *"know"* what the Bible says, the more accountable you are to obey it.

It is with this knowledge that you will be attacked, relentlessly victimized to forfeit your knowledge of the *"good"* Christ calls you to do and disobediently refuse it. This is sin! As a disciple, it will ruin your witness for Christ, damage your integrity, and cause you to suffer loss at the Bema. Beware of this assault from the devil. Satan wants to make your reward as scarce as possible, but this defeat is unnecessary for you as a disciple. Stand up and fight with the Word of God! You are a conqueror (**Romans 8:37**). Do not let the enemy take your reward (**2 John: 8**).

THE COMMAND INDESTRUCTIBLE:

Satan is a liar (**John 8:44**), but the Word of our God is *truth* (**John 17:17**). Granted, you will be interrogated, but you don't have to be intimidated. Praise God, He alone fights for you, awaiting your decision to point the Word at Satan when he so viciously attacks you. The perfect memory verse to daily boost your morale for the Judgment Seat of Christ is **Hebrews 11:24-26**. It says, *"By faith Moses, when he became of age, refused to be called the son of Pharaoh's daughter, choosing rather to suffer affliction with the people of God than to enjoy the passing pleasures of sin, esteeming the reproach of Christ greater riches than the treasures in Egypt; for he looked to the reward."*

Glory be to God! Praise unto the Lamb of God, slain for our sins! In Jesus is the reward. In Christ is the fullness of eternal blessing. Like Moses, day by day, refuse to integrate yourself with *"Pharaoh's"* company (**2 Corinthians 6:14**) and choose to embrace your cross alongside the *"people of God"* (**1 Peter 5:9**). Disown the indulgent *"pleasure of sin"* (**2 Thessalonians 2:12**) so that you may joyfully set your gaze upon the treasure you have in Christ (**Luke 12:21**). Daily, as a faithful disciple, keep *"looking to the reward"* (**Hebrews 6:10; 10:23**). The Day will come when Christ declares to you, *"Well done, good and faithful servant; you were faithful over a few things, I will make you ruler over many things. Enter into the joy of your*

Lord" (**Matthew 25:21**). Until then, serve the Lord!

THE COMMAND INQUIRED:

What cannot be measured cannot be evaluated. Therefore, it is essential to measure your comprehension of Christ's command in this teaching, or else the devil will snatch away the "seeds" of Scripture sown into your heart (**Matthew 13:19**). To keep this from occurring, write down your answers to the following questions as they correlate with the teaching this week:

In what passage(s) of Scripture do you find Christ's commandment on His **judgment**?

_____

_____

_____

What is the accurate interpretation of Christ's **judgment** you have discovered?

_____

_____

_____

_____

_____

In your own words, what are some real-life examples in Scripture of Christ's **judgment**?

_____

_____

_____

_____

_____

_____

What steps of initiation did you learn to take in order for Christ's **judgment** to transform your life?

_____

_____

_____

_____

_____

How will Satan attack you to hinder your preparation for Christ's **judgment**?

_____

_____

_____

_____

_____

What memory verse will you use to protect Christ's command about His **judgment**? Write it out.

_____

FINAL THOUGHTS

"A disciple is not above his teacher, but everyone who is perfectly trained will be like his teacher" (**Luke 6:40**). You have been *"perfectly trained"* by the exact commands that Jesus gave His disciples, making you *"like"* Christ. This Scripture reminds us to contemplate the relationship between a disciple and his Teacher. Rob Bell accurately depicts such a relationship with incredible detail:

> Jesus is a Jewish Rabbi with Jewish disciples living in a first century Jewish world. Now Jesus grew up in a region called the Galilee. And the Jewish people in the Galilee believed that God had spoken to Moses, one of the great historical leaders, and had given him the first five books of the Bible. They called these first five books the Torah...Most Jewish boys or girls around the age of six would go to school for the first time to learn the Torah...This first level of education was called Bet's Affair and lasted until the kid was around ten years old...But the best of the best would keep going, they would continue their education into the next level which was called Bet Talmud...The best of the best of the best would continue on to the next level of education, which was called Bet Midrash. They would go to a Rabbi and they'd apply to that Rabbi to become one of that Rabbi's disciples...A Rabbi's set of interpretations was called that Rabbi's *yoke*. So when you went and applied to a Rabbi to become one of that Rabbi's disciples, what you wanted to do is you wanted to take that Rabbi's yoke upon you, so that you could learn to know what the Rabbi knows, in order to do what the Rabbi does, in order to be like the Rabbi...You would leave your family, your friends, your synagogue, your village, and you would devote your entire life to being

like your Rabbi, learning to do what your Rabbi does. This is what it means to be a disciple...If you're a disciple, by the end of the day, with your Rabbi traveling on these hot, dusty, dirty roads, you've got whatever your Rabbi stepped in just caked all over the front of you. So this saying developed among the wise men and the sages, you would say to a disciple, "*May you be covered in the dust of your Rabbi.*"[1]

By the grace of God, you too have officially been discipled. You have been the student; Christ has been the Teacher. What you have been given from Christ in the form of His commands is the greatest treasure you will ever possess in your life. You have learned truths that go beyond informing to transforming—inspiring your passion while chiseling away the rough edges of your old life. Through the Scriptures, you have renewed your mind! Thus, you have established a godly environment within your heart for Christ to reign as your Lord and Master. You are His disciple, His body, and His ambassador, and you are equipped with His every command. So, it's your turn. Go make more disciples. May you also be covered in the dust of your Rabbi, Jesus Christ.

ACKNOWLEDGMENTS

Above all, I give thanks and praise to my Lord Jesus Christ for making a wretch His treasure, a rebel His disciple.

I am forever grateful for disciples of Jesus placed into my life early, such as my grandparents, Dean and Leo Treat, who loved me to Christ; my Uncle Michael Treat, who led me to Christ; and my Uncle Steve Horton and Aunt and Uncle, Mark and Merla Hill, who always encourage me to keep persevering for Christ.

Just as the Apostle Paul remembered the multitude of brothers and sisters in Christ in his life and ministry, I am beyond thankful for the host of Kingdom-minded, cross-carrying couples and individuals in my life, each of whom have invested in me by walking alongside me as we followed Jesus together: Eric and Carolann Capaci, Shane and Katrina Robertson, Rick and Judy Bolin, David and Theresa Dillard, Sonny Tucker, Billy and Melanie Stringfellow, Ken and Jody Key, Wayne and Edwina Daniell, Carley and Tina Davis, Sam and Kathy May, Jody and Joyce Tillery, Jerry and Amy Holland, Lee and Lauren Denton, Ray and Brenda Traylor, Aaron and Angela Leggett, Tommy King, Matt Green, Jacob Ricker, Mark and Erin Smith, Tracy and Lori Payne, Mike and Kimberly McKenzie, Doyle Malcom, Miles and Kim McKenzie, Brian and Vickie McWethy, Brad and Jennifer Pittman, Jeff and Laura Ardissone, Scott and Julie Brandon, David and Aamie Mason, John Ballinger, Jay and Amanda Hill, Bill and Aletha Chaney, Damon and Tammy Leggett, Tom and Rhonda Simmons, Ralph and Gail Goza, Joey and Amanda Newton, Don and Julie Stahler, Ed and Deb Fahs, Marci Kasmar, Walt and Angel Pigott, Rodney and Deanne Russell, Johnny and Wilma Johnson, Keith and Samantha Axsom, Jean Morgan, Elaine Cofer, and Pat Ballinger. All of them have been God-sent refreshers the Lord has used to strengthen and encourage me.

For my editor, Ashlyn Ohm, my heart is full of thanksgiving for her stellar diligence in pouring a countless number of hours upon days into examining every word with pristine, relentless devotion. I especially appreciate her personal value as a follower of Jesus for the content of the book, fortifying the editing appeal far beyond mere professionalism.

Finally, I have a deep gratitude beyond description for my bride by my side since 2002—Jillian, my beloved wife. She has been my constant companion in the ministry of furthering the gospel. Her Kingdom-minded life inspires me! She gave me the honor of taking her through the commands of Christ in this book as my first disciple to make for Jesus. I love you, Jillian.

NOTES

DEDICATION

[1] Bill Hull, *The Disciple-Making Pastor* (Grand Rapids: Revell, 1988), 19.

[2] Not his real name.

[3] Hull, The Disciple-Making Pastor, 20, 23.

[4] Hull, The Disciple-Making Pastor, 53.

[5] Hull, The Disciple-Making Pastor, 58-60.

CHAPTER 1

[1] Dr. Charles Stanley, *The Blessings of Brokenness* (Grand Rapids: Zondervan, 1997), 102-103.

[2] Dr. Warren Wiersbe, *The Bible Exposition Commentary*, (Colorado Springs: Chariot Victor Publishing, 1989), 1:21.

[3] Andrew Murray, *Humility: The Journey toward Holiness* (Minneapolis: Bethany House, 2001), 47-49.

[4] Mike Nappa, The Courage to Be Christian: Entering a Life of Spiritual Passion (West Monroe: Howard, 2001), 50-52.

[5] Dr. John MacArthur, *Unleashing God's Word in Your Life* (Nashville: Thomas Nelson, 2003), 113, 115.

[6] Troy Cartmill, *It's Time for Pure Hearts* (USA: Xulon Press, 2003), 38-39.

[7] Janet Kobobel Grant, *Trusting That God Will Provide* (Grand Rapids: Zondervan, 1999), 17-18.

[8] Max Lucado, *The Inspirational Study Bible* (Dallas: Word Bibles, 1995), 747-748.

[9] Max Lucado, *God's Inspirational Promises* (J. Countryman, 2001), 199.

[10] Dr. Billy Graham, *Peace with God* (Nashville: W Publishing Group, 1984), 272-273.

[11] W. E. Vine, et. al., *Vine's Complete Expository Dictionary* (Nashville: Thomas Nelson, 1996), 381-382.

[12] Chuck and Nancy Missler, *The Way of Agape* (Coeur d'Alene: The King's High Way Ministries, 1994), 63.

CHAPTER 2

[1] J. Oswald Chambers, *The Joy of Following Jesus* (Chicago: Moody Press, 1994), 26.

[2] John Foxe, *Foxe's Book of Martyrs* (Springdale: Whitaker House, 1981), 275.

[3] Dr. Ken Hemphill, *The Prayer of Jesus* (Nashville: Broadman & Holman, 2001), 9-10.

[4] Donald S. Whitney, *Spiritual Disciplines for the Christian Life* (Colorado Springs: NavPress, 1991), 159-160, 164-166.

[5] Derek Prince, *Faith to Live By* (New Kensington: Whitaker House, 1977), 14.

[6] Stephen F. Olford, *The Grace of Giving* (Grand Rapids: Kregal Publications, 2000), 46-48.

[7] Kay Arthur, *A Marriage without Regrets* (Eugene: Harvest House, 2000), 40-41.

[8] John Selby, *Jesus for the Rest of Us* (Charlottesville: Hampton Roads Publishing, 2006), 106-107, 111-112.

[9] Dr. C. S. Jenne, *The Power Filled Life: Abiding in Christ* (1st Books Library, 2002), 12-17.

CHAPTER 3

[1] James and Martha Reapsome, *Discipleship: The Growing*

Christian's Lifestyle (Colorado Springs: Shaw Books, 2002), 1, 3, 23, 67.

[2] Andrew L. Singletary, *Conquering the Flesh* (Charleston: Armour of Light, 2005), 15-16.

[3] Randy Alcorn, *Money, Possessions, and Eternity* (Wheaton: Tyndale House, 2003), 33, 38-39.

[4] Richard Foster, *The Celebration of Discipline* (New York: Harper San Francisco, 1988), 80-81.

[5] Dr. Manickam Chandrakumar, *Overcoming Temptation* (San Giovanni Teatino, Italy: Destiny Image Europe, 2004), 4-5.

[6] Alcorn, Money, Possessions, and Eternity, 19.

[7] Dr. Robb Thompson, *Give Up Worry Forever* (Tulsa: Harrison House, 2005), 24-25.

[8] Hunt, Dr. T. W., *The Mind of Christ* (Nashville: Broadman & Holman, 1995), 17.

[9] Gary Whetstone, *Make Fear Bow* (New Kensington: Whitaker House, 2002), 113-115.

[10] Tod Bolsinger, *Showtime: Living Down Hypocrisy by Living Out the Faith* (Grand Rapids: Baker Books, 2004), 37-38.

[11] John Fischer, *12 Steps for the Recovering Pharisee (Like Me)* (Minneapolis: Bethany House, 2000), 94-95.

CHAPTER 4

[1] Todd Tomasella, *Deceivers & False Prophets Among Us* (Bloomington: Authorhouse, 2005), 85-88.

CHAPTER 5

[1] Donald Posterski, *Enemies with Smiling Faces* (Downers Grove: InterVarsity Press, 2004), 127, 131.

[2] Terry Cooper, *Making Judgments Without Being Judgmental* (Downers Grove: IVP Books, 2006), 19-20.

[3] John De Gruchy, *Reconciliation* (Minneapolis: Fortress Press, 2002), 52-53.

[4] Terry Rush, *The Miracle of Mercy* (West Monroe: Howard Publishing, 1999), 41, 44-45.

[5] Johann C. Arnold, *Seeking Peace* (Farmington: Plume Publishers, 2000), 30-31.

[6] Alexander Strauch, *The Hospitality Commands* (Littleton: Lewis & Roth Publishers, 1993), 36-37.

[7] Phyllis J. Le Peau, *Kindness: Reaching Out to Others* (Grand Rapids: Zondervan, 2001), 9-10.

[8] R.T. Kendall, *Total Forgiveness* (Lake Mary: Charisma House, 2002), 20.

CHAPTER 6

[1] David Walters, *Kids in Combat* (Macon: Good News Ministries, 1992), 25-28.

[2] Dr. T. W. Hunt, *The Mind of Christ* (Nashville: Broadman & Holman, 1995), 66-67.

[3] O. S. Hawkins, *Drawing the Net* (Dallas: Annuity Board, 2002), 33-35.

[4] Dr. Robert E. Coleman, *The Master Plan of Evangelism* (Grand Rapids: Spire, 1994), 62-63.

CHAPTER 7

[1] Clarence Larkin, *The Second Coming of Christ* (Philippines: Life Line, n.d.), 5, 7.

CHAPTER 8

[1] E. W. Bullinger, *The Resurrection of the Body* (United Kingdom: Open Bible Trust, 2006), 15-16.

CHAPTER 9

[1] Jim Henry, *In Remembrance of Me* (Nashville: Broadman and Holman Publishers, 1998), 3-5.

CHAPTER 10

[1] Erwin W. Lutzer, *Your Eternal Reward* (Chicago: Moody Press, 1998), 23-25.

FINAL THOUGHTS

[1] *NOOMA*, 008, "Dust," featuring Rob Bell, aired 2005, on NOOMA.com.